MERIWETHER LEWIS

MERIWETHER

LEWIS
A Biography

BY RICHARD DILLON

WESTERN TANAGER PRESS
Santa Cruz

Library of Congress Catalog Card Number: 65-10888

ISBN: 0-934136-39-4

Cover: *Up the Jefferson* by John Clymer
Cover design: Lynn Piquett
Maps: Eagle Eye Maps

Printed in the United States of America

Western Tanager Press
1111 Pacific Avenue
Santa Cruz, CA 95060

Produced on acid-free paper

First cloth edition published in 1965 by Coward-McCann

To
William Hogan
Amicus Scriptoris

CONTENTS

CONTENTS

Maps of the Lewis and Clark expedition follow page 108

FOREWORD

THERE IS NOTHING like writing biography to get you close to a person. You live with the character during the day, at your desk or typewriter, and at night, in your dreams. You get so you know your historical subject better than you do your contemporary associates, and even friends. In the process, you look for positive and likeable traits, or admirable ones, if only because who would want to spend all that time with an unlikeable person, or an incompetent one?

I've written seven biographies—Henry Halleck, Emory Upton, Crazy Horse, Custer, Milton Eisenhower, Dwight Eisenhower, and Richard Nixon—and have a varying degree of admiration and liking for each of them. Ike stands out, partly because he was who he was and did what he did, but mainly because he was such a fine human being, and so extraordinarily competent, especially in a crisis.

But the American figure I admire most, and like the best, and spent the most time with, is a man I've never written on, Meriwether Lewis. The only reason I have not written his biography is that Richard Dillon did it first, and his is such a model biography there is no need for another. *Meriwether Lewis* is indeed one of the classics of American literature; all Lewis and Clark buffs will welcome this new edition from the Western Tanager Press.

The reasons I like and admire Lewis so much emerge in Dillon's biography—Lewis' keen intelligence, his strong character, his leadership abilities, his hot temper when anger is appropriate, his cool consideration of all points of view when caution is called for, his superb writing, his flexibility in thought and action, his gentle-ness,and his decisiveness.

I also envy him, more than any other American, for two things. First and most obviously, because he was the first to cross the Continent, on the greatest exploration of American history. Along with my family, I've spent ten summers on the Lewis and Clark Trail, camping where they camped, canoeing where they canoed, backpacking where they had to hike it. (Incidentally, I urge readers to get out and camp on the Trail; you can see what Lewis saw, except for the buffalo, in many spots, especially Montana).

But of course we were following in the Expedition's footsteps; no one but Lewis and his men can ever be the first to see the fabulous country of the upper Missouri, the Rocky Mountains, and the Columbia.

The other thing I envy is this: Meriwether Lewis dined, on innumerable occasions, alone with Thomas Jefferson in the White House. Ah, that they would have had a tape recorder! But the fact that Jefferson selected Lewis as his private secretary and dinner companion, and then to lead the Expedition to explore the Louisiana Purchase, tells more about Lewis than anything I could write.

I can sum up my own feelings about Lewis best by saying that if I were ever in a life-threatening situation, whether in armed combat, or in a ship sinking at sea, or an airplane in difficulty, Meriwether Lewis is the man I would want for my leader. He would even come ahead of Ike.

You will find out why in this wonderful biography of this great man, who came to such a tragic end.

STEPHEN E. AMBROSE
Alumni Distinguished Professor of History
University of New Orleans

INTRODUCTION

There is properly no History; only Biography.
—RALPH WALDO EMERSON

THE HISTORY of the opening of the trans-Mississippi frontier is but the collective biography of a handful of westering Americans of a century and a half ago. Marching at the head of this column are Meriwether Lewis and William Clark. (A good forty yards to the rear of this wraithy queue trudges the self-appointed and widely advertised Pathfinder, John C. Frémont.) But the man who actually leads this spirit column on its route of march toward the Far West looks strangely out of place. He is a red-haired gentleman, like Clark, but of great bearing, dressed in mufti—the plainest of dress—in contrast to the rest of the spectral company, which is attired in military uniforms or plainsmen's buckskins. This man is obviously an Easterner, or a Southerner. He is a Virginian, in fact, and a man who was probably never west of the Shenandoah Valley, for all of his travels abroad.

The man is Thomas Jefferson, the Sage of Monticello. The architect of American democratic government, third President of the United States, linguist, amateur scientist, philosopher, statesman, inventor, educator, lawyer, gentleman-farmer, author of the Declaration of Independence—and vicarious explorer.

If George Washington is the father of our country, then surely Jefferson is the father of our American West. He is seldom

xiii

thought of in these terms but only because the claim is swamped in a welter of other prior honors and contributions to our country's history. Jefferson was first familiar with, and interested in the development of, the "lesser West," the trans-Appalachian agrarian area. He was dogmatic on the subject of free navigation of the Mississippi by American vessels and served notice on Spain that the young republic considered possession of New Orleans to be a necessary guarantee of that freedom. At first he cajoled Spain with assurances which appear specious at this remove but which may simply have been naïve. Jefferson told Madrid that the United States would guarantee her possessions on the right bank of the Mississippi and, indeed, would have no interest, "for ages," in crossing the river toward the West. But Jefferson was fooling no one, not even himself, for he could not help adding a veiled threat to his friendly overtures. He warned the Spaniards that should their king be reluctant to transfer New Orleans to the United States, the latter could not be responsible for the often precipitate actions of its citizens, especially the hotheaded frontiersmen of the left bank of the great river. Had President Thomas Jefferson been completely honest, he would have been obliged to say that no president and no king—even Canute himself—could turn back the waves of westward-bound Americans breaking upon the low eastern shore of Louisiana Territory.

But the role which the Virginian played in the development of the American West was far more important than simply that of securing control of the Father of Waters. Jefferson evolved a grand design of a connective route from the Mississippi Valley to the far Pacific, a route which would eventually transform a smallish and quarrelsome confederation of fifteen semi-independent states into a two-ocean power among nations. Had not Jefferson been equal to the challenge of the critical times in which he lived, the United States might today be a Balkan-like country hemmed in on all sides by British, French and Spanish possessions.

Jefferson, however, was alert to the problem and promise of the West, of the great expanse of prairie which rolled its way west to the Rockies. Long before a single *hectárea* of these Spanish borderlands west of the 90th meridian belonged to the United States, he planned the area's exploration and its eventual settlement and acquisition. A reticent man when it was politic to be so, for all his prolific writings, Jefferson did not reveal with his pen all that was in his head. But one can read much between the lines of such letters as one he wrote James Ross: "I experience great satisfaction at seeing my country proceed to facilitate the intercommunication of its several parts, by opening rivers, canals and roads. How much more rational is this disposal of public money than that of waging war." By his actions, if not by his words, Jefferson would show himself obsessed with the opening of one particular road—the river road of the Missouri.

Since Jefferson was, at best, a vicarious Westerner, he had to delegate his responsibility and vision to someone whom he could trust. This delegation was difficult; it involved a search of more than twenty years. Two decades before Louisiana was placed on the block by Napoleon, he was looking for the right man to be his agent of empire in that great tract. He would select four men in all, but only the last—Meriwether Lewis—would not disappoint him. Conversations and preparations in the cases of George Rogers Clark, John Ledyard and André Michaux all proved to be abortive. But with the selection of Lewis, success would be assured.

If any *one* man deserves to be considered as the person who opened the Far West, it is Lewis. With his companion, William Clark, he led the way through a terra incognita and proved the feasibility of transcontinental travel. The California Trail, the Oregon Trail, and Manifest Destiny were all but matters of time once Meriwether Lewis returned safely to St. Louis from Clatsop Beach.

Lewis is a major figure in the pageant of America and yet he has been neglected in a curious fashion. Not consigned to obscurity like so many forgotten men of American history, he is, oddly, remembered as half of a partnership at best and, at worst, as if he were 50 percent of a two-headed exploratory freak called Lewisandclark. Biographies of the two men have traditionally been joint affairs, suggesting that these two rugged individualists were Siamese twins of the Western trails. Both men deserve better than to be lumped together like Mason-Dixon or Gallagher and Sheean. They were not inseparable except for the years on the march, 1804–1806, for all the duo-biographical accounts which suggest a Damon-and-Pythias-in-buckskins relationship. Moreover, while their joint adventure was definitely the high point in each man's career, it encompassed in time but a small part of their lives, especially in the case of Clark.

Both Lewis and Clark have suffered from this shotgun marriage of convenience, brokered by lazy historians more content with image than reality. Justice has not been done to either man by this treatment. In this book, Clark will be a background figure in terms of importance not only because he was in no real sense the equal of Lewis but also because this is Meriwether Lewis's story and Clark must wait his biographical turn.

Up to now there has been no adequate full-length biography of Meriwether Lewis. Since Thomas Jefferson's fourteen-page sketch of 1814, there has been but one book-length biography of the explorer from Virginia. This is the work by Charles Morrow Wilson, published in 1934 and entitled *Meriwether Lewis of the Lewis and Clark Expedition*. Vardis Fisher, a keen student of Lewis's life, has described this volume as "a farrago of errors."

An estimable book on the two explorers as a team appeared in 1947. This was the volume *Lewis and Clark, Partners in Discovery*. The author was John Bakeless. But, despite his productive research, much new material has come to light since its publication.

Interest in the exploits of the two adventurers remains high and *Books in Print* lists some sixteen works, including juvenile titles, on the two men. But almost all of these are extenuated narratives of the Missouri River expedition or the opposite, editings of their long journals, such as the well-known Bernard De Voto condensation, rather than attempts to see the whole careers of the two men separately and completely.

The work in hand, then, is an attempt at a full reappraisal of Meriwether Lewis the man, not the half-a-legend which he has, even in history textbooks, become. Wherever possible, I have quoted his own words, his own thoughts, his own feelings. I have tried, in this book, to reinterpret his life and the role he played as a prime mover in setting this nation on the road west, on the course of empire. With all due regard to William Clark, the two men were not co-equals although, once in the field, by Lewis's decision they acted as coadjutors. President Jefferson chose *one man*, Lewis, to head his long-desired Corps of Discovery. He left the selection of a second-in-command to Lewis. The latter's first choice for his adjutant was Clark and the Kentuckian eagerly joined his friend. Captain Lewis tried to get Second Lieutenant Clark a raise in rank for the trip, but failed. He therefore gave Clark an unblessed promotion, considering him to be "Captain Clark" as far as he and the expedition were concerned. Although Lewis was supreme commander of the expedition, he preferred to treat his friend as an equal and not as a subordinate. Because of this, a lot of divided-command nonsense has crept into accounts of the expedition. But the Army, the Secretary of War, the President, all recognized Lewis as commander and Clark as his subordinate. For all the egalitarianism of the historians, the ultimate authority, the decision maker in every major matter, was Lewis.

The Missouri River expedition was by no means Lewis's whole life, though he died tragically young, at thirty-five, only three years after his return from the Pacific. Prior to being given the command by Jefferson, he was a militiaman and Regular Army officer, then private secretary to the President. After carrying out the most important and successful government expedition in our national history, Lewis was honored with the governorship of Upper Louisiana Territory. This was all that land of the Louisiana Purchase lying north of the present-day state of Louisiana—a sort of Greater Missouri Territory. But in a lonely woods in Tennessee, Governor Lewis met a mysterious death in 1809. To this day no one has been able to prove beyond the shadow of a doubt whether he was a victim of murder or a suicide.

Lewis stands as the greatest pathfinder or trailblazer of this continent. He led a small band through unknown country with great tact and firmness and almost without bloodshed. He and his men traversed an ululating wilderness firmly held by hostile Indians who had nothing to fear from a feeble American government and army, far away, much less the firepower of a handful of men cut off from civilization. Lewis's success was a triumph of will and skill. During the entire time of the exploration his party was involved in only one skirmish of consequence; only two Indians were killed; none of his men were killed; only one man was wounded (himself), accidentally; and but one man died, of illness. One of the greatest tributes to Lewis's ability in handling his own men, who were anything but docile and who were, at first, not even well disciplined, was the lack of scuffling among them and the absence of collision with the Indians they met. The higher the incidence of narrow escapes and "adventures" on the part of a frontiersman, the lower his level of competence, just as the best sailor is not the one with the most shipwrecks to his career.

For two other characteristics Lewis should be remembered. His grace with the English language was considerable. The meaning of the "literary pursuit" which he headed was, indeed, a politico-commercial-scientific expedition but the narrative and description of our national epic of exploration are worthy of rescue from the national ignorance caused by the veiled paraphrase and transmutations of Messrs. Biddle and Allen in editing Lewis's journals for publication.

Finally, Lewis's prowess as an Indian nation diplomat has been shamefully neglected. Just as in the case of his expedition, the best testimony to his skill as an Indian administrator is the record: the record of Missouri in the War of 1812. There were Indian raids in the territory which he had governed; a crack troop of Rangers, reminiscent of the Louisiana Spies which Lewis had formed, were necessary to patrol the frontier from Fort Mason to L'Outre Island. But Lewis's groundwork, and the building on his foundations by Governors Howard and Clark, kept battles and even skirmishes to a bare minimum in what had been upper Louisiana—the engagements of Portage des Sioux, Fort Madison and Prairie du Chien—although British agent Robert Dickson offered £2,000 worth of trade goods for the head of American agent Thomas Forsyth and tried to hire a Sauk to assassinate William Clark.

After Lewis's death, a country which had cheered him wildly only two years earlier as a conquering hero forgot him with shameful speed and callousness. He was buried alongside the Natchez Trace in a virtually unmarked grave where he fell. His remains were never removed to his home in Virginia. There was never a real government inquiry into his death. When pioneer ornithologist Alexander Wilson made a pilgrimage to the death site of his explorer-friend, Grinder's Stand, he was so ashamed of the treatment of one of America's great men that he paid, out of his own pocket, for a rude fence around the grave to keep wolves and rooting hogs away from Lewis's last resting place.

Few remembered the captain from Virginia and his contributions until his journals finally appeared in print in 1814, in a paraphrase by Nicholas Biddle and edited for the press by Paul Allen. The work carried a brief biography by his paternalistic friend, ex-President Jefferson. Jefferson's eulogy of his trailblazing friend, who was almost a son to him, partially restored Lewis to public esteem although a suitable monument was not erected over his lonely grave until 1848.

On this monument, in an oak copse near Hohenwald, Tennessee, are engraved some of Jefferson's heartfelt words describing Lewis:

OF COURAGE UNDAUNTED, POSSESSING A FIRMNESS AND PER-SEVERANCE OF PURPOSE WHICH NOTHING BUT IMPOSSIBILITIES COULD DIVERT FROM ITS DIRECTION.

What more fitting, if belated, epitaph could we compose for the man who opened up and secured the Far West to the United States at such small cost, a mere $38,722.25 (according to War Department Accountant Simmons)—and Lewis's life.

RICHARD DILLON

San Francisco

CHAPTER I

JEFFERSON'S GRAND DESIGN

The Federalists alone still treat it [the Expedition] as a philosophism and would rejoice in its failure. Their bitterness increases with the diminution of their numbers and despair of resurrection. I hope you will take care of yourself and be the living witness of their malice and folly.
— THOMAS JEFFERSON to Meriwether Lewis,
January 13, 1804

THOMAS JEFFERSON was but one of a long line of men of varied nationality, both seamen and landsmen, who sought the fabled Northwest Passage which was said to connect the Pacific with the settled portions of the North American continent. When he first approached George Rogers Clark with a proposition to explore westward to the sea along the Missouri River, it was only after defeat had crushed the efforts of Major Robert Rogers, the Indian-fighting Ranger, and his protégé, explorer Jonathan Carver. The latter made it no farther west than Minnesota in his 1766 expedition. But the British were not ready to give up. This Jefferson knew and he wrote Clark: "I find they have subscribed a very large sum of money in England for exploring the country from the Mississippi to California. They pretend it is only to promote knowledge. I am afraid they have thoughts of colonizing in that quarter. Some of us have been talking here in a feeble way of making the attempt to search that country. How would you like to lead such a party?"

Clark begged off, saying he could not afford the command.

1

This rebuff did not discourage Jefferson; the project was too important to abandon. He kept his plans simmering like stock on the back of a kitchen range while he collected books, documents and maps on the mysterious region called Louisiana. All the while he sought the perfect agent for his dream of empire. For Jefferson was not content just to mark a route west; he meant to settle the West with Americans. He had a sense of what later Americans would call Manifest Destiny. Jefferson believed that when the density of population on the east bank of the Mississippi reached ten persons per square mile, the Americans would spill over into Louisiana and push west "in great numbers to search for a vacant country." Very likely, too, he dreamed of wresting control of the fur trade in North America from the British by means of occupancy of the upper Missouri country. Jefferson was taken in by the writings of men like Daniel Coxe, who insisted that only a short portage across a slim mountain chain blocked an all-water (river) passage to the Pacific. He did not dream that the Rockies were sometimes a tangled knot of *cordilleras* 200 miles wide. But if his knowledge of the ground was uncertain, his imagination and vision were magnificent. He fixed in the American mind the idea of a transcontinental road so firmly that false starts, failures and the hostility of Spaniards, French, British and Indians did little to arrest the eventual outcome.

While Minister to France in 1786, Jefferson met the man who seemed ideal for the task of pioneering the Missouri route to the Pacific Northwest. He was a born wanderer named John Ledyard. Jefferson described him as "a man of genius, of some science, of fearless courage and enterprise . . . and of a roaming, restless character." Ledyard, who had been a Royal Marine with Captain Cook in Hawaii, was in Paris seeking capital to engage in the fur trade in North America. When the U.S. Minister proposed that he go to Kamschatka, cross the Bering Sea by a Russian vessel to Nootka Sound and then explore western America by foot, Ledyard eagerly embraced the idea. Although Ledyard was something of an eccentric (he thought he could walk across America with no more equipment than two dogs, an Indian pipe, and his winning ways), he was a good choice. By

2

March 19, 1787, he had reached St. Petersburg, on foot, and by July 29th shanks' mare had taken him to Barnaul in Siberia. From there he wrote, "When you read this—perhaps two months before you do—if I do well, I shall be in Okhotsk." But winter halted him in Tobolsk and he was arrested there on orders of Empress Catherine the Great. She bundled Ledyard off to Poland under close guard. The American finally reached London where Sir Joseph Banks offered him an opportunity to explore North Africa. He took it and Jefferson had to wait. He had worked out another plan with Ledyard: "He has promised me to go to America and penetrate from Kentucke to the Western side of the Continent." But Ledyard did not emerge from Africa; he died of sickness in Cairo.

Independent of Jefferson, Secretary of War Henry Knox tried to mount an ultrasecret Missouri River reconnaissance in 1790, sending young Lieutenant John Armstrong to pose as a fur trader. But Armstrong got no farther than Ste. Genevieve on the Missouri.

Jefferson was not one to lose hope simply because his carefully primed plans had misfired twice. Back in the United States, his plans were recharged in 1792 by the news of Captain Robert Gray's discovery of the Columbia River. He shortly proposed to the American Philosophical Society of Philadelphia, the scientific body of which he was then vice-president, that a subscription be taken to engage a daring traveler to explore the Far West from east to west. Among the first to subscribe were George Washington, Robert Morris, and Alexander Hamilton. Possibly the first man to solicit the post was Jefferson's young friend, Meriwether Lewis. "I told him it was proposed that the person engaged should be attended by a single companion only, to avoid exciting alarm among the Indians. This did not deter him." But because of his youth (eighteen years) and lack of scientific knowledge, Jefferson passed him over for another volunteer, the French botanist André Michaux. He had arrived in the United States in 1785 to study American timber but he purchased land in South Carolina and became an explorer and scholarly botanist, traveling over southern Appalachia, Spanish Florida and the Carolina mountains. He had, himself, the idea of exploring west along the

3

Missouri River, so there was a true meeting of minds when Jefferson encountered him.

Jefferson tried to ignore the close ties between Michaux and the notorious Minister of France to the United States, Citizen Genêt. Perhaps he placed his reliance on the wisdom of La Rochefoucauld's maxim—"It is more disgraceful to suspect our friends than to be deceived by them." Although he trusted Michaux, Jefferson did not give him anything like carte blanche. Instead, he gave him detailed and specific instructions: "The chief objects of your journey are to find the shortest and most convenient route of communication between the United States and the Pacific Ocean, within the temperate latitudes and to learn such particulars as can be obtained of the country through which it passes, its productions, inhabitants, and other interesting circumstances. As a channel of communication between these States and the Pacific Ocean, the Missouri, so far as it extends, presents itself under circumstances of unquestioned preference. It has, therefore, been declared as a fundamental object . . . that this river shall be considered and explored as part of the communication sought for." Jefferson then ordered him to pass the Mississippi above the Spanish settlements to avoid being stopped, follow the Missouri, cross the mountains and search out the largest and shortest stream flowing into the Pacific—possibly the Oregon River of some of Jefferson's maps—then return by the same, or any other, route. "You will," ordered Jefferson, "in the course of your journey take notice of the country you pass through, its general face, soil, rivers, mountains, its productions, animal, vegetable and mineral—so far as they may be new to us, and may also be useful or very curious; the latitudes of places or material for calculating it by such simple methods as your situation may admit you to practice, the names, members and dwellings of the inhabitants, and such particulars as you can learn of their history, connection with each other, languages, manners, state of society, and of the arts and commerce among them. Under the head of animal history, that of the mammoth is particularly recommended to your inquiries, as it is also to learn whether the llama or alpaca of Peru is found in those parts of this Continent, or how far north they come."

Michaux started from Philadelphia on July 15, 1793. He was in Kentucky when word reached Jefferson that the Frenchman was a secret agent of Minister Edmond Charles Genêt. Although involving George Rogers Clark and Benjamin Logan, Genêt's plot to revolutionize Spanish Louisiana, using American filibusters, failed, and Michaux returned to botany in the East.

Once again Jefferson had been thwarted. This time the pill was particularly bitter, for he had to read in the newspapers of Britain's success. On July 21, 1793, Alexander Mackenzie had reached the Pacific. The only consolation to Jefferson was that the Scot had traversed the continent at too high a latitude for an effective commercial route, that his way had been blocked by a maze of mountains, and that the rivers he had followed—the Mackenzie, Peace and Parsnip—were hardly the broad highway which the Missouri was.

Jefferson bided his time for almost a decade, a period in which the United States was split on political lines over the desirability of exploring—much less occupying—Louisiana. Many of Jefferson's party saw the territory as a desirable acquisition. The Federalists, on the other hand, looked upon it as a Great American Desert (before Stephen Long coined the term to describe the High Plains) and John Lowell, in his book *The New England Patriot*, described the northern reaches of Louisiana Territory as "a tract of country beyond the Lake of the Woods which will not be inhabited by any beings but bears and buffaloes for five hundred years."

In 1802, President Jefferson was of the firm belief that free navigation of the Mississippi was absolutely necessary to preserve American commerce. Half of the country's produce already passed through Spanish New Orleans. Therefore, when he suddenly learned that Spain was being pressed into transferring New Orleans and Louisiana Territory back to France, the President rushed into action to secure the key Mississippi River delta and to explore, and perhaps secure, the immense hinterland which shut off the United States from the Pacific. He hurried his agents to France to dicker with Napoleon for the purchase of New Orleans and he sought, again, a man whom he could trust to open a route from the Mississippi to the Pacific.

This time he knew exactly the man—Meriwether Lewis.

5

CHAPTER II

———•·•———

LOCUST HILL AND BROAD RIVER

*He [Lewis] was always remarkable for perseverence . . .
a martial temper and great steadiness of purpose, self-
possession and undaunted courage.*

— PEACHY RIDGWAY GILMER,
schoolmate of Meriwether Lewis

MERIWETHER LEWIS was born, August 18, 1774, in Albemarle
County—Thomas Jefferson's county—in Virginia. He grew up a
neighbor of the Piedmont elite, the Jeffersons, Randolphs, Mad-
isons and the many other Lewises, not all of whom were closely
related. The boy was named for his mother, née Lucy Meriwether, a cousin of his father, William Lewis. His birthplace was
Locust Hill, a rustic frame building squeezed between two tall
chimneys and facing a green slope picketed with pear trees. The
house lay just north of Ivy and about seven miles west of Charlottesville, in the heart of the Ivy Creek district of Albemarle red
clay from which sprang lush bluegrass, catalpas, oaks, maples
and mimosas, as well as the locusts which gave their names to
Lewis's estate. Locust Hill itself, one of a series of rolling heights
which lay on the Three Notches Road to Waynesboro and the
old buffalo trail through Woods's and Rockfish gaps, stood like a
sentinel on the edge of a modified frontier. It was by no means
an unknown wilderness but still an area of unsettled mountains
fifty-eight years after Governor Alexander Spotswood first penetrated the Blue Ridge.

On the heels of Spotswood had come hunters and trappers,

who left lean-to structures and log huts. Then came the first settlers with their cabins and loopholed frame houses. Among them were the Meriwethers and the Lewises. They found Albemarle to be a lovely land, a hillocky paradise. Of it, Jefferson wrote: "Where has nature spread so rich a mantle under the eye? Mountains, forests, rocks, rivers. With what majesty do we there ride above the storm! How sublime to look down into the workhouse of nature, to see her clouds, hail, snow, rain, thunder, all fabricated at our feet! And the glorious sun, when rising as if out of a distant water, just gilding the tops of the mountains and giving life to all nature."

Locust Hill was close enough to Monticello for Jefferson to signal to his young friend Meriwether Lewis, when he wanted him, with a mirror reflecting the sun's rays. It was but one of several estates of the Lewises and Meriwethers located at the foot of the Blue Ridge. Other rustic manors of these Welsh Americans were Clover Fields, the Music Hall, Belvoir, the Farm, Buckeye Land, and Castle Hill. All flourished in a land of fertile pastures alternated with swelling hills and mountain spurs.

The Lewises were mainly of Welsh stock; the Meriwethers of both English and Welsh descent. On the English side they were Devonshire men and their patronymic probably came from their ancestors' enjoyment of Britain's most charming climate, that of Devon. Whatever the temperamental tendencies of Devonians, the Welsh have a strong urge toward clansmanship, like the Scots and Irish, even when far removed from their Celtic haunts. Thus the Meriwethers, Lewises, and such "kissing kin" as the Minors, Thorntons and Walkers were very close. So close, indeed, that cousin tended to marry cousin.

Among Meriwether Lewis's ancestors were many illustrious men of the Virginia Piedmont, such as Colonel Nicholas Meriwether. As commander of a Virginia regiment in Braddock's disastrous campaign of 1755, he personally helped his wounded and hapless commander off the field. Braddock's sister rewarded the colonel for saving her brother's life by sending him a fine gold-laced, embroidered military coat from Ireland. Nicholas married Margaret Douglas, daughter of the Scots Episcopalian parson, William Douglas, who was the tutor of three Presidents—Jefferson, Madison and Monroe. She was the granddaughter of the composer of "Annie Laurie" and niece of the great surgeon Dr. John Hunter. For all the rough edges on hilly, woodsy Albemarle County, its leading lights were gentry. The Meriwether and Lewis families were said to have picked up their traditional hot temper not from some redheaded Irishman who blundered into the lineage but from the bloodline of the fiery Scots parson. Another of the clan who was prominent when Meriwether Lewis was a child was Fielding Lewis, called "the Gunmaker of the Revolution." Meriwether undoubtedly visited him as a boy, calling at his Kenmore House, Fredericksburg, where he lived with his wife, Betty, George Washington's sister.

But young Meriwether Lewis was proudest of his own father, although he scarcely had time to get to know him. William Lewis, born in 1733, died in 1779 when the boy was only five years of age. He served without pay through the Revolution, considering the shouldering of arms to be his patriotic duty, not work for pay. He first came into local prominence when he marched with Lieutenant George Gilmer's Company to seize Lord Dunmore, who had confiscated the state's powder supply. This occurred on July 11, 1775, just four days after the Continental Congress declared war on Great Britain. The sortie was unsuccessful but the master of Locust Hill found military service to his liking and by September 1775 was a first lieutenant in the Albemarle County Minute Men. He was active in John Fleming's Company in February 1776 and on July 21st of that year was again dogging the trail of the elusive Lord Dunmore. When the Virginia state troops integrated with the Continental Line, Lieutenant Lewis became a Regular Army officer. He was also the third signer of the Albemarle County Declaration of Independence in 1779.

Lieutenant Lewis returned from the wars in 1779 to see his wife, daughter and two sons. Toward mid-November, he had his horse saddled and he prepared to rejoin his command. He said his good-byes, swung onto his mount and rode to the Secretary's Ford of the Rivanna River, swollen in flood. He was able to swim his horse across but he reached Clover Fields drenched to the skin. His kinfolk prevailed on him to stay over and dry out, but the damage was done. Pneumonia set in and in two days he was dead. As he lay dying, he asked to be buried at Clover Fields rather than at Locust Hill, probably because the foul weather, sodden roads and raging streams would make transportation of his body even ten miles difficult if not impossible. His wishes were honored and he was buried alongside his brother-in-law, Nicholas, under a white marble headstone.

Perhaps Meriwether Lewis's recurring distaste for the British, evident far up the Missouri River some twenty-six years later, dated from the sad event at Clover Fields. A youngster would be likely to blame his father's death in wartime not on chills and fever but on the redcoats whom his father was fighting. His father's untimely death, the near capture of his idol, Thomas Jefferson, and the occupation and looting of family property by the British in 1781 were enough to make any young Virginian into an impassioned hater of John Bull.

The Revolutionary years were exciting ones in Albemarle. In 1779–1780, some 4,000 British officers and men captured at Saratoga were kept in a compound called the Barracks, on George Carr's old farm on the north bank of Ivy Creek. And, although Albemarle had been a green paradise of fields, orchards of peaches and pippins, cornfields and bulging tobacco barns, war turned it into a depressed area. The people, on short rations themselves, became alarmed at the presence of so many of the enemy (the prisoners or Convention Troops) in their midst, especially when a total failure of provisions might occur and drive the redcoats to drastic action. Because of this threat, and British raids, the prisoners were removed to the Winchester Valley. But there was no quiet in Albemarle, for a much more real threat appeared in the person of Cornwallis's "Hunting Leopard," Colonel Banastre Tarleton. Cornwallis sent him and his Legion into a June sweep through the Piedmont in 1781. The 180 cavalrymen and 70 mounted infantrymen swept everything before them. Tarleton's Legion already had won a reputation for cruelty, and Virginia's makeshift militia units melted away before the striking force. On June 3, 1781, Tarleton left the North River near Hanover Courthouse and pushed swiftly on, bent on capturing the entire Virginia Legislature. The legislators moved from Rich-

9

mond to the presumed safety of Charlottesville but Tarleton raced after them. He captured Belvoir and Castle Hill and might have closed his trap were it not for a procrastinating and patriotic cook at Castle Hill who managed to delay Tarleton's breakfast so long that he was thrown behind schedule. The legislators were alerted and fled to safety.

The Paul Revere who carried the word to Albemarle of the approach of the Hunting Leopard was John Jouett. Captain Jack Jouett of the Virginia militia happened to be in the Cuckoo Tavern having a stirrup cup when Tarleton's dragoons came thundering through on the main road. Jouett immediately sized up the situation, mounted his horse and, using his spurs liberally, outflanked the British column to reach a little-used shortcut to Albemarle. After a forty-mile ride, he reached Monticello at sunrise to warn all there of the oncoming dragoons. The Speakers of both Houses, and members continued their leisurely breakfast, to the astonishment of Jouett. Riding like the wind came Tarleton and his men on captured blooded Virginia racehorses, destroying American army supplies and detaching a party to surprise ex-Governor Jefferson at Monticello while the main party galloped on toward Charlottesville. But they found their quarry had eluded them; Jefferson hiding on Carter's Mountain, most of the others fleeing to Staunton.

Jouett may very well have been Meriwether Lewis's boyhood hero, even after the erstwhile captain settled down to run the red brick Old Swan, one of Charlottesville's taverns. For not once but twice Jouett had to save the dillydallying legislators. When Tarleton sped in pursuit of them from Charlottesville, Jouett led him on a wild-goose chase while the lawmakers managed to slip away.

Colonel Tarleton behaved with uncharacteristic restraint at Monticello, giving orders to his men that no property was to be injured. At Charlottesville, too, he was on his best conduct. A real soldier, Tarleton shared the hardships of his troopers. At the Farm, he slept on the floor, wrapped in his cloak, with his saddled horse at the door, ready for action. While he was there, he complimented Colonel Nicholas Lewis's wife on her choice of residence, saying, "Madame, you dwell in a little paradise." But as the militia began to close in on him, Tarleton decided to convert the paradise into a hell. He moved the Legion back to Elk Hill, a Jefferson property, and let the soldiers run wild. Barns and fences were burned. Crops were destroyed in the field in a scorched-earth program. All useful cattle and horses were driven off and slaves were rounded up and taken along. Animals too young to be useful were slaughtered by the British, even the blooded colts. Tarleton left the Elk Hill area a wilderness. Some three million pounds sterling in property damages was the result of raids such as Tarleton's; small wonder that Lewis grew up to hate and to distrust the British, or that many Albemarle men moved out of the country to try their luck in unravaged Georgia after the war.

Meriwether was probably ordered to stay close to his mother during the dangerous days in Albemarle. But this was not the safest place in the land. He once saw his courageous mother shoo away a party of British officer-prisoners from the Barracks who had taken over Locust Hill. Lucy Lewis was not only a skilled herbalist and cook (from whom Jefferson bought his hams), she was also spunky and at home with firearms. Once when a hunting party gathered at Locust Hill they returned empty-handed from the chase only to find platters of succulent (if unhung) venison awaiting them. A big buck had been flushed from the woods into Lucy's yard. She drove the deer into the corner of the yard—right up against the chimney, in fact—shot it, butchered and cooked it in time for the arrival of the hungry hunters. Meriwether, when still a lad, began to reach for his gun and clothes when awakened in the middle of the night by the baying of the hounds. He would slip out of the house and join the dogs in a merry chase through the dark woods and across the streams, even when frozen in winter, of the Blue Ridge foothill country. One day, returning from a hunt and a visit to Clover Fields, Meriwether was crossing a lot in which a ferocious bull was penned. The snorting beast lowered its head and charged the boy. Instead of running for cover, Lewis stood his ground, cocked the heavy hammer of his flintlock rifle and shot the animal dead in its tracks. It is unlikely that the county's wolves

11

frightened him, either, and he probably collected the bounty of tobacco and money for wolf scalps more than once.

Young Meriwether found himself in a hunter's paradise. The place names of Albemarle County still suggest this—Wolf Trap Creek, Elk Run, Buck Mountain, Buffalo Meadow, Beaverdam Creek, Turkey Run, Red Bear Hollow, and Black Fox Branch. Fat bears hibernated in the Blue Ridge; flocks of turkeys thronged the woods and, in the fall and spring, wild ducks and geese sojourned on the rivers. Shad and herring ran the streams and pigeons roosted in the trees in such numbers that they broke the limbs with their weight. The buffalo were gone by Lewis's day, but the elk and deer were still there. With little money in the county, skins and tobacco became the media of exchange. In fall and early winter, deer hunting pushed aside all other business for Meriwether and his companions. When the hunting was slack, he mastered birdcalls, especially the gobble-gobble of the wild turkeys.

Governor George Gilmer of Georgia described the boy as having inherited the energy, courage, activity and good understanding of his mother. According to Gilmer, from that admirable woman Meriwether acquired in his youth the hardy habits, firm constitution and other traits which would mark him as a man—a man of courage, faithfulness, patriotism, ability, a sense of duty and self-possession in times of danger. By the time he was eight he liked to hunt, alone except for his dog, and by night. There is a story of his Georgia days that once, when the Cherokees were on the warpath, he was with a body of settlers hiding in the woods. One of the men stupidly kindled a fire, giving away their location to the Indians. A shot was heard; the men panicked. Here and there they ran, grabbing up rifles while silhouetted by the dancing flames of the bright cookfire. Only young Meriwether Lewis had the presence of mind to dash a bucket of water on the fire to prevent his elders from becoming sitting-duck targets for the hostiles.

Perhaps young Lewis paid more than lip service to the proud motto of his family's coat of arms—*Omne Solum Forti Patria Est* (To the Brave Man, Everything He Does Is for His Country). He also, perhaps unwittingly, responded to the motto of his maternal, Meriwether, line—*Vi et Consilo* (With Force and Counsel).

Before the Revolutionary War ended, Cornwallis sent Tarleton on a second raid into Albemarle, to seize stores collected at the Courthouse. This time, another boyhood hero of Lewis's rose to the occasion as Jouett had earlier done. The Marquis de Lafayette led a force out to contain Cornwallis's Leopard. The Frenchman could not hope for a victory in a musket-to-musket battle so he swung around the flank of the superior force, set his pioneers to clear out an old, long-unused road and reached the James River before Tarleton. When the Englishman arrived, he found the marquis and his Americans in an almost impregnable position between him and the supplies. The colonel was too good a soldier to throw his men away in a futile attack; instead, he marched off slowly toward the coast and Albemarle was able to breathe easily again.

Lucy Lewis had been left a widow when twenty-seven years old, with three small children. She did the sensible thing, remarrying within six months of her husband's death. Her second husband was Captain John Marks, a Virginian and a friend of Jefferson forced to leave military service because of ill health. They were married May 13, 1780.

Shortly after the Revolution, Captain Marks migrated with a number of Virginians to a colony being developed by General John Matthews in a grassland and parklike woodland on the Broad River of Georgia. The stream cut through the post oak and blackjack of Oglethorpe County to join the Savannah. Lucy made a home there on the Broad. Meriwether, though the second-oldest child, was the older boy so, according to Anglo-Saxon tradition and primogeniture, he received his father's property, some 1,000 acres at Ivy. But since he was too young to look after it, Locust Hill was managed by relatives while he went to Georgia with his mother.

Young Meriwether Lewis enjoyed the raw, new country which was inland Georgia. It was more of a frontier than Albemarle and he came to be a first-rate hunter while he still had his milk teeth. John Marks settled upstream of most of the log cabins and rifle-slitted frame houses of the ex-Virginians, preferring the very edge of the forest. There the boy gathered berries and hunted and fished and trapped beavers in the Broad. In Georgia he became proficient in self-taught natural history, mastering the native flora and fauna and nurturing a curiosity about animal and vegetable life which would be of great use on the trek west. Meriwether was interested in, if not exactly master of, the physical sciences, too. When told by a schoolmaster, for example, that the earth turned around, Lewis tried to prove it by an experiment. He jumped up in the air as high as he could. He was disappointed when he came down in exactly the same spot as his takeoff. And no one muttered, *"E puor si muove."*

As soon as he felt himself to be an adult, when he was thirteen or fourteen years old, Lewis returned to Albemarle County to manage his father's land with the help of his uncles, Nicholas and William Meriwether. Since he was a devoted son, he wrote frequent letters to his mother and to his sister and brother. He may have become a friend at this time of young Will Clark, who would accompany him to the Pacific. If he was a friend of George Rogers Clark's younger brother, however, he did not mention him in letters home.

Tutorial schooling by local pastors was the rule in the Piedmont during Meriwether Lewis's youth. Parson William Douglas had taught three American Presidents in their childhood—Jefferson, Madison, and Monroe. It was Lewis's lot to be tutored first by Parson Matthew Maury, in 1789 and 1790, in a rude log building on the lawn of Edgeworth Farm, almost on the very border of Albemarle and Louisa counties. This was Albemarle's Classical School. Maury was the father of the renowned Matthew Fontaine Maury of naval and hydrographic fame in Civil War days and of Milly Maury, on whom the always-romantic Lewis had a brief, schoolboy crush.

Lewis had a more disagreeable brush with formal education when he studied under Dr. Charles Everitt, a prominent M.D. of Albemarle, after two years of tutelage by Maury. Unluckily for the young student, the new dominie suffered from both ill health and ill temper. His discipline verged on sadism; his disagreeableness knew no bounds. He was peevish, cruel, temperamental and "atrabilious." One of Lewis's schoolmates described the bilious master and his class's attitude toward him: "We disliked the teacher. His method of teaching was as bad as anything could be. He was impatient of interruption. We seldom applied for assistance, said our lessons badly, made no proficiency and acquired negligent and bad habits."

Peachy Gilmer's pen picture of his classmate, Meriwether Lewis, is not altogether flattering. "He was always remarkable for perseverance, which in the early period of his life seemed nothing more than obstinacy in pursuing the trifles that employ that age; of a martial temper and great steadiness of purpose, self-possession and undaunted courage. His person was stiff and without grace; bowlegged, awkward, formal and almost without flexibility. It bore to my vision a very strong resemblance to Buonaparte." (This last observation does not appear to have been shared, particularly, by such artists as Peale and Saint-Mémin who portrayed him.)

Young Lewis was happy to transfer to a gentler-humored teacher, Rev. James Waddell. He was the model for the blind parson of William Wirt's novel, *The British Spy,* though not blind, yet, when Lewis knew him. The boy found him a great contrast to the cruel Everitt and, indeed, "a very polite scholar." He wrote his mother in August 1790: "I am, myself, at present with Mr. James Waddell, where I expect to continue for eighteen months or two years. Every civility is here paid to me and leaves me without any reason to regret the loss of a home of nearer connection. As soon as I complete my education, you shall certainly see me." Lewis hoped to be able to return to the gifted Maury but this was not possible. Shortly, one of his elders suggested that he terminate his formalized schooling since he had mastered grammar. He could always study geography (apparently, a pet subject) at home while he devoted himself, full-time, to the management of his late father's estate. Although he hungered for knowledge, he knew he was the man of the family and he bowed to the counsel of his guardians. Thrusting all hope of continuing on to the College of William and Mary from his mind, he settled down at Locust Hill with the only intellectual stimulation supplied by the visits of a local schoolmaster who was proficient in arithmetic. He left formal schooling to his younger brother, Reuben, who studied with Waddell and Rev. John Robertson, possessor of the finest collection of Latin and Greek books in all Virginia. Reuben became a doctor as well as an Indian agent but his career was not a notable success.

Corn and wheat, rather than Greek and Latin, came to occupy Meriwether's waking hours. "Crops are generally very sorry in this part of the country," he wrote Lucy on August 6, 1790, "in consequence of the Ivy weather, but [I] can say with pleasure that it is not generally the case. Many of the adjacent parts of the country having had a sufficiency of rain [and] ideal prospects of good crops. But our situation is now critical for if we have not rain in a few days, we shall make no corn." Like many youths on the farm, Meriwether hankered for a military career and he wistfully referred to General Charles Scott's little victory on the Wabash in the so-called Blackberry Campaign.

In 1790, Meriwether paid a visit to his mother and her brood in Georgia. The very next year she was widowed again and he had to take on the full role of master of the family. He drove a carriage, built by Jefferson's Negro artisans at Monticello, down to the Broad and brought back to Locust Hill his mother, his sister, his brother, and his half brother and half sister, John Hastings Marks and Mary Marks, of whom he had grown very fond.

Lucy Marks was happy to return to Virginia. Not only was Albemarle a more civilized and smiling area than Matthews's Goose Pond country but it was much healthier. For while the Broad cut through attractive country without underbrush, it was an unhealthy area in the 1790's. Oglethorpe County was not only filled with Virginia *émigrés* but was also host to innumerable vectors of bilious fevers which afflicted the transplanted Piedmontese.

Meriwether Lewis busied himself with farming. He ran Locust Hill, and ran it well. He acquired an 800-acre tract on the Red River in Montgomery County, took title to 180 acres of warrant land belonging to his late stepfather, and secured another parcel in Clark County. He thought his destiny was the career of a plantation manager. Jefferson noted that he was "an assiduous and attentive farmer, observing with minute attention all plants and

16

insects he met with." Later he would put these talents to work as an explorer, not as a dirt farmer. When he had to study botany and zoology his farming experience stood him in good stead. For the moment, Jefferson's young friend saw himself becoming a gentleman farmer, and he reluctantly turned his back on the life of "rambling" of which he had so long dreamed.

CHAPTER III

FROM BIVOUAC

TO THE WHITE HOUSE

*I feel my situation in the President's family an extremely
pleasant one. I very little expected that I possessed the confidence of Mr. Jefferson so far as to have produced on his
part a voluntary offer of the office of his private secretary.
However, nothing is extraordinary in these days of revolution and reform.*

— MERIWETHER LEWIS, March 1801

MERIWETHER LEWIS was eighteen when he decided to give up
formal schooling for the life of a Piedmont gentleman farmer.
But the role did not fit the restless youth any more than the
scholar's robes of William and Mary would have suited him. Just
two years later came the excuse which released him from the
tedium of plantation life. The "whiskey counties" of Pennsylvania, the western tier consisting of Fayette, Allegheny, Washington and Westmoreland, offered violent opposition to Alexander Hamilton's excise tax on spirits. Whiskey was the medium
of exchange and the tax was payable in money, of which the
farmers had but little. Protest meetings developed into attacks on
revenue officers; judges were defied and the U. S. mail robbed. A
lawyer, David Bradford, assumed leadership of the insurgents.

President Washington hoped to minimize the trouble, calling it
mere "symptoms of riot and violence," but eventually the commissioners he sent had to be reinforced with troops. The Presi-

18

dent called out 13,000 militiamen from Virginia, New Jersey, Pennsylvania and Maryland in August 1794 to quell the revolt. Among the first to join the Virginia colors was Meriwether Lewis, mustered in as a private in T. Walker's volunteer corps. The Government hoped that a show of force would stamp out the Whiskey Rebellion and although General, and Governor, Henry Lee commanded the army, Secretary of the Treasury Alexander Hamilton tagged along as a supercargo and usurped command from Light-Horse Harry. The invading army swung into Pennsylvania in two columns. The New Jersey and Pennsylvania troops gathered at Carlisle; Meriwether Lewis and his fellow Virginians after mustering at Winchester bivouacked with the Marylanders at Cumberland. Washington visited the camps himself to bolster the patriotism and morale of his green, untried troops. He even marched with them as far as Bedford. But there were no battles to test the recruits; by the time the advance units had crossed the Alleghenies and were closing in on Pittsburgh, the insurrectionists, including Bradford, were fleeing down the Ohio and Mississippi to safety in Spanish Louisiana. A handful of rebels were captured and marched east for trial but subsequently released and pardoned by President Washington.

The comic-opera campaign was no disappointment to Lewis. He was delighted with the life of a soldier. He thrived on it. There was no doubt whatsoever in his mind that he had found his true calling. He wrote to his mother on October 4, 1794, from Winchester that he and his mates were each cutting a most martial figure. He concluded with a very soldierlike observation, "We have mountains of beef and oceans of whiskey, and I feel myself able to share it with the heartiest fellow in camp."

At Fort Cumberland, on the 13th, he again wrote to his mother, telling her of the flight of the rebels and his only disappointment in the rebellion's quick collapse. He was loath to return home to the humdrum routine of running Locust Hill. So he decided to visit Kentucky to look over his mother's lands there and prevent any possible forfeiture of them to the state as vacant or abandoned lands. Meanwhile, he decided to remain with the small volunteer army of occupation, under General Daniel Morgan, which patrolled and policed Pittsburgh after the mass of

19

militia marched home. Writing on the 24th of November, he said, "I am quite delighted with a soldier's life." He told his mother not to worry about him, the Army's houses were comfortable and his life was not in danger. He then apologized for his wandering—"rambling"—as he termed it, but confessed that it was his "governing passion." He begged the forgiveness of his family and friends for all the worries and vexations he had caused them because of his Quixotic disposition. But, since the insurgents were still as rebellious at heart as ever, he felt that his place was in the army of occupation. "I can see no honour or profit to be gained by living at the expense of the public without rendering her any service." The would-be explorer, who would never marry, ended his letter with a light bit of romantic banter. He sent, via his mother, his regards to all the girls in Albemarle and asked Lucy to warn them that he would be bringing "an Insurgent girl to see them next fall, bearing the title of Mrs. Lewis."

Meriwether Lewis was eligible for discharge in May 1795 but he elected to continue in militia service with the rank of ensign. On May Day he transferred, in rank, to the Second Sub-Legion of the Regular Army. He wrote his mother in pride and delight that he had a fine, Philadelphia-made epaulet. Soon he was being swept down the Ohio to join the force of General Mad Anthony Wayne, victor over the Indians at Fallen Timbers. Lewis was present at Wayne's headquarters when the humbled chiefs of the Wyandots, Delawares, Shawnees, Ottawas, Chippewas, Potawatomis, Miamis, Kickapoos, Kaskaskias and others filed in to set their hands to the Treaty of Greenville, August 3, 1795. This treaty, "to put an end to a destructive war, to settle all controversies, and to restore harmony and friendly intercourse between the United States and the Indian tribes," erased the disgrace of the defeats of Generals Harmar and St. Clair. It also brought Lewis into close contact with Indians for the first time. He would ever after be an interested student of the red men.

The young ensign soon found that army life was not all beer and skittles, nor even mountains of meat and oceans of whiskey. November 6, 1795, proved to be a black day for Lewis, who had now exchanged the traditional red plumes of the Second Sub-

Legion for the green plumes of the Fourth. On that day he was haled before a general court-martial. Major Joseph Shaylor presided at his trial, the first such court-martial held in Wayne's Legion. Testimony began on the 6th and did not close until the 12th because of an adjournment. The charges were brought against Lewis by a Lieutenant Elliott (perhaps Surgeon John Elliott, a New Yorker). The first was an accusation that Lewis had made a direct, open and contemptuous violation of Articles One and Two of the Seventh Section of the Rules and Articles of War. To wit, that on September 24, 1795, Lewis had engaged in provocative speech and gestures in the Lieutenant's quarters and had presumed, that same day, to send him a challenge to a duel. Elliott's second charge was that of conduct unbecoming an officer and gentleman. According to the accuser, Lewis, drunk, had burst into his room, uninvited and "abruptly and in an ungentlemanly manner." He then had not only insulted the Lieutenant without provocation and offered to duel to the death with him, but also had disturbed the "peace and harmony" of the officers who were Elliott's guests that day.

The accusation was stated to Lewis and he was asked to plead. The reply from the now stone-cold sober Virginian was a resounding "Not Guilty." The officers of the court studied the testimony carefully and finally made their decision. They were of the opinion that Meriwether Lewis was not guilty of the charges exhibited against him. Their verdict was "That he be acquitted with Honor." Lewis was liberated from his arrest and returned immediately to duty.

Commander in Chief Mad Anthony Wayne confirmed the verdict of Major Shaylor's court-martial and stated that he fondly hoped the trial would be not only the first but the last in his encampment. Lewis was reassigned. He was transferred to the Chosen Rifle Company of elite riflemen-sharpshooters commanded by the man who would become his fast friend, William Clark. The latter welcomed his fellow Albemarlean. But they were not together long. Clark recalled, "Captain Lewis was appointed an Ensign and arraigned to the company which I commanded a few months before I resigned." The combination of ill health—Clark had a history of sickness and complained fre-

21

quently in his diary of vomiting—and the pleading of his family to come home to untangle brother George Rogers Clark's twisted financial affairs caused him to return to civilian life. On July 1, 1796, he resigned his commission.

The doughty, gouty Wayne considered Meriwether Lewis one of his most promising young officers. When, on November 17, 1796, he wanted dispatches rushed at horse-killing speed from Detroit to Major Isaac Craig at Pittsburgh, he chose the Albemarle ensign for the hard-riding assignment. Lewis, sagging in the saddle with fatigue, made the journey in jig time with his Indian guide, Enos, postponing a four-month furlough in order to carry out the assignment.

Meriwether Lewis had lost the companionship of Clark when he had hardly become acquainted with him. He made other friends, however; one of them, ironically, being Tarleton Bates of Pittsburgh, brother of the man who would become his deadly enemy when Lewis was Governor of Upper Louisiana. In 1796 Lewis applied for admission to the Masonic Order and on December 31 the Scribe of Door to Virtue Lodge Number 44, of Albemarle, recorded in his register that "Meriwether Lewis was recommended as a proper person to become a member." He was elected to membership on January 28, 1797, and, that same evening, initiated as an Entered Apprentice. Because he was in Virginia on only a short leave, he was advanced through Masonic degrees with dizzying speed. The very evening after his initiation, he was passed, first, to the degree of Fellowcraft and then raised to the degree of Master Mason. On April 3rd or 4th (after what must have seemed an interminable delay compared to the blazing action of January) he was the recipient of the degree of Past Master Mason. During the next few years he was on military duty in the West and unable to attend lodge meetings but in June and July 1798 he was at Locust Hill and was not only a regular attendant but held office in the Lodge. Thanks to his motion, for example, a portion of Lodge funds was earmarked for charity. By October 31, 1799, Lewis was a Royal Arch Mason in Widow's Son Lodge, Milton, Virginia.

Lewis threw himself into the military life, too, and was determined to cut a very military figure. He was more than a little vain about his appearance and once (January 15, 1798) wrote to his friend Lieutenant Frederick L. Claiborne of his exasperation with an inadequate tailor. "Of all the damned pieces of work, my coat exceeds. It would take up three sheets of paper, written in shorthand, to point out its deficiencies or, I may even say, deformities. However, let it suffice that he has not lined the body at all; he had galoon furnished for that purpose. The lace is deficient. I had it taken to pieces and altered and could I have done without it I should have returned it, beyond a doubt. For the blind button holes on the cuff he substituted lace and no part of those on the facings was worked blind. The four small buttons on the cape are deficient. . . ." So furious was Lewis that, when he conveyed his greetings to Claiborne's family, he wrote, "I am in good health. There is nothing worth relating in this quarter. Remember me to my [sic] wife and family." He added a final, exasperated postscript on another trying military matter. "No doubt you have had forwarded to you the late regulation of our generous Congress relative to the delivery and distribution of fuel and straw to the garrison on the sea coast and recruiting parties. The allowance falling so far short of what is really necessary, I am at a loss to determine what steps to pursue. Do let me know what plan you adapt as I am confident the proportion of fuel is so small that the soldiers cannot subsist on it."

In writing his mother, Lewis tried to correct the false impression of the Army which was current. "The general idea is that the Army is the school of debauchery, but, believe me, it has ever proven the school of experience and prudence to your affectionate son." Typical of the experience of which he spoke, besides his garrison duties, was his terrain reconnaissance near Louis Lorimier's old store and the St. Mary's and Auglaize rivers in the spring of 1796 and, in October of that year, a march overland from Detroit to Pittsburgh in which he became lost twice but profited much by the experience. He ran out of rations while floundering in the wilderness and was *really* hungry for perhaps the first time in his career, but not the last. When he happened upon some bear meat in an Indian camp, meat which had seen better days, he fell upon it as if it were prime steak and truffles.

The Army was well on its way to making not only a good soldier of Lewis but a first-rate woodsman, as well.

Ensign Lewis had transferred to the 1st U. S. Infantry Regiment in November 1796 and the following year saw him not only observing Indians but serving with them. One of his duties in February and March was to escort the Wyandot warrior and guide, Captain Enos Coon. Lewis put him up at the Pittsburgh inn run by W. Morrow. In May he was back at Locust Hill on leave to arrange for his mother's slaves to move from Georgia to Virginia. He also visited her Broad River property, sold some of his Ivy Creek land to his brother, Reuben, and to Clifton Rodes, and bought back some of his stepfather's old land grants. He then went to Ohio and Kentucky to secure land claims for Mary and John Hastings Marks, as their guardian. At this time, he obtained 2,600 acres, each worth twenty cents, in the Bluegrass State alone, for himself. He was well on his way to becoming a large landowner and were it not for his tragically early death he might have gone on to become as land poor as Jefferson himself.

In the latter part of 1797, he commanded an infantry company of Captain Isaac Guion's command, which took over the new post on the Mississippi, Fort Pickering, née Fort Adams. This bastion had been erected at Chickasaw Bluffs to awe the Spaniards who were starting to edge upriver again in the Memphis area in what was apparently a last gasp of moribund Spanish imperialism. There on the frontier of the Cherokee nation, Lewis schooled himself further in Indian ways and tongues. He gained valuable military experience when he had to assume command of the post upon the death of the ranking officer, Captain Douglas Pierce, of malaria at Fort Nogales, or Walnut Bluffs. During the next year and early in 1799, Lewis had a change of duty; he was stationed at Charlottesville on recruiting duty. On March 3rd of that year, "in pursuance of the Act of 16 July, 1798," he was promoted to lieutenant to fill the vacancy created by John Michael's promotion to captain.

Some time in September 1800, Lewis returned to the Indian frontier, rejoining Captain Claiborne's Company. At Detroit the lean and bowlegged lieutenant amused himself by debating hotly with Federalist officers over politics. On December 5th, he was promoted to captain, his promotion coming not because of his growing skill as a frontiersman but because he had a natural head for figures, despite his deficiencies in schooling. He was appointed regimental paymaster. This was far from being a tedious accountant's job. His duties gave him a veritable carte blanche for the rambling of which he was so fond. He was away from Colonel John Hamtramck's Pittsburgh and Detroit headquarters almost as much as he was there. His duties took him to Fort Washington (Cincinnati), Fort Wayne, Limestone or Maysville, Chillicothe and Wheeling. On one trip he prepared himself, unconsciously, for his future trial by the querulous Big Muddy. He traveled down the Ohio with a 21-foot bateau, or keelboat, and a pirogue or dugout. Another chore of Lewis's, besides paying scattered units of the regiment, which kept him on the road was his responsibility for keeping track of all the regiment's transfers, AWOLs, and deserters. (One of his original "Lists of Absentees" is preserved today in the National Archives.)

By New Year's, 1801, Captain Lewis seemed fated for a routine Army career—to which he had no objection. It was a fate, in fact, which he welcomed. But it was not to be. Suddenly his whole life was changed. One day, February 23, 1801, newly elected President of the United States Thomas Jefferson wrote him a letter inviting him to become his private secretary. Since Jefferson did not know the captain's whereabouts, he wrote a covering letter to his commanding officer, General James Wilkinson. To the latter Jefferson explained that he preferred a secretary who possessed a knowledge of both the Army and the "Western Country"—in other words, Meriwether Lewis. As the reason for his choice of Lewis, the President said, "A personal acquaintance with him, owing to his being of my neighborhood, has induced me to select him if his presence can be dispensed with, without injury to the service."

President Jefferson wished Lewis to retain his captaincy and his right to rise in rank while serving in the White House. (This was done. Lewis was kept on active status during his secretarial years. When Secretary of War Dearborn ordered Ensign Joseph Dorr on May 9, 1802, to report, it was "to Detroit for service there in the company commanded by Meriwether Lewis." It would be *his* company long after the Virginian left the West. On January 24, 1803, when Dearborn discharged Private Abraham Golding, it was "from Capt. Lewis's Company," although Jefferson's secretary was in the Executive Mansion workroom at the time, puzzling over plans for Jefferson's great expedition to the Pacific, cramming on navigation, and seeking the impossible— an interpreter proficient in all Indian tongues.)

The letter to Lewis was most flattering. Jefferson came straight to the point; he indicated that Lewis was his first choice and that he would not even consider a second for the secretarial post until he had an answer from him:

"The appointment to the Presidency has rendered it necessary for me to have a private secretary and in selecting one I have thought it important to respect not only his capacity to aid me in the private concerns of the household, but also to contribute to the mass of information which it is interesting to the Administration to acquire. Your knowledge of the Western Country, of the Army, and of all its interests and relations has rendered it desirable for public as well as private purposes that you should be engaged in that office. In point of profit it has little to offer; the salary being only 500 D., which would scarcely be more than an equivalent for your pay and rations, which you would be obliged to relinquish while withdrawn from active service, but retaining your rank and right to rise. But it would be an easier office, would make you known, and be known, to characters of influence in the affairs of our Country, and give you the advantage of their wisdom. You would, of course, save also the expense of subsistence and lodgings, as you would be one of my family.

"If these or any other views which your own reflections may suggest should present the office of my private secretary as worthy of acceptance, you will make me happy in accepting it. It has been solicited by several, who will have no answer till I hear from you. Should you accept, it will be necessary that you should wind up whatever affairs you are engaged in as expeditiously as your own and the public interest will admit, and adjourn to this place; and that immediately on receipt of this you inform me by letter of your determination. It would also be necessary that you wait on Genl. Wilkinson and obtain his approbation and his aid in making such arrangements as may render your absence as little injurious to the service as may be."

Four days after receiving Jefferson's letter, via Tarleton Bates, Lewis responded. "You have thought proper so far to honour me with your confidence as to express a wish that I should accept the place of your private secretary. I most cordially acquiesce, and with pleasure accept the office, nor were further motives necessary to induce my compliance than that you, Sir, should conceive that in the discharge of the duties of that office I could be serviceable to my Country, or useful to yourself. Permit me here, Sir, to do further justice to my feelings, by expressing the lively responsibility with which I received this mark of your confidence and esteem. . . . Not a moment has been lost in making the necessary arrangements in order to get forward to the City of Washington with all possible dispatch. Rest assured I shall not relax in my exertions."

In letters to friends, Jefferson made it clear that he was seeking not only a secretary but an aide-de-camp. Hence his choice of Lewis. Lewis's duties would seldom be that of amanuensis but he would have to take care of company at the White House, execute commissions in the city occasionally, carry Presidential messages to Congress, and take part in conferences with members of Congress and other officers of government.

In the absence of General Wilkinson, Colonel Hamtramck ordered Lewis east. On March 9, 1801, he asked the Quartermaster General to provide the captain with packhorses. Lewis set out as soon as he could but a combination of circumstances made his progress slow. Spring rains turned country roads into wallows; one of his horses came up lame. These delays put off his arrival in the capital until April Fool's Day. Jefferson had gone to Monticello that very day, leaving word for Lewis to follow him after resting a few days in Washington. Lewis therefore felt free to remain long enough to transfer his paymaster's records to Lieutenant Ninian Pinckney before joining the President in Albemarle County. Meriwether Lewis had missed the Inauguration on March 4 and did not hear the President deliver his long and rhetorical address in the Senate Chamber. It embodied most of his political faith but was chiefly remarkable for its omission of any reference to the subject so close to Jefferson's heart—the Far West. In the welter of appeals for unity and cooperation between Republicans and Federalists, there was only one phrase which might have caught Lewis's ear, had he been there—"a rising nation spread over a wide and fruitful land." Mum was still the word on the President's plan to spread the nation wider. The time was not yet ripe to broach his plan of exploration to Congress.

When the President returned to the White House, Lewis helped him to plan the new order of things there. Jefferson wanted none of the caste-conscious protocol of his predecessors. He hoped to make Washington society as egalitarian as himself. Lewis was his shadow, lightening his burdens. He was kept busy helping the President answer the hundreds of letters which poured in. Some were congratulatory; some were begging; many were both. Lewis, like his chief, ignored the disgust of the ceremony-loving, titled Europeans who found the capital a mudhole village and the President a gentleman in carpet slippers. Shortly after taking up residence in the White House, with its leaky roof, unplastered walls, and the nearest stable for his and Jefferson's horses at 14th and G streets, Lewis was overseeing most of the domestic arrangements of the household. Widower Jefferson's daughters were grown up and married, so they could help him only infrequently. Although he scorned ostentation, state dinners and other entertainments were still fairly lavishly affairs which Lewis had to arrange. Luckily, he was abetted by an able and efficient force of eleven servants transferred from Monticello to the White House.

The White House served as an ideal finishing school for Lewis, thanks to the long dinner conversations in which he participated. The exchanges between Jefferson and such guests as poet Joel Barlow or Thomas Paine seldom descended into small talk. The President maintained an open house for scientists, just as he had done at Monticello, while not neglecting diplomats, Congressmen and politicians. Lewis was privy to affairs of state and secrets of diplomacy. The President would dismiss the servants to secure privacy, then quiz his guests on critical subjects while his confidential secretary stood by. No one was closer to Jefferson during his first years in the Presidential office—unless it was the President's pet mockingbird. Many of Lewis's rough intellectual edges were smoothed by the cultural atmosphere of the Executive Mansion.

Frequently Lewis had to help with affairs of state. For example, on December 8, 1801, when the President broke a strong precedent by not delivering personally the State of the Union message to Congress, it was Captain Lewis who conveyed it to Capitol Hill. When the President made his semiannual visits to Monticello, Lewis accompanied him. Jefferson quartered him in the clapboard house on the estate called Franklin, home of Ben Franklin's grandson, William Bache. From time to time, the President sent him on errands but, quartered at Franklin, he was always close to both Monticello and to his own home at Locust Hill.

Occasionally Lewis had to handle rather sticky personal matters for Jefferson. One such case was the Callender affair. James Thompson Callender, an anti-Federalist writer, was a victim of the Alien and Sedition Laws, which Jefferson abhorred. To help him, he sent Lewis to Callender with a gift of $50 and word that the journalist's fine would be remitted as soon as it could be arranged. Lewis was shocked by the man's attitude. Instead of being grateful to Jefferson, he responded with insolent language —"high toned" Lewis called it—and "intimated that he was in possession of things which he could, and would, make use of in a certain case; that he received the fifty dollars not as charity but as a due, in fact, as hush money." The ingrate was a blackmailer! He intended to rake over publicly an old love affair of Jefferson's in order to embarrass the President. Jefferson was not the man to bow to an extortionist. He told his aide-de-camp to have no more dealings with Callender. "He knows nothing of me which I am not willing to declare to the world, myself," said Jefferson.

Although Lewis would have liked to convert Callender's face into a spittoon, Jefferson forbade his taking any action. He let the rogue keep the $50 and remitted his fine. The wretched Callender tried to spread the scandal and manufactured others to blacken Jefferson's name but the President was soon rid of his problem, for Callender fell into a few feet of water while, apparently, dead drunk. No questions were asked; Dame Fortune was simply thanked for the drowning.

There was good company in Jefferson's circle. Peachy Gilmore called it "the most accomplished and elegant society that has been anywhere, at any time, within my knowledge in Virginia. . . . Meriwether Lewis was, too, sometimes with us, sometimes absent." Lewis made many new friends at this time, among them Mahlon Dickerson of Philadelphia.

Sometime in 1802, probably in the President's downstairs, map-lined workroom-study, Lewis and Jefferson sat down to actually begin the planning of the Lewis and Clark Expedition. In order to dispatch Lewis on his way, the President had to secure funds from Congress for the expeditionary corps' expenses. On January 18, 1803, therefore, he submitted a secret message to Congress. He camouflaged his real intent by persuading the Congress that he was concerned with two other matters—continuing the Indian trading posts established by act of Congress, and acquiring more Indian lands by purchase. The latter subject was the ostensible reason for the confidential nature of the message; the red men were believed to be hostile to further cession of their lands.

But in the last paragraph of his message, Jefferson finally put on paper what was really weighing on his mind: "The River Missouri and the Indians inhabiting it are not as well known as is rendered desirable by their connection with the Mississippi and, consequently, with us. It is, however, understood that the country on that river is inhabited by numerous tribes, who furnish great supplies of furs and peltry to the trade of another nation carried on in a high latitude, through an infinite number of portages and lakes shut up by ice through a long season. The commerce on that line could bear no competition with that of the Missouri, traversing a moderate climate, offering, according to the best accounts, a continued navigation from its source and, possibly, with a single portage from the Western Ocean. . . . An intelligent officer with ten or twelve chosen men, fit for the enterprise and willing to undertake it, taken from our posts where they may be spared without inconvenience, might explore the whole line, even to the Western Ocean, have conferences with the natives on the subject of commercial intercourse, get admission among them for our traders as others are admitted, agree on convenient deposits for an interchange of articles, and return with the information acquired in the course of two summers."

The whole expense, said Jefferson, would be their arms and accouterments plus the grant of lands, upon the soldiers' return, for their services. The only cash needed was an appropriation of $2,500 "for the purpose of extending the external commerce of the U. S." He justified the expense. "While other nations have encountered great expense to enlarge the boundaries of knowledge by undertaking voyages of discovery and for other literary purposes, in various parts and directions, our nation seems to owe to the same object, as well as to its own interest, to explore this, the only line of easy communication across the Continent, and so directly traversing our own part of it. The interests of commerce place this principal object within the constitutional powers and cares of Congress, and that it should incidentally advance the geographical knowledge of our own Continent cannot but be an additional gratification. The nation claiming the territory, regarding this as a literary pursuit which it is in the habit of permitting within its dominions, would not be disposed to view it with jealousy, even if the expiring state of its interests there did not render it a matter of indifference." Whatever Congress's feelings about advancing the geographical knowledge of North America, they were almost unanimous in wishing to break Britain's fur monopoly. Therefore they gave the President a go-ahead.

Ten days later, Jefferson wrote his friends Caspar Wistar, Benjamin Smith Barton, and Benjamin Rush about the expedition, but warned each man to keep the information strictly confidential. The reason for this secrecy he made clear in another letter, to Robert Patterson: "I think it advisable that nothing should be said of this til he [Lewis] shall have got beyond the reach of any obstacles which might be prepared for him by those who would not like the enterprise." His letter to Rush was typical of

31

all the others; in it Jefferson sketched his plan. "About 10 woodsmen, headed by Captain Lewis, my secretary, will set out on it immediately and probably accomplish it in two seasons. Captain Lewis is brave, prudent, habituated to the woods and familiar with Indian manners and character. He is not regularly educated but he possesses a great mass of accurate observation on all the subjects of nature which present themselves here and will, therefore, readily select those only in his new route which shall be new."

Lewis was, by this time, competent in determining longitude and latitude, but Jefferson wanted Rush to prepare a memorandum on other matters which would help him in the field. Rush replied on March 12 that he would see Lewis in Philadelphia in a few days and would furnish him with a list of questions whose answers would increase America's knowledge in many fields. The President hoped Wistar, Professor of Anatomy at the University of Pennsylvania, would give Lewis advice. Of Barton, physician and naturalist at the University, Jefferson had a specific request. "In order to draw his [Lewis's] attention at once to the objects most desirable, I must ask the favor of you to prepare for him a note of those in the lines of botany, zoology, or of Indian history which you think most worthy of inquiry and observation. He will be with you in Philadelphia in 2 or 3 weeks and will wait on you."

On the 28th, Lewis received his British passport from Edward Thornton, Chargé d'Affaires of His Britannic Majesty, and a French passport on March 1 from Louis André, Baron Pichon, Chargé d'Affaires of the French Republic. All subjects of the two countries were asked to aid Lewis and his command in their endeavor, which was to advance scientific objects of interest to all civilized countries.

The perfect man, if he existed, was not available to command Jefferson's long- and often-postponed expedition. Jefferson described this super being as a man skilled in botany, natural history, mineralogy, astronomy, and other subjects and yet at the same time a man of great firmness of mind and strength of body, expert in woodcraft and familiar with the Indians. "I know of no such character who would undertake an enterprise so perilous," admitted the President. "[But] to all the latter qualifications Captain Lewis joins a great stock of accurate observations on the subject of the three [animal, vegetable and mineral] kingdoms." Thornton felt like Jefferson, saying, "The gentleman he has selected for the journey is his secretary, Captain Meriwether Lewis, a person in the vigour of his age, of a hardy constitution, and already acquainted with the manners of the Indians by his residence in the Western settlements."

Lewis was not "the ideal man" to lead such an expedition, for he was no scientist. But he was the closest thing to the ideal person. And he was Thomas Jefferson's unqualified choice.

CHAPTER IV

―――――――

CORPS OF DISCOVERY

*The gentleman he [Jefferson] has selected for the journey
is his secretary, Captain Meriwether Lewis, a person in the
vigour of his age, of a hardy constitution, and already
acquainted with the manners of the Indians by his residence
in the Western settlements.*
> —EDWARD THORNTON, British Chargé d'Affaires,
> to Lord Hawkesbury, March 9, 1803

SOMETIME IN 1802, late in the year, President Thomas Jefferson
gave Meriwether Lewis the word to proceed with the outfitting of
the Corps of Discovery. Meanwhile Jefferson prepared the top-
secret message to Congress which, through suggestion and dis-
simulation, would pry sufficient funds from that reluctant body
to finance Lewis's enterprise. Jefferson had planned to ask for
the necessary money in his regular annual Message to Congress,
scheduled for December 15, 1802, but he had been dissuaded by
Secretary of the Treasury Gallatin, to whom he had shown a
draft of his speech. Gallatin felt very strongly that the proposal
for the expedition should be held tightly confidential because it
contemplated the exploration of an area beyond the borders of
the United States. Jefferson had quickly seen the wisdom of his
friend's counsel. He was less eager to apprise his political enemies in the United States of his grandiose scheme than he was to
inform the Spanish, French and British governments. As a cover,
Lewis and Jefferson agreed that the story should be leaked that
the former's plan was to ascend the Mississippi River.

34

As Jefferson worked on the subterfuges of his communiqué that camouflaged his real intent with plans for continuation of Indian trading posts and the purchase of more Indian lands, Lewis prepared an estimate of the expenses of his secret journey. The biggest sum of money, $696, he earmarked for presents for the Indians—grease to ease his passage to the Pacific. The next largest amount, $430, would be needed, he felt, for means of transportation. He estimated that $217 would cover the cost of purchasing the mathematical instruments which were needed, and $81 the arms, ball and powder for protection and hunting. Camp equipment would run to $225, and packing and medicines, oddly combined in his estimate, to $55. Provisions for the trip would cost $224 and material for making up portable packs another $55. An important factor in the success of the project was the securing of competent hunters, guides and interpreters. For their services Lewis allotted $300. He also needed $100, in silver coin, to take care of his party's expenses from Nashville, Tennessee, to the last white settlement on the Missouri River. Finally, for all other contingencies he budgeted $81, no more, no less. This neat figure, plucked by Lewis from the crisp air of wintry Washington, brought the total to the exact sum he and the President had agreed upon as minimal for the success of the expedition—$2,500. Lewis's head for figures and his paymaster's experience in the Army stood him in good stead. Jefferson figured that the lower the figure, the better the chance of passage of the money bill. The expedition would ultimately cost more than the sum with which Lewis came up but it would serve its purpose to get the Corps of Discovery under way. And the total cost of Lewis's efficiently run survey can hardly be said to have been extravagant or a reckless squandering of public funds—$38,722.25.

Before Captain Lewis could select men for his party he had to see to his own requirements and select equipment for the trek. Jefferson had been the Prince Henry the Navigator of the plan; now it was time for Lewis to become a Columbus-Cortés-Balboa of a planner. Everything would depend on him once he left St. Louis. There would be little or nothing the President could do to help, once his boats were breasting the current of the Big Muddy.

One of the first things he did to prepare for the journey was to work out with the President a cipher, based on one evolved by mathematician Robert Patterson, with the key word "artichokes." Lewis learned to compose cryptic messages in the Executive Mansion which Jefferson translated into such practice communiqués as "I am at the head of the Missouri. All well, the Indians, so far, friendly." Lewis could not know, as he sweated over the puzzling block of ciphers, that he would never be forced to make use of the code in reporting back on the terra incognita of the Far West.

Meriwether Lewis knew himself well. He was completely confident of his Indian craft, his leadership and his knowledge of military discipline and logistics. But he was well aware that for a leader of a "literary"-scientific expedition he was more than a shade weak in science. Accordingly, he was eager to follow Jefferson's suggestion that he immerse himself completely in the subject in Philadelphia and Lancaster, Pennsylvania. His tutors there, all friends of Jefferson, would be from the intellectual elite of the nation. Most were associated with the University of Pennsylvania and the American Philosophical Society. (The latter was the first scientific body to be organized in the United States, having been founded by Benjamin Franklin in 1743.) The professors included Benjamin Smith Barton, naturalist, physician and lecturer at the University of Pennsylvania; Caspar Wistar, professor of anatomy at the University and president of the American Philosophical Society; and Benjamin Rush, the leading physician of the United States as well as a professor of medicine at the University. Jefferson also committed Meriwether Lewis to cryptologist-mathematician Robert Patterson of Lancaster, for further instruction in celestial observations and the determination of longitude and latitude. Patterson would also help him select the proper instruments to take west, such as theodolites, Hadley's sextants, Arnold's chronometers, and artificial horizons. He also prepared a set of astronomical formula for Lewis for computing longitude by lunar observations. Lewis was also to visit Andrew Ellicott, of Lancaster, in order to secure more advice on taking observations and selecting instruments.

Before he set out for Pennsylvania, Captain Lewis began acquiring maps for his journey. With the help of Jefferson, Gallatin and others, he soon secured those of Britishers Aaron Arrowsmith, Alexander Mackenzie, John Mitchell and John Thornton. He also picked up the maps made by the Frenchmen Jean Baptiste d'Anville and Guillaume Delisle. Secretary Gallatin had Nicholas King, the American surveyor of Washington, D.C., and an excellent draftsman-cartographer, project a blank map on which Lewis could enter the new geographical information which he would acquire while on the expedition west.

Gallatin urged that Lewis size up all Spanish posts in Upper Louisiana, determine the best sites to occupy in the territory in order to prevent the British from taking over the area, and to discern, as far as possible, the precise extent of the country drained by all the waters emptying into the Missouri River. In Gallatin's mind, Louisiana Territory, or at least Upper Louisiana, would be the first and perhaps the only large tract of land lying outside United States boundaries to be settled by people of that country. He hoped that Lewis would be able to evaluate the area in terms of its extent and fertility, in order to ascertain if it would support a large population. He also hoped that Lewis would be able to collect information on the area to the south of his actual route of travel, the country of the Kansas River and Rio Grande.

April 20th found Lewis in Lancaster, whence he reported on his progress to the President. He had asked John Conner for his services as scout and interpreter for the proposed expedition. According to the plan, Conner, sworn to secrecy, was to join him, bringing two Indians with him, at one or another of several military outposts on the Mississippi and Ohio where Lewis would call en route to the Missouri. Captain Lewis had also written to Major William McRea, commanding the Army post at South West Point, Tennessee, in hopes of securing some good recruits for the expedition through McRea's kind offices. Lewis also wrote to the commanding officers of Kaskaskia and Fort Massac, where he would also touch while en route to St. Louis.

Meriwether Lewis was severely handicapped in his recruiting because he could not reveal the actual destination of the Corps of Discovery to interested men. He told the Army officers that his journey would be up the Mississippi, and wrote Jefferson to remind him of the white lie—"which we agreed upon as the most proper to be declared publicly."

Lewis also contacted Congressman William Dickson of Tennessee, asking him to supply him with the name of a "confidential" boatwright at Nashville who would construct a boat for him and who would purchase a light canoe for him. He wrote to General William Irvine, Superintendent of Military Stores, Philadelphia, too, asking him to prepare certain articles for the expedition.

Lewis had designed a collapsible canoe and he hurried to Harper's Ferry to personally supervise its construction. To his disgust, his projects there stretched his stay from the week he had planned to a full month. The strange craft which was his brainchild was too much for the boatbuilder alone although it was simply an iron frame which came apart in sections, over which was stretched a covering of hide or bark. Lewis and the boatwright finally finished the portable canoe and Lewis tested it. To his delight he found that it carried the load of a comparable rigid craft of 1,770 pounds burden. And his framework, a mere 99 pounds of metal, would make child's play of portaging!

In the meantime, while he was at Harper's Ferry, Lewis looked into the matter of rifles, tomahawks and knives. He found them "in a state of forwardness that leaves me little doubt of their being ready in due time." He hoped to reach the mouth of the Missouri by August 1, 1803, but it was growing late. It was not till April 20th that Lewis arrived in Lancaster to begin his lessons with Ellicott's instruments, lessons which would run for twelve days. Jefferson expected him back, his studies completed, around the 20th.

Lewis's unforeseen delays caused talk in the capital. Jefferson had to explain to Lewis Harvie, Meriwether Lewis's successor as private secretary to the President: "I have delayed writing to you because my great regard for Captain Lewis made me unwilling to show a haste to fill his place before he was gone, and to counteract also a malignant and unfounded report that I was parting with him from dissatisfaction, a thing impossible either from his conduct or my disposition towards him."

On April 23rd, on the excuse of asking Lewis to run a few errands for him—including the purchase of a leopard or tiger-skin saddle cover and a llama or vicuña robe—a worried Jefferson wrote to his aide in Philadelphia, asking him to reply as soon as possible. On the 25th the President heard from Lewis, their letters having crossed in the mails. Two days later, he wrote Lewis again and sent him a rough draft of his instructions for the expedition, asking him to consider them and propose any modifications he thought useful or necessary. Jefferson gave Lewis permission to show the instructions to Doctors Wistar, Rush and Barton, since they were in on the secret, but to no one else for, as the President said, "the idea that you are going to explore the Mississippi has been generally given out. It satisfies public curiosity and masks sufficiently the real destination." For his own part, Jefferson asked Gallatin and Attorney General Levi Lincoln, and perhaps others, for suggestions in the line of changes or additions to Lewis's instructions. Lincoln hoped that the young captain would collect as much information as he could on Indian history, religion, morals, property, crime and punishment, diseases and medicines. He urged Lewis to secure seeds of any medicinal plants he might encounter and he advocated that he take along "kine pox matter" (cowpox serum) in case some of his men should come down with variola. The only tinkering with the instructions themselves by Lincoln was his suggestion of a change in phraseology because of Lewis's personal daring— "From my ideas of Captain Lewis, he will be much more likely in case of difficulty, to push too far than to recede too soon. Would it not be well to change the term 'certain destruction' into 'probable destruction'?" Jefferson took Lincoln's advice on the cowpox serum and placed in the instructions this specific point but he rewrote entirely the section having to do with difficulties, dangers and destruction. The President contented himself with saying: "To your own discretion therefore, must be left the degree of danger you may risk, and the point at which you should decline, only saying we wish you to err on the side of your safety and to bring back your party safe even if it be with less information."

By May 10th, Lewis was hard at work in Philadelphia, securing a gold chronometer, a surveyor's compass and chain, and plotting instruments, but almost abandoning the idea of taking a theodolite along after being advised by both Ellicott and Patterson that the delicate instrument would not survive many days of his rugged journey. Lincoln's suggestions on gathering information on the Indians were seconded by Dr. Rush, who gave Lewis a questionnaire with which he could elicit information in three general areas: physical history and medicine, morals, and religion. Ideally, Lewis was to sound the Indians out on such matters as suicide and homicide rates, sex, disposal of the dead, medicine, food preservation and "the affinity between their religious ceremonies and those of the Jews." (At this period, when the red men were not being suspected of being long-lost Welshmen they were accused of being wandering Jews.)

Back and forth flew the letters between the President and his secretary, all of them brimming with plans and news. Lewis sent sketches of the Pacific Northwest coast which he had made from Vancouver's maps. (The folio set of Vancouver's *Voyage* was too expensive and too heavy to purchase for the expedition but Lewis drained it of its most important information.) He told the President that he hoped to leave Washington for the West on June 6th or 7th although his attempts at recruiting men were most disappointing. "Out of twenty men who have volunteered their services to accompany me," he lamented, "not more than three or four do, by any means, possess the necessary qualifications for this expedition. . . . This I must endeavour to remedy by taking with me from that place [South West Point] a sufficient number of the best of them to man my boat and, if possible, select others of a better description as I pass the garrisons of Massac, Kaskaskia and Illinois [Cahokia.]."

Lewis was feverishly busy. He asked William Linnard, Military Agent, to supply him with a wagon and five horses to transport his 3,500 pounds of stores to Pittsburgh. He drew all the equipment possible from the Schuykill Arsenal in Philadelphia. What was not in stock he requested of Israel Whelen, Purveyor of Public Supplies, in the same city. By the time he had put together his List of Requirements, Lewis found that he had spent $2,160. He grouped his equipment into ten categories—mathematical instruments, arms and accouterments, ammunition, clothing, camp equipage, provisions and means of subsistence, Indian presents, means of transportation, medicine, and materials for making up the various articles into portable packs. In the general area of instruments alone he had sufficient variety of material to stock a country store—quadrant, compass, plotting instruments, surveyor's poles and chains, microscope, hydrometers, the fragile theodolite, artificial horizons, planispheres, ink powder, pens of both brass and silver, slates and pencils, crayons, sealing wax, various books including an edition of Linnaeus, maps, charts, blank vocabularies, writing paper and a pair of large brass scales. He also bought several thermometers although there has been a hard-to-kill legend that makeshift thermometers were made for him at St. Louis by Doctor Antoine Saugrain, using mercury scraped from the back of his wife's mirror. (However, it was Saugrain who supplied him with sulphur matches twenty years before they were "invented" in Britain by John Walker.)

Even more important than the scientific instruments was the outfitting of his party with adequate arms and ammunition. For upon them depended the survival of his men and himself. Captain Lewis was not satisfied with the arms available at Schuykill Arsenal. He bought, through Israel Whelen, his personal side arms—a pair of pocket pistols with secret triggers—from Robert Barnhill of Philadelphia. But he depended mostly on the Arsenal at Harper's Ferry. On March 14, Secretary of War Henry Dearborn ordered Joseph Perkins, superintendent of the Arsenal, to make for Lewis whatever arms and "iron work" he might request, and to do so with the least possible delay. The result was that Lewis, seemingly, was able to conquer the North American continent for about $80 worth of arms and ammunition. Actually, he requisitioned many hundreds of dollars' worth of supplies, in this area and the others, from the Schuykill Arsenal and Israel Whelen, beyond the $81 he had budgeted, of his $2,500 total, for firearms.

Although there would be only one skirmish in which the weapons were used against Indians, the arms which Lewis chose not only kept his men and himself fed for twenty-eight months, but also sufficiently awed the Indians to prevent any test of strength except for the single case of the thieving Piegan Blackfeet. The expedition's armory ranged from cannon to pistols, from guns to be mounted on the keelboat and two pirogues being constructed to the flintlock pocket pistols (cost, $5 each) which both Lewis and Clark carried. Captain Lewis selected a variety of arms so that if one model should fail him he could fall back on others. The superiority of a given model would be demonstrated in the most exacting field trials possible. Therefore, his men carried not only military muskets (fusees or fusils) but also rifles and even blunderbusses. They not only carried powder horns and bullet pouches to feed their arms but Lewis, a great innovator, had his 176 pounds of gunpowder put up in 52 watertight lead canisters which could be melted down and molded into rifle balls. (When Lewis prepared to leave Fort Clatsop on the Pacific for his homeward march he inspected all of his equipment before setting out. He found that of 35 canisters remaining, all but five—which had cracked during the crossing of the continent —were dry and in good order for all the rain and damp of the Oregon coast in winter.) Lewis even prepared for the frightening possibility of running out of powder altogether. He bought, with money from his own pocket, one of the newfangled air rifles which had just come on the market.

The expeditionaries carried tomahawks and scalping knives, and Lewis even included the obsolescent espontoon in his armament. This was a combination short pike and rifle rest, such as Renaissance matchlock infantrymen used when taking aim with their clumsy pieces. They would not prove of great use, though Clark killed a wolf with his and Lewis had to defend his very life with his espontoon from a charging grizzly bear. Israel Whelen turned over to Lewis the pocket pistols, powder canisters, 15 powder horns, bullet pouches and gun slings, 30 brushes and wires for cleaning the arms, 15 cartouche boxes to hold made-up paper cartridges for the pistols ("fixed ammunition"), 15 knapsacks, 500 English flints for the rifles and 125 for the muskets, 420 pounds of sheet lead to mold into balls, a pair of horse pistols, and 50 pounds of the best rifle powder. Since American powder was often of inferior quality, Lewis saw to it that his riflemen had good, imported powder. (The Du Pont de Nemours factory had not yet turned out its first powder.) The horse pistols were probably of the North and Cheney Model of 1799. These were made at Berlin, Connecticut, by Simeon North, the first official U. S. pistol manufacturer. They were of .69 caliber and were based on a French army handgun of 1777. They were about three pounds in weight and almost 15 inches long.

Since Whelen was not able to fill his order for 15 rifles, 30 bullet molds, 30 ball screws, extra rifle and musket locks and gunsmith's repair tools, Lewis had these all made especially for him at Harper's Ferry. Lewis was meticulous in his choice of rifles for the expedition. He realized the superiority of rifled arms over smoothbore muskets. They were far more accurate and had greater range. But he also knew that the long Kentucky rifles were more fragile than the shorter martial weapons. His solution to this problem was to develop a new rifle. Lewis's "Harper's Ferry Rifle" resembled the Kentucky rifle but he had the easily damaged stocks reduced to half length and the overall length of the .54 caliber piece was only 47 inches. Lewis had a rib soldered to each barrel to carry the ramrod and he rounded off the heavy barrel for about half of its length to reduce the weight. He designed patch boxes, guards and stock thimbles of brass. So efficient was Captain Lewis's design that the rifles were used as models for the first "mass-produced" Army rifle in the United States. On May 25, 1803, the Secretary of War found the new arms so functional that he ordered 4,000 of them manufactured for the troops. Only one or two minor changes were made in Meriwether Lewis's original design.

Lewis was unwilling to accept ordinary weapons; only the very best of equipment was good enough for him and nowhere was this more the case than in the arms he chose. Even the fusees which he bought were not regulation, Army-issue arms but lighter, less-clumsy muskets. However, he could do nothing with the blunderbusses, hangovers from Renaissance times. He felt these heavy pieces were needed to back up the swivel cannons in defending men and boats from possible mass charges of savages. The enormous, bell-mouthed scatter-guns were incapable of innovation. But since they could do enormous damage at close range he deemed them necessary in order to increase the fire-power of his limited band of men. In the summer of 1803, Lewis could not foresee that the blunderbusses would be nearly dead weight, useful only for firing salutes and impressing Indians with the thunder of their voices. Still larger and more cumbersome were the light cannon he procured, three swivel guns with which he would arm his little fleet for the long voyage upriver. Each could be loaded with up to 16 musket balls and this horizontal hail of lead, he knew, could cut down any massed, charging foe as a scythe topples wheat stalks. He planned to use the swivels to enforce respect for his tiny force when cooped up in the boats and in winter quarters upriver.

On July 7th Lewis was finally able to test his armory. All went well and the next day he sat down and wrote Jefferson: "Yesterday I shot my guns and examined the several articles which had been manufactured for me at this place [Harper's Ferry]. They appeared to be well executed."

The captain tried to secure the warmest, most durable clothing available. He requisitioned (in quantities of 15 each, for early plans envisaged a party no greater in number) blankets, hooded and belted coats, woolen overalls, "rifle frocks" of water-repellent cloth and 20 "fatigue frocks" or hunting shirts. Since his band had to travel light, he provided each man with only two pairs of socks (which was cutting things a bit fine) and two linen shirts. To make up new clothing, or patch up the old, he ordered 30 yards of flannel, too.

In camp equipage, Lewis had the same problem—how to out-fit his party well yet not burden them unnecessarily. He ordered kettles, axes, knives, augers, bitts, vises, rasps, spades, files, chisels, nails, saws, adzes, rope, cord, fishhooks, fishing line, and an oilstone, to make up a veritable mobile hardware store. But that was not all. He also purchased what he called trumpets and what the seller, Thomas Passmore, called tin horns, also spoons, cups, flint and steel sets, needles, awls, lamps, oilcloth sheets and bags to protect equipment from dampness, and one "sea grass hammock."

Since Captain Lewis intended that he and his men would live off the land, that is, off the accuracy of their Harper's Ferry rifles, he bought relatively little in the way of provisions. The only major food item, besides salt and spices, which he purchased in Pennsylvania was a dehydrated staple which he had concocted with the help of a Philadelphia cook, François Baillet—"portable soup." He had 150 pounds of this dried, instant soup made up, at a cost of $1.50 per pound.

Because everything depended on the reception he would receive from the Indian tribes whose lands he would traverse, Lewis was unskimping in his selection of presents for the red men. He laid in a great supply of blue, white, red, yellow and orange beads, wampum, calico shirts, striped, checked and solid-red handkerchiefs of muslin and silk, eyeglasses, burning glasses, looking glasses, bells, scissors, flint and steel sets, needles, vials of phosphorous, thimbles, red lead, vermilion, scalping knives, pipe tomahawks, brass and iron wire, ribbons, tinsel bands, 130 pigtails of tobacco, fish spears or gigs, awls for making moccasins, axes, fishhooks, gunpowder, sheets of copper, tin and iron, costume jewelry, copper kettles, finger rings, earrings, brooches, brass curtain rings (to be used as finger rings), and a dozen fine peace medals, each bearing on one side the likeness of President Jefferson and, on the other, clasped hands in the symbol of friendship.

Lewis's river flotilla consisted of a 60-foot keelboat or bateau, his pet iron-framed canoe, about 40 feet long, and a wooden canoe or pirogue. Hardware for the boats, such as chains, padlocks, boathooks, spiked setting poles and similar gear, he held to a minimum in order to keep down the weight of goods which he had to transport west.

Thanks to Dr. Rush's role as his pharmaceutical adviser and overseer, Lewis was able to fit out a compact medicine chest which, although it took little space, would have stacked up well against the dispensary of a good-sized Army post of the day. It ran a little heavy on purges and emetics but they formed, with leeches, the mainstay of medical practice of that era. Lewis took epsom salts, calomel, "powdered bark" (cinchona quinine?), opium, laudanum, tartar emetic, borax, ipecac, jalap, nutmeg, cloves, cinnamon, rhubarb, vitriol, sulphur, balsam, niter, copperas, ointments, asafoetida, gun camphor, and tragacanth, not to mention such tools of the trade as lancets, syringes, tourniquets, bandages ("patent lint")—and 50 dozen bilious pills made up especially for Lewis by Dr. Rush himself.

At the end of his List of Requirements, which totaled hundreds of items, cost $2,160.41, and required the services of thirty merchants in addition to Israel Whelen, Lewis collected the materials necessary for making portable packs—sheepskins, rawhide, etc.—then ended his supply list with some miscellaneous reminders. He noted the Indians' esteem for blue beads and their liking for brass buttons, which they valued second only to beads; he remarked their fondness for scalping knives with red-stained wooden handles and their preference for brass nests of camp kettles over the iron type.

Lewis returned to Washington from Pennsylvania on June 17, 1803, a month and a half after Livingston and Monroe had signed the final draft of the treaty ceding Louisiana Territory to the United States. He lost no time in writing to his old friend, Will Clark, to fill him in on the expedition. Lewis took Clark into his confidence after asking him to keep the contents of his letter inviolably secret. He told his old friend about the act of Congress for exploring the Missouri River—Columbia River area, the enterprise confided to him by President Jefferson. Lewis told Clark that he had been working on the outfitting of the expeditionary corps since March and that he expected to leave Washington for Pittsburgh at the end of June. He hoped to see Clark about August 10th or so, depending on the state of the river. He observed that he was instructed to select from any corps of the Army not more than twelve noncoms and privates who might volunteer for duty, and that he could hire civilians as well. The non-soldiers would receive six months' pay in advance and a bounty; the Army men would be given the six months' pay, immediate discharge upon their return, if they so desired, and not only their arrears in pay and clothing but a grant of land equal to that given veterans of Revolutionary service.

Lewis could not help asking Clark for aid in recruiting men for his Corps of Discovery. "I shall embark at Pittsburgh with a party of recruits, eight or nine in number, intended only to manage the boat and not calculated on as a permanent part of my detachment. When descending the Ohio it shall be my duty by enquiry to find out and engage some good hunters, stout, healthy, unmarried men accustomed to the woods and capable of bearing bodily fatigue in a pretty considerable degree. Should any young men answering this description be found in your neighbourhood, I would thank you to give me information on them on my arrival at the falls of the Ohio." Lewis suggested to Clark that he tell any interested men that the Lake of the Woods and the source of the Mississippi were the destinations of the Corps, and that they should be prepared for an eighteen-month absence from civilization. If they were eager for such an exploration, Lewis felt they would be even more avid to engage in the real design, which he assured Clark he would tell them about before actually engaging any of them for the trip.

The Virginian explained his plan of attack on the Big Muddy. He would descend the Ohio in his keelboat to its mouth, move up the Mississippi to the mouth of the Missouri, and then up that great tributary as far as the boat could go. Where the Missouri shoaled he would take to canoe and pirogue and in them proceed to the Missouri's source before crossing the mountains to the Oregon or Columbia River. Lewis thought that it would be easy to obtain passage home to the United States, via the East Indies, on one of the fur trade vessels accustomed to visit Nootka Sound. He explained to his friend that in the first major leg of his journey he hoped to go 200 to 300 miles up the Missouri before wintering; then he would resume his journey in the spring and reach the Western Ocean by the summer or autumn. "In order to subsist my party with some degree of comfort during the ensuing winter, I shall engage some French traders at Illinois [Cahokia] to attend me to my wintering grounds with a sufficient quantity of flour, pork, etc., to serve them plentifully during the winter and thus be enabled to set out in the spring with a healthy and vigorous party."

As for the objects of the expedition, Lewis explained that the Louisiana Territory was expected to become United States property within a twelvemonth. "But here let me again impress you with the necessity of keeping this matter a perfect secret," he warned. He made the point that the Government wanted an

47

early, friendly and intimate acquaintance with the Indian tribes of Upper Louisiana but that the United States was also interested in such scientific objects as the mapping of the country, the naming and locating of the tribal inhabitants of it, and the describing of the languages, traditions and occupations of the various Indian nations as well as a description of the land, the soil, and its flora and silva.

Finally, Lewis got down to brass tacks. "If there is anything under those circumstances in this enterprise which would induce you to participate with me in its fatigues, its dangers, and its honours, believe me, there is no man on earth with whom I should feel equal pleasure in sharing them as with yourself."

Lewis went on. "I make this communication to you with the privity of the President who expresses an anxious wish that you would consent to join me in this enterprise. He has authorized me to say that in the event of your accepting this proposition, he will grant you a captain's commission. . . . Your situation, if joined with me in this mission, will, in all respects, be precisely such as my own. . . ." Actually, Jefferson had no right to promise anything of the kind. He could only nominate officers like Clark for appointment; the Senate had to confirm them. In poor Clark's case, his appointment to captain did not even get further than Secretary Dearborn and the War Department. William Clark never did receive this promised captaincy which Lewis, under Jefferson's spellbinding, promised him so rashly. Will Clark finally got his official appointment on March 30, 1804, but it was as a mere second lieutenant of artillery whereas Lewis was confident in the summer of 1803 that he would be given a captain's bars in the Corps of Engineers. This shoddy treatment of Clark by the War Department was a source of bitterness to both Lewis and Clark, though not between them.

Historians have wrangled for decades over just what was Jefferson's intent in sending Lewis and Clark—exploration, commerce or conquest? It was clear enough to Lewis from his orders. While he awaited Clark's decision before contacting his second choice as a companion, Lieutenant Moses Hook, he read and reread the amended instructions drawn up and given him by the President. "The object of your mission is to explore the Missouri River, & such principal stream of it as, by its course and communication with the waters of the Pacific Ocean, whether the Columbia, Oregon, Colorado or any other river, may offer the most direct and practicable water communication across this Continent for the purposes of commerce."

The President continued, "Your mission has been communicated to the Ministers here from France, Spain and Great Britain, and through them to their governments; & such assurances given them as to its objects as we trust will satisfy them. The country of Louisiana having been ceded by Spain to France, and possession by this time probably given, the passport you have from the Minister of France, the representative of the present sovereign of the country, will be a protection with all its subjects; and that from the Minister of England will entitle you to the friendly aid of traders of that allegiance with whom you may happen to meet."

Jefferson ordered Lewis to fix, by coordinates of longitude and latitude, all "remarkable" points on the Missouri, such as rapids, islands, and the mouths of tributaries, the variations of the compass, the exact location of the portage between the Mississippi and Pacific drainages. He urged Lewis to make his observations with great care and to record them, as well as all of his notes, in several copies for safety against loss. "A further guard," advised the President, "would be that one of those copies be on the paper of the birch, as less liable to injury from damp than common paper."

The President ordered his agent to become acquainted with the Indian nations, to determine their numbers and the extent of their possessions. He wished to know their languages, traditions and occupations, including agriculture, fishing, hunting, war and the arts. He was interested in their relationship with other tribes, their food, clothing and tools, their diseases and remedies, their laws and customs and the articles of commerce they possessed or desired, all to encourage future trade and their ultimate civilization by the United States.

"Other objects worthy of notice," wrote the President, "will be the soil and face of the country, its growth and vegetable productions, especially those not of the U. S.; the animals of the country generally, and especially those not known in the U. S.; the remains or accounts of any which may be deemed rare or extinct; the mineral productions of every kind, but more particularly metals, limestone, pit coal and saltpetre, salines and mineral waters, noting the temperature of the last and such circumstances as may indicate their character; volcanic appearances; climate, as characterized by the thermometer, by the proportion of rainy, cloudy and clear days, by lightning, hail, snow, ice, by the access and recess of frost, by the winds prevailing at different seasons, the dates at times of appearance of particular birds, reptiles or insects."

Next, a word about his course. "Although your route will be along the channel of the Missouri, yet you will endeavour to inform yourself by enquiry of the character and extent of the country watered by its branches and especially on its southern side. The North River or Rio Bravo, which runs into the Gulph of Mexico and the North River or Rio Colorado, which runs into the Gulph of California, are understood to be the principal streams heading opposite to the waters of the Missouri and running southwardly. Whether the dividing grounds between the Missouri and them are mountains or flat lands, what are their distance from the Missouri, the character of the intermediate country, and the people inhabiting it, are worthy of particular enquiry. The northern waters of the Missouri are less to be enquired after because they have been ascertained to a considerable degree and are still in the course of ascertainment by English traders and travelers. But if you can learn anything certain of the most northern source of the Mississippi and of its position relatively to the Lake of the Woods, it will be interesting to us."

Jefferson insisted that Lewis's entry into the Far West be a peaceful one. "In all your intercourse with the natives, treat them in the most friendly and conciliatory manner which their own conduct will admit; allay all jealousies as to the object of your journey, satisfy them of its innocence, make them acquainted with the position, extent, character, peaceable and commercial dispositions of the U. S., of our wish to be neighbourly, friendly and useful to them, and of our dispositions to a commercial intercourse with them; confer with them on the points most convenient as mutual emporiums, and the articles of most desirable interchange for them and us. If a few of their influential chiefs, within practicable distance, wish to visit us, arrange such a visit with them and furnish them with authority to call on our officers on their entering the U. S. to have them conveyed to this place at the public expense. . . ."

The ultimate, critical, decisions Jefferson left to Lewis. "As it is impossible for us to foresee in what manner you will be received by those people, whether with hospitality or hostility, so it is impossible to prescribe the exact degree of perseverance with which you are to pursue your journey. We value too much the lives of citizens to offer them to probable destruction. Your numbers will be sufficient to secure you against the unauthorized opposition of individuals or of small parties, but if a superior force, authorized or not authorized, by a nation should be arrayed against your further passage, and inflexibly determined to arrest it, you must decline its further pursuit, and return. In the loss of yourselves we should lose also the information you will have acquired. By returning safely with that, you may enable us to renew the essay with better calculated means. To your own discretion, therefore, must be left the degree of danger you may risk, and the point at which you should decline, only saying we wish you to err on the side of your safety, and to bring back your party safe even if it be with less information.

"Should you reach the Pacific Ocean, inform yourself of the circumstances which may decide whether the furs of those parts may not be collected as advantageously at the head of the Missouri (convenient, as is supposed, to the waters of the Colorado and Oregon, or Columbia) as at Nootka Sound, or any other point of that coast, and that trade be consequently conducted through the Missouri and U. S. more beneficially than by the circumnavigation now practiced. On your arrival on that coast, endeavour to learn if there be any port within your reach frequented by the sea vessels of any nation, and to send two of your trusty people back by sea in such a way as they shall judge shall appear practicable, with a copy of your notes, and should you be of opinion that the return of your party by the way they went will be eminently dangerous, then ship the whole and return by sea, by the way either of Cape Horn or the Cape of Good Hope, as you shall be able. As you will be without money, clothes or provisions, you must endeavour to use the credit of the U. S. to obtain them, for which purpose open letters of credit shall be furnished you, authorizing you to draw upon the Executive of the U. S. or any of its officers, in any part of the world, on which draughts can be disposed of, and to apply with our recommendations to the consuls, agents, merchants or citizens of any nation with which we have intercourse, assuring them in our name that any aids they may furnish you shall be honourably repaid, and on demand. Our Consuls, Thomas Hewes at Batavia in Java, Wm. Buchanan in the Isles of France and Bourbon [Mauritius and Reunion], and John Elmslie at the Cape of Good Hope will be able to supply your necessities by draughts on us. . . ."

The sixty-year-old Jefferson was vicariously enjoying the planning and outfitting of the expedition with Lewis but he also worried over his young friend's fate. He had to plan for all contingencies, so he ordered Lewis "to provide, on the accident of your death, against anarchy, dispersion and the consequent danger to your party and total failure of the enterprise. You are hereby authorized by any instrument signed and written in your own hand to name the person among them who shall succeed to the command on your decease. . . . I have only to add my sincere prayer for your safe return."

Mostly Jefferson was optimistic and enthusiastic, however. In fact, he was overoptimistic. Whereas Lewis told Clark that he hoped to get 200 to 300 miles up the Missouri before winter should set in, Jefferson talked in terms of a 700–800-mile advance to winter quarters. Both men were agreed that only twelve to fifteen men need be mustered, although thirty-one, plus Sacajawea and her baby, eventually made the long march.

As Lewis's preparations neared completion, he put together a peripatetic library. He bought three nautical almanacs and a volume of tables for finding his latitudes and longitudes; Richard Kirwan's *Elements of Mineralogy;* Benjamin Barton's *Elements of Botany;* Patrick Kelly's *Introduction to Spheres and Nautical Astronomy.* Dr. Rush sent him his memorandum on "Rules of

Health" and the President presented him with a small octavo edition of Mackenzie's *Voyage.*

Captain Lewis hoped to leave Washington by the end of June but it was, fittingly, July 4th—Independence Day—when he actually set forth on the grand adventure. Before he set out, he wrote to his mother to place her mind at ease. He told her how sorry he was that circumstances prohibited his making a last visit to Locust Hill to see her before his departure. Once again, as he had done when he first entered Army service, he sought to allay her fears as he embarked on his hazardous exploit. He went to great lengths to reassure her: "My absence will probably be equal to [but] 15 or 18 months. The nature of this expedition is by no means dangerous. My route will be altogether through tribes of Indians who are perfectly friendly to the United States. Therefore, consider the chances of life just as much in my favour on this trip as I should conceive them were I to remain at home for the same length of time." If he was something less than honest about the dangers of the expedition, he was frank about his pride and confidence. "The charge of this Expedition is as honourable to myself as it is important to my Country. For its fatigues I find myself perfectly prepared nor do I doubt my health and strength of constitution to bear me through it. I go with the most perfect pre-conviction in my own mind of returning safe and hope, therefore, that you will not suffer yourself to indulge any anxiety for my safety."

Jefferson, through Henry Dearborn, sought to smooth the way west for Lewis as far as possible. He ordered Lieutenant Moses Hook, commanding Fort Fayette, Major William McRea, South West Point, Captain Amos Stoddard, at Cahokia, and Captains Russell and Daniel Bissell at, respectively, Kaskaskia and Fort Massac, to give Lewis all the aid in their power and to provide volunteers for his unit. Secretary Dearborn also authorized the Paymaster to advance Lewis money for recruiting purposes. Besides a dozen men for his permanent party, the Virginian needed men on temporary, detached duty to get him and his gear to the Missouri River jumping-off place before the ice should block the river. Dearborn ordered Stoddard and Russell Bissell to take care of this by turning over to Lewis the best boat at Kaskaskia

53

and by detaching eight men who knew how to row to Lewis for special duty.

Finally, Dearborn wrote to Lewis, himself. He instructed the captain to call on the commanding officers at Massac and Kaskaskia for such noncoms and privates as he needed but also ordered him to recruit men himself, bearing in mind that no more than twelve volunteers were to be accepted. He also gave Lewis a blank commission, leaving it up to him to select a man to be second in command and to fill it in with the name of his choice, who would be an ensign or second lieutenant. Lewis had, by now, settled on William Clark as his first choice and Moses Hook as his alternate.

On Independence Day, 1803, President Jefferson sent Lewis one of the most amazing letters in American history. It was a letter of credit to be used to secure a passage home should a return overland be too dangerous. This letter amounted to a carte blanche, a blank check, on the credit of the United States. "I hereby authorize you to draw on the Secretarys [sic] of the Treasury, of War, and of the Navy of the U. S. according as you may find your draughts will be most negotiable for the purpose of obtaining money or necessaries for yourself and your men, and I solemnly pledge the faith of the United States that these draughts shall be paid punctually at the date they are made payable. I also ask of the consuls, agents, merchants and citizens of any nation with which we have intercourse or amity to furnish you with those supplies which your necessities may call for, assuring them of honourable and prompt retribution. And our own consuls in foreign parts where you may happen to be are hereby instructed and required to be aiding and assisting you in whatsoever may be necessary for procuring your return back to the United States. And to give more entire satisfaction and confidence to those who may be disposed to aid you, I, Thomas Jefferson, President of the United States of America, have written this letter of general credit for you with my own hand and signed it with my own name."

At Harper's Ferry, Lewis encountered delays. The arms and articles made up for him there had not been picked up by his wagoner, who protested overloading his team, already hauling Lewis's accumulation of supplies from Philadelphia. So Lewis had to scout out another wagon in Fredericktown. This time the teamster did not even put in an appearance. Lewis persevered and hired still another man and team. Then he set out for Pittsburgh via Charlestown, Frankfort, Uniontown and Redstone Old Fort. Frantic haste was becoming second nature with him; he left Washington so hurriedly that he forgot not only his bridle and dirk, but even his pocketbook! Jefferson wrote him that he hoped the dagger would pass through the mails, and that the wallet was on its way, but that the bridle was too bulky to send.

CHAPTER V

PRELUDE TO ADVENTURE

*It [low water] shall not prevent my proceeding, being deter-
mined to get forward though I should not be able to make
a greater distance than a mile a day . . . [even] should I
not be able to make greater speed than a boat's length
per day!*
—MERIWETHER LEWIS, on the Ohio River,
July 1803

CAPTAIN LEWIS arrived in Pittsburgh on July 15, 1803, at two in
the afternoon, after a hot journey over dusty roads. Since the
mail closed at 5 P.M., he dashed off an optimistic note to Jefferson before 3 o'clock, although he had not yet checked on the
progress of his boat. His journey had been uneventful but a welcome change after the weeks of study. He told the President, "I
feel myself much benefitted by the exercise the journey has given
me."

Exactly a week later he wrote Jefferson again, this time in disgust, to report his having been "most shamefully detained by the
unpardonable negligence of the boat builder." The man had
promised completion by the 20th of July; on that date the boat
was hardly begun. Lewis was so desperate to be on his way that,
momentarily, he toyed with the idea of abandoning the unfinished keelboat, buying two or three pirogues, and proceeding
down the Ohio in them, trusting to luck to find a purchasable
keelboat somewhere lower down the river. He was dissuaded
from this plan not so much by the rumpot boatbuilder's repeated

56

promises of speedy completion of the boat as by the opinion of well-informed Pittsburghers who advised him that his chances of finding a suitable and available keelboat on the lower river were slim. Moreover, he did not want a secondhand craft. Lewis was an innovator; his keelboat, or barge, was of his own special design. In it he tried to anticipate every possible contingency. Not only did it have ten-foot decks at the bow and stern with a forecastle and cabin atop them for shelter, but the center of the vessel was protected by lockers which could be raised to form a breastwork to protect the complement from Indian arrows during an attack. He also provided a heavy tarpaulin to cover the entire amidships area. When the tarp was in place, the boat would not take in water although subjected to the worst blow and heaviest seas the Missouri could throw at it.

The best thing that Lewis could do was to hound, pitilessly, the negligent boatwright. "I exacted a promise of greater sobriety in future, which he took care to perform with as little good faith as he had his previous promises with regard to the boat, continuing to be constantly either drunk or sick. I have prevailed upon him to engage more hands. I visit him every day and endeavour by every means in my power to hasten the completion of the work. I spend most of my time with the workmen, alternately persuading and threatening."

Lewis was in agonized impatience to be on his way, and not solely because of eagerness to begin his great adventure. He knew that the delays were distressful to Jefferson. He was already running behind schedule and the lowering water of the Ohio threatened to strand him in Pittsburgh. Day by day, he saw the current slackening. He feared his progress would be impeded or stopped by shoals and the driftwood jams which Ohio rivermen called wooden-islands. But he refused to be intimidated by the old-timers who predicted he would be hung up, high and dry, in the lowest-ever, unnavigable Ohio. He swore that the river would not stop him. "It [low water] shall not prevent my proceeding, being determined to get forward though I should not be able to make a greater distance than a mile a day . . . [even] should I not be able to make greater speed than a boat's length per day!"

The captain arranged for Lieutenant Moses Hook to join him

at the mouth of the Missouri, to act as his second in command should Clark decline his invitation. But on July 29th, Hook's hopes—and chances of fame—were dashed as Lewis's spirits were recharged with enthusiasm. For Will Clark, that day, accepted his friend's offer of the position, and with gusto. "I will cheerfully join you," he wrote Lewis, "my friend, I do assure you that no man lives with whom I would prefer to undertake such a trip as yourself. My friend, I join you with hand and heart." The delighted Lewis immediately fired back a reply. "I could neither hope, wish, nor expect from a union with any man on earth more perfect support or further aid in the discharge of the several duties of my mission than that which, I am confident, I shall derive from being associated with yourself."

Lewis then instructed Clark to hire volunteers, but only on the basis of his final approval or disapproval. He instructed Clark to turn down soft-palmed gentlemen who were dazzled into volunteering by dreams of high adventure. "We must set our faces against all such applications and get rid of them on the best terms we can. They will not answer our purposes." He urged Clark, on the other hand, to try to secure a hunter or two but to be careful to explain that the hunters would have to turn to for duty like the rest of the company. Lewis was still eager to secure John Conner as his scout and he asked Clark to find him. (Clark was able to find Conner eventually, but the latter was not interested in the expedition.)

Captain Lewis's campaign of nagging the flagging boatbuilders finally paid off. Although the "incorrigible drunkards" took twelve days just to prepare the oars and poles, the last day of August saw Lewis preparing hurriedly to leave Pittsburgh. He had eleven hands aboard the keelboat, including a pilot, T. Moore, seven soldiers as an escort, and three volunteers for his Corps of Discovery, including John Colter and George Shannon. Always the thorough planner, Lewis lightened the bateau for the shoal water ahead by chartering two wagons, loading them and dispatching them to a rendezvous at Wheeling and deeper water, where he could reload the heavy equipment as cargo. He wasted not a precious second in getting under way. Though the keelboat was not finished until 7 A.M. of August 31st, he had it loaded by 10 A.M. and was casting off by 11 o'clock.

Lewis's great adventure started badly. Only three miles below Pittsburgh, at Brunot's, or Hamilton's, Island, he halted and went on shore. There, he demonstrated the newly purchased and newfangled air gun. He showed his marksmanship by firing seven rounds at a range of 55 yards, "with pretty good success." Blaze Cenas asked to handle the piece so Lewis gave it to him. Cenas, unacquainted with the strange new arm, accidentally discharged it. Lewis's blood chilled in horror as he saw a woman spectator stagger, cry out and fall to the ground, bleeding from her head. He recalled the scene that evening as he wrote in his log. "The ball passed through the hat of a woman about 40 yards distant, cutting her temple about the fourth of the diameter of the ball. She fell instantly, the blood gushing from her temple. We were all in the greatest consternation and supposed she was dead, but in a minute, she revived, to our inexpressable satisfaction and, by examination, we found the wound by no means mortal or even dangerous."

It was a shaken Lewis who hurried his hands aboard the bateau to cast off from the scene of the near tragedy. He navigated his craft to the first obstacle in the river, a "ripple" off McKee's Rock. There, for the first of many, many times, his eleven men had to turn amphibian, plunging into the river to lift the boat along for some 30 yards. Lewis and his crew met two more riffles that day, and it was a sodden and tired group to whom he doled out whiskey before an 8 o'clock lights-out.

Lewis wanted an early start next day but he found the river veiled in a thick fog at dawn. His eyes could not penetrate it for 40 paces so he took his pilot's advice and settled down to wait for the sun to burn it off. This ocurred at 8 A.M. To Lewis, the fogs and dews were the heaviest he had ever seen in his life. He noted they were "more remarkable for their frequency and quantity than in any country I was ever in. They are so heavy, the drops falling from the trees from about midnight until sunrise give you the idea of a constant, gentle, rain. This continues until the sun has acquired sufficient altitude to dissipate the fog by its influence."

On September 1st, Lewis met Little Horse Tail Riffle, which forced him and his men to spend two hours in the water to manhandle the boat over the barrier. Big Horse Tail Riffle was worse; he had to order his men to unload the barge and then lift it, bodily over the reef. Loading up again, he pushed on to run afoul of Woolery's Trap. Again the craft was unloaded but all the strength of the men failed to budge the boat and Lewis was forced to hire a team of oxen whose strength, with that of his men, finally overcame the Trap. But Lewis found that he had netted only ten miles by camping time. Each day became a repetition of the ones gone before. Logstown Riffle detained him four hours near the old chimneys marking the site of Mad Anthony Wayne's Legionville of 1792–93. Stranded there, Lewis had to pay a man for the services of his horse and ox to tow the bateau off. He did not come to revere the Logstonians. "The inhabitants who live near these riffles," he commented, "live much by the distressed situation of travelers, are generally lazy, charge extravagantly when they are called on for assistance and have no philanthropy or conscience." Lewis was as tired as his sodden men and his impatience knew no bounds, for he saw the buckeyes, gums and sassafras trees signaling the advent of winter with the changing color of their leaves.

The boat rubbed on Alfour's Run but by ordering the men over the side he got through, and over Walker's Riffle. Lewis glanced at the thermometer in his cabin and found the temperature a reassuring 76°. That meant that winter was still some distance off.

Delayed again by morning fogs, Lewis was heartened when he fell in with Guy Bryant, who assured him that if he could get over Georgetown Bar, 24 miles below, he would make it successfully to the Mississippi. As soon as a dense condensation fog lifted, Lewis pushed on, passed Atkin's Riffle "with tolerable ease," and reached McIntosh, site of old Fort McIntosh. But below here the boat stuck fast although he unloaded all cargo. Lewis hired enough horses to get the craft loose, but when he set up camp that night he had made a mere six miles. Before turning in, he fixed a watermark on the riverbank. When he rolled out of his blankets the next morning, he groped his way through the fog to the stake to find that the river had fallen an inch overnight! Before the fog was dispersed he was on his hurried way. Now the pirogue, overloaded to lighten the deeper-draft bateau, sprung a leak and nearly filled. "This accident was truly distressing," Lewis confided to his diary, "as her load, consisting of articles of hardware, intended as presents to the Indians, got wet and, I fear, are much damaged." Patching, paddling and poling, he got his little fleet past Georgetown Bar and set up camp where the 60-foot swath in the timber marked the Virginia-Pennsylvania boundary on the east bank and the Pennsylvania-Ohio line on the west side.

Lewis took advantage of this enforced stop to dry out all his goods, oil all hardware and put it up in oilcloth bags in casks. He also hired another deckhand and he let some of his men go fishing with gigs, or spears. Although the water was low and clear, and he could see sturgeon, bass, catfish and pike in the Ohio's holes, his men did not catch many. "We had too much to attend to, of more importance than gigging fish," he explained.

The little fleet surmounted several riffles without recourse to horses or oxen before halting at the fourteenth island below Pittsburgh, Brown's Island, on September 5th. His prayers for rain were answered that day and the river ceased to drop. But the next day he had to hire horses to drag the boat over three of the five riffles he met. Lewis felt that the teamsters' charge of two dollars, each time, was exorbitant. As the boats passed Steubenville, he was able to hoist the sail on his little flagship for the first time. His oarsmen relaxed as the wind swept them along but it freshened and became so strong that Lewis had to haul in sail for fear it would carry his mast away. He loosed it again when the wind abated but it was a trick; a squall screamed down on him, nearly toppling the mast. He took in the mainsail and scudded along under the furled sail and the awning. When the bateau struck, he hoisted sail in hope of getting her off but the squall broke the sprit and he had to fall back on the muscles of his men. All of their efforts were in vain and he went in search of horses or oxen once more. In thriving Steubenville he found oxen which drew badly but which freed the boat from the ledge and allowed a day's run of ten miles.

By the time Lewis reached Wheeling, a bustling village of fifty houses, he was averaging twelve miles per day. This was not disappointing when he considered that he and his men had walked almost as much distance on the Ohio's bed as they had floated on its bosom. He had battled weirs of tangled driftwood and gravel bars turned into dams by low water. He was delighted to see the little port at the mouth of Wheeling Creek. He knew why the post roads converged there—"the water from hence being much deeper and the navigation better than it is from Pittsburgh or any point above it."

Captain Lewis went ashore to see Mr. Caldwell, the merchant to whom he had consigned the wagonloads of goods. He found them in good order and purchased another pirogue to keep his fleet as light and shallow of draft as possible. He also hired another hand. While he was in Wheeling, he met Colonel Thomas Rodney, one of the Commissioners appointed to adjust the land claims of Mississippi Territory, also his old Army friend, Major Ferdinand L. Claiborne, and a young law student. Claiborne was a member of Rodney's Commission. On the evening of the 8th, Lewis had his new friends to a watermelon feast on the bateau. He also met at this time Dr. William Ewing Patterson, son of Dr. Robert Patterson of the University of Pennsylvania, one of Lewis's science tutors. The young man was burning to join him on his expedition to the Pacific. "I consented," Lewis later advised the President, "provided he could get ready by three the next evening. He thought he could and instantly set about it. I told the Dr. that I had a letter of appointment for a second lieutenant which I could give him but did not feel myself altogether at liberty to use it as it was given me by the President to be used in the event of Mr. Clark's not consenting to go with me, but, as he had, I could not use it without the previous consent of the President. However, if he thought proper to go on with me to the Illinois, where I expected to winter, I could obtain an answer from the President by the spring of the year or before the Missouri would be sufficiently open to admit of my ascending it." Lewis would have welcomed a physician to his corps but the doctor was not ready, so Lewis sailed without him—which was undoubtedly fortunate, for according to historian Milo Quaife, the young M.D. was a black sheep and drunkard who would have brought the corps naught but trouble.

Captain Lewis offered Rodney a ride but he declined. His own boat drew only eight inches so he expected to pass the Virginian easily. But Rodney reckoned not with Lewis's amphibious diligence. After a last-minute delay over securing fresh bread, Lewis left Wheeling and soon showed his heels to Rodney as the river began to deepen. No longer did he have to hire teams to tow him off sandbars although it was still necessary to order all hands over the side to cut passages through sand and gravel bars on the summer-sapped Ohio. On many of these bars the water in the deepest part did not exceed six inches—and Lewis's barge drew three feet of water! But the current was now strong enough to ease the men's work. Floundering in the water, they made an initial cut with spades and shovels, then a rush of water scoured it quickly to form a channel if there was no clay or driftwood mixed with the pebbles and cobbles to compact them. Lewis proudly reported that he could cut a 50-yard passage through an Ohio riffle in the course of a single hour.

Between Wheeling and Marietta, the river lived up to its French name, La Belle Rivière, being lined with enormous—sequoian—sycamores and adorned with grapevines which, suspended from treetops, formed junglelike canopies over the banks. Twelve miles below Wheeling, Lewis explored the Indian mounds at Little and Big Grave creeks, acquiring good experience in natural history and archaeology. He reported to the President, "I was informed that, in removing the earth of a part of one of the lesser mounds that stands in the town, the skeletons of two men were found and some brass beads were found among the earth near these bones. My informant told me the beads were sent to Mr. Peale's Museum in Philadelphia." Continuing on, Lewis camped at Sunfish Creek to make a good 24-mile run despite his stay at the mounds.

On September 11th, Lewis entered the Long Reach, called thus because the Ohio ran in a ruler-straight course for 18 miles. It was a pleasant area although a watch had to be kept for the five islands in its course. The Long Reach also afforded the captain and his men a welcome change of diet—fried squirrel. "I

observed a number of squirrels swimming the Ohio and universally passing from the west to the east shore. They appear to be
making to the south. Perhaps it may be mast or food which they
are in search of but I should rather suppose that it is climate
which is their object as I find no difference in the quantity of
mast on both sides of this river, it being abundant on both except
the beechnut, which appears extremely scarce this season. The
walnuts and hickory nuts, the usual food of the squirrel, appear
in great abundance on either side of the river. I made my dog
[Scammon, or Scannon] take as many each day as I had occasion
for. They were fat and I thought them, when fried, a pleasant
food. Many of these squirrels were black. They swim very light
in the water and make pretty good speed. My dog was of the
Newfoundland breed, very active, strong and docile. He would
take the squirrels in the water, kill them and, swimming, bring
them in his mouth to the boat."

Leaving camp at Grand View Island next day, the boats met
such a stubborn riffle that, for all their plying of spades and
canoe paddles, it took four hours to entrench a passage. So much
of the men's energy was gone that Lewis had to call an early halt
near the home of a "yankey farmer" who traded fresh corn and
potatoes to the Virginian for several pounds of lead.

The next day, Lewis reached the Muskingum River's mouth,
and Marietta, where he lay over all night to rest his men. He took
the occasion to write a letter to the President after meeting Colonel Griffin Green, one of the town's founders. ("He appears to
be much of a gentleman and an excellent Republican.") Lewis
also discharged two hands but allowed a young fellow to join
him, to work his way west. The captain's departure was delayed
by the fleshpots of Marietta. He found two of his men absent
without leave. "I finally found them and had them brought on
board, so drunk that they were unable to help themselves." Although squirrels still swam the river for Scammon to fetch and
clouds of pigeons filled the sky, Lewis did not take to this stretch
of the river. He found it an unhealthy area, the people afflicted
with goiter and other disorders. He noted, "The fever and ague
and bilious fevers here commence their baneful oppression and

continue through the whole course of the river with increasing violence as you approach its mouth."

On and on went the boats, past Belpré, Amberson's Island Riffle and Old Town Bar. Lewis took the time to hunt squirrels ashore and to dry out all his cargo at various stops. At Old Town Bar, all hands worked from 10 A.M. till sunset repairing water damage. It was anything but a rest stop, the commanding officer himself not finding time to eat until after dark. The next day, the winds, regular as trades, and the current of the Ohio brought Lewis to Letart's Falls, second in extent only to those at Louisville, but he got through safely. Looking back on the long series of riffles which he had cleared, he remarked to Jefferson, "Horses and oxen are the last resort. I find them the most efficient sailors in the present state of navigation of this river, although they may be considered somewhat clumsy."

At Cincinnati, Lewis and his crew had put 500 miles of river behind them. Since he was short on provisions and his men were again very fatigued, he laid over in port from September 28th until October 3rd so that his hands might recuperate. When he was ready to continue, he sent the boats on and traveled across country to meet them at Big Bone Lick, a fossil site of great interest to the President's mammoth curiosity.

Lewis explored the paleontological site and was given specimens of elephant and mammoth tusks and teeth by Dr. William Goforth, the M.D. who was excavating the site. The explorer sent them on to Jefferson but they were lost in transit, by shipwreck. He also asked the President for more smallpox serum, since his supply had "lost its virtue," and for a copy of the treaty of cession of Louisiana to show to the people of the territory to win their support for his project. He closed his dispatch by telling the President that he hoped to keep Congress in good humor by means of a horseback tour of the Kansas River area, and perhaps by a ride down to Santa Fe, since the acquisition of knowledge about the Spanish frontier had been urged on him by Jefferson. It was in reply to this letter that Jefferson quickly shot back a note, absolutely forbidding him to make either side trip. "One thing we are decided in; that you must not undertake the winter excursion which you propose in yours of October 3. Such an excursion will be more dangerous than the main expedition up the Missouri and would, by an accident to you, hazard our main object."

After his flat order, the President relaxed and offered Lewis a selection of extracts from the journal of Jean Baptiste Truteau, agent of the Spaniards' Illinois Trading Company. These concerned the Indians of the Missouri Valley, the river itself—"there is depth sufficient to carry a frigate . . . it has no cataracts, no portages"—and the land—"the soil of the Missouri is the most fertile in the Universe."

At Louisville, Lewis welcomed Clark aboard and resumed the journey on October 26th. They reached the yellow banks marking Fort Massac, rich in iron ore, salt licks—and invalids—near Paducah, on November 11th. There, Lewis hired half-breed George Drouillard as his scout, getting William Swan, assistant military agent there, to give him $30 in advance pay, and sent him to South West Point to pick up the volunteers there from McRea's detachment. While he waited for them, the Virginian practiced celestial observations in earnest in preparation for the westward journey. Fort Massac commanded a magnificent view of the river from its high and dry bank. Lewis could see along the great bend as far as the Tennessee River's mouth. However, his enjoyment of the area was short-lived. He was seized with a violent ague which lasted four hours and was followed by a high fever. Zadok Cramer, author of *The Navigator,* the Bible for Ohio boatmen, blamed Massac's bad reputation on its swampy ponds and their miasma. Lewis wondered if there was any connection between fever and mistletoe, which seemed to go together on the Ohio. Dosing himself with Dr. Rush's pills, Lewis soon convinced himself that he was better, and pushed on. He landed in the evening at the junction of the Ohio and Mississippi where Clark determined the widths for him, since he was still weak. His seventeen-day run from Pittsburgh was excellent; perhaps a low-water record. Cramer gave fifteen days as good time with high water and some were lucky to make it as far as Limestone in twenty days.

The next morning, to better his acquaintance with the Indians of the new frontier, Lewis visited a party of Shawnees and Delawares camped on the Mississippi. A respectable-looking Shawnee offered him three beaverskins for his dog, Scammon, but Lewis, who had paid $20 for the Newfoundland, declined the offer with his customary politeness. "I prized him much for his docility and qualifications generally for my journey and, of course, there was no bargain." When he returned to camp he was astonished at the size of the catfish the men had caught for supper, one weighing 128 pounds. He observed, "I have been informed that these fish have been taken in various parts of the Ohio and Mississippi weighing 175 to 200 pounds weight which, from the evidence of the subject above-mentioned, I have no doubt is authentic."

On the following day, Lewis took Clark and eight men up the Mississippi taking frequent observations and drawing sketches of the islands and bars in the Tyawapatia Bottom area. The Virginian was becoming a keen and skilled observer and he jotted his botanical and zoological notes dutifully in his journal, bird-watching and collecting geological specimens while he nursed a sick Clark and hunted a lost Sergeant Pryor.

Cape Girardeau, the post which the Spaniards had established in 1793 to blunt the threat posed by the Americans intent on carving out a new state in the Mississippi Valley, was Lewis's next landfall. There, he called on the commander, Louis Lorimier, to deliver letters of introduction from Captain Daniel Bissell and George Drouillard, nephew of the commandant. Lewis found Lorimier at the racetrack, where he was entering several horses. The main contest had just ended as the Virginian arrived and he found the Missourians excitedly settling various betting disputes. "This scene reminded me very much of the small races in Kentucky among the uncivilized backwoodsmen. Nor did the subsequent disorder which took place in consequence of the decision of the judges of the race at all lessen the resemblance. One fellow, contrary to the decision of the judges, swore that he had won and was carrying off not only his own horse but that also of his competitor. But the other, being the stoutest of the two, dismounted him and took both horses, in turn. It is not extraordinary that these people should be disorderly. They are almost entirely emigrants from the frontiers of Kentucky and Tennessee and they are the most dissolute and abandoned even among these people. They are men of desperate fortunes but have little to lose, either character or property. They bet very high on these races in proportion to their wealth. It is not uncommon for them to risk the half or even the whole of their personal property on a single wager. Their property consists principally in horses and black cattle."

The Virginian found that Lorimier had lost four horses, valued at $200, on the main race but that he bore his loss quite cheerfully. Lewis was a little surprised, after seeing this family setback, to observe Lorimier's son placing a wager of $600, in horseflesh, on another race. But then, the Lorimiers were re-markable men. The commandant was a French-Canadian who had originally settled in Ohio, where he became a violent Tory during the American Revolution and, ultimately, *persona non grata* in the Thirteen States. It was Lorimier who had led the Indian war party which captured Daniel Boone in 1778 and it was he who had to flee for his life when George Rogers Clark swooped down on his post in a retaliatory raid of 1782. He lost $20,000 in the burning of his Ohio property. Wiped out, he moved west to Louisiana to start over again and was soon flush.

The French-Canadian invited Lewis to dinner and Lewis en-joyed his hospitable family very much. The Virginian was most impressed with his host. "He is a man about 5 feet, 8 inches high, dark skin, hair and eyes. He is remarkable for having once had a remarkable suit of hair. He was very cheerful and I took occa-sion to mention this to him. He informed me that it was once so long that it touched the ground when he stood erect nor was it much less remarkable for its thickness. This I could readily be-lieve from its present appearance. He is about 60 years of age and yet scarcely a grey hair in his head, which reaches now, when queued (the manner in which he dresses it) nearly as low as his knees and it is proportionately thick. He appears yet quite active. This uncommon queue falls down his back to which it is kept close by means of a leather girdle confined around his waist."

If Lorimier and his coiffure were remarkable and his Shawnee squaw handsome and interesting, his daughter was absolutely dazzling to the romantically inclined young captain. He found her "remarkably handsome. . . . She dresses in a plain yet fashionable style or such as is now common in the Atlantic states among the respectable people of the middle class. She is an agreeable, affable girl and much the most decent-looking female I have seen since I left the settlement in Kentucky a little below Louisville."

Shortly after Pryor found his way back to the party, Lewis led his little fleet past the peculiar rock called Grand Tower. Of the cubical monolith, almost surrounded by water, Lewis wrote, "There seems among the watermen of the Mississippi to be what the Tropics or Equinoxial Line is with regard to sailors. Those who have never passed it before are always compelled to pay or furnish some spirits to drink, or be ducked." He also investigated the Great Eddy and the nob which he called Sugarloaf Point, near Cape Cinque Hommes, which his men bastardized into St. Comb. Upon his arrival at Kaskaskia, Lewis selected enough men from the troops there to bring the strength of his detachment to twenty-five men. On the 28th he left that post and marched overland, accompanied by an officer, to Cahokia, opposite St. Louis. He left Clark in complete command of his force.

In Cahokia, on December 5th, he secured the services of Postmaster John Hay and a trader, Nicholas Jarrot, both of whom were fluent in French. He rushed over to St. Louis with them on the 8th to present his compliments to Don Carlos Duhault Delassus, the commandant of the town and military and civil governor of Upper Louisiana. The polite Spanish official had hardly returned Lewis's letters of introduction before the young Virginian was bombarding him with questions through the two translators. Governor Delassus, with great courtesy, wished Lewis's expedition every success, since he was sure it was harmless to His Catholic Majesty's interests. But, whatever his personal feelings might be, his duty as an officer was clear and his orders anything but ambiguous. The udeviating policy of the Spanish Government with regard to the admission of foreigners into the interior of its provinces forbade his granting Lewis permission to ascend the Missouri River.

Delassus advised Lewis to remain at Cahokia, promising to ask permission of the Governor General in New Orleans for

Lewis to continue west. He was sure that, by spring, when the river was again navigable, all diplomatic obstructions would be removed. Lewis had an alternate plan prepared should he be refused permission to enter Spanish territory. He had already discussed the possibility of a camp in Illinois. However, he told Delassus that he would not camp in Cahokia but somewhere nearby. Since business detained him in St. Louis he left the selection of a site entirely in his comrade's hands. On December 12th, Clark picked a campsite on the Rivière Dubois, or Wood River, about eighteen miles from St. Louis and (in 1804) directly opposite the Missouri's mouth. It was good game country, abounding in turkeys and opossums.

While axes rang in the Wood River bottom, Lewis busied himself in St. Louis, gathering every shred and shard of information he could find on the Missouri and its Indian nations. Secretary Gallatin had suggested that Lewis ascend the Missouri with traders to the Indians to winter with the latter as high as possible on the river, "so that his band should be fresh and in good spirits in the spring." Since this was now impossible and he would not be able to acquire a knowledge of the river by experience until the spring thaw, Lewis determined to learn as much as he could about Louisiana Territory from St. Louis sources.

A windfall was his meeting Antoine Soulard, Surveyor General of Upper Louisiana. At first, Soulard was going to let him make abstracts from the census of 1800 but, at the last minute, he panicked and retrieved the document for fear that Delassus would disapprove. But he estimated that there were 10,000 souls in Upper Louisiana, of whom 2,000 were Negro slaves. Two-thirds of the remainder were Americans and all but a handful of the balance were French or French-Canadian. There were few Spaniards although Spain had held the territory for forty-one years. When Lewis wished to copy a manuscript map of the land between New Mexico and the Missouri, Soulard at first agreed then again lost his nerve and demurred. Lewis soon found that he had to clear with Delassus on almost every matter of business he took up. He wrote to Jefferson, "These people are so much accustomed to elude the eye of despotic power that they can do no act but this principle seems, in some measure, to have inter-

70

woven itself with the actuating motive. . . . They move more as though the fear of the Commandant, than that of God, was before their eyes. They have some reason to fear Col. Delassus; he has been pretty tyrannical with them. With regard to the more wealthy part of the community, the Col. seems to have differed from his predecessors in office in respect to the policy he has observed towards them. Formerly, this class of people escaped punishment for almost every crime, but he has, for the very slightest offense, put some of the most wealthy among them into the Carraboose. This has produced a general dread of him among all classes of the people." But Lewis was sure that once Louisiana became American territory, people would come forward with information. Until then, he would have to obtain what knowledge he could by subterfuge. He could only guess at the number of Americans who yearly emigrated into the territory but he was sure that it was no less than double the figure of common opinion, which was 100 families.

While in St. Louis, Lewis, usually honest with himself and others, because of his unswerving loyalty to Jefferson, practiced some wishful thinking. To please his patron and friend, he told the President that his plan to withdraw the white population to the east side of the Mississippi, leaving the west side a vast Indian preserve, was a workable idea. Lewis was more likely deceiving himself than dissimulating when he observed that the project could be effected in a few years if the U. S. Government were liberal in its donation of lands to the *émigrés*. He admitted the French were little inclined to move, particularly because they feared their slaves would be taken away. (Adjacent Indiana Territory forbade the further introduction of slaves.) Luckily for Lewis, Jefferson had, long before, abandoned his unworkable plan.

Jefferson was pleased with the reports and suggestions he received from his agent of empire. In his fact-finding, Lewis was, unwittingly, taking the first steps toward eventual occupancy of the post which Delassus held. Not all of his recommendations were palatable to Jefferson, of course, such as his recommendation that Louisiana be merged with William Henry Harrison's territory. "I trust I shall be pardoned for giving it as my opinion, that of office hunters to the contrary notwithstanding, that Upper Louisiana can be governed more for the happiness of and justice to the people with less expense to the mother government and with better prospects of inforcing her future policy, by dividing it into about three counties and incorporating it with the Indiana Territory, than by establishing it into a separate Territory or continuing it as a part of the Government of Lower Louisiana, in any shape." This recommendation Jefferson, fortunately, did not take.

Captain Lewis found that Indian traders like Auguste Chouteau possessed the most information on upriver matters but lacked the leisure or the literacy to convey it to him in intelligible form. He therefore worked up a list of questions and circulated copies of it to those who, he felt, had something to contribute to knowledge. Surprisingly, Delassus offered no objection. Lewis also zealously collected all maps of the area which he could find, for the upper river was still a cartographic blank. He also sought journals which might throw light on the Indians to the westward.

Via his questionnaires, Lewis received a mass of information which he crowded into his notebooks and passed on to his colleagues of the American Philosophical Society. He learned about the territory's population, the number of Yankee immigrants, slaves, and people of color who were free. He secured data on the quantity of land granted and claimed, the wealth of the citizenry, the location, extent—and even the nicknames—of settlements, the condition of agriculture and of trade. He sought to determine the amount of goods, in dollar value, annually brought into Upper Louisiana from Canada, New Orleans and the United States. The young captain secured a list of the animals, birds and fishes of Louisiana, their form, appearance, habits—even their dispositions. (But by this he meant their range, not their temperaments.) He asked also, "What are your mines and minerals? Have you lead, iron, copper, pewter, gypsum, salts, salines, or other mineral waters, nitre, stone-coal, marble, limestone, or any other mineral substance? Where are they situated and in what quantities found? Which of these mines or salt springs are worked? And what quantity of metal or salt is annually produced?" Ironically, neither Jefferson nor Lewis thought to ask after silver and gold, although the Spaniards of New Mexico were already frantic over the Virginian's supposed designs on their El Dorado. Several of his men would become miners (Willard and Sacajawea's baby, Baptiste) in the California gold rush, but Lewis himself apparently was never seized with gold fever as, months after he tallied his questionnaires, he walked over Rocky Mountain territory, which became the scene of frenzied rushes and bonanzas in the mid-nineteenth century.

Lewis was very thorough. He was also as pleasant as he was persistent and instead of being dismissed as a spy or, at least, an annoying busybody, he made friends with everyone in St. Louis from Delassus on down. He was careful not to inspect military sites (until March 1804, when the territory became American) but secured a great quantity of useful information as a result of his diligence. The answers to his questionnaires helped him prepare for his spring journey into the mysterious territory which his Gallic informants called *Le Pays Inconnu*—the Unknown Land.

CHAPTER VI

INNOCENT PASSAGE

My most sincere and cordial congratulations on the very happy acquisitions you have made for our country on the Missouri. Altho' no one here appears to know the extent or price of the cession, it is generally considered as the most important and beneficial transaction which has occurred since the Declaration of Independence and next to it most likely to influence or regulate the destinies of our Country.

—Caspar Wistar to Thomas Jefferson,
July 13, 1802

Had an indecisive or bumbling U. S. Army officer descended upon Upper Louisiana in the winter of 1803, with a proposition which amounted to bald trespass of His Catholic Majesty's territories, Lieutenant Governor Carlos Delassus would have been somewhat alarmed. But when the dedicated and aggressive Captain Meriwether Lewis burst upon St. Louis, Delassus and the other officials of Spain's Internal Provinces went off like Congreve rockets. Fortunately for Lewis, most of their fulminating resulted only in showers of memoranda rather than any direct military precautions.

In a sense, Delassus had been expecting Lewis or, at least, a similar visitor. Spanish Louisiana had long feared Yankee aggression and, for a solid year, the little city of 180 stone houses and log cabins had been aware of Jefferson's designs on the Far West. No breach of security in Washington was responsible; Jefferson hid his actual plans only from the public and, particularly, the Congress with its hostile "Feds." He openly wrote to such friends as the French naturalist, Bernard de Lacépède, "We are now actually sending off a small party to explore the Missouri to its source and whatever other river, heading nearest with that, runs into the Western Ocean."

Reaction was swift. The Spanish Minister to the United States, Don Carlos Martínez de Yrujo, wrote his Minister of Foreign Affairs at the Spanish Court, Don Pedro Cevallos, as early as December 1802. He warned him of Jefferson's plan to penetrate to the "Southern Ocean" via the Missouri. When Jefferson frankly asked him if Spain would oppose the exploration, Martínez, with equal candor, replied that it could not fail to give umbrage to his government. The President had no success although he leveled a barrage of argument at the Minister, repeatedly assuring him that the expedition would have no other view than the advancement of geography and commerce. When the President tried another tack, suggesting that Lewis would determine, once and for all, whether a Northwest Passage actually existed, the Spaniard rebuffed him with the claim that this point had been already settled, negatively, by the fruitless searches of Cook, Vancouver, Mourelle, Bodega and Malaspina.

When the two parted, Martínez felt that he had won the battle of words. But he wisely warned Madrid that there was still a chance that President Jefferson might proceed with his plan. "The President has been, all his life, a man of letters, very speculative and a lover of glory and it would be possible he might attempt to perpetuate the fame of his administration . . . by discovering or attempting, at least, to discover the way by which the Americans may, some day, extend their population and influence up the coasts of the South Sea."

How little did Martínez really know Jefferson. The President could no more discard his favorite project than he could give up his love of country—with which his plan was much entangled. The Spanish Minister had evaluated Jefferson's plan as a device to continue the fame of his administration, whereas the President was actually obsessed with the perpetuation of his young republic. However confused he might be over the Northwest Passage, living mastodons and Philip Nolan's Mountain of Salt, Jefferson's early enthusiasm for an overland exploration had hardened by 1803 into an urgent determination. Martínez should have known as much, from the tenor of the President's message to Congress. Jefferson assured the lawmakers that Spain would not be jealous of Lewis's strictly mercantile and "literary" pursuit—even if "the expiring state of its interests there did not render it a matter of indifference."

Jefferson, upon occasion, could change his mind as mercurially as a barrister. But in this case, it was made up forever. He told Lewis to go ahead. "Without waiting for permission, we shall enter into the exercise of the natural right we have always insisted on with Spain, to wit, that of a nation holding the upper part of streams having a right to innocent passage through them to the ocean. We shall prepare her to see us practice on this and she will not oppose it by force."

Martínez wrote Madrid again to report that the President had presented his plan to the Senate but that the good judgment of the Upper House failed to see the advantages which the President proposed. On the contrary, Martínez reported with delight, the Senators feared it might offend certain European nations. "Consequently," wrote the Minister, "it is very probable that the project will not proceed." Shortly after the Court read this communiqué, Cevallos scrawled across the document these words—"His Majesty has seen with satisfaction that by their [i.e, Congress's] erudite reflections, the President's project has been abandoned."

His Majesty was not only premature in his judgment, he was dead wrong. The Jefferson-Lewis project proved to have more lives than Talleyrand. Now, Secretary of the Treasury Albert Gallatin threw his support behind it. He suggested that the United States secure a perfect knowledge of Spain's posts and military forces in Louisiana, determine the key sites to control the territory, and seize it before Great Britain swallowed it up.

At their St. Louis meeting, Lieutenant Governor Delassus told Lewis that he could not permit him to pass upriver into His Majesty's domains. Lewis took the rebuff with good grace. There was little else he could do; he did not even possess a Spanish passport. Although he had French and British documents, his lack of a

Spanish *pasaporte* was more than an oversight, it was a serious blunder by Jefferson and himself. They had been lulled into carelessness by overoptimism, thinking the transfer of Louisiana from Spain to France would be effected speedily.

It was actually only twenty days after Lewis confronted Delassus that the Spanish Government reported, officially, to the Lieutenant Governor on the forthcoming transfer of sovereignty. But in the meantime Lewis had made a graceful and diplomatic change of plan which saved face in both Washington and St. Louis and which earned him Delassus's respect and friendship. Lewis abandoned the idea of wintering at La Charrette, beyond St. Louis, and instead set Clark to locating a suitable campsite on U. S. Territory across the Mississippi from St. Louis. He did not want any diplomatic difficulties to loom up to block his "innocent passage" in the following spring and he wanted to get settled before the Midwest winter closed its cold fist tightly on the Missouri and Mississippi. He wanted snug cabins and he wanted hunting parties out to stock the corps' larder for winter. Since Delassus had promptly asked his superiors for a decision on Lewis's spring passage, Lewis was most amicable and agreeable in waiting upon the Spanish Government's decision. The two men struck it off well, from their very first meeting.

Delassus reported the strength of Lewis's party as only twenty-five men. The Virginian had more like forty-five or fifty during his early weeks at the Wood River site Clark selected. But he planned to shrink his force to a core of some twenty-five men. (The shrinkage, however, never came to pass.) Lewis may have been dissimulating a bit but Delassus's low estimate was really based on his own idea of the optimum number of soldiers for such an expedition. Less than that number would mean insecurity from Indian attack; if the party set out overstrength, provisioning the men would be difficult. Lewis eventually built his party up to almost double Delassus's optimum figure simply by deciding to worry about problems of logistics and sustenance once he was on the march, and not before. He had an idea that some of the men whom Clark was putting through their paces— Drouillard, Reuben and Joseph Field, John Colter—would shape up as excellent hunters. He would have to depend on them.

Delassus's respect for Lewis was evident in his reports to his superiors. While other Spaniards were suspicious of the Virginian's motives, the Lieutenant Governor wrote: "I believe that his mission has no other object than to discover the Pacific Ocean by following the Missouri, and to make intelligent observations, because he has the reputation of being a very well educated man, and of many talents." But the Spanish Government remained uneasy. Part of this may have been due to the obvious discrepancy between Lewis's appraisal of his detachment as twenty-five men and the half a hundred the Spanish saw chopping timber in the Rivière Dubois bottom. Perhaps, too, a rumor of Lewis's abortive plan to explore to Santa Fe leaked out. In any case, they linked Lewis with Jefferson's interpretation of Louisiana Territory as including the lands astride *all* of the tributaries of the Missouri, many of which, they knew, headed in the indistinct upper reaches of New Mexico.

The first of several Spanish alarms occurred when word of Lewis's feverish preparations for winter, coupled with the normal immigration of American frontiersmen into Louisiana, became so garbled that Juan Ventura Morales, Intendant of Louisiana, warned Don Miguel Cayetano Soler in New Orleans that Delassus was arming the militia to repulse 500 Americans arriving with Captain "Wheather." Martínez, in Washington, was not yet a member of this worried group of Spaniards. He mistakenly relied on Jefferson's clinging to his old and discarded idea of restricting white settlement in Louisiana Territory to the left bank of the Mississippi. The river, the Indians, and the no-man's-land would prove a powerful barrier between the pressuring Americans and New Mexico.

While Martínez was deluding himself, the outgoing governor of Louisiana was finally writing Delassus (January 28, 1804) to compliment him on his actions in regard to Lewis during the time he had been without specific orders. Now he instructed his lieutenant governor not to place any obstructions in the explorer's way, but to allow him to proceed up the Missouri whenever he chose to embark.

Although news of the purchase of Louisiana reached the

United States by the end of June 1803, and although Napoleon's letter with official word of the transfer reached New Orleans by June 6th, the ceremonies of transfer did not take place until November 30th and December 20th. On the first date, a dreary, gray, winter's day, the Spaniards turned the keys to the Crescent City over to the French in the crowded Plaza before the Cabildo and absolved the population of allegiance to Spain. The Spanish flag came down and the French tricolor was run up. Less than a month later, Act II opened with the formal transfer, this time, of Louisiana Territory from France to the United States. The slippery General James Wilkinson headed the U. S. Commission, with Governor C. C. Claiborne of Mississippi Territory assisting. On December 20th, the tricolor sagged to earth and the Stars and Stripes was hoisted up into the warm sunshine of a fine winter day. The two ceremonies marked the transfer of all Louisiana Territory to the United States but it was thought best to reiterate the transfer in isolated and thinly populated Upper Louisiana by means of an additional ceremony in St. Louis.

The Prefect of New Orleans wrote Delassus that Captain Amos Stoddard of the U. S. Army was authorized to accept Upper Louisiana for France and the U. S. Commission notified him that Stoddard would also receive the territory when France tendered it to the U.S.A. On February 18, 1804, Stoddard wrote various messages to Delassus concerning the cession, entrusting them to a sergeant en route to Meriwether Lewis's cantonment. After stationing his men in Cahokia, Stoddard followed the noncom to the Upper Louisiana capital to confer with Delassus on arrangements for the transfer. The latter canceled all leaves and ordered his troops to be in full, clean uniforms and knapsacks, ready for Sergeant Juan Robyna's verbal orders to shoulder arms and evacuate the fort in good order and with proper military bearing.

It was not till March 9th, however, that Lieutenant Stephen Worrell, Stoddard's regular adjutant, who was displaced for the next several days by Meriwether Lewis, led the U. S. troops across the river to St. Louis. Meriwether Lewis, in his best uniform, had already joined Stoddard at the old Government House, to assist him as his aide and to act as the President's personal envoy. The moment Lewis and Stoddard entered Government House, a Spanish soldier stationed at the corner of the building waved his hat as a signal to the fort. A cannoneer applied a lighted match to a touchhole and the first of several cannon blazed in a salutatory salvo which was maintained at regularly spaced intervals. Lewis, with the others, stood at attention, listening to Delassus make his last proclamation as lieutenant governor of *Alta Luisiana* as the last booming echoes of the cannon died in the river bottom.

For a Latin, he came to the point quickly. Addressing all the inhabitants of Upper Louisiana, he proclaimed: "By the King's command I am about to deliver up this post and its dependencies. The flag under which you have been protected for almost thirty-six years is to be withdrawn. From this moment, you are released from the oath of fidelity you took to support it. The fidelity and courage with which you have guarded and defended it will never be forgotten and, in the character of representative, I entertain the most sincere wishes for your perfect prosperity."

Delassus then placed Stoddard in possession of Government House, and the Spanish battery punctuated the proceedings with another salute. Next, Delassus and Stoddard signed the formal document of transfer, in triplicate. It was then witnessed; first by Meriwether Lewis, then by Antoine Soulard, and finally by Charles Gratiot.

Delassus then addressed Stoddard again, saluting him in the King's name as Commissioner of the French Republic and congratulating him on behalf of the United States for the purchase of the rich territory. He then presented his officers to Stoddard and Lewis, and to some of the leading citizens of St. Louis, assuring the American officers that they all were ready to receive the new laws under which they would henceforth reside.

Stoddard responded in English, solemnly—and slowly, so that Gratiot could translate his words for Delassus and the Franco-Spanish population. The captain expressed his gratitude for the kind reception given him and ventured that the civilities of the day were a favorable omen for future harmony. He reflected his government's gratitude for the confidence the Louisianans were placing in their new country. He ended, "I salute the officers of

His Catholic Majesty with the urbanity and affection which forms the characteristic of military men."

After exchanging these amenities, the representatives of the two countries fell silent and watched the proxy troops of Napoleon, courtesy of the U. S. Army, march to the fort on the hill and take possession of it. The Spanish soldiery filed out and the culmination of the day's colorful and stirring ceremony was the dipping of the Spanish flag and the hoisting of the French colors. The wishes of the old French settlers, expressed to Stoddard and Lewis by Gratiot, were that the tricolor be allowed to fly for one day. Lewis watched as Delassus took the Spanish ensign, threw it over his shoulder and wrapped it around him like a cloak or serape.

One incident of that day the Virginian did not see. Black Hawk, chief of the Sauks and Foxes, who would later threaten Lewis's Indian plans—and American settlement in general—in the Mississippi Valley, related it in his autobiography: "A few days afterwards, the Americans arrived. I took my band and went to take leave, for the last time, of our Father [Delassus]. The Americans came to see him also. Seeing them approach, we passed out at one door as they entered another and immediately started in canoes for our village on Rock River, not liking the change any more than our friends appeared to at St. Louis. . . . We had always heard bad accounts of the Americans from Indians who had lived near them and we were sorry to lose our Spanish Father, who had always treated us with great friendship."

As Black Hawk indicated, not all of the population of Upper Louisiana was eager for a change of masters. The capital was quiet and its citizenry either indifferent or apathetic, but there were difficulties and scuffles elsewhere. However, in Mine à Burton, later Potosi, there were cries of *"Viva Gifferson!"*

On March 10th, again with Lewis's help, Stoddard officially lowered the French tricolor to end Franco-Spanish sovereignty over Upper Louisiana forever. He raised the Stars and Stripes and formally took possession in the name of the United States.

Lewis did not return immediately to his military camp at Wood River but assisted Stoddard for the last time when Delassus called an Indian council at Lewis's and Stoddard's request. The powwow was intended not only to confirm, in Indian eyes, the transfer of the territory but to smooth the way west for Lewis's expedition. Delassus addressed the gathered Delawares, Abanakis, Shawnees, Sauks and others on the 12th of March, saying: "Your old Fathers, the Spaniard and the Frenchman, grasp by the hand your new Father, the Head Chief of the United States. By an act of their good will, and in virtue of their last treaty, I have delivered up to them all these lands. They will keep and defend them and protect all the white and red skins who live thereon. You will live as happily as if the Spaniard were still here. . . ."

After complimenting the Indians on their record of peace during Spanish jurisdiction over Louisiana, he bade his wards adieu. "For several days past we have fired off cannon-shots to announce to all the nations that our Father, the Spaniard, is going, his heart happy to know that you will be protected and sustained by your new Father, and that the smoke of the powder may ascend to the Master of life, praying him to shower on you a happy destiny and prosperity in always living in good union with the whites."

Lewis returned to Wood River, put away his good uniform, and settled down to the routine of preparations for his embarkation.

The amity existing between Don and American, as exemplified by the cordiality of the transfer, was anything but universal. While Delassus was clasping hands in friendship with Lewis and Stoddard, the Marquis of Casa Calvo was taking steps to detain the explorer and prevent any discoveries on the Missouri or on the South Sea shore, where, he said, Lewis and Jefferson planned to have a port within five years. He asked the Commanding General of the Internal Provinces, Brigadier Don Nemesio Salcedo y Salcedo, in Chihuahua, to order the arrest of Lewis to prevent "the hasty and gigantic steps which our neighbours are taking towards the South Sea [i.e., Pacific], entering by way of the Missouri River."

Casa Calvo cried out that the crisis was at hand, that Captain "Merry"—whom he sometimes called "Leivis Merry Whethez"

—must be restrained or a chain of American establishments would be set up to make the Yankees masters of Spain's rich New Mexico. On March 17, 1804, Manuel de Godoy, the Spanish Minister and so-called Prince of the Peace, made it clear that Spain hoped to hang on to much of what Jefferson considered now to be American territory. No boundary had been run in the interior (or would be until 1819) but he made it known that the Spanish Court considered that the confines of Texas and New Mexico extended beyond the Missouri River and included not only both banks of that stream but its confluence with the Mississippi at St. Louis! On April 6th he also insisted that the Texas-Louisiana boundary line ran between Los Adaes and Natchitoches—and on north across the Red River to the Missouri. This was a barrier beyond which Lewis must not pass. The Prince of Peace suggested to his own government that forts be set up on one or both rivers to assure Spain's monopoly on their navigation.

The Spaniards were not able to move fast enough to catch Lewis at Wood River but after he set out they followed his progress as closely as possible from the reports trickling downriver to St. Louis. By late September 1804, the Spanish estimated that he was 300 leagues above the city and well advanced into Spain's Internal Provinces. Casa Calvo busily routed clippings from such newspapers as the New Orleans *Gazette*. On January 22, 1805, the *Gaceta de Madrid* lamented that, thanks to Lewis, it would not be long before the immense lands of the red men to the west of U. S. territory would be incorporated into the United States. The tension in Madrid led the King of Spain himself that month to instruct his Minister Plenipotentiary to complain to the United States Government against "so manifest an offense against the sovereignty of the King as Captain Merry Weather's expedition."

Brigadier Salcedo had no more idea of where the Missouri headed than any other man of his day. Perhaps it burbled out of a mountain spring in New Mexico. A number of geographers conveniently delineated all the major watercourses of western America—the Missouri, Columbia, Colorado and Rio Grande —as flowing out of a tight continental nexus in the Rockies, a watershed ganglia on the very border of New Mexico if not wholly within that province. In any case, Salcedo doubted strongly that Lewis's sole interest lay in tracing the Missouri as close to the Pacific as possible. Perhaps he had heard from Regis Loisel that the Americans claimed the sources of the tributaries of the Missouri, even should they rise in the *plazas* of Spanish settlements. Salcedo suspected that Lewis's real goal was the wealth of New Mexico, if not Sonora and Sinaloa.

Spain was plainly uneasy. The Americans made no secret of what they would, one day, term their Manifest Destiny. The London *Morning Post* as long before as December 1782 had prophesied that all Spanish possessions on the Mississippi would fall before the Americans and that their power would reach to the Pacific, to dispossess the Europeans of every hold upon the continent. Suspicion was mixed with fear, too. Madrid suspected that Lewis was linked with Philip Nolan, who had been killed in 1801 on a mysterious expedition into Spanish territory.

Casa Calvo urged Salcedo to take immediate and drastic action to preserve undamaged the King's permanent domains in North America, and to prevent particularly the ruination of New Mexico by Meriwether Lewis. He reiterated, "The only means which presents itself is to arrest Captain Merry Weather and his party, which cannot help but pass through the nations neighbouring New Mexico, its *presidios* and *rancherías*. . . . I do not doubt that Your Excellency will give orders that the most efficacious steps be taken to arrest the referred-to Captain Merry and his followers who, according to notices, number twenty-five men, and to seize their papers and instruments that may be found on them. This action may be based on the fact that, without the permission of the Spanish Government, they have entered its territory. Since the line of demarcation has not been determined as yet, they cannot infer that it already belongs to the United States. . . . Although there be no motive or pretext whatsoever, nevertheless, it is absolutely necessary, for reasons of state, to carry out the arrest of the said Captain." Casa Calvo's sense of urgency was indicated by his use of such expressions as "We must not lose a moment to deliver a decisive and vigorous blow" at Lewis's expedition.

Salcedo's first answer was that he would restrict the Americans to former French settlements on the Ouachita, Arkansas and Missouri rivers and that he would keep them far from New Mexico. His eventual response was dramatic, if not speedy. He asked the governor of New Mexico, Joaquín del Réal Alencaster, to send a party of Spain's Indian allies to capture Lewis. He wanted Alencaster to win the friendship of the Otos, Loups, Pawnees and other tribes of the Kansas, Platte and Arkansas rivers. Salcedo wanted the chiefs, especially the Pawnees, to visit Santa Fe to engage in a council which would infuse the Indians with horror (the word was Salcedo's) for the Americans. He insisted, "The Ideas of the Americans can be nothing other than, once the friendship of the Indians is secured, to destroy them in a few years, by making themselves the possessors of the River and their lands."

By now, even Lewis's friend Delassus was fearful that the United States was going to extend its borders into Mexico. But he did not think that Lewis was an *agent provocateur* of this American imperialism and he continued to defend Lewis from loose charges in Spanish circles, insisting the Virginian's plan to discover the Pacific Ocean via a Missouri route was no pretext for territorial aggrandizement.

Salcedo wrote Viceroy Iturrigary on October 6, 1805, to damn Lewis for his extraordinary proceedings and his suspicious conduct. He claimed—falsely—that the American was handing out rifles and powder to the Indians as well as medals and flags to capture the good will of the Missouri River tribes. Alencaster moved as fast as possible but it was almost a week after Salcedo wrote the viceroy before he could report that he had an expedition ready to march in pursuit of Lewis. The governor sent as co-commanders Don Pedro Vial and the man who kept the Pawnees from treating with Lewis, Interpreter José Calvert (alias Jarvet and Chalvet). With them went two *carabineros* of the Santa Fe Presidial company, Corporal Juan Lucero and Private Francisco García, and fifty militia troopers as an escort. The two officers also took along as scouts four French traders and trappers, Lorenzo Durocher, Juan Bautista Lalanda, Dionisio Lacroix and Andrés Lacroix.

Vial marched by way of Taos, traveling by night to escape

detection and attack by Indians, intending to meet with the Pawnees at the head of the Kansas River. He would find out if the American's wiles had worked on them and send information back with the militiamen while the Frenchmen, acting as spies, would make canoes and drift down the Kansas and Missouri rivers to St. Louis. Vial and Calvert intended to winter with the Pawnees, to consolidate the friendship of that tribe. The Spanish plans were well laid.

Passing through great herds of buffalo, the Spanish expedition reached the Arkansas River on November 5th. But Indians whose tribal allegiance Vial was never able to determine now began to dog his steps. Late that night, a force of 100 of them split into three parties and attacked his detachment. All his men, militia, Regulars and Frenchmen, fought well and drove the Indians off after three hours, but only after they had pillaged his camp. And when he tried to resume his march, they attacked again. With his ammunition and other supplies looted, Vial had to retreat to Santa Fe. As Meriwether Lewis, ignorant of the drama far to the southeast of him, slept in his cold and sopping blankets on the Columbia River's shore, Vial turned his back on the Arkansas and retraced his steps to Santa Fe. There he urged that a fort be constructed on the Arkansas to protect New Mexico's flank from Lewis, and begged that larger forces, with more munitions, be sent out to prevent such a disaster as had overtaken him.

Lewis never realized that he was being stalked. There was no confrontation. Soon, Spain was so preoccupied with the Florida boundary quarrel and the expeditions of Dunbar and, particularly, Pike that Lewis was largely forgotten. But it was his threat, at least in Spanish eyes, which caused Madrid to build up its military strength in Texas to an all-time high of 1,273 men under arms, not counting Plains Indian allies and auxiliaries such as Melgares's Pawnees and Juan Lucero's Kiowas, in a belated attempt to restrict American Louisiana to the narrowest possible proportions.

CHAPTER VII

THE ADVANCE BASE

Every individual of the party is in good health and excellent spirits, zealously attached to the enterprise and anxious to proceed. . . . With such men, I have everything to hope and but little to fear.
—MERIWETHER LEWIS, April 7, 1805

IF EQUIPMENT for the Corp of Discovery was important, Lewis realized that personnel was the critical factor. At the start of winter, he was sure of only one member of the expedition besides Clark and himself—his big Newfoundland dog, Scammon. To test the mettle of the volunteers, he turned on them as a hard-driving taskmaster. The Beau Brummel officer and gentleman who had earned the sobriquet of "the sublime dandy" transformed himself into a fair likeness of Mad Anthony Wayne. His stringent physical examination, his brusque handling of the men, paid off. The ungainly mob of volunteers was soon reduced to a manageable company of forty-five men. If there was any fat left in the detachment, Will Clark would work it off with his hard drilling on the Wood River bottom.

Lewis was not surprised as the enthusiasm of some of the men waned. Many, like Corporal John Robinson, or the thief Leakins, made it as far as Wood River but no farther. He could not yet size up his boat crews. They constituted an unknown quantity and he could not even test the nine French watermen from Kaskaskia and St. Louis, who would get him to the Mandan villages, because, as he complained to Clark, they were not amenable to military discipline. "They will not agree to go farther [than the Mandan country] and I find it impossible to reduce them to any other engagement than that usually made with these people." Thus, Lewis had to depend heavily on the *patron* of the *engagés,* Baptiste Deschamps, to get the most out of his countrymen.

Captain Lewis felt he could rely on the noncommissioned officer who commanded his escort, a mere corporal's guard of a half-dozen Regulars, which was to see him safely through the dangerous Sioux country. Corporal Richard Warfington was a tobacco-chewing noncom with the unmistakable stamp of a real soldier on him. His men were not much, however, and Lewis must have ruminated on the low state of the U. S. Army as he looked over Privates John Boley, John Dame, Alexander Carson, Isaac White, Ebenezer Tuttle, and Robert Frazier.

As for the members of his permanent party, those who would go all the way to the Pacific, unlike Warfington's and Deschamps's men, Lewis had to admit that the civilian volunteers were shaping up much better than the Regulars he and Clark had recruited. The backbone of his detachment, already, was the group called "the nine young men from Kentucky." He had enlisted two of them himself, John Colter and young George Shannon, on his voyage down the Ohio with the cumbersome bateau, while Clark had selected the other seven from applicants at Louisville and at Clarksville, Indiana Territory. John Colter, who would become a great mountain man, was one of the "sooners" of the expedition, having joined Lewis on October 15, 1803, at Limestone, now Maysville, Kentucky, thereby beating even Clark in seniority of service. He was a twenty-eight-year-old frontiersman who had been a Ranger with Simon Kenton. Blue-eyed like Lewis, he also resembled his commander in that he was a pleasant and ingenuous Virginian, quick in mind and muscle, and as brave or braver than the captain from Ivy himself.

Meriwether Lewis found George Shannon one of the most promising of his volunteers. He was a blue-eyed Pennsylvanian of only eighteen years of age—the youngest man in the party. He, like Colter, had joined Lewis as the latter made his way down the Ohio. The likable young Protestant Irishman was handsome, clean-shaven in a hirsute age, intelligent and well-educated for his youth. He would prove to be the only one of the expedition, other than Lewis, with an intellectual bent but his age and private's station prevented him from displaying it on the march. Unfortunately, he was not well versed in woodcraft. He made up for this weakness, in Lewis's estimation, with his great courage, perseverance and loyalty.

William Bratton would pass muster; he was the expedition's third-best gunsmith. The Kentuckian, William Warner, was a good cook and since Lewis, as well as Napoleon, realized that an army—or a detachment—traveled on its stomach, he was important. Joseph Whitehouse was handy at making and repairing clothes with buckskin; John Shields was the best gunsmith and blacksmith at Wood River and a valuable boatwright and handyman, to boot. Second only to Shields as a gunsmith was the giant twenty-six-year-old from New Hampshire, Alexander Hamilton Willard—no relation to Jefferson's old enemy. Willard was probably the strongest man of the party barring the herculean York, Clark's negro servant, and was one of the better hunters of the corps.

In the two Field brothers, Reuben and Joseph, Lewis saw that fate had dealt him a pair of aces. As woodsmen they were excelled by only one man, Lewis's scout, Drouillard. He knew, too, that he could count on them to be dependable soldiers. Moreover, Joseph was a fine handyman and Reuben was the fleetest runner of the entire detachment.

The ninth Kentuckian was Sergeant Charles Floyd, a young man highly respected by Lewis and Clark. They had no worries about his ability. He came of good stock. Floyd was the son of the Charles Floyd who had soldiered with George Rogers Clark and Daniel Boone.

Both captains must have had some misgivings about Collins, Hall, Newman and Reed of the Regulars. John Collins behaved so badly when he first arrived at Wood River that Clark described him to Lewis as a blackguard. He began to shape up after Lewis prescribed a flogging for what ailed him, and was soon an acceptable soldier as well as a good hunter and cook. Hugh Hall was a tosspot but he stayed out of trouble more than Collins, even when he was in his cups. Both Lewis and Clark were fooled by John Newman and Moses B. Reed, and La Liberté of the *engagés*. These were the only really weak links in the chain of command which stretched from Lewis to (eventually) a half-breed baby and its Indian mother, Sacajawea. All three—Newman, Reed and La Liberté—turned out to be deserters once they were deep in Indian country.

Hugh McNeal, Richard Windsor and the German, John Potts, had little to distinguish themselves but seemed to Lewis to be acceptable soldiers. John B. Thompson was an ex-surveyor but an even better cook. Peter Wiser, another soldier-cook, was responsible enough for Lewis to make him his quartermaster.

Lewis had selected two sergeants in addition to Charles Floyd. One was Floyd's cousin, Nathaniel Pryor, and the other was John Ordway. Both were solid, intelligent men. Ordway, in Lewis's opinion, was the most dependable of the noncommissioned officers.

Among the enlisted men, Patrick Gass was outstanding. He was a barrel-chested Irishman from Pennsylvania. Ruddy-faced like so many Irishers, he hid the fact behind a bushy beard. Gass became Lewis's head carpenter. As a civilian he had helped build a house for the father of future President James Buchanan. Uneducated, having had only nineteen days of schooling, he was intelligent and an experienced Indian fighter. Stationed at Kaskaskia, he applied for Lewis's expedition but his commander—not wanting to lose his best carpenter—refused. He then came directly to Lewis, who persuaded Captain Russell Bissell to let Pat Gass go west.

Lewis welcomed Silas Goodrich to the corps because he found that the man was an expert fisherman. A prairie Izaak Walton would be provident, to vary the monotonous diet of meat. An even better morale builder was George Gibson, who played the violin. Lewis planned to use that fiddle as an instrument of diplomacy with the Indians, as well as of morale with his men. To his delight, Lewis found a waterman, Peter Cruzatte, an even superior fiddler.

The most important person in the entire detachment, after

Lewis and Clark, was a private. George Drouillard had a responsibility second only to that shared by the commanders. He was Lewis's scout, interpreter and chief hunter. He made Lewis thank God that his first choice for the post, John Conner, had let him down and led him to choose Drouillard. The scout's mates Anglo-Saxoned his name to Drewer or Drewyer but he was a *métis,* a French-Indian half-breed. His mother was a Shawnee; his father, Pierre, a friend of George Rogers Clark. Lewis exempted him from guard duty, promised him extra pay upon the completion of the expedition—and got it for him. Drouillard was to Lewis what Kit Carson was to Frémont. He was the eyes—and often the commissary—of the whole party. His accuracy with a rifle was uncanny. The *métis* was tall and ramrod straight in posture. He had inherited his mother's stoicism and reserve as well as her jet-black hair and dark brown eyes. He was second only to Reuben Field as a strong and fast runner and his proficiency in woodcraft, or plainscraft, made even such men as Colter and the Field brothers look like rank amateurs. Unlike many of his full-blood French colleagues, Drouillard could write tolerably well and he was fluent in Indian sign language, which Lewis knew was the lingua franca of the plains and Rockies. To Lewis, the services of Drouillard as nimrod, dragoman and dactylologist at $25 per month was just about the best bargain he had ever made.

From the many French Canadians who were available to him, Lewis singled out two *engagés* to be his permanent boatmen for the entire journey to the Pacific and back. Chief waterman was Private Pierre Cruzatte, a wiry, one-eyed Creole whom the irreverent soldiers immediately nicknamed St. Peter. He was an ex-trader with the Chouteaus, spoke the Omaha language, and was well liked by the detachment, especially because he scraped an even meaner fiddle than Gibson. With only one eye, and that one nearsighted, he could con boats through the worst rapids or shoals better than any of the watermen blessed with two eyes. His companion, Private François Labiche, not only was second boatman but Lewis named him second interpreter behind Drouillard because he knew English, French and several Indian dialects. Another bonus surprise was Labiche's talent as a tracker, second only to Drouillard.

Clark's Negro servant, York, was an obsidian-black man, a jolly giant of a fellow whose wit made a long and hard journey seem shorter to the men.

By and large, Lewis—and Clark—had chosen well. On the eve of his departure for the Far West, Lewis felt no compunction in joining Amos Stoddard in the sentiments he expressed to Secretary of War Henry Dearborn—"His [Lewis's] men possess great resolution and are in the best health and spirits."

As winter melted into spring, Lewis had to leave the problem of personnel, more and more, to Clark as he attended to the many tasks incidental to getting the expedition under way by May. There was the need to collect rations in St. Louis and Cahokia in order to stretch his expeditionary stores; there was his urge to secure every tidbit of information on Louisiana from such journals as those of James Mackay and John Hay. Correspondence also had to be attended to. Jefferson wrote to tell him that he had been elected to the American Philosophical Society on October 21st. This news delighted Lewis, always sensitive to honors and glory, as much as did the maps and translations of Spanish journals of exploration which the President sent him.

But a constant strain and annoyance to Lewis was the nonarrival of Clark's commission. Finally, on February 10th, he wrote to Secretary Dearborn, reminding him of the promised commission and of the gentleman's agreement that it should be for a captaincy in the Corps of Engineers. (He forbore reminding Dearborn that one of the gentlemen concerned was currently resident in the White House.) The answer which the Secretary penned and sent him must have called forth some choice Piedmont cursing from the Virginian. "Sir," was Dearborn's salutation. "The peculiar situation, circumstances and organization of the Corps of Engineers is such as would render the appointment of Mr. Clark a Captain in that Corps improper. . . ."

A furious Lewis read on. "Consequently, no appointment above that of a lieutenant in the Corps of Artillerists could with propriety be given him, which appointment he has received and his commission is herewith enclosed. His military grade will have no effect on his compensation for the service in which he is engaged." To make his cut even unkinder, Dearborn or one of his bureaucrats had dated Clark's commission March 26, 1804, as if to deliberately reduce his seniority. Clark had accepted Lewis's offer in July 1803 and had joined his friend at Louisville in October. Lewis did his best to correct this unfair situation by writing Dearborn, but failed.

Work continued to come before pleasure. On Valentine's Day, Lewis received a Kickapoo chief when he would have preferred being with Clark at the gala holiday ball in St. Louis. He postponed visits to that city and Cahokia in order to meet with Major Nathan Rumsey, agent for Elisha G. Galusha, contractor for Army rations, in order to better fit out his boats. Lewis approved of Clark's plan to secure men from fur trader Manuel Lisa and arranged for Pierre Chouteau to bring an Osage Indian delegation down the river to see him in St. Louis. Chouteau agreed to escort them but wanted the affair kept secret so that other tribes would not become jealous. Lewis agreed but asked Chouteau to shepherd the Osages all the way to Washington, to see Jefferson; he wrote letters to William Preston and Major George Croghan to smooth Chouteau's way to the seat of government.

By February, Lewis had selected Ordway to be his acting first sergeant, keeping the roster and orderly books. On the 20th he had him parade the men and read them his Detachment Orders. The troops were notified that in the absence of Lewis and Clark, Sergeant Ordway was in command. Since Lewis knew that soldiers preferred specifics to generalities, he had Ordway read off a number of duty orders concerning the sawyers, sugar makers, blacksmiths and hunters. Ordway himself was to remain in charge of Lewis's "practicing party" and would reward the top marksman of each session with an extra gill of whiskey. To conserve powder and ball for the march, Lewis ordered Ordway to restrict the men to one round per day from the offhand position at fifty yards from the target. Lewis placed Floyd in charge of the officers' quarters and stores in their absence; forbade any absences from camp, except for hunters; and ordered that no whiskey be delivered from the contractor's store except for the legal ration.

Ordway and Floyd did their best but discipline sagged badly when Lewis and Clark were absent from the cantonment. Upon his return, Lewis had to call out the detachment and tongue-lash the men, particularly Wiser, Colter, Shields, Boley, Robinson and Reuben Field. He read the riot act to them, through Ordway. "The Commanding Officer feels himself mortified and disappointed at the disorderly conduct . . . [and] the want of discretion . . . in the absence of Captain Clark and myself." Lewis restricted the miscreants to camp for ten days and reiterated that all men were to obey Ordway's orders, in his own absence, as if they were his own.

Lewis realized why the men had run wild. They were bored with the long winter, and chafing to be on their way up the Big Muddy. He was himself impatient—more so than the most of them. But he could not allow himself to hurry the expedition into hasty action. He continued his meticulous planning, his study, his interviewing of anyone and everyone who might be able to shed a little light on the little-known country upstream.

Nor did Captain Lewis ever forget his role of minister without portfolio to the Indian nations of the Missouri. Jefferson had written him to say, "We become their fathers and friends." Lewis was the personal representative of the Great Father on the Western frontier of the United States, and he never once lost sight of this fact. In March he took time from his other duties to write and send a speech to the Sauks and Foxes. The communiqué, carried by a Sauk chief to the truculent tribes, was his first Indian address. Its results were hardly what Lewis expected. But he learned that the Sauk had turned the document over to an English trader to translate and the Briton had twisted Lewis's tongue to the great disadvantage of the United States. When word of this trick seeped back to Lewis, he immediately responded by sending his own personal interpreter upriver to repeat the address of friendship, correctly this time.

Lewis followed this up with a parole and speech addressed to the Iowas and Sioux of the Des Moines River. He had the trustworthy Indian trader Lewis Crawford carry it to the Indians. This time there was no tinkering with the message in translation and the word began to spread among the tribes that the Spaniard had, indeed, been replaced as sovereign of Upper Louisiana. The Virginian took advantage of Crawford's trip and his knowledge

and experience to procure, via the trader, vocabularies of the
Iowa and Sioux languages for his own use as well as to copy and
forward to Jefferson. On March 15th, together with other documents, he sent a copy of his address to the Secretary of War, plus
a recommendation that John Hay be appointed Indian Agent. At
the same time, he wrote Governor William Henry Harrison of
Indiana Territory and Secretary Dearborn on the measures necessary to place Louisiana Territory into a proper state of defense.

Still weak in taxonomy, Lewis prepared for the trip ahead of
him by botanizing, whenever possible, in the Rivière Dubois bottom. Among the specimens he collected and sent to the President
in March were slips of the Osage plum and Osage orange. He
was still an amateur, though a very gifted one, as a botanist and
he described the latter plant in citric terms—"this fruit is the size
of the largest orange, of a globular form and of a fine orange
color"—but then called the plant the Osage apple! However im-
precise he might be in terminology, Lewis was most informative
about the specimens he collected. He told the President that animals ate the Osage orange but the Osage Indians did not, considering it to be poisonous. He suggested that it would make a
fine hedge if domesticated, and described the spiny shrub as being of great economic importance to the Indian nations although
its fruit was considered toxic. The Osage nation used almost no
other wood for bows, he explained. "So much do the savages
esteem the wood of this tree that they will travel many hundreds
of miles in quest of it."

Lewis was Jefferson's field zoologist as well as botanist, of
course. One of the quadrupeds which fed on the Osage orange
interested him, the ungainly but swift caricature of a rabbit which
he termed "the large hare of the plains," meaning the prairie
jackrabbit. Lewis was eager to see one of these beasts in action
and he wrote the President, "It is said to be remarkably fleet and
hard to be overtaken, on horseback, even, in their open plains."

Not until April Fool's Day were the noncommissioned officers'
appointments ratified. The sergeants were all to have equal powers unless Lewis specifically ordered otherwise. This amounted to
a demotion for acting top sergeant Ordway. At the same time,

Lewis decided upon the final composition of the Corps of Discovery. To insure order and discipline and to promote proper policing of camp, he divided his detachment into three formal squads or messes under Sergeants Pryor, Floyd and Ordway. The captain also retained Corporal Warfington in service.

Both Lewis and Clark were extremely busy in April 1804 with last-minute preparations. Lewis failed to find red lead or paint in St. Louis, so the keelboat's lockers had to remain unpainted. However, he was successful in securing 200 nails to use on the locker hinges and in May he came up with flags and shirts and a real windfall in 19 mosquito bars. Clark was doing his share of the planning and it was he who suggested that the two blunderbusses be mounted on swivels in the stern of the bateau in the same fashion as the bow cannon. Lewis answered Clerk's query on this with a brief "Do as you please on this subject."

The two officers worked together superbly. There was no cabin fever during the winter. Lewis did not always go along with his aide-de-camp's advice, however. When Clark suggested that they take along with them an Indian of the Missouri tribe who had attached himself to the party at Wood River like a stray dog, Lewis vetoed the idea. Clark thought that the man would help the corps make a favorable and peaceful impression on his Missouri tribe. Lewis said no. But his negatives to Clark's ideas were never peremptory. In this case, he explained his decision to his colleague in a brief note: "On inquiry, I find he is not a character that can render us any service."

The commander tried to unravel a number of tangled personnel and pay problems, with varying success. Ex-Paymaster Lewis knew the importance of pay to soldiers so he tried to secure some back pay for Private Whitehouse. He failed, though he got a statement from Zebulon Pike that the man was entitled to the money. He granted all of the men an advance of $5 on their special $10 per month salary in order that they might secure any clothing they might need beyond that furnished by the Government. Lewis was as unsuccessful in Clark's case as in Whitehouse's; on May 6th, with the expedition almost under way, he had to forward a lieutenant's commission rather than a captaincy to his friend. Dejected and angered, Lewis wrote, "It is not such as I wished or had reason to expect, but so it is. A further explanation when I see you. I think it will be best to let none of our party—or any other persons—know anything about the grade. You will observe that the grade has no effect upon your compensation which, by God!, shall be equal to my own!"

During early May, Lewis was frenetic with the last-minute logistics of the great voyage. He asked Clark to send the smaller pirogue down to him in St. Louis in order to have way strips laid along its gunwales; he sent, with Reed and Colter, a horse to join the one already in camp; he dispatched tallow and hog's lard by Colter and Reed, asking Clark to put it in some of the kegs he had originally intended for whiskey. "Not a keg can be obtained in St. Louis," he complained, "nor are they to be expected from Mr. Contractor. We must, therefore, do the best we can." His impatience kept pace with his energy. The slightest delay annoyed Lewis and reminded him of the drunken, malingering boatwrights of Pennsylvania who had detained his journey down the Ohio. He hit it off badly with the greatest of the Missouri River fur traders, Manuel Lisa, and his partner, François Marie Benoît. The Virginian was never one to pussyfoot and he expressed his contempt for the Spaniard and his French colleague in some prime Lewisiana: "Damn Manuel and triply damn Mr. B. They give me more vexation and trouble than their lives are worth. I have dealt very plainly with these gentlemen. In short, I have come to an open rupture with them. I think them both scoundrels and they have given me abundant proofs of their unfriendly disposition towards our Government and its measures. These gentlemen—no, I will scratch it out—these puppies are not unacquainted with my opinions and I am well informed that they have engaged some hireling writer to draught a petition and remonstrance to Govr. Claiborne against me. Strange, indeed, that men to appearance in their senses will manifest such strong symptoms of insanity as to whetting knives to cut their own throats."

Lisa lost no love on Lewis, either. He disparaged the explorer as a man "fond of exaggerating everything relative to his expedition and . . . a very headstrong and, in many instances, an imprudent man." On May 13th, Lewis, still detained in St. Louis, received word which made him forget, if not forgive, Manuel Lisa. Clark sent him the news that he had been waiting for so long. All the goods and equipment were stowed in the 22-oared keelboat, the seven-oared Frenchmen's pirogue and the six-oared soldiers' pirogue. All men were in good health, each man was armed with plenty of powder and 100 ball, and everyone was eager and ready to embark.

An exultant Lewis gave Clark the order, "Sail!"

CHAPTER VIII

———•◆•———

THE BIG MUDDY

I set out at 4 o'clock, P.M., in the presence of many of the neighbouring inhabitants, and proceeded on under a jentle brease up the Missourie. . . .
—WILLIAM CLARK, May 14, 1804

THE WINTER at Wood River had convinced Lewis that he could trust Clark as he could trust himself. Accordingly, he left the next step in the expedition entirely to his friend. While he took care of the unfinished business of the visit of the Osages to Washington, Clark led the little flotilla out into the mainstream of the Missouri on Monday, May 14, 1804.

Lewis arranged to meet Clark and the fleet at St. Charles, only seven leagues up the river. The voyage to that point would be a shakedown cruise to determine if the lading of the vessels was proper; to test the keelboat's square sail and the oars and the towrope. Clark tested the setting poles, too. These were necessary when crossing the breadth of the river or when passing the mouths of tributaries where the *cordelle,* or towrope, could not be used. Ashore, Drouillard led the party's two horses along the riverbank.

Clark waited out a rainy forenoon, then departed late in a showery day. He made only four miles before camping at the mouth of Coldwater Creek just above Cantonment Bellefontaine. Ridiculously short as the run was, it did mark a start and the men were enthusiastic. Patrick Gass noted that the corps was unanimously determined, resolute and confident even though

99

campfire gossip that evening predicted the expedition would "pass through a country possessed by numerous, powerful and warlike nations of savages of gigantic stature, fierce, treacherous and cruel, and particularly hostile to white men."

On the 15th, Clark made only nine miles. The keelboat struck concealed logs in the river three times as it slowly made its way past geese and goslings flocking under the crumbling banks. He fired a gun at 2 P.M. the next day to announce his arrival but the commander had not yet arrived at St. Charles. However, the whole village turned out to greet the little squadron. Before giving his men liberty, he warned the high-spirited fellows that he would retire from the village to some distant camp if they misbehaved during "shore leave." The impatient men, hungry for excitement, quickly forgot his words and at 11 A.M. on the 17th, in Lewis's absence, Clark had to convene a court-martial on the quarterdeck of the barge. He gave Privates Warner, Hall and Collins a lashing, each, for being AWOL and disorderly at a dance.

Back in St. Louis, Captain Lewis left Amos Stoddard his power of attorney as he wound up his affairs. Stoddard would act as his agent in getting the Indian chiefs to Washington, paying off the French *engagés* upon their return from the Mandan villages, and drawing bills on the Secretary of War in Lewis's behalf. Should Stoddard have to absent himself from St. Louis, Lewis wanted him to transfer the power of attorney to Charles Gratiot.

Lewis did not quite give Stoddard a carte blanche. He was too cautious and careful for that. He spelled out in a memorandum the manner of handling the Indian deputations, since they were matters of the utmost concern of the President, and advised his brother officer to be particularly watchful for a delegation of Sioux and Iowas from the Des Moines River. Through Lewis Crawford, he had already invited chiefs of the two tribes to visit Washington.

At St. Charles, Clark did not wait for Lewis to attend to the correcting of the lading of the bateau, which had run aground on snags three times. He had his men reload it to make it heavier forward, bringing up the stern so that the bow would not swallow so many waterlogged tree trunks. He knew that Lewis would approve; the short run had been planned for just such a purpose.

When the Virginian set out from St. Louis to rejoin Clark, he did not travel unescorted. He had made many friends in the frontier capital and some of them accompanied him toward St. Charles—Governor Amos Stoddard, Lieutenant Stephen Worrell, Lieutenant John Milford, Charles Gratiot, Auguste Chouteau, David Delaunay, Sylvester Labbadie, James Rankin, Dr. Antoine F. Saugrain and other leading citizens of the Missouri frontier. Lewis bade his hostess, Mrs. Pierre Chouteau, a sad adieu and asked her to remember him to his "fair friends of St. Louis." He then began America's greatest Western expedition with all the drama of a Sunday picnic. At 1:30 he and his convivial friends were traveling along pleasantly. When a violent thunderstorm roared out of the northwest, they found shelter and broke out a cold picnic lunch which they had packed. After an hour and a half stop, some of the gentry deserted Lewis but eight of them went on with him through a rain which drenched the beautiful level prairie. They arrived at St. Charles at 6:30, just in time for Lewis to change into something dry and then join Clark and a visitor, Ensign Carlos Tayón, ex-Spanish commandant of St. Charles, at Sunday supper. After dining, Lewis went to the barge at an early hour to rest.

The next morning, Lewis examined St. Charles. He found it to be a mile-long strip of some hundred dwellings and a chapel. The one street paralleled the river on a narrow plain just high enough to escape the flooding of the Big Muddy. The inhabitants were poor, illiterate and lazy but polite and hospitable. He observed in a note to Jefferson that they lived in harmony, obeying their priest and Commandant Tayón, adding: "The men in the vigour of life consider the cultivation of the earth a degrading occupation and, in order to gain the necessary subsistence for themselves and families, either undertake hunting voyages on their own account or engage themselves as hirelings to such persons as possess sufficient capital to extend their traffic to the natives of the interior parts of the country. On those voyages, in either case, they are frequently absent from their families or homes the term of six, twelve, or eighteen months, and always subjected to severe and incessant labour, exposed to the ferocity of the lawless savages, the vicissitudes of weather and climate, and dependent on chance or accident alone for food, raiment or relief in the event of malady. These people are principally the descendants of the Canadian French and it is not an inconsiderable portion of them that can boast a small dash of the pure blood of the aborigines of America."

After consulting with Clark, Lewis postponed their departure until 2 P.M., May 21st. But it was more like 3:30 or 4 before the boats cast off to breast the turgid Missouri again, the captains having been delayed by a going-away party. As they steered into squalls of wind, waving their good-byes, the entire population of St. Charles, some 450 persons from the cradle to the lip of the grave, gathered at the landing to wish them bon voyage via three resounding cheers.

Some Kickapoos came into Lewis's camp at Femme Osage Creek on the 22nd, bringing deer meat. Lewis overpaid them for the venison—two quarts of whiskey for four deer—perhaps because he was so delighted to be finally under way. Upriver, he could have had a whole herd of deer for half a gallon of uncut liquor. His jollity was tempered that evening when his surprise inspection of arms and ammunition disclosed that, already, some of the weapons in the pirogues were in bad order. He set the men to making them right.

On the following day, Lewis had a narrow escape. Exploring Indian pictographs in and around a cave called the Tavern, he almost fell to his death over a 300-foot cliff. He lost his balance, slid over the precipice and dropped but caught himself on a ledge 20 feet below. Shortly, the entire detachment was put to its first test when the boats struck the dangerous stretch of water called the Devil's Raceground. The Devil almost had his due as the keelboat was on the point of upsetting on a sandbar. It broke its towrope and forced all hands to jump overboard to manhandle the boat to safety in deep water. But the little fleet raced through safely.

On the 24th, Lewis led his men into La Charrette, civilization's last outpost on the Missouri. A scattering of thirty to forty families lived in the area of the seven-house settlement. The most famous citizen was seventy-year-old Daniel Boone but apparently neither Lewis nor Clark was aware that he lived only a few miles from town in a cabin on Femme Osage Creek. Lewis did talk with Regis Loisel, a partner of Hugh Heney in the Indian trade and an informant highly recommended to him by Louis Labeaume in St. Louis. Loisel gave him information on the disposition of the Sioux and on the condition of the river in the area of Cedar Island.

Lewis was pleased with his progress. The expedition's speed varied from three miles a day to as much as twenty-eight miles, but the average of fifteen was more than adequate. In fact, when Amos Stoddard received a note from Lewis, then sixty miles up, he was so impressed that he wrote Secretary Dearborn to tell him that Lewis was making "a velocity seldom witnessed on the Missouri, and this is the more extraordinary as the time required to ascertain the courses of the river and to make the other necessary observations, must considerably retard his progress."

Actually, most of the credit for the speedy and safe navigation of the cluttered and treacherous Missouri, which the Indians justly called "the Troubled Waters," was due Clark. By the time La Charrette was astern, Lewis realized that his comrade was the better waterman and navigator and he willingly let him command the squadron while he reconnoitered the shore, made natural history observations, determined the latitude and longitude of points, and collected specimens. This came to be the normal order of things as the days drifted by, although Lewis took the quarterdeck often enough to keep his hand in and to give Clark a chance to stretch his legs and hunt. Too, when repairs to the boats had to be made, Lewis delegated the responsibility of supervision to Clark. Thus it was the redhead who sent a party ashore under Sergeant Pryor to cut ash for new oars and who mustered another fatigue detail to repair the anchor cable and the towrope.

Ashore, Lewis was toughening up his legs and developing that ground-eating gait which would wear out his scouts and hunters when they accompanied him in advance parties. He checked his maps, too, the Evans chart of the lower Missouri sent him by President Jefferson and another of the serpentining river as far as the Mandan villages which Governor William Henry Harrison had given Clark. Also, he began to fill his notebooks with his observations on the riparian flora and fauna. While the hunters filled the boat's larder with deer meat, Lewis explored the cobbled or sandy beaches, the mouths of tributaries and the low cliffs. He kept the hunters busy because he did not allow all venison to be eaten fresh, but had a certain portion made into jerky for future use as emergency rations.

On May 26, 1804, Lewis issued orders to his detachment which formally required each sergeant to maintain a daily journal and urged the privates to do likewise. Gass, Whitehouse, Shannon, Frazier and possibly Willard imitated the noncoms and at the end of each day thereafter, the campfires were surrounded by men industriously scrawling in diaries the events of the day as the twilight faded. Lewis also reorganized the detachment. He put the three squads of infantry to crewing the bateau, or barge; the French to manning the red pirogue; the guard squad of Warfington handling the white pirogue. Labiche and Cruzatte were to alternate at the larboard bow oar, the one not at the oar to act as bowsman. One sergeant was placed at the helm to steer, one stationed amidships to command the guard, maintain security and oversee the oarsmen and to manage the sails. The midship sergeant also had the job of looking for creeks and islands, issuing spirits, setting embarkation and halt times, and posting sentinels at each stop. Part of this last duty involved reconnoitering, with two of his guard, each landing place and potential campsite. The sergeant stationed amidships was also sergeant of the guard for the night, in charge of six sentries. He had to place one picket behind the camp on the landward side if they camped on the bank and not on an island, as Lewis often ordered for security, and another near the boats. At each relief of the guards the duty sergeant would again reconnoiter for one hundred paces around the camp with the two men going off duty, to make sure that there were no red men lurking in the weeds. They would also examine the keelboat and pirogues for their safety. The three sergeants rotated the critical guard-sergeant's position amidships so that its duties did not fall more heavily on one man than the others. The three noncoms were excused by Lewis from fire making, cooking and tent pitching because of their extra responsibilities. But Lewis was a bear for security and the only men exempted from guard duty besides Clark and himself were Drouillard, the scout, Deschamps, the *patron* of the boatmen, and Warfington. And the latter two were responsible at *all* times for the security of the pirogues in their care. Sergeant Ordway had the job of making up guard details in addition to the chore of issuing provisions to the detachment.

The job of the sergeant in the bow was to act as a lookout for river craft or any dangers, be they Indians, snags, obstructions or "strong water"—rapids. Armed with a setting pole, the forward sergeant was also to help the bowsman in poling and managing the prow of the craft when it was under way. He was also charged by Lewis's orders with the role of signalman, handling all communications between vessels as well as "ship to shore."

The same day that Lewis took his security measures, he improved the provisioning system. He sent Drouillard and Shields with the horses on the first of a continuing series of wide circuits through the countryside parallel to the river, ordering them to hunt one day and move on the next, and so on, until they reached the Osage River, which he designated as their first rendezvous with the main party.

The boats began to meet traders heading downstream. Lewis first spoke two fur-laden canoes from the Omaha nation, then two pelt-laden *cajeaux* (rafts lashed across a pair of canoes, catamaran-style) from the Grand Osages and the Pawnees of the Platte. Pressing on in drenching rain and hail in a rising river, the Corps passed another cave, Montbrun's Tavern, above the Gasconade River, then inched along a bosky area of cottonwoods, oak, hickory, sycamore and white walnut to camp in the grapevines and rushes of Grindstone Creek. Here, above the Big Muddy or Big Miry, not to be confused with the Missouri itself, they were forced to remain all of the last day of May, the prisoners of blasting westerly winds. When Lewis spied two more furpiled canoes, he hailed their occupants, a Frenchman, an Indian and a squaw, and invited them to sup and stay the night. From the Frenchman, Lewis learned the disquieting news that the letters of Auguste Chouteau to the Osages, informing them of the transfer of the territory from Spain to the United States, had been consigned to the flames by the Indians, who refused to believe the information. This news did not bode well for the reception which Lewis would receive from the Indians upriver. But he did not let it discourage him. While his men caught rats of considerable size in the woods for him, he took further advantage of the unplanned stay at Grindstone Creek to collect a number of curious plants and shrubs.

When the hunters, Drouillard and Shields, rejoined the main party at the Osage River as ordered, on June 2, Lewis saw that they were very travel-worn. They had been on foot or on horseback for seven days, in almost incessant rain, had taken five deer, had rafted or swum a number of swollen streams. But they were toughened up for future venison forays which Lewis promised he would ask them to make. They gave their inquisitive C.O. a flattering account of the countryside through which they had traveled. It was the best land they had seen so far, being well timbered with ash, oak, hickory and black walnut.

As soon as camp was set up at the junction of the Osage and Missouri rivers, Lewis had his men fell all the trees on the very point of land so that he could get a good celestial sight, in order to note down accurately the position of the important waterway. Although it was dwarfed by the gigantic, 900-yard-wide Missouri, the Osage was no rivulet. According to Clark's careful measurements, it was almost 400 yards wide where it debouched into the Big Muddy.

Continuing on, the boats passed Cedar Island safely but beyond, Ordway, at the helm of the keelboat, steered too close to shore and an overhanging sycamore limb snapped the mast off. The forced stop afforded time for some more meat to be jerked, then off went the little fleet again. They met two more Frenchmen with a *cajeau* who informed the Virginian that he would not encounter any Kansas Indians on the river since they were all on the plains hunting buffalo, having cleared most of the game from the river itself during the winter.

With the mast repaired, the keelboat made good progress, past the Salt, or Saline, River, the Big Manitou, the Bonne Femme and the Mine River. Both Lewis and Clark explored the shoreline here but found the lush weeds and vines so thick that they could not penetrate them and had to retire from the jungle to the boats. At a meadow called Prairie of the Arrows, the Missouri narrowed to 300 yards and here the barge gave Lewis some uneasy moments, running on snags twice. The current swung the boat around into a very dangerous position, broadside to the current, and he was afraid she would bilge. But the men got her off the snag and rowed the craft to the safety of an island to camp.

At the Chariton River, Lewis was forced to camp to wait out a blow. He put the time to good use, taking observations with his octant, hunting and exploring the rolling grassland on the east bank and the wooded prairie on the west. He also orderd a general overhaul of the equipment and all articles were spread out in the sun to dry. Hunters brought in bear and deer meat which was jerked for iron rations, too. Hailing a trapper, Pierre Dorion, rafting downstream with pelts, buffalo grease and tallow, Lewis bought 300 pounds of the suet from him. Although Clark thought that the tough St. Louis trader, half-wild like so many of his ilk, had little information to impart, Lewis not only questioned him closely but suggested that he return with them to the Sioux in order to persuade some of the chiefs to visit Washington. Dorion had lived with the powerful Sioux or Dakotas for twenty years and was a confidential friend of theirs. Lewis hoped to use him as an entrée to Siouxdom as well as an interpreter.

The very next day, Dorion pointed out to Lewis the site of a great village where 200 Missouris had fallen to the Sauks in battle. No vestige remained; only thirty families of the once numerous tribe survived, living under the protection of the Otos on the Platte, a tribe which was itself on the decline.

Midway through June, the keelboat was again almost wrecked, running atop one of the levering logs called sawyers. Once they escaped the snag, the men found themselves in a zone of dangerous moving quicksands with a current so strong that they could not stem it with oar power even when backed with a favoring wind. Lewis and Clark gave the order to run for the opposite bank. This immediately fell in on them as they skirted it but they were able to make a slow progress with the towrope. The men had been given a good scare and Lewis let them camp and relax near two abandoned villages, one of the Osages and one of the Missouris.

After being plagued with thick fog and another encounter with a traveling sandbar, Lewis halted to try to persuade two French traders from the Pawnees to return with him. They declined. The next day, Drouillard, cold sober, told Lewis a fantastic tale when he came in from a hunt. He had passed a small pond on the starboard side of the Missouri where he saw many deer feeding. As he approached the little lake, he saw and heard, to his astonishment, a snake in the pond making gobbling noises like a turkey. When he fired the gobbling noises did not stop but increased. Drouillard told Lewis that he had heard the Indians tell of such a creature and one of the *engagés*, who was eavesdropping, nodded his head in assent.

The Americans became increasingly adept at living off the country. On one day they secured ash timber for oars and captured a fat wild horse, probably lost by the Osages; on another, they made oars and, from a cable which Lewis had bought in Pittsburgh, fashioned another towrope. Almost every day they bagged deer and bear to eat and gathered gooseberries and raspberries. These victuals made possible a more varied diet than the rigorous one which Lewis had planned, for bare survival: hominy and grease, one day; pork and flour, the next; pork and cornmeal, the third; and back to hominy and grease on the fourth, and so on, ad nauseum.

The party reached Mackay's old post on June 16th, which Lewis took to be the site of old Fort Orleans (1723), too. It lay on an important river crossing used by Sioux, Sauks and Iowas and in a prairie of timothylike grass which, either green or as hay, would fatten horses well. The only imps in this paradise of deer, turkey, elk, bear and even pelicans were the ticks, gnats and mosquitoes. Lewis was glad that he had thought to provide mosquito bars for his men, and he broke them out at this stop.

Each day, Captain Lewis ranged farther and farther from the boats. Sometimes he was so far in advance of his little squadron that he had to spend the night, cold and alone, by a campfire on the bank, waiting for the boats to come up in the morning. Besides all his other duties, he had to play doctor to the men, curs-

Maps of the Lewis and Clark Expedition

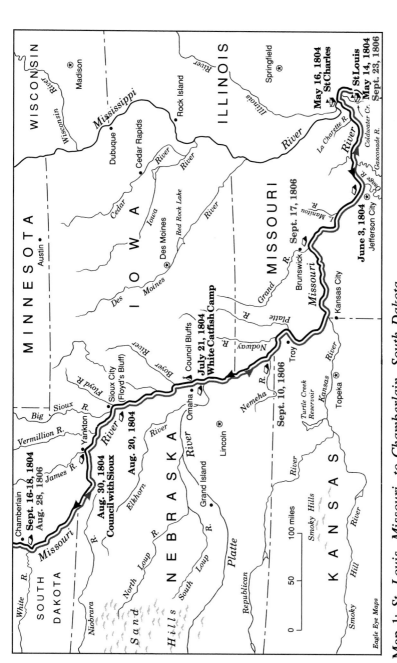

Map 1: *St. Louis, Missouri, to Chamberlain, South Dakota*
The route May 14–September 18, 1804, on the way west; and August 28–September 23, 1806, on the return.

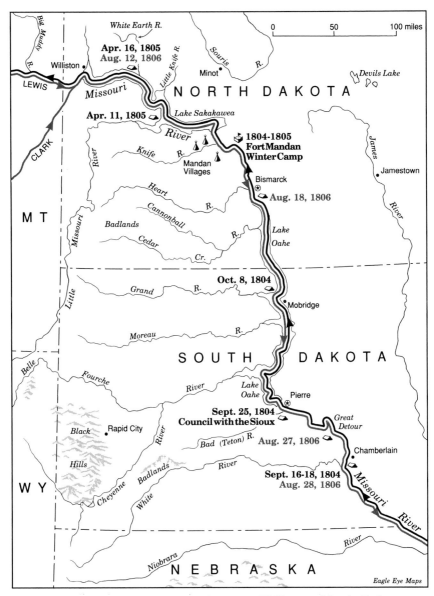

Map 2: Chamberlain, South Dakota, to Williston, North Dakota
The route September 18, 1804–April 16, 1805, on the way west; and
August 12–August 28, 1806, on the return.

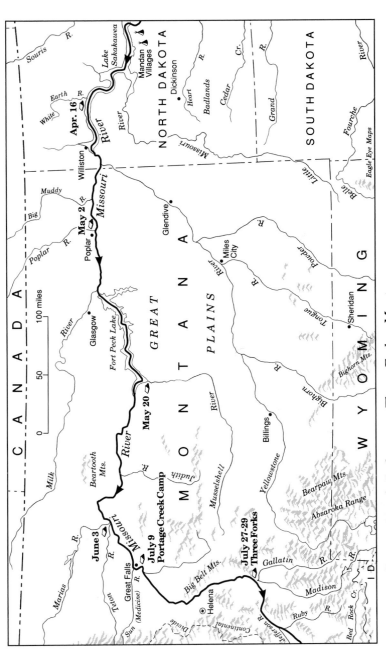

Map 3: *Williston, North Dakota, to Three Forks, Montana*
The route April 16–July 29, 1805, on the way west.

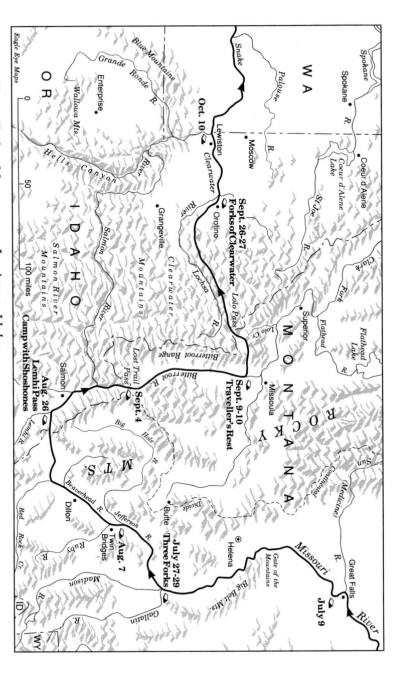

Map 4: *Three Forks, Montana, to Lewiston, Idaho*
The route July 29–October 10, 1805, on the way west.

Eagle Eye Maps

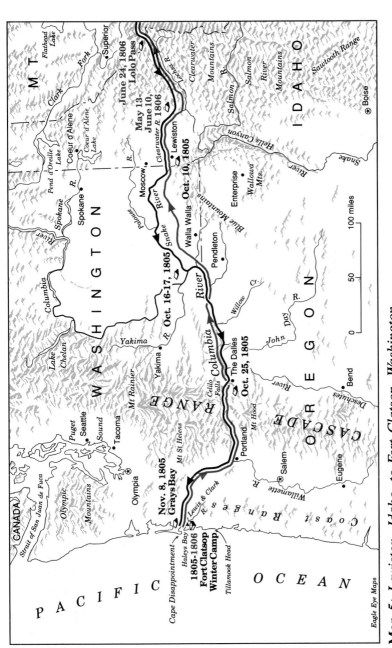

Map 5: *Lewiston, Idaho, to Fort Clatsop, Washington*
The route October 10, 1805–March 23, 1806, on the way west (winter stay at Ft. Clatsop December 7–March 23); and March 23–June 24, 1806, on the return.

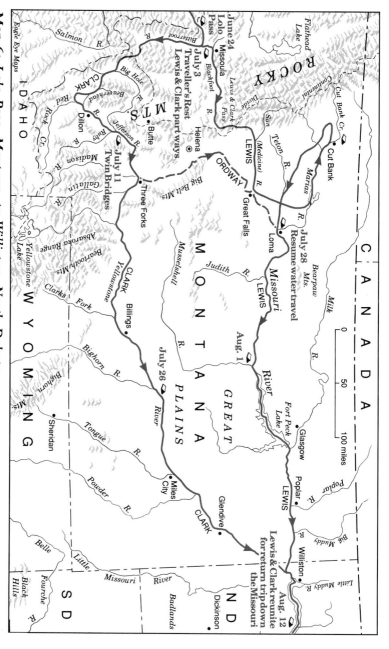

Map 6: *Lolo Pass, Montana, to Williston, North Dakota*
The separate routes of Lewis and Clark June 24–August 12, 1806, on the return. (See Map 2 for the continuation of the return route down the Missouri River.)

ing the fool who had thrown sand in York's eyes and worrying—
unnecessarily, as it turned out—over the Negro's losing the sight
of one eye as a result.

Shortly after the boats successfully negotiated a dam of driftwood at the head of a large sand island, the river threw a new
obstacle at them when it split into two channels, both of which
looked treacherous. Cruzatte was hard put to make his choice;
each was a swift race in which the water roared over rolling
sands as if it were a cataract. Finally, he chose the right-hand
channel and they ran the millrace with much difficulty though
they plied the towrope and the anchors. To Lewis's great surprise
and relief, when the boats were all safely above the trap, his inspection showed only minor damage. A cabin window was
broken and several oars had been carried away.

Lewis gave his men a well-earned rest while he looked over
the countryside. He found the Missouri flowing in a handsome
stretch of country with three distinct levels of vegetation. In the
lowlands he found cottonwoods and willows; in the intermediate
level of the prairies, mulberry, sycamore and linden. The high-
lands were dotted with oak, walnut and blue oak. Summer was
well advanced. Before his usual morning stroll, Lewis glanced at
the thermometer and found the mercury in the column standing
at 87 degrees. After leaving the River of the Fire Prairie, a hot
downriver wind was so strong that no progress could be made,
so Lewis halted his men, inspected arms, and let Clark take out
an overland exploring party. Next day, it was his turn to explore
Hay Cabin Creek.

As the blazing summer's sun sapped its strength, the river began to fall. In one night alone, Lewis observed it drop by seven
inches. On a day which began without a dawn—the night giving
way, grudgingly, to an opaque fog which shrouded the river from
bank to bank—he had to lighten the keelboat to raise it eight
inches to clear a shoal. But when he called a halt, it was to camp
in an island paradise, a natural garden of wild plums, raspberries and wild apples. Great numbers of deer fed on the apples
as well as upon young willows and other staple riverbank herb-
age. But the idyll did not last. Low water meant more trouble the
next day on a sandbar near the Big Blue, and the towrope broke

twice. At the Missouri's mouth, Clark had marveled at the mighty river which seemed "to dispute the preeminence of the Mississippi." Now, he and Lewis cursed it for emulating the shallow Platte.

Lewis decided that a real layover was in order at the mouth of the Kansas, or Kaw, River. They reached it on the 26th and he gave orders that they would not move out till the 29th. While the hunters were out getting a mixed bag—seven deer, a rattler and a wolf—he had others pitching tents and erecting bowers for shade from the hot Missouri sun. When he was not examining the young wolf which some of the hunters captured, writing in his diary, or bird-watching (paroquets), Lewis supervised, with Clark, the drying out of all baggage and another arms inspection. He found some of the provisions spoiled by damp. He had the pirogues hauled up on the beach, emptied of cargo and bilgewater, turned over, dried out and repaired. Although he had seen no Indian sign, he was enough of a soldier to take the precaution of erecting a redoubt all the way from the Kansas River across the point of land to the Missouri. And this breastwork was no line of wattles; he had his men pile up a barricade of logs and bushes to the height of six feet. While they were doing this, Lewis took the specific gravity of samples of Missouri River and Kansas River water and, with Clark, gave them a taste test. They found the Kansas water to be very disagreeable.

The rest at the mouth of the Kansas unfortunately led to slackened discipline, and the day on which they shoved off again Lewis had to call another court-martial. He continued the tradition, which he was starting in the U. S. Army, of having enlisted men sit in judgment of their peers. Collins was charged with getting drunk on the whiskey he was guarding and allowing Hall to steal some of it. Hall's plea of guilty caused his punishment to be reduced to fifty lashes. But the not-guilty plea of guardhouse lawyer Collins did not sway the Court and he was sentenced to 100 lashes. As soon as the flogging was finished, Lewis gave the order to cast off and the expedition was resumed. Soon the men were in enough trouble to make even Collins forget his stripes. The boat turned broadside opposite a large sandbar and was, literally, within six inches of striking but miraculously escaped.

The next day the boat was dismasted again but the men were in such an interesting and pleasant country that the accident did not faze them in the least. They found the Little Platte, or Shoal River, boasted a number of falls which appeared suitable for mills. It coursed through handsome land inhabited by all kinds of game. The only drawback to the Little Platte was the heat. It enfeebled the men and they wilted over their sweeps when the temperature hit 96 degrees in the afternoons. Lewis had to give his detachment a three-hour siesta on a driftwood-covered island off Biscuit Creek as they were virtually overpowered by the intense heat of the Leavenworth, Kansas, area.

July opened as they passed the Iles des Parques where, one of the *engagés* told Captain Lewis, the French used to keep cattle and horses for their river trading posts. Near it, the boats met the dangerous, snaggy armada of logs and driftwood which had been released when a logjam gave way upstream. After camping near old Fort Chartres, they stopped at a deserted trading post just above Buffalo Cow Island on Independence Day's Eve. Here they met the first sign of the creature which would change the history of the American West when they found the first beaver pond of their journey.

CHAPTER IX

―――――＊●＊―――――

THE POWWOW

The Great Chief of the Seventeen Great Nations of America, impelled by his parental regard for his newly adopted children on the Troubled Waters, has sent us out to clear the road, remove every obstruction, and to make it the road to peace. . . .

—MERIWETHER LEWIS, to the Otos and
Missouris, August 3–4, 1804

THE BOOMING of the bow gun at sunup not only ushered in the Fourth of July, it signaled the beginning of a new stage in the journey. The corps was entering beaver country, which also meant Indian country. Lewis had long anticipated meeting his first red nation and delivering his first speech in behalf of the White Father in Washington, but each day dawned and died disappointingly without any contact with Indians. Near Fourth of July Creek and Independence Creek, where the officers gave the men some corn as a holiday treat, Joseph Fields further enlivened the day by getting bitten by a rattlesnake. After attending to his swollen foot with a poultice of bark and gunpowder, Lewis walked up to the top of a high mound toward which three Indian trails led. From the top he had a fine view of the Missouri bottom and the prairie, dotted with copses of timber. But, as usual, there was not a sign of Indians and he retraced his steps sadly to camp, where he doled out an extra gill of whiskey to the men to celebrate Independence Day after the booming of the sunset gun.

The river continued to fall and the keelboat almost came to

grief on a quicksand bank and on a raft of driftwood. But the towrope got the barge through safely, once more. Some of the men were not well now and Lewis blamed their ills on the filthy river water they had to drink. On July 7th, Lewis was called upon to play surgeon again. This time it was not dysentery, tumors, boils, abcesses or felons, but sunstroke. He bled Frazier, who had collapsed, and gave him some niter, after which he recovered considerably. The tedium of the hot day was broken when the bowsman spied a wolf asleep on the riverbank. The splashing of the oars awakened the animal but did not alarm it. Lewis drew a bead and fired. The ball struck the wolf in the hindquarters but only stung it. As the wolf snapped at its hurt, John Colter fired. His ball killed the beast. And still the heat continued. In the crooked and narrowing bottom of the Missouri it was like a bake oven. "Dr." Lewis soon had five men on the sick list, all suffering from headaches and sunstroke.

At Nodaway Island, Lewis called a halt to rest the sun-dazed men. He issued another Detachment Order there to insure prudent use of provisions, appointing Thompson, Warner and Collins as regular cooks. In lieu of extra recompense, he gave them the rather exalted title of Superintendents of Provision, to go along with their enlarged responsibility for a "judicious consumption" of the provisions. He also ordered them to cook the food in the most wholesome and nutritious fashion possible. Otherwise, he let his chefs exercise their own judgment in the matter of cuisine.

Up and up the Missouri plodded the corps, past Wolf River and Pape's Creek, named for a man who had killed himself accidentally with his own rifle. When the hunters became overdue, Lewis cut a notch on a prominent riverbank tree to show them that the boats had passed that point. He could not waste precious time waiting for them to rendezvous. But when he spied a fire across the river he hurried a pirogue over. He would be happy to find his hunters, happier to find Indians. But no one was there. He fired the cannon as a signal but no response came. Since so many men were exhausted or sick, he called a halt. The missing hunters came in but his day was spoiled by his need to order yet another court-martial. And this time it was no drunken ne'er-do-well like Collins who was on trial but usually dependable Alex Willard. The big New Hampshireman's offense was so grave—sleeping while on guard duty—that Lewis thought it best for Clark and himself to compose the Court. Under U. S. Army Regulations and the Articles of War, Lewis could demand the death penalty. Both men were stern of mien as Willard was brought forward by the sergeant of the guard. He, pathetically, pleaded "Guilty to lying down, not guilty of going to sleep," but he was held guilty on both counts and sentenced to 100 lashings, to be delivered in four floggings.

Bastille Day, which none of the *engagés* celebrated, was a stormy day of rains and winds. A gust almost dashed the bateau to pieces. All hands went over the side to save their craft. They succeeded, thanks to Lewis's foresight in fitting a tarpaulin over the amidships section. This tarp threw off the water and prevented the barge from bilging. At Bald Pated Prairie, Lewis rested his men and let them gather berries or putter about beachcombing among the driftwood and pumice of the shore while he corrected his chronometer which had run down. Then he rode out through the river's skimpy, ragged fringe of hardwoods into a handsome, low but well-watered country into which the Missouri was cutting—literally—its way. Sometimes it would gnaw away up to twenty acres in one site. There were no Indians to be seen but Lewis did enjoy the lush region of wild timothy, cockleburs, wild grapes and plums. Trees were scarce but gooseberries and chokecherries plentiful, and the soldiers put up a lot of the cherries in a barrel of whiskey for dessert.

The Corps of Discovery passed the poetically named Weeping Stream, *L'Eau Qui Pleure,* and made a major stop, July 21st, at the Platte's mouth. Here Lewis set up White Catfish Camp. He found the current of the shallow tributary to be remarkably strong. A half century later it would be fabled by Argonauts as "too thick to drink and too thin to plow," but Lewis was amazed at how it bullied its way into the Missouri, creating great sandbars in the Missouri's bed, vomiting up willowy islands indiscriminately, and rolling tons of Nebraska sand and topsoil onto the shore of the Big Muddy opposite its mouth. The Platte deposited so much sediment in the Missouri's bed that Lewis and

Clark had great difficulty in getting the boats to round the vast underwater alluvial fan. Rowing up the Platte, he estimated the speed of its sand-bearing current at eight miles per hour, as compared to the Mississippi's four and the Missouri's six. "The steady, regular and incessant velocity of this stream is perhaps unequalled by any on earth," he wrote. "Notwithstanding its great rapidity, the surface of the water continues smooth except when occasionally interrupted by a boiling motion or ebullition of its waters."

The Platte, Lewis knew, was not only the boundary of Oto, Pawnee and Loup land, but was a busy waterway. The Indians navigated it in coraclelike bullboats, circular craft made of buffalo hide stretched over a frame of light poles. But Lewis decided that the river, because of its shallowness, rapid current and great quantity of rolling sand, would never be navigable for keelboats or even pirogues.

From his Platte River camp, Lewis sent Drouillard and Cruzatte to find the elusive Indians while he busied his other men with varied fatigue duties. But the scouts returned to report the Oto villages deserted. With little hope of the Otos returning from their buffalo hunting, and the cool and refreshing breezes turning into sandstorms which punished the men without driving the mosquitoes away, Lewis decided to move out. He was further annoyed by a series of petty incidents—Willard lost his tomahawk; one of the horses died; Whitehouse cut his knee badly; a man lost his gun crossing Boyer's Run on a log and Reuben Field had to dive for it. But Lewis quickly forgot these annoyances when Drouillard ran into camp. He had found an Indian!

The scout brought an elk-hunting Missouri into camp. Lewis sent him with La Liberté to the Oto camp to invite them to a council at a site he named Council Bluffs—near present-day Sioux City, rather than Council Bluffs, Iowa. After posting a guard, a delighted Lewis took a walk with Clark to the high prairie atop the bluffs. He found a beautiful plain, with grass a foot high, stretching away to the far horizon. While the men waited for the Indians, they hunted, as usual. Joseph Field killed the first "brarow" or badger they had ever seen. The Virginian was fascinated by the stocky creature with the large claws, and after studying it he skinned it and tanned its pelt as a specimen for the President. Next, Drouillard brought in a live beaver from one of his traps. It was only slightly hurt and so tame that the half-breed kept it for a pet.

On August 2nd, a trader, Mr. Fairfon (perhaps Farfan or Faufon), who resided with the Otos, brought a party of that tribe and of the Missouris to camp. Lewis was delighted although the six chiefs present were not the principal headmen. The Indians fired their rifles as they approached and Captain Lewis responded with a salute from the bow gun. As he shook hands with them, the cannon boomed again. He told them how happy he was to see them and announced he would palaver with them the next day. Then he gave them roasted meat, flour, pork and meal. The Indians reciprocated with a load of watermelons. Although he was joyous at meeting Indians at last, he took his usual precautions, for all the friendly reception they had given him, and kept a strong guard on duty. He also took the precaution of setting up the council area not in the shade of the trees, which might shelter an ambuscade, but on the open beach. To protect the conferees, he had his men stretch the barge's mainsail as an awning.

The next day, after impressing his visitors with a parade of his entire detachment in military formation, he presented packages of presents to the chiefs and a medal to Chief Petit Voleur, or Little Thief, of the Otos. This exalted personage was not present, but Lewis gave his tribesmen a packet of presents and the medal for their chief. Then he launched into his speech. It was perhaps the most important address of his career, since it would be the model for all the future powwows he would give. After an introductory greeting. Lewis went on: "Children, commissioned and sent by the Great Chief of the Seventeen Great Nations [i.e., the states of the U. S.] of America, we have come to inform you as we go also to inform all the nations of red men who inhabit the borders of the Missouri, that a great council was lately held between this Great Chief of the Seventeen Great Nations of America and your old Fathers, the French and Spaniards, and that in this great council, it was agreed that all the white men of Louisiana inhabiting the waters of the Missouri and Mississippi should obey the commands of this Great Chief. He has, accordingly, adopted them as his children and they now form one common family with us. Your old traders are of this description. They are no longer the subjects of France or Spain but have become citizens of the Seventeen Great Nations of America, and are bound to obey the commands of their Great Chief, the President, who is now your only Great Father. . . ."

Lewis then told them that Spain had withdrawn all of its troops from Louisiana, never to return, and that the Americans would now serve and protect the red men. He continued: "Children, the Great Chief of the Seventeen Great Nations of America, impelled by his parental regard for his newly adopted children on the Troubled Waters, has sent us to clear the road, remove every obstruction, and to make it the road of peace between himself and his red children residing there, to enquire into the nature of their wants and, on our return, to inform him of them in order that he may make the necessary arrangements for their relief. . . . He has commanded us, his war chiefs, to undertake this long journey, which we have so far accomplished with great labour and much expense, in order to council with yourselves and his other red children on the Troubled Waters, to give you his good advice, to point to you the road in which you must walk to obtain happiness. He has further commanded us to tell you that when you accept his flag and medal, you accept herewith his hand of friendship, which will never be withdrawn from your nation as long as you continue to follow the councils which he may command his chiefs to give you, and shut your ears to the councils of bad birds. . . ."

The Virginian then summed up.

"You are to live in peace with all the white men, for they are his children; neither wage war against the red men, your neighbours, for they are equally his children and he is bound to protect them. Injure not the person of any traders who may come among you, neither destroy nor take their property from them by force, more particularly those traders who visit you under the protection of your Great Father's flag. Do not obstruct the passage of any boat, pirogue, or other vessel which may be ascending or descending the Missouri River, more especially such as may be under cover of your Great Father's flag, neither injure any red or white man on board such vessels as may possess the flag for, by that signal, you may know them to be good men and that they do not intend to injure you. They are, therefore, to be treated as friends and as the common children of one Great Father, the Great Chief of the Seventeen Great Nations of America.

"Children, do these things which your Great Father advises and be happy. Avoid the councils of bad birds, turn on your heels from them as you would from the precipice of a high rock, whose summit reached the clouds and whose base was washed by the gulf of human woes, lest by one false step you should bring upon your nation the displeasure of your Great Father, the Great Chief of the Seventeen Great Nations of America, who would consume you as the fire consumes the grass of the plains. The mouths of all the rivers through which the traders bring goods to you are in his possession and if you displease him, he could, at pleasure, shut them up and prevent his traders from coming among you and this would, of course, bring all the calamities of want upon you. But it is not the wish of your Great Father to injure you; on the contrary, he is now pursuing the measures best calculated to insure your happiness."

After this warning, Lewis promised traders and posts, explaining that he himself was not a trader but an explorer and hence had no trade goods. He assured the Indians that those who followed him would bring goods to the Platte to trade for furs. He then urged the absent Little Thief to visit the Great Father in Washington, offering him horses, an interpreter, food and all other means necessary for the trip but warning him to carry the U. S. flag and Lewis's parole, dated August 4, 1804.

Lewis listened while the chiefs announced their approval of his sentiments in a response almost the equal of his palaver in eloquence. They promised to follow his advice. They asked him to mediate their differences with the Omahas, with whom they were at war. After hearing them out, Lewis distributed medals, gave them trinkets, a canister of gunpowder and a bottle of whiskey as presents and made their eyes bulge, before they left, with a demonstration of his accuracy with his Harrison air gun.

CHAPTER X

———◦◦———

TROUBLED WATERS

I sent a Beloved Man, Captain Lewis, one of my own household, to learn something of the people with whom we are now united, to let you know we were your friends, to invite you to come and see us and to tell us how we can be useful to you. . . . I hope your countrymen will favor and protect him as far as they extend. On his return, we shall hear what he has seen and learned, and proceed to establish trading houses where our red brethren shall think best, and to exchange commodities with them on terms with which they will be satisfied.
— PRESIDENT JEFFERSON, to the Osage delegation,
Washington, July 1804

IT WAS with good spirits that Captain Lewis bade his new Indian friends good-bye. He was buoyed up with the realization that his first bit of diplomatic duty with the Indians had gone well—very well, indeed. He was of the same mind as Sergeant Ordway, who said, "They all appeared to be glad that they got freed from all other powers."

The Americans sailed from Council Bluffs although La Liberté had not returned to camp. They passed a large beaver lodge, which Lewis dutifully examined, then the ruins of an old trading post where Cruzatte had hunted with the Omahas two years before. Here, Lewis let Moses Reed go back to the old campsite to look for a knife which he said he had lost. When the man failed to return, Lewis began to wonder if he and La Liberté had not deserted. The Virginian led the party on through a wriggling section of the cantankerous Missouri's course. In one place they had to go twelve miles by water to gain a position which they could have reached by striking overland a mere 370 yards. The Big Muddy was living up to its reputation. George Fitch described it well, just 102 years after Lewis traversed its course, as "one river that goes traveling sidewise, that interferes in politics, rearranges geography and dabbles in real estate; a river that plays hide-and-seek with you, today, and tomorrow follows you around like a pet dog with a dynamite cracker tied to his tail."

The truculent stream lashed out at everything in sight—men, boats, islands, peninsulas, the prairie, its own banks. Its Indian name, Troubled Waters, was richly deserved. Constantly changing its course, it battered and sluiced away peninsulas, overran them at high water and transformed them into short-lived islands which it then wiped out without a trace. At every bend, banks caved in, sometimes atop the men, and Lewis on his hunting forays often found himself stalking game in ghost beds of the river, old channels either bone-dry or patched with stagnant pools.

By August 6th, Lewis was forced to assume La Liberté and Reed were deserters. Although time was precious, he could not let them desert with impunity so he sent some of his best trackers to Council Bluffs and the old Oto village with orders to bring them back, dead or alive. He also gave the posse another duty, carrying a message to persuade the Otos and Missouris to send peace envoys to the Omahas. Lewis gave Drouillard a string of wampum and a carrot of tobacco to lower Oto resistance to his blandishments.

Pelican Island he found to be literally covered with the ungainly birds and for 70 yards the river's surface was carpeted with feathers and down. Private Whitehouse noticed that "Captain Lewis shot a Pellican. The Bagg that it carried its drink in contained five gallons of water, by measure." Beyond Blackbird's Hill, Lewis sent a party to the Omaha village to arrange a pow-wow but the men returned to report the village deserted. Stopping at Omaha Creek to fish, Clark and some men took 387 with a willow drag. Lewis did even better with his group. By trolling and using brush nets he got 709 fish of several kinds. He took advantage of the stopover to send Dorion and some men to investigate some smoke across the river. They reported trees left burning by Indians who had passed not long before. He now felt that his council could not be far off. He was right. Labiche came into camp as a runner, bearing the tidings that Reed was caught and eight chiefs and warriors of the Otos and Missouris were coming to camp with Drouillard. Labiche told Lewis that La Liberté had been taken from the Indians but had escaped again. Reed had tried to persuade his guard, Bratton, to let him flee but Bratton had told him he would shoot him dead in his tracks if he ran.

When Faufon, Drouillard and the Indians arrived, Lewis set fire to the prairie to bring in the Sioux and Omahas. None came, but he was delighted to meet Little Thief, at last. A dance which closed the evening of the 18th, Lewis's birthday, impressed the Indians mightily. Next day, he repeated his powwow of the 3rd. The major ceremony was bestowing presents. All went well until one brave, whose name—Big Blue Eyes—belied his black disposition, became dissatisfied with the tobacco, trinkets and certificate handed him. The ingrate rudely thrust away the diploma which, ironically, attested to his good conduct. Lewis curbed his temper and gently rebuked him for his greediness for goods instead of peace. Thinking quickly, he gave the rejected document to Little Thief, suggesting that he give it to his "most worthy warrior." There was a complete meeting of minds between Lewis and the chief and he handed the paper to Big Blue Eyes, who swallowed the bait up to the shank. The insufferable brave's pride was the chink in his armor. Peace was restored. Lewis gave a dram of whiskey to each red man as a signal to break up the assembly, then entertained his visitors with a demonstration of his skill with the novel air gun.

Lewis was so caught up in the council that he had little time to notice that Sergeant Floyd was ailing. He examined the drawn, ashen Floyd and found him suffering from diarrhea and vomiting. The feeble sergeant had almost no pulse. Lewis called an immediate halt and he and Clark tried to treat the man's violent "colic." But with his slight knowledge of medicine, Lewis might just as well have treated him with vinegar and brown paper.

Floyd was doomed and it is doubtful if even Dr. Rush himself could have saved him. He might have been suffering from appendicitis, hepatitis, or a malignant diarrhea which, like cholera, was draining away his body's fluids. He may have been afflicted with nothing more than food poisoning caused by the same staphylococcus bacteria which tortured the men with painful boils. Late in the day, the sergeant called weakly to Clark, "I am going to leave you. I want you to write me a letter." Before Clark could find pen and ink, the boy was gone. The flame of life guttered out and the first American soldier died west of the Mississippi River.

The Corps of Volunteers for North Western Discovery was saddened, almost stunned. Everything had gone so well. Death had never been a very real threat. They stood at attention as Lewis read the burial service, then helped bury their comrade at Floyd's Bluff and erected a stout cedar post to mark his grave. The silent men proceeded another mile and camped. It was a dolorous group which turned in early that night. There was no dancing, no horse play, and Cruzatte did not take up his fiddle.

Next day, the boats scudded past impressive pale cliffs before a wind which forced them to reef the sail and which filled the air with fine sand, which explained why the Missouri was sometimes called the Smoky River. But, though the bowsman could hardly see the channel ahead, the boats made a 25-mile advance. Dorion pointed out the Big Sioux River as they passed it, which flowed through a red pipestone quarry so important and sacred that it was a no-man's-land, or asylum, where all warriors were safe, much like the Cities of Refuge which Captain Cook had found on the Island of Hawaii.

The following day, the American Philosophical Society nearly lost its farthest-flung member. Lewis, playing the scientist more and more each day, became too thorough in examining the bluffs, which appeared to contain alum, copperas, cobalt and ores of various kinds. He repeatedly tested them by taste and the earths and minerals made him deathly ill, perhaps from arsenical or other metallic poisoning. But that evening an enfeebled Lewis, flat on his back, ordered his men to elect a new sergeant to replace Floyd. In this historic first American election in the

Far West, Patrick Gass won with a tally of nineteen votes, followed by Bratton and Gibson in the poll.

August 23rd was a memorable day. Joseph Field killed a buffalo, the first. The Midwest was turning into the Far West. Lewis, although still weak, led twelve men out of camp to dress the bison and to bring the meat into camp to salt it down. They were now in an area of cedar bluffs, some of them "burning." Smoke and steam from the chemical heat engendered by the decomposition of pyrites in damp shale led the voyageurs to call the area *Les Côtes Brûlées* (Burnt Bluffs) and the Americans to call it the volcanic country. Lewis found the earth too hot to poke his hand into it for any length of time. For all the hellish smoke and haze, the burning area was a land of plenty. There were elk, deer, rabbitberries and buffalo berries and hefty catfish —nine of them totaled 300 pounds in weight! But the main feature of the landscape was Spirit Mound or the Mountain of the Little People, so frightfully Big Medicine that no native dared approach it for fear of incurring the wrath of the little 18-inch-high devils in human form who lived there. Lewis was eager to bag one of these fellows, to cage or stuff and send to Jefferson, come spring, but his expedition to the mound resulted in little more than heat exhaustion for him, his dog, Scammon, and some of his party. There was a fine view from the top, and martins, or swallows, and bats congregated there, but there were no "little men" unless the ugly, winged mammals were the originators of the Indian legend.

Many of his troopers were ill again, from boils and stomach disorders. Lewis blamed these afflictions on the mineralized, scummy river water and ordered his men to agitate the water to disperse the scum and to dip deep into the river when securing a drink. They followed his advice and it seemed that the gripes and pustules declined but it may have been just good psychosomatic medicine, for the staphylococcus was more to blame than the opaque Missouri. By the time he reached Petit Arc, or Little Bow, Creek, Lewis was himself again and he attended to the formality of confirming Gass as a sergeant.

At the mouth of the Yankton River (alias the Jacques, the James, the Dakota), Drouillard brought three Omahas into camp. Since they lived with the Sioux, Lewis immediately seized upon them as envoys to the powerful confederation, to invite the Sioux to a council at Grand Calumet. He did not know what kind of a reception he would get from them. They were in bad repute in St. Louis for their insolence and rapacity, feared and respected in Washington as the most powerful nation on the Missouri. He would make them friends if it were at all possible.

Shortly after Lewis had the deserter, Reed, run a gantlet of ramrod-wielding troopers, Pryor and Dorion led sixty or seventy-five Yankton Sioux into camp across the river from the soldiers. Among them were five chiefs and Dorion's son, a trader with the Yanktons. Lewis sent them tobacco, corn and some kettles to hold them, promising them a council next day.

On the penultimate day of August, 1804, Lewis finally addressed the Sioux nation. He began at noon under an oak tree near the flagstaff, from which flew the Stars and Stripes, after the Sioux had entertained with dancing and music. He spoke along the lines of his Oto address, advising the Indians on their future conduct. He then made five of them Jeffersonian chiefs, bestowing medals and presents such as tobacco and clothing on them. He heaped presents on the Grand Chief, Shake Hand, including a U. S. artillery officer's richly laced coat and a cocked hat with a red feather in it. Private Whitehouse described the climax of the afternoon's festivities: "Captain Lewis shot his air gun, told them that there was medician in hir, and that She would do great Execution. They were all amazed at the curiosity and as soon as he had shot a fiew times, they all ran hastily to see the Ball holes in the tree and they Shouted aloud at the Site of the execution she would do." After his target practice, Lewis smoked a pipe of peace with the chiefs before they retired for a rest in the brush bower which the young braves had erected for them.

At dark, Lewis gave the Yanktons, gathered around the campfires which he had kindled for them, a grained deerskin to stretch over a half keg, to make a drum. The Indians quickly made it ready and beat rhythms on it and shook maracalike rattles of dried rawhide filled with pebbles. During the entertainment which followed, the whites tossed knives, bells, tobacco, tape and bindings to the pleased musicians and dancers. As he watched, Lewis asked himself, Can these be the people whose name, Sioux, means "Enemy"? Was the sign for them in the silent tongue (sign language) perhaps undeserved—the sawing of the edge of the hand across the throat to symbolize "cutthroat"? Could these happy and friendly folk be the fearsome Sioux who had blocked the Missouri to French and Spanish traders? Even the Dog Soldiers, the braves of the elite guard, hardly seemed the terrors which legend painted them.

After bidding adieu to the Sioux and to Pierre Dorion, Lewis led his party forth again on the first of September. He investigated a large beaver lodge and what Clark called an "ancient fortification," which turned out to be a natural phenomenon, its breastworks being piled up by drifting sand. He also stopped to send men to a Ponca village in hopes of working up another powwow but that tribe was absent, hunting buffalo. Lewis and Clark visited the round knoll called the Tower, which loomed 70 feet above the river, but the Virginian was much more taken with the prairie-dog village at its base. An attempt to secure specimens resulted in just one animal, dead, so all the men were collected from camp, except the guards, and ordered to bring with them all the kettles and cooking vessels they had. With these, and river water, the detachment attempted to flush out their quarry from their abodes. In one hole alone, they poured four barrels of water without any effect except, presumably, to raise the humidity in the tunnels. The men worked all night but caught only two animals in all, and one was dead. Lewis tried another tack. He had some men dig at the mouth of a burrow. They were down six feet when he had them run a pole into the burrow. They found that they were not quite halfway to the bottom. Finally, even Lewis was ready to quit. Before he left, he found two frogs in one hole and killed a rattler in another. This incident caused him to abort a pseudoscientific observation which has plagued the world of American natural history ever since. He opined that the "barking squirrels" were so charitable that they welcomed all manner of critters as neighbors, even the deadly rattlesnake. On the other hand, he was now enough of a scientist to know that the little animals were not dogs, but either squirrels or marmots. But he had to admit that they looked like fat and sassy puppies as they sat on their haunches, forepaws in the air, in an attitude either of prayer or dog-paddling.

More and more "gangs" of buffalo were now being seen, although the corps was still eating more venison than buffalo meat. But the animal which really excited Lewis's interest was a dead one, and a long time dead. He discovered a fossil skeleton of what he took to be an ancient fish. The petrifaction, which he collected to send to Jefferson, was 45 feet long and probably the remains of a Cretaceous reptile. Sergeant Gass could not understand Lewis's cries of delight over the fossil. To the unimpressed noncom it was just "a ruck of bones."

Shannon, who had been long lost on a hunting trip, finally stumbled into camp, without his horse and almost starving. In contrast, Colter, sent after him by Lewis, came in fat as a porcupine. Shannon had fired away all his rifle balls early and then had to subsist on wild grapes and one rabbit which he shot with a sharpened stick in lieu of a bullet. The main party, meanwhile, was living high on the hog, enjoying a rich and varied diet of buffalo humps, venison steaks and beaver tails. But as the river shallowed and the hauling on the boats' thwarts became more common, game—real game—began to follow the trees into oblivion, leaving only wolves, porcupines, beaver and the persistent mosquitoes. However, in the vicinity of White River, Clark shot the party's first antelope, which the *engagés* called goats or cabres.

On the 16th of April, camped at Crow Creek, Lewis decided not to send the pirogue back to St. Louis as originally planned. He would keep the escort of soldiers with him through the winter and then have them crew the barge home. This was a key decision and the making of it troubled him. He knew that the President would worry about him, for lack of news, but it could not be helped. Perhaps a sixth sense warned him that the other Sioux would not be as peaceable as the Yanktons. In any case, after turning the matter over and over in his mind, he decided that he had best keep his detachment at full strength through the winter.

His decision made, Lewis gave his men a day's rest, redistributed the cargo to lighten the bateau for the shoals ahead and issued flannel shirts to the men for winter. For his own part, he devoted himself to scientific observation. He investigated the cottonwoods, elms and ashes and found them all of an indifferent quality of wood. But the white oaks, he discovered, were laden with acorns of excellent flavor. The nuts were so sweet that they drew buffalo, elk, deer, bear, turkeys, ducks, pigeons and wolves to the area from afar. However, when his men killed several deer for food, they found that, nuts or not, the meat was too poor to eat. Lewis used the skins to cover the pirogues and had his men kill some buffalo. But these, too, were poor specimens and Lewis kept only the tongues, marrowbones and skins.

Lewis saw much that day. He wallowed in natural history and it was, perhaps, the most satisfying single day of his entire march. Partial proof was the fact that it was the occasion of one of the longest journal entries he ever wrote:

"Having for many days past confined myself to the boat, I determined to devote this day to amuse myself on shore with my gun and to view the interior of the country lying between the River and the Corvus [Crow] Creek. Accordingly, before sunrise, I set out with six of my best hunters, two of whom I dispatched to the lower side of Corvus Creek, two with orders to hunt the bottoms and woodland along the River, while I retained two others to accompany me in the intermediate country. One quarter of a mile in the rear of our camp, which was situated in a fine open grove of cottonwood, we passed a grove of plum trees loaded with fruit and now ripe. Observed little difference between this fruit and that of a similar kind common to the Atlantic states. The trees are smaller and more thickly set. This forest of plum trees garnish a plain about 20 feet more elevated that that on which we were encamped. This plain extends back about a mile to the foot of the hills one mile distant. . . . It is entirely occupied by the burrows of the barking squirrel. . . . This animal appears here in infinite numbers and the shortness and verdure of the grass gave the appearance throughout its whole extent of a beautiful bowling green in fine order. . . . A great number of wolves of the small kind [i.e., coyotes], hawks, and some polecats to be seen. I presume that these animals feed on this squirrel. . . ."

Encountering an area of deep ravines and intervening steep

hills from 100 to 200 feet high, Lewis climbed to a viewpoint atop one. The level plain opened up before his eyes, seeming to extend to infinity beyond the farthest horizon. "This scenery is immensely pleasing and beautiful," he recorded, "heightened by immense herds of buffalo, deer, elk and antelopes which we saw in every direction, feeding on the hills and plains. I do not think I exaggerate when I estimate the number of buffalo which could be comprehended at one view to amount to 3,000.

"My object was, if possible, to kill a female antelope, having already procured a male. I pursued my route on this plain to the west, flanked by my two hunters until eight in the morning when I made the signal for them to come to me, which they did shortly after. We rested ourselves about half an hour and regaled ourselves on half a biscuit each and some jerks of elk which we had taken the precaution to put in our pouches in the morning before we set out, and drank of the water in a small pool which had collected on this plain from the rains which had fallen some days before. We had now, after various windings in pursuit of several herds of antelope which we had seen on our way, made the distance of about eight miles from our camp. We found the antelope extremely shy and watchful insomuch that we had been unable to get a shot at them. When at rest, they generally select the most elevated point in the neighbourhood and, as they are watchful and extremely quick of sight, and their sense of smelling very acute, it is almost impossible to approach them within gunshot. In short, they will frequently discover and flee from you at the distance of three miles.

"I had this day the opportunity of witnessing the agility and the superior fleetness of this animal, which was, to me, really astonishing. I had pursued and twice surprised a small herd of seven. In the first instance, they did not discover me distinctly and therefore, did not run at full speed though they took care before they rested again to gain an elevated point where it was impossible to approach them under cover except in one direction and that happened to be in the direction from which the wind blew towards them. Bad as the chance to approach them was, I made the best of my way towards them, frequently peeping over the ridge with which I took care to conceal myself from their view. The male, of which there was but one, frequently encircled the summit of the hill on which the females stood in a group, as if to look out for the approach of danger. I got within about 200 paces of them when they smelt me and fled. I gained the top of the eminence on which they [had] stood as soon as possible, from whence I had an extensive view of the country. The antelopes which had disappeared in a steep ravine, now appeared at the distance of about three miles on the side of a ridge which passed obliquely across me and extended about four miles. So soon had these antelopes gained the distance at which they had again appeared to my view I doubted, at first, that they were the same that I had just surprised. But my doubts soon vanished when I beheld the rapidity of their flight along the ridge before me. It appeared rather the rapid flight of birds than the motions of quadrupeds. I think I can safely venture the assertion that the speed of this animal is equal, if not superior, to that of the finest blooded courser. . . ."

Lewis continued his scientific prowling the next day, looking over the site of old Fort Recovery and killing a new bird of prey similar to the magpie of the East. Almost before he realized it, his fleet was rounding the Great Detour of the Missouri. Once around the great bend be began to notice the country drying out, the grass giving way to prickly pear. The Virginian sent two men across the neck of land at the Detour to hunt and to await the boats only 2,000 yards from their present position but a long 30-mile haul by water.

At 1 A.M. that night, tragedy brushed the corps. The Sergeant of the Guard hoarsely shouted the men awake. The sandbar on which they were camped was being broken up by the treacherous Missouri. All hands fled to the boats and made their way to a safe camp on the south side of the river. As Lewis saw his campsite disappear into the roily waters, he had an expert lesson in why the Missouri came to be so muddy.

Above Cedar Island and near Reuben Creek, three Indian boys swam out to the boats to tell him of 140 Teton Sioux lodges ahead. But the day set for a talk did not begin auspiciously; the Sioux stole Colter's horse, the detachment's last animal. Lewis told the Indians he would not council with them until the mount was returned. Anchoring his little flotilla off the mouth of the Teton River, which, appropriately, the Sioux called the Bad River, he landed only his cooks and a guard. Aboard the boats, the men prepared for action. Lewis invited five Indians aboard as guests—in case he needed hostages, later. A Frenchman in the detachment was able to talk to the Sioux enough to learn that their chief was attempting to get the horse back from some of his young men.

Leery of the Sioux because of their bad reputation, Lewis once again located his council site on an open beach, safe from ambush. He had the customary flagstaff and awning erected and anchored his "flagship" offshore some 70 yards with her battery covering the site.

The first two chiefs arrived early, at 11 A.M. Things did not go well. Some of the meat which they brought was spoiled; communication between the two groups was clumsy and uncertain for want of a good interpreter among the whites. The formal ceremony began at 12 noon with Lewis smoking the peace pipe with the chiefs. He gave his accustomed speech but curtailed it because of the interpretation problem. Next, he gave a medal to the Grand Chief, Black Buffalo, whom he took to be a good man, and to four others, among whom was the insolent and treacherous Partisan against whom Regis Loisel had warned him. He then invited all of them aboard the bateau to see its curiosities and gave them each a quarter of a glass of whiskey, which he knew they liked. He was amused when they sucked on the empty bottle but his smile faded when the Indians began to act in an ugly manner, particularly the Partisan. Captain Lewis finally suggested that it was time for the chiefs to go ashore. They did so, albeit grudgingly. Lewis watched Clark herd them into a pirogue and direct it to the bank. He straightened and tensed when he saw that his friend was in some kind of difficulty. In Clark's own words, "As soon as I landed the pirogue . . . the Chief's soldiers hugged the mast and the Second Chief [the Partisan] was verry insolent both in words and justures. He pretended drunkenness and staggered up against me, declaring I should not go on, stating he had not received presents sufficient from us. His justures were of such a personal nature, I felt My Self compelled to draw my sword and made a signal to the boat to prepare for action." At this moment, Lewis ordered all his men to arms. Those with Clark showed their disposition to fight, at the same time. The Grand Chief then took hold of the rope and ordered the young man to release it.

It was a tense moment. But, with relief, Lewis saw the Indian let go of the pirogue's painter. He found it difficult to maintain his forbearance and patience in the face of such truculence but he had to dismiss any idea of addressing the Tetons with a whiff of grapeshot because his mind was full of Jefferson's counsel to make peace with the Sioux—"Of that nation we wish most particularly to make a friendly impression because of their immense power and because we learn they are desirous of being on the most friendly terms with us." A peculiar kind of friendship they were demonstrating on the beach, thought Lewis.

The Indians had strung their bows and had taken arrows from their quivers. This meant an end to bluff and a start of war, so Lewis ordered his men to aim and prepare to fire. The Sioux wavered as they saw the riflemen drawing beads on them. With great pride, mixed with apprehension, Lewis saw his comrade coolly send his men to the keelboat, except for the interpreters, while he stood his ground on the beach, surrounded by Sioux. While Clark stalled for time by persistently offering his hand in friendship to the chiefs who stubbornly resisted it, Lewis sent the pirogue back with reinforcements, a twelve-man landing party, armed to the teeth and itching for a fight to relieve the monotony of the voyage.

Lewis's show of force and Clark's courage gave the Tetons pause. They notched no arrows, knowing that such an action would be the signal for the cannons to boom and the hammers of the vigilant rifles to fall. Clark finally spun on his heel, signaling the interpreters to follow him, turned his back on the Indians and strode to the water's edge without a glance behind him. The wary Lewis, watching, noted that not a Sioux made a move to restrain the redhead. But, as he watched, Chief Black Buffalo and the third-ranking chief, Buffalo Medicine, waded into the water to ask to be allowed to go aboard with Clark. Their request was granted by the Kentuckian and the pirogue pulled away from the glowering Partisan and his warlike braves on the beach.

Captain Lewis quickly moved his boats a mile and anchored off a willow-clad island which Clark dubbed Bad Humored Island. He posted sentinels in the boats and mounted guards over the cooks ashore.

But, to the surprise of both officers, the Sioux now tried to conciliate them. Indians lined the banks for miles and when the two captains went ashore, separately, they were met by Tetons who carried them ceremoniously in a buffalo robe—a great honor—to the village, which was decorated with the Stars and Stripes as well as the flag of Spain. At the council house they ate roast dog, smoked a pipe, and heard the chiefs out. That night, the squaws assembled and danced with trophy scalps dangling from sticks until 11 o'clock, when Lewis and Clark returned to the boats with the two chiefs as their guests. The next day, Lewis returned to the lodges with the chiefs but kept a wary eye on his hosts. For all their protestations of friendship, he could not forget their long history of violence or their bad conduct of just the day before.

As Clark was returning to the bateau in a pirogue from the night dance, his steersman clumsily ran the boat across the bow of the keelboat, breaking the cable. Lewis was still ashore, so Clark loudly commanded, "All hands up and at the oars!" The men tumbled to. The Sioux chief, alarmed by the bustle, called out to his men and the bank was soon crowded with 200 warriors. When Lewis asked the Partisan why his men were drawn up in war formation, that chief explained that he thought the Omahas were attacking. Lewis had been advised by Cruzatte that several Omaha prisoners had warned him that the Sioux were determined to prevent the whites from continuing their voyage. But Lewis had to appear to accept the Partisan's explanation. He had no anchor, so he could not escape. He ordered the keelboat tied up under a bank completely exposed, all night, to the Sioux. But there was no sleep for anyone aboard that night; all hands were on guard.

The night passed quietly, however, and in the morning Lewis had the river dragged for the anchor. But it could not be found. Nevertheless, he decided to get his force out of a deteriorating situation. He ordered the crews to cast off. However, although the Grand Chief was aboard the barge, the belligerent Dog Soldiers seized the keelboat's cable and sat down on the bank with it. Clark called Black Buffalo out of the cabin and the chief joined Lewis in the bow. He told the Virginian that his young warriors wanted some tobacco. Lewis, exasperated, would not agree to be forced into paying anything to the Sioux, even tobacco sticks, for the right of passage on an American river. Lewis was seething as the Partisan asked for—demanded—a flag and *tabac*. The Virginian had the patience of neither Job nor Griselda. In a few moments he would have given the Partisan a musket ball. He absolutely refused the Indian's demand and was on the point of ordering his men to fire on the Dog Soldiers when Clark caught up a carrot of tobacco and turned to Black Buffalo. "You have told us you are a great man and have influence. Take this tobacco and show us your influence by taking the rope from your men and letting go without coming to hostilities."

Clark had touched Black Buffalo's weak spot—his pride. He took the tobacco plug, gave it to the Dog Soldiers and, at the same time, pulled the rope out of their hands. He flung it to the bowsman and Lewis immediately gave the order to set sail before a provident southeast breeze. After he had placed the Teton River two miles astern, he noticed the third chief, Buffalo Medicine, beckoning from ashore. He had followed the whites to tell them that the Partisan had egged the young hotheads on to their rash action. Next, Buffalo Medicine's son came galloping along the riverbank and he, too, was taken aboard. Lewis sent a message by him to the Tetons. He told them to stay at home, if they wished peace. If they persisted in their attemps to detain him, he was both willing and able to defend himself and his men. He would again hoist the red (war) flag. After calling a halt to let the boy go ashore, and to make a stone anchor for the keelboat, Lewis took his party on to a campsite where the exhausted Clark could hardly keep his eyes open long enough to write in his journal: "I am verry unwell for want of sleep. Determined to sleep tonight if possible."

The next day, Lewis found the Tetons still dogging his tracks. A few called for tobacco from shore but none made threatening gestures and, in fact, most were as meek as mice. Perhaps the meaning of his red flag had not been lost on them. Perhaps they understood Clark's courage and realized that Lewis was of the same kidney. Lewis went so far as to send peace offerings in the shape of tobacco sticks ashore and when the Partisan humbly *asked* if he might be ferried across the river, Lewis obliged him. But he kept a close watch on the villain. The friendly Black Buffalo remained on the barge as Lewis's guest until the boats ran headlong into a storm. The chief proved to be a landlubber. He became so frightened that the commanders took pity on him and set him ashore. Before he left them, he wished them the Siouan version of godspeed, assuring Lewis that the river ahead was free of his troublesome Tetons. Both captains thanked him for his friendship but bluntly warned him to tell his braves that, for their own good, they had best keep clear of the boats. Before he left, they gave him a knife, a blanket and some tobacco. Then the two captains turned their backs on the Sioux nation and prepared to face the Arikaras, or Rees, and the Mandans.

CHAPTER XI

MANDAN WINTER

The Missouri is much larger and affords more water than the Mississippi. Geographers and other writers here consider it as a branch of the latter, whereas it is the main river and the Mississippi a tributary stream, only.
—AMOS STODDARD, *Sketches of Louisiana,* 1812

Of all the variable things in creation, the most uncertain are the action of a jury, the state of a woman's mind, and the condition of the Missouri River.
—Sioux City, *Register,* 1868

WILL CLARK'S EAR for the Anglo-French patois of the watermen was imperfect and he understood the large stream which they met on October 1st to be the *Chien,* or Dog, River when it was the Cheyenne, more poetically known as *La Rivière Qui Parle* or Talking River. Shades of Yankee babbling brooks! Even the Spaniards retained the charming name, Hispanizing it to *El Río Que Habla.* On its surface floated such quantities of tar that Lewis thought it could be used to make a fine cement for adobe bricks to construct a fort. More important, it marked something of a limit to the Sioux nation.

When Lewis ordered a camp made, it was eleven miles above the talkative stream, opposite a trading post from which came Jean Vallé to stay the night. He told Lewis that he was waiting for the Sioux to come down from the Arikara, or Ree, villages. He also told him many tales of the upper Cheyenne country, where he said he had wintered. If he was to be believed, it was a land worthy of Lemuel Gulliver. Where he had ventured—300 leagues (750 miles) upstream—grizzlies roamed at will. In the Black Mountains he heard strange, inexplicable noises. Vallé, who spoke English well, advised his new friend that he was not likely to meet any more Indians on the Troubled Waters until he fell in with the Arikaras.

There were more attempts to slow or stop the corps' progress—not by the Sioux nation but by the troublesome Missouri. Rain and wind halted the men one day; shallow water and sandbars the next. During the enforced stops, Lewis ordered an inspection of all provisions and found a new enemy at work, mice. The rodents had cut storage bags, scattered corn everywhere, eaten clothing and shredded his stock of paper. When the stores were once again put in order, Lewis broke camp and moved out.

The men kept themselves busy hunting in a region where all of the game seemed amphibious. The hunters killed four antelope in the river ahead of the boats and let them float down to be hauled aboard. Lewis himself shot a prairie wolf, or coyote, which had followed its prey right into the river. With full stomachs and calm and pleasant evenings, the men began to relax. To help them shed their tensions, Lewis and Clark treated them all to a glass of whiskey each. He meant the treat to suggest that they were leaving the Sioux behind and approaching the friendly Arikaras.

The captain knew that he was well into Arikara country by the 6th as he led his men through the ruins of a town which the Rees had abandoned. The village bore no sign of life around the earth-covered huts but his eyes picked out buffalo-hide bullboats and the remains of gardens where the Indians had tended crops of squash, corn, beans and tobacco. The latter, he discovered, was a far cry from the Virginia leaf to which he was accustomed. It was kinnikinnik, which was mixed with shavings of sumac, red osier, dogwood and saccacomis or bearberry bark for the red man's "makings." The Americans found it tolerable for smoking but it would not answer for chewing.

The Missouri now divided its bed into several shallow channels and the men had to drag the boat over shoals much of the time as they approached the Ree villages. There Lewis got two French

136

traders, Joseph Gravelines and Antoine Tabeau, to join him. Gravelines agreed, even, to winter with the corps up at the Mandan villages.

At the Grand River Arikara village, York created a sensation. The Negro passed himself off as a tamed wild animal, not a human. He claimed that he had been captured and domesticated by his master, Clark. To prove his awesome background, the slave, who had the power of a stump puller, performed muscular feats, accompanied by horrible grimaces, which made the Indians' eyes bulge.

Lewis soon found that the Arikara squaws had many accomplishments. Not only were they skilled workers and good coracle sailors, but they were "handsome and lively and disposed to be amorous." Two squaws followed the detachment to its camp and, to put it delicately, "persisted in their civilities." One of them continued on with the men in the boats and this "maiden" was a bewildered spectator at the court-martial of John Newman for mutiny, when he was sentenced to seventy-five lashes and dismissed from the corps. Clark had never seen such friendly or persistent "squars," he told Lewis, and he wrote in his diary, "Their women are verry fond of caressing our men."

But if Lewis was somewhat disturbed by the immorality of the Ree women, he was amazed at the men. They were a nation of teetotalers! Completely unlike their hard-swigging Sioux brethren, the earthen-lodge people abhorred liquor. They told Lewis, "You are not friends or you would not try to give us what makes us fools." Perhaps sobriety equated with civility on the upper Missouri; in any case, Lewis did not press spirits on them and they treated him and his men most hospitably. The Rees offered the Americans corn, beans, squash, a kind of succotash bread made of beans and corn, mixed, and a special treat in the form of a large bean which they stole from the industrious field mice who gathered it as winter rations. The chief seemed sincerely pleased with Lewis's visit and asked him to speak a good word to the Mandans, with a view to restoring peace between the two tribes.

Lewis addressed the Arikaras on the 10th and they responded the next day. He then proceeded upriver to the second and third villages to repeat the process. His confidence in his hosts was

137

diluted somewhat by his discovery that the Indians had a predilection for petty thievery. But presents were exchanged in good grace and it was a friendly parting when the Americans took leave of the Arikaras. Before he left, Lewis administered Newman's flogging. The corporal punishment so shocked Arikara Chief Ahketahanasha that he cried out in protest. He told Lewis that in his nation he put men to death but never humiliated them by a public whipping. The commander patiently explained the cause and the necessity for the form of disciplinary action to the horrified chief.

On the 18th, Lewis hailed two French traders, Grenier and Degie, who had been robbed by a party of Mandans. He invited them to tag along with the corps, in hopes of getting their furs back. They accepted his protection eagerly and accompanied the boats past the Cannonball River to a rich country where antelope, or goats, as the men called the pronghorns, were very numerous. Clark also counted fifty-two "gangs" of buffalo in view at one time, feeding on both banks near the ruins of old Mandan villages, littered with human and animal bones, skulls and teeth.

The 21st was a black-letter day on Lewis's calendar; the first snow of the season fell. The Virginian had already noted that leaves were dropping and that animals were heading for the cover of the mountains, to winter. But a more dramatic symptom of winter's coming, to Lewis, was his partner's suddenly succumbing to rheumatic pains of the neck, pains so violent that Clark could not move. Lewis applied hot stones, wrapped in flannel, which gave his friend some temporary ease.

Coincidental with the first flurries of snow, the whites met their first Mandans. Lewis was most curious to see his prospective winter hosts. They appeared friendly enough as they sat on their horses, singing and hallooing to the Americans from the shore. The Arikara chief traveling with Lewis was received courteously by his presumed enemies and a Mandan chief smoked a calumet with him. The son of the late Great Chief of all the Mandans impressed Lewis with the depth of his grief. The mourner had cut off his two little fingers to demonstrate his sorrow at his father's death.

Lewis hurried to get his men into winter camp quickly as the snow began to fly. He knew the Missouri would soon ice up and his boats would be helpless. So the Virginian gently deposited the Arikara on shore, picked up two Mandan chiefs and walked to the first village with them. There he met many tribesmen, also Hugh McCracken and another British trader. The pair had come from the north to trade for horses and buffalo skins. They worked for the North West Company. Lewis also met René Jusseaume there, a trader to the Mandans. He hired him on the spot as an interpreter. The captain next sent three carrots of tobacco to the Mandan chiefs as a goodwill offering and invited them to a powwow on the morrow. But the day proved too stormy for a council so Lewis observed the fair-complected Mandans while Clark sought a proper wintering site.

When the gale died, Lewis fired a shot from the bow piece to impress the Mandans and Minnetarees (or Lower Gros Ventres, or Hidatsas) with the importance of his mission. Then, through Jusseaume, he delivered a speech to the chiefs, among whom was Black Cat, Grand Chief of the Mandans. He chided them for allowing the theft of Degie's furs and ostentatiously gave the Arikara chief a certificate attesting to his good conduct. Only then did he award medals to the Mandans, and uniform coats and befeathered hats. The Indians were pleased but he really read appreciation in their faces when he presented them with an iron corn mill. (He thought that they were uncommonly fond of cornmeal but, actually, they intended to break up the mill for arrow points.) At 3 P.M, he had the cannon fired again to signal the end of his conference, then astounded his audience with a demonstration of his air gun. The day closed excitingly with an evening prairie fire in which two Indians were burned to death. Lewis learned a new plainsman's trick when he found that a half-breed boy had saved himself from the flames by wrapping up in a green buffalo hide.

The next to the last day of October 1804 found Lewis still trudging along the riverbank looking for a winter's campsite. He found none but did meet Big White, or Sheheke, chief of the Mandan lower village, and belatedly hung a medal around his neck. That day, also, Lewis bade good-bye to McCracken and gave him a message to his superior, Charles Baptiste Chaboillez.

In his letter to the Assiniboin trader, Lewis again performed as a buckskin diplomat, explaining that he had been sent to explore the Missouri and the western part of the continent "with a view to the promotion of general science." To the North West Company factor Lewis explained that he intended to fortify his party at the Mandan villages. He hoped Chaboillez would send him information on the flora, fauna and geography of the countryside and, indeed, any information of use to mankind and the prosecution of his voyage. He sent him a copy of his British passport, asked that the North West Company traders be informed of his presence, and ventured that "As individuals, we feel every disposition to cultivate the friendship of all well-disposed persons, and all that we have at this moment to ask of them is a mutual exchange of good offices. We shall, at all times, extend our protection as well to British subjects as American citizens who may visit the Indians of our neighborhood, provided they are well-disposed; this we are disposed to do, as well from the pleasure we feel in becoming serviceable to good men as from a conviction that it is consonant with the liberal policy of our Government not only to admit within her territory the free egress and regress of all citizens and subjects of foreign powers with which she is in amity, but also to extend to them her protection while within the limits of her protection."

Lewis was rather pleased with his communiqué. It contained a friendly greeting, a heavily veiled threat of force, and a dogmatic reminder that the upper Missouri was now American territory.

Clark found a site which Lewis approved of, on the banks of the Missouri opposite the mouth of Knife River. He liked the way the timbered bottom there was protected by a lofty rimrock from the polar winds already beginning to whistle and sweep down the Missouri, hinting at the bitter cold of the white season to come. He had his men pitch their tents and begin to lay the foundations of the two lines of huts which would be their cantonment. While the men worked, Lewis interviewed and hired Toussaint Charbonneau as an interpreter.

On November 6th, Gravelines and four French watermen set out in a pirogue to winter with the Arikaras, while Lewis and Clark superintended construction of their fort. They did not know it, but on or about that date, the Sioux formally voted in council to go to war against the corps, the Mandans, and the Minnetarees. Trader Charles Le Raye, who was their prisoner, learned of the plan but could not escape to warn Lewis until much later. However, before the Sioux were ready to strike in the spring, Lewis had led his men on upriver.

On the 11th of November, Charbonneau's squaws, Sacajawea and Otter Woman, came to visit the fort. Next day it was Big White and his squaw, Yellow Corn, hunched under a present of 100 pounds of meat for Lewis and Clark. The commanders, in turn, gave them some presents.

For some days, Lewis had watched flights of brant, ducks and swans, and great V's of honking Canada geese winging for the Gulf of Mexico on the high-altitude flyway over the Missouri. Another wintry sign was the capture of a weasel which had just metamorphosed into a white-coated ermine. On the 13th of November, it began to snow in earnest and ice started to run in the river. During the week that followed, a last-minute rush of visitors came to the fort, not only Mandans and Minnetarees but even Assiniboins and Crees. Chief Black Cat warned Lewis of the Crees, allies of the British, who were making trouble and who might soon be "making moccasins"—that is, actively preparing for war. He described them as spoiled by a surfeit of North West Company goods and used to driving hard bargains with such river tribes as the Mandans. Lewis, thereupon, sent word to them to stay at peace. He told them that if they were patient, they would get American trade goods when the American traders should come and that, in the meantime, he would protect them.

Other Mandan visitors warned him, as winter closed in, that the Sioux of the Cheyenne River were abusing the Arikaras for making peace with the whites and were openly threatening war on the Mandans that winter. There were only some 350 Mandans and a mere 80 Omahas, plus 600 to 700 Minnetarees, so Lewis was ready to throw in his legion, if need be, and lead the allies against the Sioux. In the meantime, he made the bastion, Fort Mandan, as snug as possible, in terms both of comfort and security. Exactly a week after the first float of ice on Old Muddy,

141

the two officers moved into their new hut. The hunters brought in the first pirogueload of meat for the new smokehouse, too. The floating butcher shop was loaded with succulent cuts of thirty deer, eleven elk and a few buffalo.

The first axes had rung on November 2nd; on the 13th, Lewis took a party upstream for stone for the chimneys. It was on the 19th and 20th that the men moved into their quarters and, during the weeks which followed, they daubed the walls, calked the chinks between logs, split cottonwood timber and hewed it into puncheons. On the 27th, winter descended on them; seven inches of snow fell on Fort Mandan that one day.

With the Arikaras and Mandans, Captains Lewis and Clark ran up against a new problem. The wanton Indian girls proved themselves the match for any Tahitian *wahine* who ever plagued Cook or Bligh. To save a Mandan's squaw's life, for example, Clark had to intervene in a domestic triangle, plains style, in which Ordway was "the other man." The commanders ordered him to give presents to the offended cuckold and forbade the corps having anything to do with the woman or any other (presumably) happily married women, under penalty of corporal punishment.

During the early part of their Mandan stay, Lewis and Clark were almost constantly on the move. There was no hibernating for them. Besides hunting a great deal, they toured the Mandan and Minnetaree villages, visited and stopped with headmen like Black Moccasin. All the Indians treated them with respect and even friendship save one, Horned Weasel, who chose not to be at home when Lewis called. Some of this activity was demanded by the rumors which Lewis felt called upon to squash. One canard had the Americans readying an alliance with—of all people— the Sioux! The intent? To fall upon the big-bellied Minnetarees. Lewis invited the Paunch Indians to visit the fort where he repeatedly professed his friendship for them and argued, effectively, through Interpreters Charbonneau and Jusseaume that the talebearers all had forked tongues.

A rumor of a different kind reached Lewis's ears that November. He heard that François Antoine Larocque of the North West Company was distributing British flags and medals to the

Indians. He immediately prepared a scouting party to find Larocque and order him to desist. But Larocque saved him the
trouble by appearing at that opportune moment at Fort Mandan
with a party of "Peter Pond's Pedlars," as the Hudson Bay Company factors derisively termed their competition. (The North-
westers, in turn, sarcastically said that the H.B.C. stood not for
Hudson's Bay Company but for "Here Before Christ.") It was
easy for Larocque to reach an agreement with Lewis, since the
rumor was false. He later recalled, "As I had neither flags nor
medals, I ran no risk of disobeying those orders, of which I assured him." Lewis and Larocque had a friendly conversation in
Lewis's quarters, where the American explained the expedition's
goals to his visitor. The two men got along quite well for rivals
but an assistant clerk in Larocque's group did not hit it off with
Lewis at all. Charles McKenzie indicated how little of his love
was lost on Lewis by writing in his journal: "It is true Captain
Lewis could not make himself agreeable to us. He could speak
fluently and learnedly on all subjects, but his inveterate disposition against the British stained, at least in our eyes, all his eloquence." Perhaps this blurting out of irritation at the Virginian's
apparent Anglophobia was caused by Lewis's teasing him in relation to Chief Horned Owl's refusal to see the Americans. For, of
the owlish sachem, Lewis remarked to the Scot, "I sent word
ahead to inform *La Belette Qui Porte des Cornes* that I intended
to take up my quarters at his lodge. He returned, for answer, that
he was 'not at home.' This conduct surprised me, it being common only to your English Lords not to be 'at home' when they
do not want to see strangers, but as I had felt no inclination of entering any house after being told the landlord would not be 'at
home,' I looked out for another lodging, which I readily found.
. . ."

What particularly caused Lewis to wear his Anglophobia so
obviously was not the mere presence of the Anglo-French Canadians, nor an elephantine memory for redcoat raids into Albemarle, but, rather, current John Bullish machinations. He was
well aware that the North West party's interpreter, Batiste Lafrance, was speaking unfavorably to the Indians about the Americans' intentions while Larocque affected, and probably felt, a

143

genuine friendship for him. Lewis not only told the Indians that their acceptance of any British gifts would incur the displeasure of their Great White Father but he also peremptorily ordered Larocque and McKenzie to put a stop to Lafrance's lies—which they did.

Quite likely, too, Lewis was deliberately overplaying his role of landlord of American Louisiana, for calculated effect. He certainly had the gift of insight to realize that, on that bleak and wintry corner of history's stage, he occupied a commanding role. With magnificent presence, he played it to the hilt and carried it off triumphantly—as if he had a regiment of artillery behind him instead of a company of volunteers and a log stockade. But he had built well. His rude fortress and half a hundred fighting men impressed the Britishers. And his little legion was still the strongest military force anywhere west of the Mississippi, north of New Orleans and Chihuahua, and south of Lower Canada.

Fort Mandan was a rude stockade but it was not unimpressive in terms of its competition, for there simply was none. Larocque gave it a careful surveillance and pronounced the picketed post to be virtually cannonball-proof. He dutifully noted that Lewis kept a sentry atop the fort all night and a sentinel on the ground inside all day. The rude redoubt was composed of two rows of cottonwood log huts or sheds joined at one end to make a squared-off U. At the open end of the U ran a strong palisade of pickets, providing security and access via a barred gate. There were eight barracks rooms and the slant-roofed compound also boasted two storerooms. So secure was the post that Lewis reduced the initial guard detail to three men and a sergeant.

The American's saber rattling did not awe Lafrance completely. He remained a thorn in Lewis's side. When Lewis sent Jusseaume to Big White, although he was losing confidence in the interpreter whom he found "assuming and discontented," to find out why Charbonneau's horse had been taken, he learned that Lafrance had seized it, saying Toussaint owed him a horse. Even when Lewis tried to be obliging, he was rebuffed by Lafrance or McKenzie, though never by Larocque. When he loaned Charbonneau to the Britishers, for example, the Scot sneered that the interpreter was only "a mulatto[?] who spoke bad French and worse English." Still, Lewis let them have his interpreter, only enjoining him not to say a word prejudicial to the United States, in translating, even if ordered to do so by Larocque. He turned quickly to the latter, who was standing nearby, smiled graciously, and added, "Of course, we are far from thinking you would."

As December opened, Lewis's attention was distracted from the North West Company "pedlars." The Mandans informed him that a party of Sioux had raided their horse herd, killing and wounding several men. Clark immediately called for volunteers but he found the Mandans reluctant to take the field with him. Although they were fond of playing outdoor games when Lewis would be forced to relieve his half-frozen sentinels every hour, the earthen-mound people were not up to warring in winter. They explained, "Father, the snow is deep, the weather cold, and our horses cannot travel through the plains. The murderers have gone off. If you will conduct us in the spring, when the snow has disappeared, we will assemble all the surrounding warriors and follow you." Clark, with Lewis's blessing, gave up the punitive expedition.

The tedium of winter was not broken again until Big White informed Lewis on December 6th that the buffalo were coming to the river. He invited the Americans to join in a hunt. The soldiers eagerly accepted and bagged ten or eleven of the shaggy beasts but could get only five back to the fort on the horses, or on their backs, so bitter cold was the weather, 12 below zero. The mounted Indians managed to kill thirty or forty more.

During the coldest part of the winter, Lewis proved to be a better frontiersman than Clark. He was as much at home in the snow as an Irishman in jail. Unlike Clark's hunters, his men did not suffer from frostbite, either, though they camped in the snow at times with but a single blanket apiece, and a ground sheet of buffalo hide. Lewis and his hunters swept the area near the fort, and rushed the meat to the storehouse before the wolves could get at it. He packed it on the backs of Indians, horses and soldiers and also commandeered Mandan dogsleds. But by the 12th, the ferocity of a Mandan winter discouraged even the Eskimo of Charlottesville. With the mercury plummeting to 38 degrees below, Lewis called off hunting for the time being. But, two days later, when the temperature soared back to a cozy zero, he grabbed up his rifle and took one of his twenty-mile strolls through the snow. However, the buffalo had largely quit the area and he saw only two bulls, both too poor to shoot, so he killed two deer and returned to the fort the following day, hunting on both sides of the broad band of ice which was the Missouri. When his hunters went out, they were forced to abandon much of the meat they took because of the cruel cold, so Lewis finally ordered them to stay in garrison and keep warm. But he and Clark put the men to work making sleds for hauling meat when the cold spell should let up. To test the cold, Lewis exposed some of the corps' proof spirits to the outside air. It froze into hard ice in just fifteen minutes, proving the men's point that it was a little too cold for hunting.

The 16th of the month was warmed for Lewis by the arrival of Hugh Heney from the Assiniboine River. He brought an answer to the Virginian's letter to Chaboillez. Lewis and Heney got on famously, from the start. Heney was intelligent and helpful; not only did he convey his superior's warm greetings and offer of assistance, but he personally supplied Lewis with information, and even sketches, of the Missouri area to the west. With the temperature locked stiffly at minus 34, Lewis tried his best to make Heney's return trip as comfortable as possible. He gave him provisions and had his best carpenter, Gass, fix up a horse sled to make his journey easier.

The commanders were kept busy greeting visitors, trading with the Indians, treating the soldiers and Indians for a variety of illnesses. The press of visitors by Christmas was such that it became unpleasant; Mandans were underfoot everywhere. Lewis took advantage of the holiday to request the Indians to stay away from the fort on Big Medicine Day. This kind of religious prohibition comported beautifully with Mandan mores and they took the order with the best of grace. On Christmas Eve, the last of the pickets were driven and the fort officially completed. The soldiers laid down their tools and had themselves a little celebration, the captains contributing to the Christmas party some flour, pepper and dried apples.

The officers were awakened on Christmas morning by two blasts from the swivel cannon and three volleys from the guns of the entire detachment. They found the men "merrily disposed." Clark presented each man with a glass of the fiery taffia, variously described as brandy and as rum but probably unidentifiable scientifically. Then the American colors were hoisted to wave over the bastion for the first time. The sight of Old Glory waving in a Mandan zephyr was enough to arouse the thirst of any patriot, so another glass of spirits was served up to each man. The soldiers then cleared a room and began dancing to Cruzatte's fiddle, a tambourine, a horn and the clapping hands of the kibitzers. Halting only for another drink and for dinner, they jigged and capered until 8 P.M., to the amusement of the spectators, among whom were three potential dance partners—Sacajawea, Otter Woman and a Mandan squaw of Jusseaume's. But they were not asked to dance. The men remembered Lewis's orders and gave the squaws a wide berth. The women just watched, big-eyed.

No Indians came on Christmas Day or the day following. They were apparently loath to intrude on another possible holy day. But they were back, en masse, on December 27th when Lewis ordered his blacksmith, Shields, to the forge in the fort's smithy. Shield's skill at working iron into tools and weapons brought the Indians in droves. They were impressed by the sweating smith but his bellows literally astounded them. Shields and his smithy proved to be more of Lewis's secret weapons, like Cruzatte's fiddle, impressing even the hostile chief of the Minnetarees, upon whom the British were working. Boasted one-eyed Le Borgne, "Had I these white warriors on the upper plains, my young men would soon do for them as they would do for so many wolves." But he grudgingly had to admit that there were two sensible men among them—"the worker of iron and the mender of guns." The chief of the so-called Paunch Indians was cool toward Lewis because he did not lavish goods and presents on them. He explained that he was an explorer, not a trader, but they did not understand. All they knew was trade goods and Le Borgne groused to McKenzie, "Had these whites come amongst us with charitable views, they would have loaded their Great Boat with necessaries. It is true they have ammunition, but they prefer throwing it away idly than sparing a shot of it to a poor Mandan."

Larocque, however, seeing the Indians crowd into Fort Mandan to trade corn for the smith's services in mending axes and hoes, realized that Lewis had counted diplomatic coup. Never were Mandan-American relations better. The Anglo-Frenchman commented in his journal: "They have a very expert smith who is always employed making different things and working for the Indians who are grown fond of them, although they disliked them, at first." McKenzie, for all his dislike of Lewis, had to admit, too, that the Indians respected him and not just because of his smith. He noted, "The Indians admired the air gun, as it could discharge forty shots out of one load, but they dreaded the magic of the owner [Lewis]." When the North West pedlar paid a call on Le Borgne, he found that even that surly Minnetaree had been won over by the Americans. He overheard the chief deprecating his Canadian companions and noted in his journal, "It was most galling to me, who understood some of the Indian language, to hear them despised and the American captains, whom they had hated till then, praised."

No fool, Lewis put his bolstered position to immediate use. He discouraged two Minnetaree chiefs from their plan to war on the Shoshones to the west when spring came. He also made use of his forge-and-bellows diplomacy to ration the corps better, trading parts of the caboose, or boat's stove, which had rusted and burned out on the long upriver ascent, for food. Each piece of the metal, precious to the Mandans, brought seven to eight gallons of corn, plus the pleasure of the natives. The Indians particularly wished Shields to fashion battle-axes of a peculiar, traditional shape. To Lewis, they were of execrable design, being too clumsy and short-handled to be truly efficient weapons. But, clumsy or not, when he presented one of the war axes to Chief Black Cat, the chief was very grateful.

Lewis and Clark kept a close eye on the weather, sending hunters out when the cold lessened and dispatching horses and sleds to pick up the meat they left in caches, some as far as thirty miles from the fort. The monotony of garrison life was broken also by a quarrel between Jusseaume and Charbonneau; by a

pleurisy case and the need to bleed the patient; by the amputa-
tion, by Lewis, of several toes of a frostbitten Indian boy; and by
attempts to free his fleet from the icy grip of the Missouri.

The efforts to loosen the boats were repeated again and again.
Nothing seemed to work. Axes failed; rocks heated to melt the
water frozen inside the craft exploded as they were roasted in the
fires. As a last resort, Lewis tried iron spikes attached to poles, as
bores. He had a strong rope made of elkskin so that, with his
windlass, he could draw the boats up on the bank out of danger
once they could be freed. "The situation of our boat and pirogues is now alarming," he confided to his journal. "They are
firmly enclosed in the ice and almost covered with snow. The ice
which envelopes them lies in several stratas of unequal thickness,
which are separated by streams of water. This is peculiarly unfortunate because so soon as we cut through the first strata of ice,
the water rushes up and rises as high as the upper surface of the
ice and this creates such a depth of water as renders it impracticable to cut away the lower strata which appears firmly attached to, and confining, the bottom of the vessels."

On the next to the last day of January, Larocque asked Lewis,
for the second time, if he could accompany him west. Again
Lewis politely but firmly refused. The Canadian gave up his im-
ploring and, on February 20th, left for his home base, grateful
for Lewis's parting gesture. The Virginian devoted the greater
part of a day to the repair of the Canadian's compass for him, the
glass being broken and the needle no longer pointing due north.

The attrition of winter began to be felt. Drouillard came down
with an attack of pleurisy and Lewis bled him and gave him tea.
He was soon better but then Jusseaume became unwell. Next,
Sacajawea took to her bed, but the reason for the squaw's indisposition was not illness. On the evening of February 11th she
gave birth to a strapping and squalling son, Jean Baptiste Charbonneau. He was Sacajawea's first child, and no easy birth.
Lewis was used to playing surgeon but the role of midwife was a
new one to him. He hovered over the girl, helpless, until Jusseaume—the man Alexander Henry described as "an old, sneak-
ing cheat, more despicable than the worst of the natives"—told
him that he had frequently administered powdered rattlesnake

rattles to assuage the pangs of childbirth and to hasten the arrival of the baby. Lewis recalled, "Having the rattle of a snake by me, I gave it to him and he administered two rings of it to the woman, broken in small pieces with his fingers, and added to a small quantity of water." Sacajawea's labor pains lessened and in just ten short minutes, Baptiste was born. Lewis, always the eager scientist, was soon dutifully describing the rattlesnake powder for the edification of Doctors Rush, Barton, and others of the Philadelphia intelligentsia.

To escape the boredom of garrison life, the commanders amused themselves by touring the Mandan villages. There, Lewis saw how the Indians wintered their stock. The horses were allowed to run free by day, but were brought into the lodges at night and fed cottonwood trash. The Mandans were hard on their mounts but the beasts seemed to thrive on the tree greens, like giraffes. Lewis explained, "The Indians in our neighbourhood are frequently pilfered of their horses by the Ricaries, Sioux and Assiniboines and, therefore, make it an invariable rule to put their horses in their lodges at night. In this situation, the only food of the horse consists of a few sticks of cottonwood, from the size of a man's finger to that of his arm." It was on one of these tours of inspection that Lewis finally found a Mandan who really impressed him, Black Cat, chief of the upper village. "This man possesses more integrity, firmness, intelligence and perspicacity of mind than any Indian I have met with in this quarter and, I think, with a little management he may be made a useful agent in furthering the views of our Government." When Clark was not touring with Lewis, he kept himself busy compiling a map, with the aid of Big White's crude charts drawn in the dirt, paying particular attention to the Yellowstone area far to the west.

A major break in the winter's routine occurred on February 15th. Hunters Drouillard, Frazier, Goodrich and Newman, while about twenty-four miles below the fort, were rushed by a hundred or more Sioux. The warriors succeeded in cutting the horses loose from the sleighs and making off with three of them. Drouillard managed to get one horse back and put up enough of a bluff to prevent the Sioux from lifting the whites' scalps but he had to submit to the rustling of the horses, one of which had been loaned by McKenzie to Lewis.

As soon as word reached him, Captain Lewis called for twenty volunteers to be ready to march at midnight. He sent a hurried message to the Mandans to inform them that he was going to pursue the Sioux and to invite them to join him. His friend Big White responded immediately and another chief and a handful of warriors followed but they reported that most of the young men were out hunting and, therefore, almost no guns were left in the village. Lewis let his men rest till sunrise, then set off at the head of a 24-man detachment, reinforced by the Mandans, armed with spears, battle-axes, bows and arrows and two old fusees. It was cold—16 degrees below zero. One sub-chief was soon forced to drop out suffering from snow blindness. After a 30-mile forced march, Lewis ordered a camp set up. He pressed on, next day, toward one of the meat caches. As he closed with it, he saw smoke rising into the frosty air, as if from campfires. He had Sergeant Ordway sound his horn and his men broke into a charge. The soldiers, eager for a fight, were disappointed to find the pen torn down, the meat stolen, and the smoke arising from the embers of the hunters' huts. The Sioux were gone. From the meat depot, Lewis sent back four Mandans and a corpsman, all suffering from frostbite. He kept to the field with the remainder of his force for almost a week, following the trail of the raiders up onto the bluffs and out into the prairie, but he was not able to catch sight of them.

Resolving to put his expedition to the best use, Lewis scouted all the meat dumps and found one which the Sioux had overlooked. He then turned his force into a hunting party, sending out a great circle of beaters, safari-style. When he returned to the fort he brought no captured Sioux but he was not empty-handed. Besides the meat from the cache, he had 36 freshly killed deer and 14 elk. He estimated that one of the two sleds, alone, had 2,400 pounds of venison on it. But he was far from content with the results of his punitive expedition, for he knew that by failing to punish the raiders he had lost face in Indian eyes.

It was after the Sioux raid that Lewis discovered that Fort

Mandan was hardly impregnable. First, he had to put a lock on the gate, in addition to the bolt, because the interpreter's squaws fell into the habit of letting Indian visitors into the fort at night by unbarring the gate. Next, when Private Howard returned late one night from the village, instead of calling the guard for admittance, he scaled the wall and dropped inside. This was bad enough, but a watching Indian saw his performance and followed his example. Lewis harangued the Indian, explaining just how close he had come to joining his ancestors, then gave him a piece of tobacco and sent him packing. He reserved his rage for Howard, whom he arrested prior to calling for a court-martial. The exasperated commander wrote in his diary, "The man is an old soldier, which still heightens the offense." Perhaps because Howard was a veteran, Lewis ultimately remitted the Court's sentence of fifty lashes.

The first, premature, signs of spring came on February 22nd, when Captain Lewis noticed that the snow had changed to rain, the first drizzle to fall on the fort since November. He hurried the men who were still trying to cut the ice away from the boats, as he envisioned fleets of jagged ice floes bearing down on the frail pirogues. By the 27th of February, his minuscule fleet had been winched up the bank on rollers to safety, although the weight of the barge broke the elkskin cable on the windlass several times.

The day the boats were finally high and dry, Gravelines and Roi returned from the Arikaras. They reported that the marauding horse thieves whom Clark had hoped to pursue were 106 Teton Sioux who had boasted that they were going to wipe out the entire corps. Tabeau also sent word to Lewis, to warn him against the Sioux who were threatening war against whites, Minnetarees and Mandans. One bit of news pleased the Virginian; the Arikaras had not turned against him. They had, in fact, refused food to the Sioux raiders and had manifested their displeasure with the Tetons in other, unmistakably hostile, ways.

Winter paled but Lewis's attention to natural history research never flagged. From Gass, he learned that the superstitious Mandans offered bowls of food to severed buffalo heads, saying "Eat up!" in order to keep on the good side of all buffalodom and to insure a future supply of steaks and roasts. This ethno-anthropological note went into his journal along with observations on a total eclipse of the moon, his discovery of the secret formula of the Arikaras and Mandans for making beads, and his discussion of the predatory effectiveness of wolves even in sub-zero weather. He also laid to a well-deserved rest Jefferson's quaint daydream of a briny Quivira. Lewis found nothing resembling the Mountain of Salt which Jefferson believed lay in the West. He strongly doubted that one lay on his track to the Pacific. But he summed up his exploration of salt licks, mineral springs, saline creeks and alkaline rivers for the President before concluding, "I have obtained no satisfactory account of any fossil salt being found in Louisiana altho' repeated inquiries have been made of such as possess the best information of the interior parts of the country. I am, therefore, disposed to believe that those travelers who have reported its existence must have mistaken the massive salt formed by concretion for that substance."

Lewis worked up tables of information on the Indians of the Missouri and, via hearsay evidence, on those living toward the South Snowy Mountains, or Rockies. The Minnetarees were more helpful in this project than the sedentary Mandans. From the former he picked up details of the Flatheads, using information the Minnetarees acquired on war excursions far to the west. "They are a timid, inoffensive and defenseless people. They are said to possess an abundance of horses," reported his informants. For the most part, Lewis just accepted such information. But in the case of the Sioux, with their aggressive hostility and power, their strange, whip-bearing Dog Soldiers and raiding parties, he made an exception and editorialized. He simply could not contain himself and turned this portion of his scientific table into a diatribe: "These are the vilest miscreants of the savage race and must ever remain the pirates of the Missouri until such measures are pursued by our Government as will make them feel a dependence on its will for their supply of merchandise. Unless these people are reduced to order, by coercive measures, I am ready to pronounce that the citizens of the United States can never enjoy but partially the advantages which the Missouri presents. . . . They view with contempt the merchants of the Missouri, whom they never fail to plunder when in their power. Persuasion or advice with them is viewed as supplication and only tends to inspire them with contempt for those who offer either. The tameness with which the fur traders of the Missouri have heretofore submitted to their rapacity has tended not a little to inspire them with contempt for the white persons who visit them. . . . A prevalent idea among them and one which they make the rule of their conduct is that the more illy they treat the traders, the greater quantity of merchandise they will bring them. . . ." In describing the James River, Lewis added, "The Sioux annually hold a fair on some part of this river in the latter end of May. Thither the Yanktons of the North and the Sissetons who trade with Mr. Cameron on the head of the St. Peter's [Minnesota] River bring guns, powder and balls, kettles, axes, knives and a variety of European manufactures which they barter to the four bands of Tetons and the Yanktons *Ahnah* who inhabit the borders of the Missouri and upper part of the River Des Moines and receive, in exchange, horses, leather lodges, and buffalo robes which they have either manufactured or plundered from the Indian nations on the Missouri and west of it. This traffic is sufficient to keep the Sioux of the Missouri tolerably well-supplied with arms and ammunition, thus rendering them independent of the trade of the Missouri and enabling them to continue their piratical aggressions on all who attempt to ascend that River, as well as to disturb perpetually the tranquility of all their Indian neighbours.

"I am perfectly convinced that until such measures are taken by our Government as will effectively prohibit all intercourse or traffic with the Sioux by means of the River Des Moines and St. Peter's, that the citizens of the Unitd States can never enjoy but partially those important advantages which the navigation of the Missouri now presents. . . ." Lewis was a good prognosticator; in the 1850's the Sioux would plague General W. S. Harney; in the 1860's, they would terrorize Minnesota; in the 1870's they would destroy George Custer and his command. Not until the Battle of Wounded Knee in the '90s could the West breathe easily.

As the false spring began to merge with the real thing, Lewis ordered axmen to hew dugouts from cottonwood logs. Notwithstanding several broken axes, six new pirogues were quickly built and either floated down to the fort as the frozen Missouri's icy skin began to break up or manhandled overland to the post. Lewis tested how much weight they could carry without foundering. They would not carry as much as he had hoped, so he decided not to send the large (original) pirogue back to St. Louis with the bateau, after all.

In March, all the men were busy with last-minute preparations to resume the voyage. On the 5th, Lewis wrote Jefferson about the neatly packed specimens on the keelboat—including a root which was a sure cure for mad-dog bites. He was distracted from his work first by a return visit from Larocque, who brought the disquieting news that the North West Company and the X Y Company had ended their rivalry by a merger. Next, Charbonneau arrived back from the Minnetarees, laden with presents pressed on him by Chaboillez. Finally, Le Borgne paid Lewis a call. The one-eyed, unscrupulous villain finally gave in to his gnawing curiosity and came to the fort although the American commander had made no move to send him the large flag which he demanded. Lewis had sent him some other presents, however, which Le Borgne claimed had never arrived. Although the soldier in Lewis rebelled, the diplomat won out and he presented the scoundrel with a two-gun salute, a medal, a shirt, a gorget and armbands, some scarlet cloth, his long-sought flag, and much more. The Hidatsas' Great Man was pleased. All the chiefs were now firmly won to the American cause, as much by the Big Medicine which Lewis showed them—his quadrant, spy glass and air gun—as by the presents he lavished on them.

Conferring with Clark on March 11th, the commander regretfully decided that Charbonneau's allegiance had been corrupted by the North West Company and its presents. Nor could Lewis agree to the interpreter's impossible demands—that he be excused from guard duty on the march west, that he be allowed to take whatever provisions he pleased, that he be free to return to the Mandans whenever he liked. So Lewis released the French-Canadian from his verbal contract and signed Gravelines in his place. Charbonneau moved out of the fort in a huff and pitched his lodge beyond its walls. But shortly he changed his mind, stopped his sulking, and contritely apologized to Lewis, admitting that he had been foolish. He asked to be restored to duty on the captain's terms and Lewis took him back.

The officers collected the boats together, broke all the baggage into eight packs and loaded the recalked craft as soon as the ice broke up and the boats could be returned to the roily bosom of the Missouri. The men worked against a spectacular backdrop— the breakup was sending great quantities of ice and drowned buffalo down the river while fire and smoke rose from the prairie beyond, where the Indians were firing the plains to bring up the new grass.

April Fool's Day came and passed. Lewis paid McKenzie for the borrowed horse the Tetons had stolen, he supervised the packing of the specimens destined for Jefferson and the American Philosophical Society—mineral samples and plant specimens, all carefully labeled by him as to date and place found and any virtues his research had determined. With them went bones, fossils, skins and horns for study. With the greatest care, Lewis then oversaw the arrangements for transporting the live specimens he was sending the President—a prairie dog, four magpies and a prairie chicken.

About 5 P.M., April 7, 1805, Lewis had the swivel gun fired to officially recommence the voyage. The barge slipped downstream under the command of Corporal Warfington and he set out up-river with Clark, three sergeants, twenty-three privates, Drouillard, Charbonneau, Sacajawea, little Baptiste, York and a Mandan who wished to go west to make peace overtures to the Shoshones or Snakes. Warfington took with him Clark's notes on the expedition, since Lewis had not had the leisure time to make a corrected copy of their joint journal. Clark apologized for the rough state of his notes and Lewis promised to send a true copy back with the dispatches he intended to entrust to three or four men at the extreme point of navigation of the Missouri.

In regard to Warfington's barge and men, Lewis said, "I have but little doubt but they will be fired upon by the Sioux, but they have pledged themselves to us that they will not yield while there is a man of them living." As for his own six small canoes and pirogues, Lewis planned to leave the pirogues at the Falls of the

Missouri and proceed in the canoes and the "pirogue of skins" which he had framed up at Harpers Ferry. Incredibly optimistic, he added, "This pirogue is now in a situation which will enable us to prepare it in the course of a few hours." He estimated his party would travel at the rate of 20 to 25 miles per day until he reached the Falls. After that point, no one could tell what their progress would be.

Lewis sent his mother a letter via Warfington which was a good summary of the Lewis and Clark Expedition as far as the Mandans. In it he stated, "The near approach of winter, the low state of the water and the known scarcity of timber which exists on the Missouri for many hundreds of miles above the Mandans, together with many other considerations, equally important, determined my friend and companion, Captain Clark, and myself to fortify ourselves and remain for the winter in the neighbourhood of the Mandans, Minnetarees and Ahnaharways [Wattasoons, or Black Moccasin Indians], who are the most friendly and well-disposed savages we have yet met.

"So far, we have experienced more difficulty from the navigation of the Missouri than danger from the savages . . . , from the rapidity of its current, its falling banks, sandbars, and timber which remains wholly or partially concealed in its bed, usually called by the navigators of the Missouri and Mississippi, 'sawyers' or 'planters.' One of those difficulties the navigator never ceases to contend with from the entrance of the Missouri to this place and in innumerable distances, most of those obstructions are at the same instant combined to oppose his progress, or threaten his destruction.

"To these we may also add a fifth and not much less inconsiderable difficulty, the turbid quality of the water which renders it impracticable to discover any obstruction, even to the depth of a single inch. Such is the velocity of the current at all seasons of the year from the entrance of the Missouri to the mouth of the great River Platte, that it is impossible to resist its force by means of oars or poles in the main channel of the river. The eddies, therefore, which generally exist on one side or the other of the river, are sought by the navigator but these are almost universally incumbered with concealed timber or within the reach of the falling banks, but, notwithstanding, are usually preferable to that of passing along the edges of the sand bars, [on] which the water, though shallow, runs with such violence that if your vessel happens to touch the sand, or is by accident turned sidewise to the current, it is driven on the bar and overset in an instant, generally destroyed, and always attended with the loss of the cargo. The base of the river banks being composed of a fine, light sand, easily removed by the water, it happens that when this capricious and violent current sets aganst its banks, which are usually covered with heavy timber, it quickly undermines them, sometimes to the depth of 40 or 50 paces, and several miles in length. The banks being unable to support themselves longer, tumble into the river with tremendous force, destroying everything within their reach. The timber thus precipitated into the water with large masses of earth about their roots, are seen drifting with the stream, their points above the water, while the roots, more heavy, are dragged along the bottom until they become firmly fixed in the quicksands which form the bed of the river, where they remain for many years, forming an irregular, though dangerous, *cheveaux de frise* to oppose the navigator.

"This immense river, so far as we have yet ascended, waters one of the fairest portions of the globe, nor do I believe that there is in the universe a similar extent of country equally fertile, well-watered and intersected with such a number of navigable streams. The country as high up this river as the mouth of the River Platte, a distance of 630 miles, is generally well timbered. At some little distance above this river, the open or prairie country commences. With respect [to] this open country, I have been agreeably disappointed. From previous information I had been led to believe that it was barren, sterile and sandy, but, on the contrary I found it fertile in the extreme, the soil being from one to 20 feet in depth, consisting of a fine black loam, intermixed with a sufficient quantity of sand only to induce a luxuriant growth of grass and other vegetable productions, particularly such as are not liable to be much injured or wholly destroyed by the ravages of fire. It is also generally level, yet well watered; in short, there can exist no other objection to it except that of the want of timber, which is truly a serious one. This want of timber is by no means attributable to a deficiency in the soil to produce it, but owes its origin to the ravages of the fires which the natives kindle in these plains at all seasons of the year. The country on both sides of the river, except some of its bottom lands, for an immense distance is one continued open plain in which no timber is to be seen except a few detached and scattered copses and clumps of trees, which, from their moist situations or the steep declivities of the hills, are sheltered from the effects of fire. The general aspect of the country is level so far as the perception of the spectator will enable him to determine but from the rapidity of the Missouri, it must be considerably elevated as it passes to the northwest. It is broken only on the borders of the watercourses.

"Game is very abundant and seems to increase as we progress. Our prospect for starving is, therefore, consequently small. On the lower portion of the Missouri, from its junction with the Mississippi to the entrance to the Osage River, we met with some deer, bear, and turkeys; from thence to the Kansas River, the deer are more abundant, a great number of black bear, some turkeys, geese, swan and ducks; from thence to the mouth of the White River, vast herds of buffalo, elk and some deer and a greater number of turkeys than we had before seen, a circumstance which I did not much expect in a country so destitute of timber. From hence to Fort Mandan, the buffalo, elk and deer increase in quantity with the addition of the *cabri* [pronghorn antelope], as they are generally called by the French *engagés,* but which is the size of a small deer. Its flesh is deliciously flavoured.

"The ice in the Missouri has now nearly disappeared. I shall set out on my voyage in the course of a few days. I can see no material obstruction to our progress and feel the most perfect confidence that we shall reach the Pacific Ocean this summer. For myself, individually, I enjoy better health than I have since I commenced the voyage. The party are now in health and excellent spirits, attached to the enterprise and anxious to proceed; not a whisper of discontent or murmur is to be heard among them, but all act in unison and with the most perfect harmony. With such men, I feel every confidence necessary to insure success. The party, with Captain Clark and myself, consists of thirty-one white persons, one Negro man, and two Indians.

"The Indians in this neighbourhood inform us that the Missouri is navigable nearly to its source and that from a navigable part of the river at a distance not exceeding half a day's march there is a large river running from south to north along the western base of the Rocky Mountains. But as their war excursions have never extended far beyond this point, they can give no account of the discharge or source of this river. We believe this stream to be the principal south fork of the Columbia River and, if so, we shall probably find but little difficulty in passing to the ocean. We have subsisted this winter on meat, principally, with which our guns have furnished us with an ample supply and have by that means reserved a sufficient stock of the provisons which we brought with us from the Illinois, to guard us against accidental wants, during the voyage of the present year.

"You may expect me in Albemarle about the last of next September, twelve months [i.e., September 1806]. I request that you will give yourself no uneasiness with respect to my fate for I do assure you that I feel myself perfectly as safe as I should do in Albemarle; and the only difference between 3 or 4 thousand miles and 130 is that I cannot have the pleasure of seeing you as often as I did while at Washington. . . ."

Another letter which Warfington carried was from Lewis to Jefferson. In it he apologized for not sending a pirogue back earlier, to quiet the Chief Executive's fears. But, he reasoned, "the provision pirogue and her crew could not have been dismissed in time to have returned to St. Louis last fall without evidently, in my opinion, hazarding the fate of the enterprise in which I am engaged. Therefore, I did not hesitate to prefer the censure that I may have incurred by the detention of the papers to that of risking, in any degree, the success of the expedition."

Lewis left as little as possible to guesswork; his plans were based on his sifting and evaluating of the information he had gleaned from the Indians all winter long. He depended heavily on the Shoshones, or Snakes, and mentioned to the President, "The circumstances of the Snake Indians possessing large quantities of horses is much in our favour as, by means of horses, the transportation of our baggage will be rendered easy and expeditious overland from the Missouri to the Columbia River. Should this river not prove navigable where we first meet with it, our present intention is to continue our march by land down the river until it becomes so, or to the Pacific Ocean."

If he could conquer the one problem of transportation, Lewis was sure he could win through to the sea. The other major factor, food, scarcely bothered him at all. "Since our arrival at this place, we have subsisted principally on meat, with which our guns have supplied us amply and have been enabled to reserve the parched meal, portable soup and a considerable portion of pork and flour . . . for the more difficult parts of our voyage. If Indian information can be credited, the vast quantity of game with which the country abounds, through which we are to pass through, leaves us but little to apprehend from the want of food." Small wonder, then, that Lewis, with his plans so well laid, confidently signed off with: "You may, therefore, expect me to meet you at Monticello in September 1806."

But, before he penned his adieu to the President, Lewis predicted complete success for the great enterprise and laid praise for the eventual success of it where, in his mind, it belonged—on the shoulders of his stout volunteers. "I can see no material or probable obstruction to our progress and entertain, therefore, the most sanguine hopes of complete success. As to myself, individually, I never enjoyed a more perfect state of good health than I have since we commenced our voyage. My inestimable friend and companion, Captain Clark, has also enjoyed good health, generally. At this moment, every individual of the party is in good health and excellent spirits, zealously attached to the enterprise and anxious to proceed. Not a whisper of discontent or murmur is to be heard among them but all in unison act with the most perfect harmony.

"With such men, I have everything to hope and but little to fear."

CHAPTER XII

―•◦•―

A'WESTERING

There has existed among all the greatest harmony, and those who have returned speak in the best terms of the humaneness, care and extraordinary attention which Captains Lewis and Clark have had with all. They left them very happy and completely convinced that they will winter on the Pacific Ocean.

—New Orleans *Gazette*, 1805

SINCE LEWIS had had little real exercise for several months, he chose to walk ahead of the boats when they cast off and set out from Fort Mandan on April 7th. He told Clark that he would visit Black Cat to smoke a friendly pipe with him, and then, leisurely, he would select a good campsite and await the boats. But, before he strode out in his energetic fashion, he stood for a moment to look over the historic sight which lay before him. It impressed itself indelibly on his mind and he later reconstructed it for his journal:

"Our vessels consisted of six small canoes and two large pirogues. This little fleet, although not quite so respectable as those of Columbus or Captain Cook, were still viewed by us with as much pleasure as those deservedly famed adventurers ever beheld theirs and, I dare say, with quite as much anxiety for their safety and preservation. We were now about to penetrate a country at least two thousand miles in width, on which the foot of civilized men had never trodden, the good or evil it had in store for us was for experiment yet to determine and these little vessels contained every article by which we were to expect to subsist or defend ourselves. . . .

"The picture which now presented itself to me was a most pleasing one, entertaining as I do the most confident hope of succeeding in a voyage which had formed a darling project of mine for the last ten years. I could but esteem this moment of my departure as among the most happy in my life. . . ."

Captain Lewis's giant strides left the boats far behind as their crews found it difficult, after the long winter's layoff, to recapture the powerful rhythm of rowing necessary to stem the brawling current. To further hinder their progress, one of the canoes almost immediately bilged, nearly sinking. Small wonder, then, that Lewis had to backtrack along the riverbank to find his lagging fleet at the end of the day.

As the boats worked their way west, Lewis looked in vain for spring. Winter hurried aside directly, for summer. Some of his oarsmen stripped to breechclouts as they worked under the blazing sun of the outskirts of the Dakota badlands. Pumice and a sulphurous stench alerted them to the nearness of these *terres mauvaises*. But, though the soil and water were impregnated with salts, and alkali flats glistened like autumn fields covered with hoarfrost, game was plentiful. The men took fish, shot beaver and muskrats and even bagged a bald eagle, which was quickly plucked by a half-dozen diarists for quill pens. Scammon delighted his master by bounding into the river to retrieve geese shot by the soldiers, and Lewis, hardly believing his eyes, saw nests of wild geese in tall trees. Knowing his report would be scoffed at in the East, he sent an intrepid volunteer up a 60-foot tree to bring him an egg as a trophy.

A week out of Fort Mandan, the boats passed the farthest point Charbonneau and Lepage had ever been. They were now truly in terra incognita, where unafraid beavers swam their untrapped streams in broad daylight and where a buffalo calf attached itself to Lewis like a pet dog. Here, Lewis spied the first huge tracks of grizzlies among the carcasses of drowned buffalo on the riverbank. He assumed the bears fed on carrion. Two days later, the first of the legendary "white bears" were seen, but too far away for a shot at them. He wrote, "The men as well as ourselves are anxious to meet with some of these bears. The Indians give a formidable account of the strength and ferocity of this animal, which they never dare to attack but, in parties of six, eight or ten persons, are even then frequently defeated with the loss of one of more of their party. The savages attack this animal with their bows and arrows and the indifferent guns with which the traders furnish them. With these, they shoot with such uncertainty and at so short a distance that, unless shot through the head or heart, the wound [is] not mortal. They frequently miss their aim and fall a sacrifice to the bear. Two Minnetarees were killed during the last winter in an attack of the white bear. This animal is said more frequently to attack a man on meeting him than to flee from him. When the Indians are about to go in quest of the white bear, previous to their departure they paint themselves and perform all those superstitious rites commonly observed when they make war on a neighbouring nation."

Dutifully, Lewis took his turn conning the boats, to allow Clark a chance to explore by land. Being a master of shanks' mare, like John Ledyard, he much preferred the walks along the shore to the enforced inactivity of the boats, although the latter did furnish him with an opportunity for concentrated bird-watching. His eyes sought out bald eagles, sparrow hawks and—high above—great flights of black and white cranes, making northing. As he jotted notes in the journal balanced on his knee, he groused, "The pirogue is so unsteady that I can scarcely write." When the boats stopped at a likely place to camp, Lewis observed Sacajawea performing the role of housekeeper, Shoshone style, for the entire detachment. "When we halted for dinner, the squaw busied herself in searching for the wild artichokes which the mice collect and deposit in large hoards. This operation she performed by penetrating the earth with a sharp stick about some small collections of driftwood. Her labour soon proved successful and she procured a good quantity of this root, which resembles that of the Jerusalem artichoke. . . ."

The boats were now creeping past bluffs seamed with lignite. The low-grade coal was afire and the strata threw out smoke and a sulphurous stink over the darkened shoreline of "lava" and sluffing pumice. The soldiers fetched floating pumice from the river, as souvenirs of what they thought to be a volcanic area. Testing the water where the alkali lay in a whitish blanket on the ground, like snow, Lewis found that it tasted like a mixture of water, table salt and Glauber's salts. Unfortunately, the amateur scientist had to put up with another of the occupational hazards of the dedicated investigator. He was not poisoned this time but he did find that the mineralized water was a powerful purgative. Gass showed him petrified logs, ideal for hones or whetstones, he averred, and Lewis's hunters continued to bring him specimens of fauna, such as plovers (actually avocets), hooting owls, wolf pups, buffalo calves and high-nest goose eggs.

Although they were passing through a land which had been hunted over by Rees and Assiniboins, whose pens or corrals for antelope drives were occasionally seen, Drouillard seldom let the party down, bringing in some kind of game every day and usually providing juicy venison steaks and roasts, or beaver tails, to go with the soggy biscuit of the boats' stores and the bullet-sized wild onions which Lewis himself gleaned from the countryside. Lewis cursed the treeless plains, not for their aridity or the lack of game, but because they allowed the almost ceaseless winds to whip across the Missouri beyond the White Earth River, completely unhindered. These gales not only stopped the progress of the boats but whipped up the fine, caustic sand into clouds which resembled smoke at a distance but pepper, close up. The dust storms blinded the men, afflicted them with sore eyes for days, and stopped Lewis's pocket watch in spite of the double case protecting it. "So penetrating is this sand," he wrote, "that we cannot keep any article free from it; in short, we are compelled to eat, drink and breathe it."

On April 25th, impatient as ever, Lewis called Scammon and, taking four men, hurried overland for the mouth of the long-awaited *Roche Jaune,* the legendary Yellowstone River. He wanted to hoard every bit of time. He had been studying this river from afar, for much of the winter, piecing together bits and pieces of information and misinformation from travelers. How many times had he read and reread those notes he had written at the fort? "This river is said to be nearly as large as the Missouri but is more rapid. It takes its rise in the Rocky Mountains with the waters of a river on which the Spaniards reside, but whether this stream be the North River [i.e., Rio Grande del Norte] or the waters of the Gulph of California, our information does not enable us to determine. . . . The Yellowstone River is navigable at all seasons of the year for boats or pirogues to the foot of the Rocky Mountains. . . . If Indian information can be relied upon, the river waters one of the finest portions of Louisiana, a country not yet hunted and abounding in animals of the fur kind. . . . We are informed that there is a sufficiency of timber near the mouth of this river for the purpose of erecting a fortification and the necessary buildings. In point of position, we have no hesitation in declaring our belief of its being one of the most eligible and necessary that can be chosen on the Missouri, as well in a Governmental point of view as that of affording to our citizens the benefit of a most lucrative fur trade.

"This establishment might be made to hold in check the views of the British North West Company on the fur trade of the upper part of the Missouri which, we believe, it is their intention to monopolize, if in their power. They have, for several years, maintained a partial trade with the Indian nations on the Missouri near this place [Fort Mandan], overland from their establishment at the extreme of Mouse River on the Assiniboine, unlicensed by the Spanish Government, then the sovereigns of this country. But since the United States have acquired Louisiana, we are informed that, relying on the privilege extended to them by our treaty with Great Britain, they intend fixing a permanent establishment on the Missouri near the mouth of Knife River, in the course of the present summer.

"If this powerful and ambitious Company are suffered uninterruptedly to prosecute their trade with the nations inhabiting the upper portion of the Missouri and thus acquire an influence with those people, it is not difficult to conceive the obstructions which they might, hereafter, through the medium of that influence, oppose to the will of our Government or the navigation of the Missouri. Whether the privileges extended to British subjects under existing treaties with that power will equally affect a territory not in our possession at the time those treaties were entered into is not for me to determine. But it appears to me that in this respect Louisiana is differently situated from the other territory of the United States.

"There is also a considerable fall on this [Yellowstone] River, within the mountains, but at what distance we never could learn. . . . The Indians inform us that a good road passes up this River to its extreme source, from whence it is but a short distance to the Spanish settlements." (By the time he was on his way home again, Lewis had convinced himself that the Yellowstone reached almost to the sources of the Willamette, Snake, Rio Grande, Big Horn and Platte!)

Long before he saw the junction of the Missouri and Yellowstone, Lewis correctly predicted its eventual importance as a commercial site. Thus he hurried forward to locate it with his astronomical instruments and to explore the ground. He was not disappointed when he caught sight of the union of the two great rivers from the top of a small hill which had blocked his view until he was almost upon them. "I had a most pleasing view of the country . . . one common and boundless pasture," he wrote, "particularly of the wide and fertile valleys formed by the Missouri and Yellowstone Rivers, which, occasionally unmasked by the woods on their borders, disclosed their meanderings for many miles in their passage through these delightful tracts of country."

While Lewis made astronomical observations, he had Joseph Field explore the Yellowstone. Field found that its current followed a very crooked course, obstacled with frequent sandbars. When the main party rendezvoused with him, Lewis issued a dram of whiskey to all hands, to celebrate their safe arrival at the important milestone of their long voyage. "This soon produced a fiddle," he wrote, "and they spent the evening with much hilarity, singing and dancing, and seemed as perfectly to forget their past toils as they appeared regardless of those to come."

The men were in a new kind of country as April ended. It was a land which reared itself into the highest bluffs most of the men had ever seen. From their tops stared the first mountain sheep they had seen. Several sharpshooters tried to bring down some of the animals but their shots failed to strike their mark. For days after their first encounter with these "ibex," grizzly spoor increased and there were occasional glimpses of the bears ascending the steep hills with surprising speed and ease. Once, two of Lewis's men, unarmed, were chased into camp by one of the bears as they tried to inspect their traplines. Lewis took a man and stalked two of the grizzlies. The hunters wounded both but one escaped. "The other," Lewis explained, "after my firing on him, pursued me seventy or eighty yards but, fortunately, had been so badly wounded that he was unable to pursue so closely as to prevent my charging my gun. We again repeated our fire and killed him." It was while retreating hastily before the onrush of the bleeding beast—not fully grown, yet weighing 300 pounds —that Lewis began to reconsider his earlier discounting of Indian tales of the bear's prowess. He finally admitted, "It is a much more furious and formidable animal [than other bears] and will frequently pursue the hunter when wounded. It is astonishing to see the wounds they will bear before they can be put to death."

However, Lewis was no mean hunter and a little vain of his own prowess with the rifled long gun. He was not yet willing to concede everything to the bullying behemoth—"The Indians may well fear this animal, equipped as they generally are with their bows and arrows or indifferent fusees. But in the hands of a skilled rifleman, they are by no means as formidable or dangerous as they have been represented."

The plains were now devoid of trees except for dead and rotton cottonwoods in the river bottom. The abandoned lodges which the men found were of driftwood beachcombed laboriously by the Indians. But as trees decreased, game increased. In this area, Lewis killed the largest elk he had ever seen—five feet three inches from point of hoof to top of shoulder. The herds of antelope were so large they supported satellite "gangs" of wolves and coyotes, the packs running to six to ten animals each. The predators dragged down males still weak from winter and females big with young. Lewis commented, "We scarcely see a gang of buffalo without observing a parcel of those faithful shepherds on their skirts, in readiness to take care of the maimed and wounded. . . . Although game is very abundant and gentle," wrote Lewis (Scammon killed antelope swimming the river),

168

"we only kill as much as is necessary for food and believe that two good hunters would conveniently supply a regiment with provisions."

While Lewis and Clark agreed that the Yellowstone-Missouri confluence should have top priority as a site for an American fort, their views on the best site for the post differed radically. Clark thought the bastion should be built at the lowest point, right on the river, to command its entire breadth. "Lewis disagreed, explaining, "It is true that it is much nearer both rivers and might answer very well but I think it rather too low to venture a permanent establishment, particularly if built of brick or other durable material at any considerable expense. For, so capricious and versatile are these rivers that it is difficult to say how long it will be until they direct the force of their currents against the narrow part of the low plain which, when they do, must yield to their influence. In such case, a few years only would be necessary for the annihilation of the plain and, with it, the fortification." Therefore, he walked with Clark through the woodland to a small lake and told his friend, "At the point of the high plain at the lower extremity of this lake, I think would be the most eligible site for an establishment."

April ended and May came in like a catamount. A gale threatened to snap the sails to tatters and to drive the boats on shore. The fleet split in twain and scurried for shelter on both shores; ice froze on the oars again as the Missouri played another cruel trick from its bottomless bag; an entire day's advance became no more than ten miles in the teeth of icy winds. Men fell sick and an inch of snow on the ground contrasted crazily with wild flowers on the windswept plains, the bunting of blooms on the Osage plains, and dollar-sized fresh leaves greening the cottonwoods.

The animals seemed as tame as those in a zoological garden. Even buffalo bulls let Lewis come within fifty paces; at times, he and his men literally had to push their way past bison cows and calves. Strolling up Two Thousand Mile Creek, not only was Lewis able to slip up behind two unwary porcupines and touch the waddling, bristly creatures with his espontoon, but he found perhaps the height of carelessness in the form of a goose's nest among some driftwood, with three eggs ready for the poacher.

The industrious beavers were so fearless that they left their lodges at midday to putter about their hydraulic works—and to fall prey to the soldier-trappers. The animals were everywhere, felling trees up to three feet in diameter for the bark. *Castor* was the cause of the first quarrel in the corps. As Lewis explained it, "One beaver was caught this morning by two different traps, having a foot in each. The traps belonged to different individuals, between whom a contest ensued which would have terminated, most probably, in a serious rencounter had not our timely arrival prevented it." Small wonder a fight was brewing; the animals were superb specimens. Said Lewis, "The beaver of this part of the Missouri are larger, fatter, more abundant and better clad in fur than those of any part of the country that I have yet seen."

Although buffalo calf suited Lewis's palate ("I think it equal to any veal I ever tasted"), he preferred beaver even more. "The flesh of the beaver is esteemed a delicacy among us. I think the tail a most delicious morsel. When boiled, it resembles in flavour the fresh tongues and sounds of the codfish and is usually sufficiently large to afford a plentiful meal for two men. . . . The men prefer the flesh of this animal to that of any other which we have, or are able to procure, at the moment. I eat heartily of the beaver, myself, and think it excellent, particularly the tail and liver."

After hiking about this hunter's paradise, Lewis had to note in his journal, "It is now only amusement for Captain Clark and myself to kill as much meat as the whole party can consume. I hope it may continue thus through our whole route, but this I do not much expect." But, for the moment at least, hunting was child's play. Like most of his men, Lewis was toughened up again after the winter layoff and thought nothing of shooting a deer during one of his pre-breakfast strolls and then carrying it a mile and a half to the boats, to round out his dawn constitutional.

Lewis's attitude toward the grizzlies was speedily converted to one of healthy awe when Clark and Drouillard put five balls through the lungs of one beast and five more in other sections of its 600-pound frame, only to see it swim the wide river to a sandbar where it took twenty minutes to die. Lewis tried out six gallons of grease from the bear's fat, which he put up for lard. He examined the beast's head and estimated that its maw was ten times the size of a black bear's. "I find that the curiosity of our party is pretty well satisfied with respect to this animal. The formidable appearance . . . added to the difficulty with which they die, even when shot through the vital parts, has staggered the resolution of some of them." Yet he felt obliged to add, "Others, however, seem keen for action with the bear," and he himself continued his lone nature walks, armed with his rifle and spearlike espontoon. "Thus equipped," he told President Jefferson, "I feel myself more than an equal match for a brown [grizzly] bear, provided I get him in open woods or near the water, but feel myself a little diffident with respect to an attack in the open plains. I have, therefore, come to a resolution to act on the defensive only, should I meet these gentlemen in the open country."

Beyond the Milk River, which Lewis mistook for the stream which the Indians poetically called the River Which Scolds at All Others (actually Maria's River, ahead), and which he mistakenly thought might lead directly to the Saskatchewan, Lewis examined perhaps the strangest stream of the entire voyage, the Big Dry River. "Today we passed the bed of the most extraordinary river that I ever beheld. It is as wide as the Missouri . . . and not containing a single drop of running water." But perhaps even more wondrous than the upside-down river, the giant grizzlies, the herds of game as tame as pets, was the total absence of Indians from this happiest of happy hunting grounds. Lewis was completely unprepared for such a situation. He noted on May 10th, "We sent out several hunters to scour the country. To this we were induced not so much from want of provisions as to discover the Indians." But the hunters always returned without news or views of the Assiniboins ("a viciously ill-disposed nation") or any other redskins. Half-pleased and half-displeased with his scouts' reports, an ambivalent Lewis wasted no time worrying about them. When he found his diplomatic avenues blocked, he simply turned to his scientific pursuits, walking off alone to be spared the banal small talk of the soldiers, studying the mule deer, which he named, and the grizzlies.

One day, Lewis was astounded to see one of his sick bay patients, Bratton, running at full speed up the beach toward him. But it was no case of a miraculous discovery; he was fleeing for his life. As he collapsed, he gasped that a grizzly, which he had shot, was after him. Lewis took seven men and tracked the beast by blood spatters on the willows and wild roses. They found the bear hidden in thick brush and put two bullets in its skull, killing the animal. Lewis examined the carcass and found that Bratton's ball had gone true, yet the beast had pursued him a half mile before returning another mile to dig a bed in the earth five feet long and two feet deep. A marveling Lewis wrote, "These bears, being so hard to die, rather intimidate us all. I must confess that I do not like the gentleman and had rather fight two Indians than one bear. There is no other chance to conquer them by a single shot but by shooting them through the brains and this becomes difficult in consequence of two large muscles which cover the sides of the forehead, and the sharp projection of the center of the frontal bone, which is also of a pretty good thickness."

Around their evening campfire, Lewis and Clark labored over their twin journals. Where once they had been parallel accounts but distinctive—Lewis's polished and literate, Clark's raw and amusing—they were now becoming, virtually, two copies of a single narrative. Clark's version was a paraphrase of Lewis's, differing little except for misspellings. The duplication for safety's sake was important, not individuality. Lewis found time to insert in his journal trivia which suggest what kind of a person he was. For example, he preserved the recipe for his favorite prairie dish—Charbonneau's White Pudding, actually a sausage. Charbonneau took buffalo intestines and stuffed them with a mixture of chopped meat, suet, pepper, salt and flour. It was then, in Lewis's words, "baptized in the Missouri with two dips and a flirt, and bobbed into the kettle. . . . After it was well boiled, it is taken and fried with bear's oil until it becomes brown, when it is ready to assuage the pangs of a keen appetite, such as travellers in the wilderness are seldom at a loss for."

The persistent winter still refused to die and in mid-May the men found that their moccasins froze overnight near the campfire. But these were annoyances, not threats. Danger came from grizzlies and the river itself. On May 14th six hunters encountered a grizzly. Four fired and two held their fire in reserve. All the rifle balls took effect (two through the lobes of the beast's lungs) yet it charged, openmouthed, at the men. The two reservists fired. Again the balls struck home, one breaking a shoulder, but the beast hardly broke stride. The men gave up their fumbling for ball, powder and patches; two pushed off in a canoe and the others ran to hide in the willows. Reloaded rifles belched again but the fusillade only seemed to make bruin more furious. The bear chased two of the hiding men over a 20-foot bank into the Missouri and came into the water after them. Finally, one of the men on shore put a bullet into the bear's skull. When they examined its carcass they found that *eight* rifle balls were imbedded in it.

At approximately the same time as the great battle with bruin, Lewis was having a nervous time himself, watching a squall hit the white pirogue, heeling it over on its beam ends. Charbonneau, at the helm, panicked. He luffed and the square sail's brace was torn from Cruzatte's hands. The boat was on the verge of upsetting. Only the resistance of the awning against the surface of the water prevented its turtling bottoms-up. Lewis fired his gun to attract Charbonneau's attention, gesturing to him to cut the halyards and take in sail, but the craven Charbonneau sat paralyzed with fear except to cross himself and mutter hoarse prayers. To save the precious cargo, Lewis almost committed suicide. As he recalled it, "While the pirogue lay on her side, finding I could not be heard, I, for a moment, forgot my own situation and, involuntarily, dropped my gun, threw aside my shot pouch and was in the act of unbuttoning my coat before I recollected the folly of the attempt I was about to make, which was to throw myself into the river and endeavour to swim to the pirogue. The pirogue was 300 yards distant; the waves so high that a pirogue could scarcely live in any situation, the water excessively cold and the stream rapid. Had I undertaken this project, therefore, there was a 100-to-1 but that I should have paid the forfeit of my life for the madness of my project but this, had the pirogue been lost, I should have valued but little."

Luckily, Cruzatte took command of the endangered craft. As Charbonneau cried to God for mercy, Cruzatte threatened to shoot him if he did not take hold of the rudder and do his duty like a man. Somehow he got the boat, barely afloat, to shore. Weak in relief, Lewis saw down on the bank and called for a glass of spirits, all around. For, as he said, "This accident was very near costing us dearly. Believing this vessel to be the most steady and safe, we had embarked on board of it our instruments, papers, medicine and the most valuable part of the merchandise which we still had in reserve as presents for the Indians. We had also embarked on board ourselves, with three men who could not swim and the squaw with the young child, all of whom—had the pirogue overset—would most probably have perished, as the waves were high and the pirogue upwards of 200 yards from the nearest shore." The damage was less than it might have been, thanks to Sacajawea, of whom Lewis said, "The Indian woman, to whom I ascribe equal fortitude and resolution with any person on board at the time of the accident, caught and preserved most of the light articles which were washed overboard."

But the run of bad luck was not yet over. That night, both officers were rudely shaken awake by the Sergeant of the Guard and rousted from their beds. The river had picked up an ally in the winds of its valley, which had picked up live coals from the campfire and blown them into a tree right over Lewis and Clark's *tipi,* setting the branches afire. The men moved just in time; shortly, the blazing tree collapsed and fell on their tent site. "Had we been a few minutes later," commented Lewis, "we should have been crushed to atoms."

Just short of the Mussel Shell River, it was Scammon's turn. As the men cordelled the boats up the narrowing Missouri, now a handsome, clear stream, Lewis's dog tried to help a hunter by retrieving a wounded beaver in the river. There was still plenty of fight left in the beaver; he was in his element; he was armed with terrible cutting weapons in his teeth. The beaver bit Scammon through a hind leg, cutting an artery. Lewis fought to stop the gush of blood but sadly wrote, that evening, "I fear it will yet prove fatal to him." Fortunately his doctoring of his pet was completely successful.

In the high plains, eroded brown hills destitute even of grass and shrubs, the days rolled on like tumbleweeds, one hardly distinguishable from the last. Dangerous riffles appeared, leading Lewis to double-man the pirogues, and bison disappeared. "Buffalo are very scarce," he lamented, "and I begin to fear our harvest of White Puddings is at an end." And *still* there were no Indians.

But on May 26th, the same day that he had a narrow escape from a rattlesnake, Lewis's spirits were recharged by the sight which greeted his eyes near Cow Creek, Montana. "On arriving to the summit of one of the highest points in the neighbourhood, I thought myself repaid for my labour, as from this point I beheld the Rocky Mountains for the first time. . . . I could only discover a few of the most elevated points above the horizon, the most remarkable of which, by my pocket compass, I found bore north 65°. . . . These points of the Rocky Mountains were covered with snow and the sun shown on it in such a manner as to give me the most plain and satisfactory view. . . . While I viewed these mountains I felt a secret pleasure in finding myself so near the head of the heretofore-conceived boundless Missouri. . . . But when I reflected on the difficulties which this snowy barrier would most probably throw in my way to the Pacific, and the sufferings and hardships of myself and party in them, it in some measure counterbalanced the joy I had felt in the first moments in which I had gazed upon them. But, as I have always held it a crime to anticipate evils, I will believe it a good, comfortable, road until I am compelled to believe differently."

The crews successfully passed the dangerous shallows of Lone Pine Rapids and camped. In the middle of the night, the whole party was turned out by an alarm but the threat was not a skulking grizzly or an Indian war party, but a blundering bull buffalo. The shaggy animal ran up the bank after swimming the river, clambering right over the unlucky white pirogue, and galloped into the camp. Its hooves dug into the ground less than 18 inches from the heads of some of the sleeping men. In Lewis's words, "When he came near the tent, my dog saved us by causing him to change his coarse a second time, which he did by turning a little to the right, and was quickly out of sight, leaving us, by this time, all in an uproar, with our guns in our hands." Miraculously, not a man was even scratched. But, said the Virginian, "It appears that the white pirogue, which contains our most valuable stores, is attended by some evil genie."

The morning after the buffalo came calling, Lewis explored the mouth of a clear-flowing, timbered river which he called the Bighorn. When Clark asked that his young lady fair, Julia (Judy) Hancock, of Fincastle, Virginia, be remembered cartographically, Lewis gladly renamed the stream Judith's River. He examined the remains of 126 recent campfires and a litter of mussel shells and abandoned moccasins, which showed that the red men had not vanished from the earth entirely, then treated his men to a dram of tipple. He was surprised at the results: "Notwithstanding the allowance of spirits we issued did not exceed one half-gill per man (and a full gill was but a quarter-pint), several of them were considerably affected by it. Such is the effects of abstaining for some time from the use of spiritous liquors. They were all very merry."

The explorer was pleased to see Ash Rapid, where the hills closed ranks about the river. The dangerous, shoaly waters were clearer, heralding the mountains. Near here, Lewis's attention was caught by a powerful stench. He then noted an inordinate number of lazy and tame wolves, fat as Strasbourg geese and so lethargic that Clark killed one with his espontoon. The reason for their sloth explained the stink. The boats were drawing up on a 120-foot precipice whose base was littered with the remains of buffalo which had gone over the edge. "The water appeared to have washed away a part of this immense pile of slaughter and still there remained the fragments of at least a hundred carcasses. They created a horrid stench."

Lewis named the neighboring stream Slaughter River, then explained to Jefferson the phenomenon of the buffalo cliffs. "In this manner, the Indians of the Missouri country destroy vast herds of buffalo at a stroke. For this purpose, one of the most active and fleet young men is selected and disguised in a robe of buffalo skin, having also the skin of the buffalo's head, with the ears and horns fastened on his head in the form of a cap. Thus caparisoned, he places himself at a convenient distance from a herd of buffalo and a precipice proper for the purpose, which happens in many places on this River for miles together. The other Indians now surround the herd on the back and flanks and, at a signal agreed-upon, all show themselves at the same time, moving forward towards the buffalo. The disguised Indian or decoy has taken care to place himself sufficiently nigh the buffalo to be noticed by them when they take to flight, and, running before them, they follow him in full speed to the precipice, the cattle behind driving those in front over and, seeing them go, [they] do not look or hesitate about following until the whole are precipitated down the precipice, forming one common mass of dead and mangled carcasses. The decoy, in the meantime, has taken care to secure himself in some cranny or crevice of the cliff which he had previously prepared for that purpose. The part of the decoy, I am informed, is extremely dangerous. If they are not fleet runners, the buffalo tread them under foot and crush them to death and, sometimes, drive them over the precipice where they perish in common with the buffalo."

With the mountains nearing, the current of the river was now too strong for the oars and the men had to struggle with the tow-rope in cold water up to their armpits. They abandoned their slick moccasins though the rocks cut their bare soles. Lewis was never more proud of his volunteers—"Their labour is incredibly painful and great and yet these faithful fellows bear it without a murmur." At noon respites, he showed his appreciation by treating them to whiskey.

The straining men at the cordelle had little time for sight-seeing but Lewis and Clark, while hardly men of leisure, were able to gaze for hours on the enfolding panorama of the river front. Grotesquely eroded and castellated bluffs led Lewis to describe them as lofty structures and towers, parapeted and stocked with nature's statuary and sculptured columns. In his imagination they resembled elegant ruins with broken pedestals and capitals rather than cliffs etched by wind and rain and plastered with the mud-daub nests of martins, or bank swallows. Bedazzled by these bluffs, Lewis wrote, "As we passed on, it seemed as if those scenes of visionary enchantment would never have an end. . . . So perfect, indeed, are those walls that I should have thought that Nature had attempted here to rival the human art of masonry had I not recollected that she had first begun the work."

By June 2nd, the bluffs were lowering, the current gentling. Towing was easier and game became plentiful again. Lewis and the hunters secured elkskins as well as meat that day, so that he could cover his iron boat frame. Drouillard and Charbonneau had a narrow escape from a grizzly that day and the following day was even more memorable; the corps reached a fork in the Missouri and perched there on the horns of a dilemma. No Indian had scratched a map in the sand at Fort Mandan to show this junction. No information had told Lewis which branch he should take up from this critical confluence.

CHAPTER XIII

———◆●◆———

THE HIGH ROAD

Before the cession of Louisiana to the United States, this was the region of fable. Fancy peopled it, and a thousand miraculous tales were related. The mammoth, that wonder of creation, it was thought might be there, and Welsh Indians, with remnants of the Jewish tribes.
—ZADOK CRAMER, *The Navigator,* 1814

ENCAMPED at the puzzling forks in the river, Meriwether Lewis realized that his next decision, should it be the wrong one, might be disastrous. Two months of the traveling season were already gone. If he led his men off on a wild-goose chase up the wrong fork, he would have to backtrack and ascend the other branch, losing days and perhaps weeks. A blunder like this, he warned Clark, "would not only lose us the whole of this season but would probably so dishearten the party that it might defeat the expedition."

Lewis carefully curbed his natural impetuosity and impatience because of the gravity of the decision he alone had to make. He and Clark compared the two forks in depth, width and rapidity of current, then surveyed the terrain which was "one vast plain, in which innumerable herds of buffalo were seen, attended by their constant shepherds, the wolves. The solitary antelope, which now had their young, were distributed over its face; some herds of elk were also seen. The verdure perfectly clothed the ground, the weather was pleasant and fair; to the south we saw a range of lofty mountains."

Because Lewis found the north fork to be deeper but more turbid and slower flowing, most of the corpsmen voiced the opinion that it was the true Missouri. But Lewis confided to Clark and his journal: "If we were to give our opinions, I believe we should be in the minority. Certain it is that the North Fork gives the colouring matter a character which is retained from hence to the Gulf of Mexico [but] I am confident that this river rises in, and passes a great distance through, an open plain country. I expect that it has some of its sources on the eastern side of the Rocky Mountains, south of the Saskatchewan, but that it does not penetrate the first range of those mountains and that much the greater part of its sources are in a northwardly direction towards the lower and middle parts of the Saskatchewan in the open plains. Convinced I am that if it penetrates the Rocky Mountains to any great distance, its waters would be clearer, unless it should run an immense distance, indeed, after leaving those mountains, through the level plain, in order to acquire its turbid hue."

Lewis knew that there was but one sure way to identify the correct course of the Missouri—by finding the legendary Great Falls, of which the Indians spoke with awe. He was still puzzled that the Indians had not mentioned the forks where he stood: "What astonishes us a little is that the Indians, who appeared to be so well acquainted with the geography of this country, should not have mentioned the river on [the] right hand, if it be not the Missouri." The truth was that the North Fork, Maria's River, or River Which Scolds at All Others, had simply been misplaced downstream in the memory of Lewis's informants.

While their commander pondered his dilemma, the men dressed skins for clothing and moccasins for the rugged mountains ahead. Some made double-ply soles for their moccasins to thwart the bruising ground which, cut by buffalo hooves when wet, baked into sharp ridges under the hot sun. Against the stabbing prickly pears there was no sure protection. Lewis eyed his men and noticed that "many of them have their feet so mangled and bruised with the stones and rough ground over which they passed barefoot that they can scarcely walk or stand; at least, it is with great pain they do either. . . . But, notwithstanding the difficulties past, or those which seem now to menace us, they remain perfectly cheerful."

The information his scouts brought back from a reconnaissance proving inconclusive, Lewis decided that he and Clark would have to explore the two forks. For the first time, incredibly, in a long career on the frontier, Lewis had to fix himself an enlisted man's pack. Although he had tramped over half of America and camped alone of nights, he had done so, before, with only a coat or blanket as duffle. This time he took a regular pack, like the other men . . . "the first time in my life that I had ever prepared a burthen of this kind and, I am fully convinced that it will not be the last."

Early on June 4th, the two reconnaissance parties set out, Lewis taking the North Fork, Clark the other. By the next day, Clark had seen enough to convince him he was following the real Missouri. On the 6th, some sixty miles from the stream's mouth, Lewis knew beyond the shadow of a doubt that the river he was following did not lead west. He had his men build rafts but they were unseaworthy because of the slender poles which had to be used, for want of better timber, and they were abandoned. Therefore, Lewis led his men off across the rain-spattered plain in a gait that ate up twenty-three miles by camping time, although the ground was almost as slick as ice from the incessant rain. The treacherousness of the slippery soil underfoot was brought home forcibly to Lewis: "In passing along the face of one of these bluffs today, I slipped at a narrow pass of about thirty yards in length and but for a quick and fortunate recovery by means of my espontoon, I should have been precipitated into the river down a craggy precipice of about ninety feet. I had scarcely reached a place on which I could stand with tolerable safety, even with the assistance of my espontoon, before I heard a voice behind me cry out, 'God! God! Captain! What shall I do?' On turning, I found it was Windsor, who had slipped and fallen about the center of this narrow pass and was lying prostrate while he was holding on with the left arm and foot as well as he could, which appeared to be with much difficulty. I discovered his danger, and the trepidation which he was in gave me still further concern, for I expected, every instant, to see him lose his strength and slip off. Although much alarmed at his situation, I disguised my feelings and spoke very calmly to him and assured him that he was in no kind of danger; to take the knife out of his belt behind him with his right hand and dig a hole with it in the face of the bank to receive his right foot; which he did and then raised himself to his knees. I then directed him to take off his mockersons [sic] and to come forward on his hands and knees, holding the knife in one hand and the gun in the other. This he happily effected and escaped."

Lewis took to the river itself to avoid the dangerous ravines, floundering in the water or slithering along the muddy bank at the head of his men. When the bottom dropped off beneath their feet, they swam, and when the water near the sheer bluffs was over their heads, Lewis laboriously cut footsteps in the bank with his knife so that they would not have to swim all the way back to the Forks. The only bright spot was that the bottomland woods were natural aviaries. The Virginian was delighted with them. "When the sun began to shine today, these birds appeared to be very gay and sung most enchantingly. I observed among them the brown thrush, robin, turtle dove, linnet, goldfinch, the large and small blackbird, wren and several other birds of less note."

The mud-spattered captain could not convince his men that they were not floundering in the Missouri itself. "The whole of my party, to a man—except myself—were fully persuaded that this river is the Missouri but, being fully of the opinion that it was neither the main stream nor that which would be advisable for us to take, I determined to give it a name and, in honour of Miss Maria Wood, called it Maria's River." Miss Wood was Lewis's cousin and, quite likely, the object of his affections at the time. "It is true that the hue of the waters of this turbulent stream but illy comport with the pure, celestial virtues and amiable qualifications of that lovely fair one, but, on the other hand, it is a noble river, one destined to become, in my opinion, an object of contention between the two great powers of America and Great Britain with respect to the adjustment of the northwestwardly boundary of the former, and that it will become one of the most interesting branches of the Missouri in a commercial point of view, I have but little doubt, as it abounds with animals of the fur kind, and most probably furnishes a safe and direct communication to that productive country of valuable furs exclusively enjoyed at present by the subjects of His Britannic Majesty; in addition to which, it passes through a rich, fertile and one of the most beautifully picturesque countries that I ever beheld. . . ."

At five o'clock he led his sodden, muddied cohorts into camp where Clark anxiously awaited him, worried because he was two days overdue.

Lewis was gratified that his men, all of whom thought he had chosen the wrong branch, were ready to follow him. He decided to hurry forward and find the Falls, to convince them. He was in very poor shape to make an assault on the Falls. "I felt myself very unwell this morning," he wrote, "and took a portion of salts from which I feel much relief." But because time was of the essence, he determined to set out in two days. While he "rested," he established a ropewalk, to make a towline of elkskin, sent out hunters, and inspected Cruzatte's cunningly hidden caches, as well as the hiding place for the red pirogue on an island in the mouth of Maria's River.

While he was not so ill that he felt it necessary to join Sacajawea in being bled by Clark, Lewis was still feeble from dysentery when he swung up his pack and led Drouillard, Joseph Field, Gibson and Goodrich to the Teton (Tansy or Rose) River, where he halted. "I determined to take dinner here but before the meal was prepared, I was taken with such violent pain in the intestines that I was unable to partake of the feast of the marrow bones. My pain still increased and, towards evening, was attended with a high fever. Finding myself unable to march, I determined to prepare a camp of willow boughs and remain all night. Having brought no medicine with me, I resolved to try an experiment with some simples and the chokecherry which grew abundantly in the bottom and first struck my attention. I directed a parcel of the small twigs to be gathered, stripped of their leaves, cut into pieces of about two inches in length, and boiled in water until a strong black decoction of an astringent taste was produced. At sunset, I took a pint of this decoction and, about an hour after, repeated the dose. By 10 in the evening, I was entirely relieved from pain and, in fact, every symptom of the disorder forsook me. My fever abated, a gentle perspiration was produced and I had a comfortable and refreshing night's rest."

Another tot of chokecherry extract on June 12th not only put him on his feet but enabled Lewis to help kill two grizzlies. "These fellows leave a formidable impression in the mud or sand," he noted, after examining a series of great paw prints made by one of the beasts. "I measured one this evening which was eleven inches long, exclusive of the talons, and seven and one-fourth inches in width." Still weak from his bout with the intestinal disorder, Lewis had to call a halt to his march after "only" a 27-mile advance. But he was able to eat heartily and to join his Izaak Walton, Private Goodrich, in some fishing. He also scanned the mountains on the horizon. "They appear to be formed of several ranges, each succeeding range rising higher than the preceding one until the most distant appear to lose their snowy tops in the clouds. This was an august spectacle and still rendered more formidable by the recollection that we had them to pass." He also sized up isolated, monolithic Square Butte and Crown Butte like a prairie Vaubin, remarking, "These inaccessible heights appeared like the ramparts of immense fortifications. I have no doubt but [that], with very little assistance from art, they might be rendered impregnable."

Beyond the buttes, he split his party, sending Field, Drouillard and Gibson to the flanks to hunt while he and Goodrich hewed to the river, seeking some sign of the Falls. Before they could see them they heard their thunderous rush. "My ears were saluted with the agreeable sound of a fall of water and, advancing a little further, I saw the spray arise above the plain like a column of smoke, which would frequently disappear again in an instant, caused, I presume, by the wind which blew pretty hard from the southwest. . . . I hurried down the hill, to gaze on this sublimely grand spectacle . . . the grandest sight I ever beheld . . . the irregular and somewhat projecting rocks below receive the water in its passage down and break it into a perfect white foam which assumes a thousand forms in a moment, sometimes flying up in jets of sparkling foam to the height of 15 or 20 feet and are scarcely formed before large rolling bodies of the same beaten and foaming water is thrown over and conceal them. In short, the rocks seem to be most happily fixed to present a sheet of the whitest beaten froth for 200 yards in length and about 80 feet perpendicular. The waters, after descending, strike against the butment . . . on which I stand and seem to reverberate and, being met by the more impetuous current, they roll and swell into half-formed billows of great height which rise and again disappear in an instant."

Lewis wished he had the descriptive talent of a poet or painter in order to better record the scene so long concealed from civilized man. In fact, he admitted, "After writing this imperfect description, I again viewed the Fall and was so much disgusted with the imperfect idea which it conveyed that I determined to draw my pen across it and begin again. But then I reflected that I could not perhaps succeed better than penning the first impression of the mind. . . . I most sincerely regretted that I had not brought a *camera oscura* with me, by the assistance of which even I could have hoped to have done better but, alas, this was also out of my reach. . . . I hope still to give to the world some faint idea of an object which, at this moment, fills me with such pleasure and astonishment and which, of its kind, I will venture to assert is second to but one of the known world."

After marveling at the sight some more, Lewis finally broke away and designated a camping place while he set off to find a landing point from which to begin the portage around the Falls. Although he was disappointed in his quest for dockage for his little fleet, it was a most exhilarating day which drew to a close, and Lewis keenly enjoyed his dinner. "My fare is really sumptuous this evening—buffalo's humps, tongues and marrow bones, fine trout, parched meal, pepper and salt, and a good appetite. The last is not considered the least of the luxuries."

The next morning's sun saw Lewis striding out of camp to see what new wonders might unfold before his eyes. "Hearing a tremendous roaring above me, I continued my route across the point of a hill a few hundred yards further and was again presented by one of the most beautiful objects in nature, a cascade of about 50 feet, perpendicular, stretching at right angles across the River from side to side to the distance of a quarter of a mile. Here the River pitched over a shelving rock with an edge as regular and as straight as if formed by art, without a niche or break in it. The water descends in one even and uninterrupted sheet to the bottom where, dashing against the rocky bottom [it] rises into foaming billows of great height and rapidly glides away, hissing, flashing and sparkling as it departs. . . . I now thought that if a skilful painter had been asked to make a beautiful cascade, he would most probably have presented the precise image of this one. Nor could I for some time determine on which of those two great cataracts to bestow the palm, on this or on that which I had discovered yesterday. At length, I determined between these two great rivals for glory, that this was pleasingly beautiful, while the other was sublimely grand." Pushing on, he found two more, smaller, falls, one (Black Eagle Falls) remarkable for the island below it—"a beautiful island, well timbered, is situated [in] the middle of the River. On this island, on a cottonwood tree, an eagle has placed her nest. A more inaccessible spot I believe she could not have found for neither man nor beast dare pass those gulfs which separate her little domain from the shores."

Climbing a hill, he found a vast and beautiful plain spread out before his eyes. The great sweep of terrain was blotched with black herds of buffalo. Above the Falls, toward the Medicine River, now called the Sun River, the unruffled sheet of water which was the Missouri was dotted with great flocks of geese. So bewitched was Lewis with the fantastic Eden that, after shooting a buffalo for his lonely supper, he completely forgot what had become a reflex action to him—the reloading of his rifle. The lapse came near being, literally, the mistake of his life. The succession of events which followed this careless omission was stamped on his memory for the rest of his life:

"While I was gazing attentively on the poor animal, discharging blood in streams from his mouth and nostrils, expecting him to fall every instant . . . a large white, or rather, brown [i.e grizzly] bear had perceived me and crept up on me, within twenty steps before I discovered him. In the first moment I drew up my gun to shoot but, at the same instant, recollected that she was not loaded and that he was too near for me to hope to perform this operation before he reached me, as he was then briskly advancing on me. It was an open level plain, not a bush within

miles nor a tree within less than three hundred yards of me. The
river bank was sloping and not more than three feet above the
level of the water. In short, there was no place by means of
which I could conceal myself from this monster until I could
charge my rifle. In this situation, I thought of retreating in a
brisk walk as fast as he was advancing until I could reach a tree
about 300 yards below me but I had no sooner turned myself
about [than] he pitched at me, open-mouthed, and at full speed.
I ran about 80 yards and found he gained on me, fast. I then ran
into the water. The idea struck me to get into the water to such
depth that I could stand and he would be obliged to swim and I
could, in that situation, defend myself with my espontoon. At
this instant, he arrived at the edge of the water within about 20
feet of me. The moment I put myself into this attitude of defense,
he suddenly wheeled about, as if frightened, declined the combat
on such unequal grounds and retreated with as great precipitation as he had just before pursued me. As soon as I saw him run
off in that manner, I returned to the shore and charged my gun,
which I had still retained in my hand throughout this curious
adventure.

"I saw him run through the level, open plain about three miles
till he disappeared in the woods on Medicine River. During the
whole of this distance, he ran at full speed, sometimes appearing
to look behind him as if he expected pursuit. I now began to
reflect on this novel occurrence and endeavoured to account for
this sudden retreat of the bear. I at first thought that he had not
smelt me before he arrived at the water's edge so near me, but
then I reflected that he pursued me for about 80 or 90 yards
before I took to the water and, on examination, saw the ground
torn up with his talons immediately on the impression of my
steps. And the cause of his alarm still remains with me mysterious and unaccountable. So it was, and I felt myself not a little
gratified that he had declined the combat. My gun reloaded, I felt
confidence once more in my strength and determined not to be
thwarted in my design of visiting Medicine River but determined
never again to suffer my piece to be longer empty than the time
she necessarily required to charge her."

After exploring a stretch of the Medicine River, Lewis returned toward the "shoots" (chutes, or falls) of the Missouri. On the way, he surprised a strange animal and, resting his rifle on his espontoon as if it were an ancient firelock, he fired at it, but it disappeared into a burrow. He described it as "of the tiger kind"; perhaps it was a carcajou, or wolverine. Whatever it was, the animal gave him quite a start, for "it crouched itself down like a cat, looking immediately at me as if it designed to spring on me. . . . It now seemed to me that all the beasts in the neighbourhood had made a league to destroy me, or that some fortune was disposed to amuse herself at my expence, for I had not proceeded more than three hundred yards from the burrow of this tigercat before three bull buffalo, which were feeding with a large herd about half a mile from me on my left, separated from the herd and ran full speed towards me. I thought at least to give them some amusement and altered my direction to meet them. When they arrived within a hundred yards they made a halt, took a good view of me, and retreated with precipitation.

"I then continued my route homewards, passed the buffalo which I had killed but did not think it prudent to remain all night at this place which, really, from the succession of curious adventures, wore the impression on my mind of enchantment. At sometimes, for a moment, I thought it might be a dream, but the prickly pears which pierced my feet severely once in a while, particularly after it grew dark, convinced me that I was really awake and that it was necessary to make the best of my way to camp."

Lewis arrived in camp after dark and found the party uneasy over his safety. "They had formed a thousand conjectures, all of which equally forboding my death." But the "victim" ate a hearty supper and, much fatigued, rolled into his blankets for a good night's sleep. When he awoke next day, he found a large rattlesnake coiled, some ten feet from him, on the leaning trunk of the tree under which he slept. He killed it.

Rejoining Clark and the main party, Lewis set up Portage Creek Camp and Clark reconnoitered the 18-mile portage route. Lewis then set his men to work to make a rude cart to haul the canoes and baggage over the portage trail. He also doctored Sacajawea, who was ill. When Clark returned, he reported a portage impossible on the south side because of deep ravines.

Lewis begged to differ. "Good or bad, we must make the portage," he reminded his friend. "Not withstanding this report, I am still convinced that a good portage may be had on this side, at least much better than on the other, and nearer." The wagon-making party brought better news. The problem of making Mexican *carreta*-like wheels was solved. Recorded Lewis, "We were fortunate to find one cottonwood tree just below the entrance to Portage Creek that was large enough to make our carriage wheels, about 22 inches in diameter. Fortunate, I say, because I do not believe that we could find another of the same size, perfectly round, within 20 miles of us." He had the pirogue's mast cut to form two axletrees and the groaning, clumsily wheeled cart was soon being hauled by the men overland.

Portaging was slow. The mud was deep, axles broke. A freak hailstorm bombarded everyone, knocking some of the hatless men down and cutting and bruising them. Lewis scooped up many of the stones, which covered the ground in an icy sheet, and used them to cool the drinking water of the hard-working men. He wrote of them in admiration again. "At every halt these poor fellows tumble down and are so much fatigued that many of them are asleep in an instant. In short, their fatigues are incredible. Some are limping from the soreness of their feet; others faint and unable to stand for a few minutes, with heat and fatigue. Yet, no one complains; all go with cheerfulness."

The tired men were made uneasy in camp by the grizzlies which hung about, once stealing 30 pounds of buffalo suet from the camp. Lewis believed their presence was not due to curiosity or ferocity but simply because he and his men had camped in the middle of the animals' normal scavenging ground. Skeletons of bison clung to the shore like macabre driftwood, marking where the currents washed dead buffalo "to afford fine amusement for the bears, wolves and birds of prey. They may be one reason, and I think not a bad one, either, that the bears are so tenacious of their right of soil in this neighbourhood. . . . The white bears have become so troublesome to us that I do not think it prudent to send one man alone on an errand of any kind, particularly where he had to pass through the brush. . . . They come close around our camp every night but have never yet ventured to attack us and our dog gives us timely notice of their visits. He keeps constantly patrolling all night. I have made the men sleep with their arms by them, as usual, for fear of accidents. . . . My dog seems to be in a constant state of alarm with these bears and keeps barking all night. We have, therefore, determined to beat up their quarters tomorrow and kill them or drive them from these haunts."

The next day, Lewis launched his anti-grizzly campaign via a frontal assault. Sergeant Gass played war correspondent, reporting the engagement as follows: "In the evening, the most of the Corps crossed over to an island to attack and rout its monarch, a large bear, that held possession and seemed to defy all that would attempt to besiege him there. Our troops, however, stormed the place, gave no quarter, and its commander fell. Our army retired the same evening to camp without having suffered any loss on their side."

Independence Day was celebrated by an alfresco banquet which caused the commander to write, "We had no just cause to covet the sumptuous feasts of our countrymen on this day." He and his men tore into bacon, beans, buffalo beef, and suet dumplings. At 4 P.M. the officers gave a party, serving out the last of the spirits to the men except for a modest reserve in Lewis's medicine chest. The soldiers, after toasting the Glorious Fourth, danced to the fiddle until a 9 P.M. shower dampened their enthusiasm. But even in their blankets they continued the mirth, exchanging songs, jokes and banter until late at night. The next morning, Lewis let the men relax and many visited the Falls.

The Fourth of July marked for Lewis another irrevocable decision—not to send a canoe back with dispatches. His reasons? "Not having seen the Snake Indians, or knowing, in fact, whether to calculate on their friendship or hostility, we have conceived our party sufficiently small and, therefore, have concluded not to dispatch a canoe with a part of our men to St. Louis, as we had intended earlier in the spring. We fear, also, that such a measure might possibly hazard the fate of the expedition. We have never hinted to anyone of the party that we had such a scheme in contemplation, and all appear perfectly to have made up their minds to succeed in the expedition or perish in the attempt."

CHAPTER XIV

———◆•◆———

THE SKY-PROPPING MOUNTAINS

We shall have much geographical information from our Western travellers. Really, to have journeyed from the seat of our National Government quite across the Continent to the great Western Ocean is a rare performance. It does honour to our national enterprize and will afford the most substantial additions to Natural History. I anticipate much delight from the conversation of Captain Lewis relative to his successful expedition.

—DR. SAMUEL E. MITCHELL to John Vaughan,
November 5, 1806

BY INDEPENDENCE DAY, 1805, Lewis was ready to rename his folding boat—from *Experiment* to *Fiasco*. He had been very optimistic at first: "She has assumed her shape and looks extremely well. She will be very light, more so than any other vessel of her size that I ever saw." Unfortunately, the trim craft leaked like a sieve. Had Lewis put his boat in the water for long, she would have submerged like Bushnell's *Turtle* or Fulton's *Nautilus*. He hoped that the skin of the hull would hold together if he payed the seams more heavily. But here, too, fate dealt him another unkind cut. "Our tar kiln," he lamented, "which ought to have begun to run this morning, has yielded no tar as yet and I am much afraid will not yield any. If so, I fear the whole operation will be useless. I fear I have committed another blunder also in sewing the skins with a needle which has sharp edges. These have cut the skin and, as it stands, I discover that the thong does not fill the holes as I expected, tho' I made them sew with a large thong for that purpose." A little later he added a forlorn footnote: "No appearance of tar yet, and I am now confidant that we shall not be able to obtain any, a serious misfortune."

But Lewis was stubborn and the metal brainchild was his next of kin. He could not yet disown it although he almost despaired of its ever floating on the surface of the Missouri. He turned the craft over, placed it on a scaffold, keel to the sun, then kindled fires beneath it to dry it out. He recalled later, "I then set a couple of men to pounding of charcoal to form a composition with some beeswax which we have, and buffalo tallow, now my only hope and resource for paying the boat. I sincerely hope it may answer, yet I fear it will not. The boat in every other respect completely answers my most sanguine expectations. She is not yet dry and [yet] eight men can carry her with the greatest ease. She is strong and will carry at least 8,000 pounds with her suite of hands." But he was quickly forced to add, "The stitches began to gape very much since she has begun to dry." He applied two coats of the sticky composition, which added much to the craft's appearance, and launched it on July 8th. "She lay like a perfect cork on the water," he exulted.

A windstorm whistled in to put an end to Lewis's launching ceremony and, in the end, sounded a requiem for the *Experiment*. For when he was able to return from the shelter he had sought from the storm, it was to find that his boat had sunk like a plummet. The composition over which he had labored had separated from the hides, cracking, scaling off and exposing the skin beneath, and letting water into the boat from seams and awl and needle holes. She leaked like a colander.

Bitterly, Lewis conveyed his frustration and disappointment: "She will not answer. I need not add that this circumstance mortified me not a little. . . . I now find that the section formed of the buffalo hide, on which some hair had been left, answered much the best purpose. . . . Had I formed her with buffalo skins, singed not quite close as I had done those I employed, she would have answered even with this composition. But to make any further experiments in our present situation seemed to me madness.

The buffalo had principally deserted us and the season was advancing fast. I bade *adieu* to my boat and her expected services." Lewis sank the vessel to loosen the skins from the frame so that he could salvage and cache the metal, ordered axmen to hew out two dugouts to replace his collapsible craft, then gave the frame decent burial.

July 15th was the day on which to proceed. The two new pirogues gave him a fleet of eight boats, all heavily laden with dried meat, pemmican and "grease." He urged the men to discard or cache unnecessary gear in order to make more room for victuals. In his diary he noted, "We eat an immensity of meat. It requires four deer, an elk and a deer or one buffalo to supply us plentifully twenty-four hours. Meat now forms our food, principally, as we reserve our flour, parched meal and corn as much as possible for the Rocky Mountains, which we are shortly to enter and where, from the Indian accounts, game is not very abundant."

To lighten the canoes further, Lewis walked the first day, taking his almost-constant hunting companion, Drouillard, and two invalids. They marched to the very base of the Rockies where the Missouri's waters wrenched themselves loose from the grip of the mountains and swung around the foot of the great monolith which Lewis named the Tower. From this starting mark, they began a mad dash. When they made camp, Lewis squatted on his haunches like the other men to wolf down a frugal meal. The onetime Beau Brummel of Ivy, Virginia, was beginning to look like an Indian. Deeply tanned, wearing greasy buckskins, he saluted Drouillard's cooking: "For the first time I ate of the small guts [of the buffalo] in the Indian style, without any preparation of washing or other cleaning, and found them very good." For dessert he had yellow or black currants, finding the wild berries far superior to anything cultivated in the States.

Now the Missouri and its shelves narrowed until Lewis felt hemmed in by cliffs on which bighorn mountain sheep bounded. "Every object here wears a dark and gloomy look," he observed. "The towering and projecting rocks in many places seemed ready to tumble on us. The river appears to have forced its way through this immense body of solid rock for the distance of five and three-quarters miles and where it makes its exit below, [it] has thrown on either side vast columns of rocks, mountains high. . . . From the singular appearance of this place, I called it the Gate of the Rocky Mountains."

Assuming that the reports of his hunters' rifles were alarming the Indians, Lewis decided to send Clark forward with a small squad of scouts to contact the Snakes before the discharges should cause them to melt away. Suddenly, Lewis spied smoke about seven miles ahead. It was the Shoshones, at last! But when he came up, he found that the Snakes had just fired the tall grass to warn their fellow tribesmen of the onset of the whites. He ordered small flags flown from the canoes to show spying eyes that their occupants were whites and not the dreaded Blackfeet. When he arrived at Clark's camp, Lewis offered to take over the redhead's scouting assignment but Clark insisted on continuing, despite his fatigue and blistered feet.

While Clark forged ahead, Lewis remained in charge of the boats. The river exited from the gorge and entered an extensive plain. It relaxed, spread out and filled with islands. So many islets and sandbars did the Missouri spawn that Lewis had to take to a rise on foot to find a channel for his flotilla. But still the river kept its crystalline clarity. When Lewis shot an otter, the animal sank to the cobbled bottom but he could see it clearly in eight feet of water. He dove in, retrieved it and had a refreshing swim, to boot, in 80° weather. Sacajawea recognized more and more of this terrain. It was her native Snake country. She showed Lewis where she had gathered wild onions as a girl and in a lush area of rabbitberries pointed out the bank of red earth where Shoshone warriors secured pigment. Wrote Lewis, "The Indian woman assures us that this is the river on which her relations live; and that has cheered the spirits of the party who now begin to console themselves with the anticipation of shortly seeing the head of the Missouri, yet unknown to the civilized world."

Unknown to the Virginian, he and his men were passing over a gold-rich area, Montana's El Dorado of the 1860's. He had not time to prospect, in any case. His eyes were completely occupied with seeking Indians on the horizon and in piloting the boats up the narrowing river. "I fear every day," he confessed, "that we shall meet with some considerable falls or obstruction in the river, notwithstanding the information of the Indian woman to the contrary, who assures us that the river continues as we see it. I can scarcely form an idea of a river running to a great extent through such a rough, mountainous, country without having its stream intercepted by some difficult and dangerous rapids or falls." But Sacajawea's memory held; aside from beaver dams in the sluices, or channels, only small riffles interrupted the smooth sheet of water passing the clusters of small islands.

Game again was thinning out, so Lewis forbade his men to shoot at geese. They were too small to subsist the party and so hard to hit that he felt he could not afford the waste of ammunition. From droppings and old bones he saw that buffalo occasionally struggled up as far as the valley. But he pointed out to his men, "There is no fresh sign of them and I begin to think that our harvest of white puddings is at an end, at least until our return to buffalo country." On the other hand, he remarked ruefully, "Our trio of pests still invade and obstruct us on all occasions. These are the mosquitoes, eye gnats and prickly pears; equal to any three curses that ever poor Egypt laboured under, except the Mahometan yoke. The men complain of being much fatigued. Their labour is excessively great. I occasionally encourage them by assisting in the labour of navigating the canoes and have learned 'to push a tolerable good pole,' in their phrase."

On July 27, 1805, Lewis finally reached the Three Forks of the Missouri. It was a grand site, one which made his spirits soar. "The country opens suddenly to extensive and beautiful plains and meadows which appear to be surrounded in any direction with distant and lofty mountains." Their arrival was none too soon. Looking about him at his men, exhausted from fighting the current with cordelle and setting pole, he observed, "They begin to weaken fast from the continual state of violent exertion." While he awaited Clark's return, he rested his worn men and examined and sketched the Three Forks area.

If Lewis's men were run-down, Clark's were worn out. When the Kentuckian came into camp he was staggering. Lewis caught him and ordered him to bed. He found that the redhead had pushed himself too hard in his zeal to find the Shoshones. He was near complete exhaustion. Lewis needed no further inducement to call for an extended halt at Three Forks while he treated his friend with Dr. Rush's pills, footbaths and bark tonics. The unexpected layover meant time on his hands, and Lewis began to worry again. But he wrote his concerns down, since this act always seemed to release him from tensions, setting his mind at ease and preparing himself, mentally, for action. It was a subconscious purgative of worry. "We begin to feel considerable anxiety with respect to the Snake Indians. If we do not find them, or some other nation who have horses, I fear the success of our voyage will be very doubtful or, at all events, much more difficult in its accomplishment. We are now several hundred miles within the bosom of this wild and mountainous country, where game may rationally be expected, shortly, to become scarce and subsistence precarious without any information with respect to the country, not knowing how far these mountains continue or where to direct our course to pass them to advantage or intercept a navigable branch of the Columbia. . . . Even were we on such a one, the probability is that we should not find any timber within these mountains large enough for canoes, if we judge from the portion of them through which we have passed."

Halfway through his worrying, Lewis, as usual, began to cheer up. "However, I still hope for the best and intend taking a tramp myself in a few days to find these yellow gentlemen, if possible. My two principal consolations are that, from our present position, it is impossible that the southwest fork can head with the water of any other river but the Columbia and that if any Indians can subsist in the form of a nation in these mountains with the means they have of acquiring food, we can also subsist."

While Clark mended in a shady bower almost on the very spot where Sacajawea had been captured by the Minnetarees four or five years earlier, Lewis proceeded (July 30th) on foot and alone up the Jefferson River, the southwest fork. The others he named the Madison and Gallatin rivers. The canoes followed him but could not keep up with the fast-moving officer, although his path led him through an obstacle course of sloughs, bayous and beaver dams. Dosing himself with Glauber's salts because of a recurrence of dysentery, the prodigious hiker still made marches of 28 miles in a day! But he still caught no sign of Sho-shones. Early in August, he and a few companions reached and named the Philosophy and Wisdom rivers. At the latter, now called the Big Hole, he left a note on a stick for Clark, advising him to take the left-hand fork. When he retraced his steps, he found that Clark had missed the note and gone up the wrong branch. In the rough water a canoe overturned and Whitehouse was almost killed. To his dismay, Lewis learned that the delay and accident were his own fault. They were caused by his care-lessness and a freakish joke of nature. "They arrived at the con-fluence of the two rivers where I left the note," he later recapitu-lated. "This note had, unfortunately, been placed on a green pole which the beaver cut down and carried off, together with the note!"

On the 8th, Lewis noted, "The Indian woman recognized the point of a high plain to our right which she informed us was not very distant from the summer retreat of her nation on a river, beyond the mountains, which runs to the west. This hill, she says, her nation calls the Beaver's Head [near Dillon, Montana], from a conceived resemblance of its figure to the head of that animal. She assures us that we shall either find her people on this river or the river immediately west of its source which, from its size, cannot be very distant. As it is now all important with us to meet these people as soon as possible, I determined to proceed tomorrow with a small party to the source of the principal stream of this river and pass the mountains to the Columbia and down that River until I found the Indians. In short, it is my resolution to find them or some others who have horses, if it should cause me a tramp of one month."

The quartet of scouts passed Rattlesnake Bluffs, Prairie Creek and Red Rock Creek, where the Indian trail they were following petered out just about where canoe navigation ended. Lewis camped in Horse Prairie and observed, "The mountains do not appear very high in any direction although the tops of them are partially covered with snow. This convinces me that we have ascended to a great height since we have entered the Rocky Mountains, yet the ascent has been so gradual along the valleys that it was scarcely perceptible by land. I do not believe that the world can furnish an example of a river running to an extent which the Missouri and Jefferson Rivers do, through such a mountainous country and, at the same time, so navigable as they are." An unquenchable optimist, Lewis could only conclude, "If the Columbia furnishes us with such another example, a communication across the Continent by water will be practicable and safe." (The Columbia was not that obliging, but Lewis was only a few miles from Upper Red Rock Lake, source of the Missouri—2,714 miles from St. Louis.)

The captain moved out on August 11, sending Drouillard and Shields as flankers and keeping McNeal with him. He wanted no signal shots fired; if a man spied something, he was to place his hat on the muzzle of his gun, held in the air, as a sign. After five miles of marching in this extended order, Lewis saw a mounted Indian descending a slope toward him, two miles away. "With my glass, I discovered from his dress that he was of a different nation from any that we had yet seen and was satisfied of his being Shoshone. . . . I was overjoyed at the sight of the stranger and had no doubt of obtaining a friendly introduction to his nation, provided I could get near enough to him to convince him of our being white men. I therefore proceeded towards him at my usual pace. When I had arrived within about a mile, he made a halt, which I did also, and, unloosing my blanket from my pack, I made him the signal of friendship, known to the Indians of the Rocky Mountains and those of the Missouri, which is by holding the mantle or robe in your hands at two corners and then throwing it up in the air higher than the head, bringing it to earth as if in the act of spreading."

The Indian kept his place, as if suspicious of Shields and Drouillard who were still walking toward him. Lewis prayed that they would stop. They were too far away to hail. All he could do was to hurriedly drop his gun and stride forward, displaying beads, a looking glass, and other trinkets. But when he drew within 200 paces of the man, to his dismay he saw the warrior turn his horse and move off, all the while eying Lewis's men. Desperately, Lewis signaled to them to halt. Drouillard caught his gestures but Shields plodded on. "I now called to him [the Indian]," Lewis remembered, "in as loud a voice as I could command, repeating the word *Ta-ba-bone,* which, in their language, signified white man. The Indian halted again and turned his horse about as if to wait for me and I believe he would have remained until I came up with him had it not been for Shields, who still pressed forward. When I arrived within about 150 paces, I again repeated the word, *Ta-ba-bone,* and held up the trinkets in my hand and stripped up my shirt sleeve to give him an opportunity to see my [white] skin."

But when Lewis closed the gap between them to less than 100 yards, the Snake wheeled his mount, gave it the whip, and horse and rider disappeared from the cove in an instant, into the willow brush. "With him vanished all hopes of obtaining horses for the present," wrote Lewis in disgust. "I now felt quite as much mortification and disappointment as I had pleasure and expectation at the first sign of this Indian. I felt sorely chagrined at the conduct of the men, particularly Shields, to whom I principally attributed this failure in obtaining an introduction to the natives. I now called the men to me and could not forbear upbraiding them a little for their want of attention and [their] imprudence on this occasion."

However, there was no time to waste in recrimination and Lewis knew it. He fixed an American flag to a pole which he gave to McNeal to carry and fanned the men out to pick up the horseman's trail. To avoid frightening the Indians, he did not make too vigorous a pursuit. But when he camped, Lewis had his men kindle a bright fire which would have warmed a platoon. He laid out trinkets, too. But no Indians approached the well-lit camp and next morning the four men continued their tracking. Their path took them, in Lewis's words, to "the most distant fountain of the waters of the mighty Missouri, in search of which we have spent so many toilsome days and restless nights. Thus far, I have accomplished one of those great objects on which my mind had been unalterably fixed for many years. Judge, then, of the pleasure I felt in allaying my thirst with this pure and ice cold water which issues from the base of a low mountain or hill of a gentle ascent for half a mile. . . . Two miles below, McNeal had stood exultantly with a foot on each side of this little rivulet, and thanked his God that he had lived to bestride the mighty and heretofore deemed endless Missouri."

Refreshed, Lewis led his men, via Lemhi Pass, over the top of a ridge which was the Continental Divide. He descended the mountain and drank at a head of Lemhi River, a tributary of the Snake, saying, "Here, I first tasted the water of the great Columbia River." On August 13th, the scouts encountered three Indians who fled and then, suddenly, three squaws who had no time to run. Resigned to their fate, they bowed their heads, awaiting death. Lewis laid down his gun. "I took the elderly woman by the hand and raised her up, repeated the word *Ta-ba-bone* and stripped up my shirt sleeve to show her my skin to prove to her the truth of the assertion that I was a white man, for my face and hands, which had been constantly exposed to the sun, were quite as dark as their own. They appeared instantly reconciled and, the men coming up, I gave these women some beads and a few moccasins, awls, some pewter looking-glasses and a little paint."

As the women were guiding the whites to their camp, some sixty warriors galloped up, all armed with bows and arrows save for three with trade muskets. They came in a bellicose manner and almost at full speed but Lewis laid down his gun and coolly advanced toward them, bearing the flag. The braves reined up sharply and their chief addressed the women, who chattered excitedly and, with obvious delight, showed him their presents. Lewis sketched the scene: "These men advanced and embraced me very affectionately in their way, which is by putting their left arm over your right shoulder, clasping your back, while they apply their left cheek to yours and frequently vociferate the word *ah-hi-e, ah-hi-e,* that is, 'I am much pleased, I am much pleased.' Both parties now advanced and we were all caressed and besmeared with their grease and paint until I was heartily tired of the native hug."

Before giving out presents, Lewis smoked a calumet with the chief, Cameahwait, and accepted his hospitality. Once at the Shoshone camp, however, he found the Indians reluctant to accompany him back to meet Clark. They feared a Piegan Blackfeet trap. Lewis considered his situation to be critical. "The transition from suspicion to confirmation of the fact would not be very difficult in the minds of these ignorant people . . . accustomed from their infancy to view every stranger as an enemy."

In desperation, Lewis made a chiding speech, translated by Drouillard into sign language, to try to shame the Snakes into going back with him. "I told Cameahwait that I was sorry to find that they had put so little confidence in us though I knew they were not acquainted with white men and, therefore, could forgive him; that among white men it was considered disgraceful to lie or entrap an enemy by falsehood. I told him that if they continued to think thus meanly of us that they might rely on it that no white man would ever come to trade with them or bring them arms and ammunition and that if the bulk of his nation still entertained this opinion, I still hoped that there were some among them that were not afraid to die, who were men and would go with me and convince themselves of the truth of what I had asserted."

Stung, Cameahwait proudly told Lewis that *he* was not afraid to die; that *he* was determined to accompany him. "I soon found that I had touched him on the right string," observed the explorer. "To doubt the bravery of a savage is to put him on his mettle." But after a harangue from the chief, still only six or eight braves followed him and Lewis as they headed eastward. Then, suddenly, all of the Indians ran to join them. Shaking his head in amazement at how fast the situation changed with the mercurial Shoshones, Lewis commented, "This may serve in some measure to illustrate the capricious disposition of these people who never act but from the impulse of the moment. They were now very cheerful and gay and, two hours ago, they looked as surly as so many imps of Satan."

Reaching Shoshone Cove at sunset, Lewis held the Shoshones by giving them the last of his flour but next morning he thought all was lost. His heart sank when, as he recalled the scene, "We saw one of the spies [scouts] coming up the level plain under whip. The Chief paused a little and seemed somewhat concerned. I felt a good deal so, myself, and began to suspect that, by some unfortunate accident, perhaps, some of their enemies had straggled hither at this unlucky moment. . . ." But no, the In-

dian scout was the bearer of glad tidings for the hungry Shoshones. Drouillard had killed a deer. All of the braves whipped
up their steeds, including the man behind whom Lewis was riding. Southern horseman that he was, the captain could barely
keep his seat atop the jostling withers. When he cursed his pro-
tests to the wind, his co-rider abandoned the horse to him and
ran at full speed for a full mile, on foot, to the kill. "They [all]
dismounted and ran in, tumbling over each other like a parcel of
famished dogs, each seizing and tearing away a part of the intestines which had been previously thrown out by Drouillard." So
Lewis sketched the bloody scene. "The scene was such when I
arrived that had I not a pretty keen appetite, myself, I am confident I should not have tasted any part of the venison. Each one
had a piece of some description and all eating most ravenously.
Some were eating the kidneys, the melt and liver and the blood
running from the corner of their mouths, others were in a similar
situation with the paunch and guts. . . . I really did not until
now think that human nature ever presented itself in a shape so
nearly allied to the brute creation. I viewed these poor starved
devils with pity and compassion." Lewis directed McNeal to
keep only a quarter of the deer and to give the balance to the
famished Snakes. Drouillard brought down two more animals to
hold the friendship of the suspicious—but hungry—Shoshones
for another day.

When the Indians began to hang back and desert again, Lewis
gave one of them the flagstaff to carry, then took off his cocked
hat and placed it on Cameahwait's head. It was almost his last
symbol of civilization—"My overshirt being of the Indian form,
my hair disheveled and skin well-burned with the sun, I wanted
no further addition to make me a complete Indian in appearance. Although he had told the chief that Clark might not yet be
at the fork of the Wisdom and Jefferson rivers, Lewis's heart
sank when he saw they had not arrived. Out of the corner of his
eye he saw the still-suspicious Indians slacken their pace as their
distrust of him was again aroused. "I now determined to restore
their confidence, cost what it might, and therefore gave the Chief
my gun and told him that if his enemies were in those bushes
before him that he could defend himself with that gun [and]

that, for my own part, I was not afraid to die and if I deceived him he might take what use of the gun he thought proper; in other words, that he might shoot me." At Lewis's command, his men followed suit, turning over their arms to the Snakes.

But even this desperate gesture was not enough. As Lewis's mind raced, he clutched at a straw. "I thought of the notes which I had left and directed Drouillard to go with an Indian and bring them to me. . . . I now had recourse to a stratagem in which I thought myself justified by the occasion but which, I must confess, set a little awkward. . . . After reading the notes—which were the same I had left—I told the Chief that this note was left here today [i.e, by a messenger from Captain Clark] and that he informed me that he was just below the mountains and coming along slowly. . . ."

Not all of the Snakes were taken in by Lewis's trick but enough swallowed his explanation of Clark's absence to keep the party together while he got a brave to accompany the *coureur de bois* downstream with a note asking Clark to hurry, lest all be lost. The explorer prayed that the river had not become impassable for the canoes below Rattlesnake Bluffs and he practically sweated blood during the next several hours of Drouillard's absence, as the fate of the entire expedition hung in a delicate balance. "I knew that if those people left me that they would immediately disperse and secrete themselves in the mountains where it would be impossible to find them or, at least, in vain to pursue them, and that they would spread the alarm to all the bands within our reach and, of course, we should be disappointed in obtaining horses, which would vastly retard and increase the labour of our voyage and, I feared, might so discourage the men as to defeat the expedition altogether. My mind was, in reality, quite as gloomy all this evening as the most affrighted Indian but I affected cheerfulness to keep the Indians so who were about me. . . . I slept but little, as might be expected, my mind dwelling on the state of the expedition which I have ever held in equal estimation with my own existence and the fate of which appeared, at this moment, to depend in a great measure upon the caprice of a few savages who were ever as fickle as the wind."

To try to hold the Shoshones, Lewis told them Clark had trade goods galore and was accompanied not only by a woman of their own tribe but by a man whose hair was curly and whose skin was black. He noted, "They seemed quite as anxious to see this monster as they were [to see] the merchandise which we had to barter for their horses." The agony of waiting was short. Drouillard and his Indian companion were gone only a short time before another Snake rushed into camp to report the detachment of white men in sight. Cameahwait, as relieved by his scout's report as was Lewis himself, repeated his fraternal embrace. This time, Lewis had no complaints over the Shoshone greeting, for all its grease and smearing paint.

As the two groups approached each other, a squaw pushed her way through the crowd of Shoshones to run and embrace Sacajawea. She had been a Minnetaree captive with Charbonneau's wife, but had escaped. When things quieted down, Lewis began his powwow with Sacajawea interpreting. To his complete astonishment, the girl jumped up and ran, weeping, to Cameahwait. When Lewis was able to get an explanation he learned that the chief was her long-lost brother! Having learned from experience that powwows should not be fatiguing, he kept this one short and sweet, explaining he wanted only horses and guides, for which he would pay, and that trade goods and firearms would make their way up the Missouri to the Snakes later. He then treated the Indians to some hominy and shot his air gun which, even more than York or sagacious Scammon, "was so perfectly incomprehensible that they immediately nominated it the Great Medicine."

Later, Lewis and Clark held a private powwow and decided the Kentuckian should take eleven axmen over the Divide to explore the Lemhi as a possible route and report to him whether further progress would be via canoes or horses.

On August 18th, Lewis was not so busy bartering for horses to forget to celebrate his birthday with a little soul-searching. "This day I completed my thirty-first year and conceived that I had in all human probability, now existed about half the period of which I am to remain in this sublunary world. I reflected that I had as yet done but little, very little indeed, to further the happiness of the human race or to advance the information of the succeeding generation. I viewed with regret the many hours I have spent in indolence and now sorely feel the want of that information which those hours would have given me had they been judiciously expended. But, since they are past and cannot be recalled, I dash from me the gloomy thought and resolve in future to redouble my exertions and, at least, [to] endeavour to promote those two primary objects of human existence by giving them the aid of that portion of my talents which nature and fortune have bestowed on me or, in future, to live *for mankind* as I have, heretofore, lived *for myself.*"

Lewis saw the first frost whiten the ground the day after his birthday. It was a chilling, frank warning and one which was repeated just two days later when deerskins froze stiff as boards where they lay in the grass, ink froze in his writing stand, and ice stood a quarter of an inch deep atop the cooking pans. Hurrying his preparations, he tried to get more geographical information out of Cameahwait but all answers about the way due west were the same—impassable. An old Indian suggested another route. It led to a great lake of water of bad taste. Lewis thought that this "stinking lake" of the Indians might be the Gulf of California rather than the Pacific so he waited for Clark before making any decision. Meanwhile, he had the inspiration to ask Cameahwait how the Nez Percés got over the mountains to the Missouri to hunt buffalo. The Snake chief told him that it was by a northerly route and very bad, being rocky, heavily timbered, and lacking in game. "However," said Lewis, "knowing that Indians had passed and did pass at this season on that side of this river, to the same below the mountains, my route was instantly settled in my own mind. . . . I felt perfectly satisfied that if the Indians could pass those mountains with their women and children, that we could pass them."

Lewis tried to spoil the Shoshones as much as possible since he had to depend on them so much. He treated them to dinners of fish (after his men caught 828 specimens with a brush drag), boiled corn and beans and squash. Cameahwait liked the vegetables better than anything else except sugar, a small lump of which Sacajawea had given him. As Lewis wrote, "The Chief wished that his nation could live in a country where they could provide such food. I told him that it would not be many years before the white man would put it in the power of his nation to live in the country below the mountains, where they might cultivate corn, beans and squashes. He appeared much pleased with the information."

The feasting made for amity, but uneasiness still gnawed at Lewis's peace of mind. "Most of them [the Shoshones] were thus far on their way down the valley towards the buffalo country and observed that there was a good deal of anxiety on the part of some of those who had promised to assist me over the mountains to accompany this party. I felt some uneasiness on this subject but they still said they would return [west] with me, as they had promised. I said nothing to them but resolved to set out in the morning as early as possible."

Clark had found the Lemhi and Salmon rivers equally impracticable for horses or canoes so Lewis decided to follow the northerly, Nez Percé, trail advocated by the guide, Toby. "The Shoshones all opposed it," he noted. "They said there was a river but that the road led over to the fish weir, but not across the mountains. The guide persisted and we determined to try." The corps set out with nine purchased horses, two more on loan, and a mule which Lewis bought. It was not a good start. Only six miles were made that first day and Drouillard could find no game. Moreover, Lewis was almost killed again when a ball fired by Frazier at a duck in a pond ricocheted off the water and passed within inches of the commander's head. But Lewis quickly forgot the petty annoyances of the day and his close call when a real blow befell his plans. The exasperating Charbonneau casually mentioned to him that the Shoshones were going back on their word and would not go west with him but were going to head east for the buffalo range. Lewis was not only alarmed over the success of the expedition but furious at the stupidity of Charbonneau. "I was out of patience with the folly of Charbonneau, who had not sufficient sagacity to see the consequences. . . . Although he had been in possession of the information since early in the morning, when it had been communicated to him by his Indian woman, yet he never mentioned it to me until afternoon.

THE SKY-PROPPING MOUNTAINS

I could not forbear speaking to him with some degree of asperity."

Without a moment to lose, the Virginian frantically sought to reverse the alarming trend of events. He smoked with Cameahwait and two other chiefs, then suddenly released an impassioned torrent of embarrassing questions. "I asked them if they were men of their words and whether I could depend on the promises they had made to me. They readily answered in the affirmative. I then asked them if they had not promised to assist me with my baggage to their camp on the other side of the mountains. . . . They acknowledged they had." By the time Lewis was through with them, all three chiefs wore hangdog expressions of shame. Cameahwait confessed after Lewis's diatribe that he had done him a wrong, but only because his people were so hungry, so needful of buffalo. Lewis could hardly blame him. "I observed the Indian women collecting the root of a species of fennel [dill], which grows in moist ground," he recalled, "and feeding it to their poor, starved children." But he overcame his remorse over the gaunt youngsters to quickly get whites and red men back on the trail west again. When they camped, he gave the Shoshones the only deer his hunters brought in, while he and his men went to sleep supperless except for a little parched corn.

At Cameahwait's village, Lewis fired a salute to the Shoshones and presented flags to ranking chiefs, then sent out hunters and played his trump card in his grim little battle to win the Shoshones to him. Knowing from experience that when all else failed, music still had charms to tame the savage breast, he ordered Cruzatte to play his fiddle. "The party danced very merrily, much to the amusement and gratification of the natives though, I must confess that the state of my own mind did not well accord with the prevailing mirth, as I somewhat feared that the caprice of the Indians might suddenly induce them to withhold their horses from us, without which my hopes of prosecuting my voyage to advantage was lost. However, I determined to keep the Indians in a good humour, if possible, and to lose no time in obtaining the necessary number of horses."

CHAPTER XV

WHERE ROLLS THE OREGON

There is something peculiarly interesting in the narrative of the adventures of men who . . . break their way through the unvisited deserts of a Continent, exploring the hidden sources of some immense river or penetrate to the remote confines of an exterior ocean. The strange perils that continually await them, the privations, hardships and the sufferings they are exposed to, and the fund of courage and fortitude necessary to encounter and surmount them make them appear to us in the light of champions and heroes.

—EDITOR, *Analectic Magazine*, February 1815

As AUGUST ENDED, the time seemed ripe to Lewis to make the push over the Bitterroot Mountains. He and Clark were ultimately forced to trade knives, musket balls and even the redhead's pistol but they reached their goal of thirty horses, although many of them were poor pack animals and others suffered from sore backs. Leaving the Lemhi River and the Shoshones, the Americans reached a flat, naked moor in good order, from which rose Lost Trail Pass to Bitterroot Valley and the Lolo Trail to the west. The stony hill country, thicketed with brush and "balsam fir," through which they had to cut their way, soon turned into genuine mountains. Sharp stones bruised the horses' feet and animals and men slipped and fell innumerable times on the slopes of the Bitterroots, some of which were as steep as the roof of a house. It was a hellish country in every way, leading both Lewis and Clark to describe it as the worst road—if it could so be called—that was ever traveled by man. It led over and through deadfalls, beaver dams and a slough of despond so miry that Lewis dubbed it Dismal Swamp. Rain and sleet made the march even more wearying and discomforting. Five miles became a good day's advance and eleven miles exceptional. But Lewis's guide, Toby, assured him that in ten days they would be on the west-flowing river and in fifteen at salt water. So the Americans pushed doggedly on.

Parched corn did not seem so bad after the Yankees saw Flatheads eating the inner bark of pines. But these Indians, destitute of food and most goods, were as "horse poor" as many of Lewis's Virginia gentry were land poor. Clark bought eleven horses from their herd of 500 and exchanged seven mounts for fresh animals. Meanwhile, Lewis made four Flatheads into Democratic, or Jeffersonian, chiefs by the laying on of medals and handing out of shirts and flags. He then set about a truly impossible task, the compilation of a Flathead vocabulary for Jefferson. Theirs was the most curious tongue he had ever heard; it was as if each Flathead had a brogue and a speech impediment. To Lewis, of Welsh descent himself, the constant lisp or burr suggested the ancient language of Cambria. The Indians even began to look like Welshmen to him, for they were light-complexioned. Powwowing with them was very difficult, his ideas going through five languages in the process, from his English to the guttural gargles of sound, occasionally relieved by a fowl-like clucking, which was Flathead.

Since snow was already smothering the peaks and frost limning the lowlands, Lewis did not tarry with these "likelyest and honestest Savages we have ever yet seen" [Whitehouse], but hurried along the Bitterroot, or Clark's, River to camp with another group of Flatheads at Traveller's Rest Creek, near modern Missoula. From here they struck over rugged Lolo Pass, through empty-gut country where even cranes were welcomed to the diet. Finally, Lewis had to break out the emergency rations of so-called portable (i.e., dried) soup which he had made up in Philadelphia. It was not a howling success but Lewis only said, "Some of the men did not relish the soup and agreed to kill a colt, which they immediately did and set about roasting it, and which appeared to me to be good eating."

Four hunters staggered over Lolo Pass into the Pacific drainage in advance of the main party, with its straggling pack train and hungry handlers. Somehow, perhaps by some instinct, the corps found its way through the maze of narrow, rocky cañons, clogged with underbrush, and over steep-slanting mountain slopes. From the hills of Glade and Lochsa creeks several of their jaded horses fell, cartwheeling into the gorges, one of them dashing Lewis's field desk to smithereens. Other beasts staggered off to lose themselves and their cargoes, including his portmanteau and clothing. "Dinner" now meant parched corn, portable soup, colt veal and water. On the 16th, the first flurries of snow began to fly and by nightfall it lay six to eight inches deep. The men truly feasted when they had crayfish and wolf meat, but more often they dined on portable soup, snow water, bear oil and candles. Still, they ground out seventeen or more miles a day, though they were now gaunt rather than lean. Most were without stockings and some had rags wrapped around their feet like Washington's soldiers at Valley Forge. They lurched their way over trails alternately covered with patches of snow or awash with meltwater.

When Lewis and Clark spied a level plain from a lofty ridge, they joyfully took it to be the Columbia Valley. It was actually Camas Prairie of the Clearwater, or Kooskooskee, River. The men were flagging badly, beset with incipient starvation atop their dysentery and Job's plague—boils. Their horses were afflicted with sore hooves and backs and tortured by stinging wasps. After calling a halt, Lewis wrote by the light of one of the last uneaten, guttering candles: "I directed the horses to be hobbled, to prevent delay in the morning, being determined to make a forced march tomorrow to reach, if possible, the open country. . . . We killed a few pheasants and killed a prairie wolf which, together with the balance of our horse beef and some crawfish which we obtained from the creek, enabled us to make one more hearty meal, not knowing where the next was to be found. . . . I find myself growing weak from the want of food and most of the men complain of a similar deficiency and have fallen off very much." But he was able to lead his men down Glade Creek and the Lochsa River to the flat, where he halted at the Nez Percé village of Chief Twisted Hair to exult, prematurely, "The pleasure I now felt in having triumphed over the Rocky Mountains and descending once more to a level and fertile country where there was every rational hope of finding comfortable subsistence for myself and party, can be more readily conceived than expressed, nor was the flattering prospect of the final success of the expedition less pleasing."

The corpsmen, camped on the prairie, filled their bellies too quickly and too fully and were soon ill. The bread made from camas roots disagreed violently with them. Clark dosed the sick, including the commander, with Dr. Rush's pills but for ten or twelve days Lewis was too ill to mount even the gentle animal Twisted Hair provided. The whole camp resembled the shambles of a field hospital, with the men sick, enfeebled and emaciated. Some troopers lay like dead men along the trail; others had to be helped aboard their horses.

By October 1st, however, rest and an improved diet had worked wonders. Lewis reassumed his duties and the men were busy burning out log canoes, Indian fashion. On the 5th, Lewis rounded up his horses prior to taking to the Clearwater. In the first trans-Rocky roundup, he branded 38 horses with a hot iron reading US. CAPT. M. LEWIS. (The original iron is now in the possession of the Oregon Historical Society.) He gave his horse herd to the care of Twisted Hair until he should call for it in the spring, and launched the canoes. One canoe was sunk and another damaged in white water, or rapids, and the Shoshone guide, Toby, deserted, but Twisted Hair and another Nez Percé joined Lewis as guides to the Columbia and the canoes skimmed swiftly down the Clearwater and then the Snake, through rapids and smooth water, halting only long enough to give the men a hasty rest and time to buy fish and dogs. The Virginian was beginning to enjoy a predominantly canine diet. "Most of our people, having been accustomed to meat, do not relish the fish, but prefer dog meat which, when well cooked, tastes very well."

211

Clark could not stand it, however, so his diet was the most restricted—roots, dried fish and Adam's ale.

Lewis took chances with the river because he knew that the big gamble was with winter; delays, not rapids, were his worst threat. The season was so far advanced that it was a worse hazard *not* to take chances on immediate obstacles. He spurned portages which a more prudent waterman would have taken; on a single day the canoes passed eleven islands and shot seven rapids. Several times, canoes were sunk but luck continued to ride with him and all the men bobbed up safely each time in the vexed water, and the wrack of the filled canoes was salvaged.

When an Indian told him he was four days from the Falls of the Columbia, Lewis began to scramble up hills to scout ahead. Far off, he saw a mountain range, probably the Blue Mountains of Washington. On and on flew the canoes until the 16th, when they reached the broad Columbia. The river was crowded with fish but they were migrating salmon, spent and dying; the poorest excuse for food. His men preferred anything to the flaccid fish— hares, grouse, dogs. The trip down the Columbia was monotonous, its boredom relieved only slightly by rapids and the thievery of the Indians of the fishing villages. When the toper, Collins, made some beer from moldy camas-root bread, it became the highlight of the whole journey. Ducks, gulls and cormorants became more common and Lewis, noting dentalium shells through aboriginal noses, and seeing an Indian in a sailor's pea jacket, knew that the Pacific could not be far.

The Chinook Indians not only stole everything which was not bolted down, they planned to kill the whites, so the Nez Percé guides took their leave. Lewis could not take the cowardly Chinooks seriously but he maintained his usual security precautions. He regarded them as disagreeable kleptomaniacs rather than potential murderers. Far more dangerous than the thieving Chinooks were the Columbia's many rapids. He halted, studied each chute, and then ran it. But Celilo Falls could not be run. The men carried all their goods around the pitch by a portage, then hauled and floated their canoes down a narrow channel and lowered them on elkskin cables into the river below the falls, where they bobbed safely among the curious sea otters. They next encountered the Short Narrows, or Dalles, where Cruzatte's skill as a boatman got the canoes through safely, to the astonishment of the watching natives, eager for flotsam and jetsam. He ran the canoes through the pinched gut of the Columbia, the Long Narrows, and, on the 30th, Lewis and Clark surveyed the Great Chute, or Upper Cascade. This was the first of a series of rapids making up the Cascade or Great Rapids of the Columbia, the last real barrier to overcome. Again with great skill, they slipped the canoes around the cascades on poles, portaged all equipment over an Indian trail of 940 yards, and by November 2nd were in tidal water. Brant, geese, ducks and swans filled their larders and stomachs; it was a far cry from the rotten salmon and bowel-griping camas of the upriver country. Indians with kettles and other trade items told Lewis he was within two days of the sea. So, when the canoes reached wide Gray's Bay on the 8th, Clark took it to be the Pacific and exclaimed in his log, "Ocian in view. O, the joy!"

The incessant chop of the waves made many of the men seasick and Lewis had to coast twenty miles to make a bare nine miles of straight-line distance. Desperately he sought a beach for a landing but there was not so much as a shelf. Finally, a landing had to be made on the boulders and driftwood of the rugged shore. It was a wet, uncomfortable and dangerous camp. The river water was too salty to drink; those who persisted found it a purgative. The only sweet water was that caught in the kettles during rainstorms. Violent winds and waves forced emergency landings and kept the men prisoners on huge logs or boulders beneath steep cliffs. For eight days, the hungry men were never dry, trapped in their camp crannies by tides and rain. Lewis had to sink the canoes with parcels of stone to keep them from being smashed to kindling by the ramming drift logs. But, though the men's buckskins rotted on their backs, all were healthy during the frustrating halt just short of their goal. They were cheerful, too, perhaps because the roaring of the breakers on the coast ahead signaled, dramatically, the end of their long westering quest.

At low tides, Lewis broke camp to seek higher and drier camps but without success. The men he sent around Blustery

Point were driven back but a second group finally reached the seashore. Colter returned to report no ships in sight but the theft of his gig, knife and basket by Indians. The culprits, at that moment, decided to pay Lewis a visit and he ordered his soldiers to advance on the thieves at double time, guns at the ready. He soon retrieved Colter's articles. Then he curtly ordered the Chinooks to clear out. At 3 P.M., Lewis set out for the shore to see if Trader Haley was about. He caught up with Willard and Shannon just in time. The Indians had stolen their rifles from their grasp as they slept. The explorer descended on the Chinook camp like Attila and made short work of recovering the arms. But not one shred of sail did he see lying offshore as he stared toward the horizon, so he rejoined Clark and the troopers after a reconnaissance of Haley's Bay, passing around Cape Disappointment and following the tideline to the north. He blazed a prominent tree en route, carving his name and the date, in imitation of Mackenzie. When he found, upon his return to camp, that the Indians had tried to steal guns from the main party, he ordered them barred from the camp. The news spread among the Indians and a sort of password was speedily evolved by them. Whenever a native wished to visit the American camp, he would shout loudly as he advanced, "No Chinook!"

While Clark took ten men to have a look at the Pacific, Lewis collected specimens of the Chinook language, awarded medals and bought a beautiful robe of sea-otter skins with Sacajawea's help. The quiet of camp life was disrupted when a Chinook madame brought her troop of a half-dozen girls up to the camp. They were an unprepossessing lot of camp followers and Lewis shuddered as he chose the lesser evil of giving his men ribbons to exchange for the attentions of the women in order to prevent them giving away knives or other valuable articles. One or two of the damsals could have been considered handsome by men who had been on the trail nearly two years but most of them had lumpy, misshapen legs, flattened skulls, and were badly blighted with smallpox and/or venereal disease. One was literally covered with scabs and ulcers; another had a sailor's, or trader's, brand—J. Bowman—tattooed on her arm.

In keeping with his democratic philosophy, shaped by his

great admiration for Jefferson, Lewis now called for a vote on the choice of a site for winter headquarters. Even York, the slave, and Sacajawea, the Indian squaw, were given an equal vote by Lewis. Only two members of the party were not consulted—Scammon and Baptiste, the baby asleep in his sling on Sacajawea's back. Some of the soldiers preferred to return to the Quicksand River; the squaw urged a site where there were plenty of wild potatoes (wappato roots). Most, like Lewis, wanted to winter on the south side of the Columbia near its mouth. He wished to make salt on the ocean beach and to be able to speak any vessel which might call at the river. Moreover, the Indians had told him elk congregated in that area. Clark was willing to go along with Lewis, although he thought salt water was unhealthy. But the less rigorous climate and the chance of sighting a ship outweighed his prejudice against the sea air and he voted with Lewis and the majority.

Lewis searched for an adequate campsite on the south shore so long that Clark began to worry. "Captain Lewis's long delay below has been the cause of no little uneasiness on my part for him. A thousand conjectures have crowded into my mind respecting his probable situation and safety. . . ." But the very day that the Kentuckian penned his apprehensions, his comrade returned to announce that he had found a good situation on a small river which entered the Columbia from the south. Storms delayed their move but Lewis could not tolerate such inaction and he hurried ahead, by land, with four men to set up camp on the site for the main party in the canoes. His efforts to bag some game for a welcoming dinner were fruitless and the men were forced to starve along on pounded salmon. Soon, however, they were getting elk in their sights.

Piloting the men up the little Netul River, now the Lewis and Clark, the Virginian led them to a spring on a high point of land west of the Netul. Here the men began clearing a space and trimming trees into logs for huts. Clark, meanwhile, blazed a trail to the coast through bogs which "the wate of a man would shake for ½ an Acre." A number of men were ailing from colds, tumors, boils and dysentery; Werner had a strained knee and Pryor a dislocated shoulder. So Lewis was eager to get a roof over their heads before winter. He was pleased with the site he had selected when Drouillard and Shannon returned to camp after killing and butchering sixteen elk nearby. Moreover, ex-carpenter Gass approved of the straight and easily split timber—the balsam pine, or fir—which he said made the best puncheons he had ever seen.

By Christmas Eve, the men finished the eight huts which composed Fort Clatsop, named for the Indian tribe of the locality. The fort closely resembled its Missouri River model, Fort Mandan, being composed of a row of three huts along one wall and of four along the opposite. A single gate in the south wall gave into the compound, or parade ground, between the structures. Christmas Day was cloudy and wet but it was a happy holiday, nevertheless, for the expeditionaries. They moved from their sodden camp into the relative comfort of Fort Clatsop's cabins. After a parade, the men fired a round apiece from their arms and shouted and sang outside Lewis and Clark's headquarters, to wish them a Merry Christmas. Clark collected almost the last twelve carrots of tobacco and gave them to the men. Nonsmokers and nonchewers were each given, instead, a handkerchief. Unfortunately, there were no spirits left for toasts and the meat, though plentiful, was poor and unsalted.

Clark wrote on Christmas: "Our Dinner today consisted of pore Elk boiled, spilt [spoiled] fish and some roots, a bad Christmas dinner." The huts smoked; the fleas bit; the men's stomachs rumbled and belched in rebellion; Lewis's smokehouse, patterned after Jefferson's at Monticello, did not work and the meat spoiled in the mild climate. Yet the men were happy. They were snug in their billets, ready to sit out another winter. When the festivities of his third Christmas in the field were over, Lewis sent five men to the shore to make salt. The other enlisted men put the finishing touches on the fort, completing chimneys, bunks, gates and the great pickets of the stockade. The last work, on the very last day of 1805, in a warm rain which evoked no memories of sub-zero Yuletide, 1804, at Fort Mandan, was the digging of sinks and the construction of a sentry box.

CHAPTER XVI

———◆◆———

ADIEU TO OURIGON

We feel a deep concern for their personal safety; are astonished at their fortunate escapes from apparently inevitable fatalities and are filled with admiration at their enterprising spirit and persevering energy while, at the same time, our curiosity is gratified by the development of new views and traits of Nature and her children.
—EDITOR, *Analectic Magazine*, February 1815

A ROLL of rifle reports awakened Meriwether Lewis and William Clark on New Year's morn, 1806. They looked out from their quarters to find the entire detachment drawn up by the noncommissioned officers and firing a salute, "the only mark of respect which we had it in our power to pay this celebrated day," noted Lewis. "Our repast of this day [elk tongues and marrowbones, presented them by the hunters], tho' better than that of Christmas, consisted principally in the anticipation of the first day of January 1807 when, in the bosom of our friends, we hope to participate in the mirth and hilarity of the day. . . . A present, we are content with eating our boiled elk and wappato and solacing our thirst with our only beverage, pure water."

The commander found the local Indians to be avaricious pilferers, fond of haggling over barter—"If they conceive you anxious to purchase, they will be a whole day bargaining for a handful of roots." For safekeeping from the kleptomaniac Clatsops, Lewis had to deposit most of the axes in the room he shared

217

with Clark, and he warned his troopers that anyone caught trading tools to the Indians would be summarily court-martialed.

Although beaver and otter were plentiful, to the delight of Drouillard and the others with traps, game animals were scarce. So many elk hunts ended as fiascos that they "reminded us of the necessity of taking time by the forelock," to use Lewis's words, "and keeping out several parties while we have yet a little meat beforehand." Hunting failures also directed his attention to the securing of both whale blubber and meat for eating, as well as the dogs to which they were by now accustomed. Chief Comowool, or Kobaiway, and his Clatsops esteemed blubber highly but Lewis clung to his preference of dog meat. "Our party," he observed, "from necessity having been obliged to subsist some length of time on dogs, have now become extremely fond of their flesh. It is worthy of remark that while we lived principally on the flesh of this animal we were much more healthy, strong and more fleshy than we had been since we left the buffalo country. For my own part, I have become so perfectly reconciled to the dog that I think it an agreeable food and would prefer it vastly to lean venison or elk."

He tried some blubber from a whale beached in the Tillamook Head area. "It was white and not unlike the fat of pork, though the texture was more spongy and somewhat coarser. I had a part of it cooked and found it to be very palatable and tender. It resembled the beaver or the dog in flavour. It may appear somewhat extraordinary, tho' it is a fact, that the flesh of the beaver and dog possess a great affinity in point of flavour." He was pleased with the improvement in all viands when Willard and Wiser presented him with the first salt manufactured by Americans on the Pacific. "This is a great treat to myself and most of the party, not having had any since the 20th ultimo. I say most of the party, for my friend, Captain Clark, declares it to be a mere matter of indifference with him whether he uses it or not. For myself, I must confess I felt a considerable inconvenience from the want of it. The want of bread I consider as trivial provided I get fat meat; as to the species of meat, I am not particular, the flesh of dog, the horse and the wolf having, from habit, become equally familiar with any other, and I have learned to think that if the cord be sufficiently strong which binds the soul and body together, it does not so much matter about the materials which compose it."

Although Fort Clatsop was, quite possibly, located in California—New Spain's province of Alta California had the most vague of boundaries but presumably extended all the way up the coast to Nootka Sound—Lewis was sure that few, if any, trading vessels which called at the Columbia were Spanish. The best evidence of this was the exotic vocabulary of the Indians. It consisted, in its entirety, of the King's English—"musket, powder, shot, knife, file, heave the lead, damned rascal and son of a bitch." For their otter, elk, sea otter, beaver, fox and "tyger-cat," or lynx, skins, plus root biscuit and pounded salmon, the natives got from the sea traders old American or British muskets, ball, shot, kettles, coffeepots, teapots, blankets, plates, sheets of copper and brass, cloth, wire, knives, tobacco and beads. When Lewis asked the natives where the ships came from, they always pointed to the southwest quadrant, leading him to anticipate the important way station to the Pacific Northwest which Hawaii would become. "I am sometimes induced to believe that there is some other establishment on the coast of American southwest of this place, of which little is known to the world, or it may be, perhaps, on some island in the Pacific Ocean."

Food continued to be Lewis's major concern all winter. The smokehouse had failed him; the men ate prodigious quantities of meat when it was fresh and six pounds of jerky lasted no more than two and a half days. "At this rate," he warned himself, "our seven elk will last us only three days longer, yet no one seems much concerned about the state of our stores; so much for habit. We have, latterly, so frequently had our stock of provisions reduced to a minimum, and sometimes taken a small touch of fasting, that three full days allowance excites no concern. In these cases, our skill as hunters affords us some consolation for if there is any game of any description in our neighbourhood, we can track it up and kill it. Most of the party have become expert with the rifle. . . . The Indians witnessed Drouillard's shooting . . . some elk, which has given them a very exalted opinion of us as marksmen. . . . I scarcely know how we should subsist were it not for the exertions of this excellent hunter."

The last candles sputtered out on January 13th but Lewis made new ones of elk tallow. He put a fatigue detail to jerking elk meat to try to prevent a constant feast-or-famine existence. His sick list came to be larger than at any time since Fort Mandan, as he treated Goodrich for venereal disease, Bratton for lumbago, and Ordway, McNeal and Willard for a variety of illnesses. Gibson was so ill that neither Lewis nor Clark could cure him and he had to be carried about in a litter, although the commander gave him heroic treatment—dosing him with diluted niter, laudanum and Rush's pills, pouring pints of sage tea into him and bathing his feet in warm water. But luckily most of his cases ran to colds and influenza rather than serious illnesses.

Lewis himself was in good health and enjoyed a fine appetite. He wrote, "Our fare is the flesh of lean elk boiled with pure water and a little salt. The whale blubber, which we have used very sparingly, is now exhausted. On this food I do not feel strong but enjoy the most perfect health. A keen appetite supplies in a great degree the want of more luxurious sauces or dishes and still renders my ordinary meals not uninteresting to me, for I find myself sometimes inquiring of the cook whether dinner or breakfast is ready." A few days after writing this, he commented, "This evening we had what I call an excellent supper. It consisted of a marrow bone, apiece and a brisket of boiled elk that had the appearance of a little fat on it. This, for Fort Clatsop, is living in high style."

Life at Fort Clatsop was a humdrum affair, without even the pain of Fort Mandan frostbite to joggle the men out of their boredom. Lewis did not find the free time of Fort Clatsop oppressive. He whiled away the hours botanizing or studying coastal fauna, from the Oregon badger to the California condor. He was especially taken with the frolicksome, lush-coated sea otter. "It is the richest and, I think, the most delicious fur in the world. At least, I cannot form an idea of any more so. It is deep, thick, silky in the extreme, and strong." The sewellel, or mountain beaver, also interested him; a bizarre animal, to him it appeared to be halfway between a squirrel and a beaver. He lined his fine lynx-skin coat with sewellel pelts. The men appreciated particularly some of his fishy discoveries, such as the eulachon or ulken, which they called anchovies. This smeltlike surf fish or candlefish, one of the most delicious in the world, became the Virginian's nightly *pièce de résistance*. "I find them best when cooked in Indian style, which is by roasting a number of them on a wooden spit without any previous preparation whatever. They are so fat they require no additional sauce and I think them superior to any fish I ever tasted, even more delicate and lucious than the white fish of the [Great] Lakes which have, heretofore, formed my standard of excellence among the fishes. I have heard the fresh anchovy much extolled but I hope I shall be pardoned for believing this quite as good. The bones are so soft and fine that they form no obstruction in eating this fish." Although he was living in a hungry land, he could observe, "We live sumptuously on our wappato and sturgeon. The anchovy is so delicate that they soon become tainted unless pickled or smoked." Of the mallards of the Columbia he wrote, "They are abundant and are found on every part of the River below the mountains. They remain here all winter but I believe they do not continue during winter far above tidewater. A beautiful duck and one of the most delicious in the world." Like a bush Escoffier, he eulogized the canvasback or shelldrake of Oregon also: "To the epicure of the Union, where this duck abounds, nothing need be added in praise of the exquisite flavour of this duck. I have frequently eaten of them in several parts of the Union and I think those of the Columbia equally delicious."

With difficulty, the gourmet of the Corps of Discovery dragged his thoughts away from food to begin the planning of the return passage across the continent. "We could even travel now on our return, as far as the timbered country reaches, or to the Falls of the [Columbia] River. But further would be madness for us to attempt to proceed until April, as the Indians inform us that the snows will be deep in the plains of the Columbia during the winter and in those plains we could scarcely get as much fuel of any kind to cook our provisions as [when] we descended the River. And, even were we happily over the plains and again at the woody country at the foot of the Rocky Mountains, we could not possibly pass that immense barrier of mountains on which the snows lie in winter to the depth, in many places, of twenty feet. . . . We shall not leave our quarters at Fort Clatsop until the first of March unless the want of subsistence compels us to that measure. . . . Earlier than April we conceive it a folly to attempt the open plains where we know there is no fuel, except a few small, dry shrubs."

In preparation for the return journey, Lewis bought another canoe, but was forced to trade his fine laced uniform coat for it. "It seems that nothing except this coat would induce them to dispose of a canoe which, in their mode of traffic, is an article of the greatest value, except a wife, with which it is equal. . . . I think the U' States is indebted to me another uniform coat, for that which I have disposed on this occasion was but little worn." (Whether Lewis meant this remark as a joke or not, Washington took it as a serious claim and on August 5, 1807, the U. S. Army's accounting office credited him with $135 for the coat, one silver epaulet, a dirk, belt and hanger, a horse pistol and a fowling piece, all private property which he was forced to swap for canoes, horses, roots or dogs—"for public service during the Expedition," as the accountant put it.) Worse luck, Lewis was running out of trade articles. "Two handkerchiefs would now contain all the small articles of merchandise we possess. The balance of the stock consists of six blue robes, one scarlet ditto, one uniform artillerist's coat and hat, five robes made of our large flag, and a few old cloths trimmed with ribbons. On this stock we have wholly to depend for the purchase of horses and such portion of our subsistence from the Indians as it will be in our power to obtain; a scant dependence, indeed, for a tour of the distance of that before us."

At least the Indians posed no real martial threat to his corps; for this Lewis was thankful. But he did not drop his vigilance. "We determined always to be on our guard as much as the nature of our situation will permit us and never to place ourselves at the mercy of any savages. We all know that the treachery of the aborigines of America and the too great confidence of our countrymen in their sincerity and friendship has caused the destruction of many hundreds of us. So long have our men been accustomed to a friendly intercourse with the natives that we find it difficult to impress on their minds the necessity of always being on their guard with respect to them. This confidence on our part we know to be the effect of a series of uninterrupted friendly intercourse but the well-known treachery of the natives by no means entitles them to such confidence and we must check its growth in our minds as well as those of our men by recollecting, ourselves, and repeating to our men that our preservation depends on never losing sight of this trait in their character, and being always prepared to meet it in whatever shape it may present itself."

But Lewis was not prepared for the kind of attack the Indians planned and he groaned when he saw Chief Delashelwit come into view, trailed by his squaw, who doubled as an aboriginal madame. In her tow were six simpering girls. Lewis sternly warned his men to give the old bawd and her harlots a wide berth. He reminded them that their ilk were responsible for the afflictions of McNeal and Goodrich; what he really worried about was the men trading off priceless equipment for the favors of the girls. The old whore was not one to give up easily. Patience was her sole virtue. She and her chief, with the flirting girls, made camp near the fort, determined to lay close siege to the corps. "But," wrote Lewis, "I believe, notwithstanding every effort of their winning graces, the men have preserved their constancy to the vow of celibacy which they made on this occasion to Captain Clark and myself." The belles of the Lower Columbia had no sex appeal for Lewis himself. "The most disgusting sight I have ever beheld is these naked dirty wenches."

When it was time to leave Fort Clatsop, Lewis drew up a document to post on the wall of his room in the little bastion before he turned the fort over to his friend Chief Comowool, of whom he said, "We have found him much the most friendly and decent savage that we have met in this neighbourhood." It was a list of the names of the men of his expeditionary force, prefaced by this statement: "The object of this list is that, through the medium of some civilized person who may see the same, it may be known to the informed world that the party consisting of the persons whose names are hereinto annexed and who were sent out by the

Government of the U' States in May 1804 to explore the interior of the Continent of North America, did penetrate the same by way of the Missouri and Columbia Rivers to the discharge of the latter into the Pacific Ocean where they arrived on the 14th of November 1805 and from whence they departed on the 23d day of March 1806 on their return to the United States by the same route they had come out."

This modest document was of the utmost importance in American history. With it, Lewis staked a claim for the U. S. Government on the Oregon country which the Astorians and Oregon Trail overlanders would consolidate. Copies of the notice were found, eventually, and sent back to the United States via Canton.

Lewis gave up the idea of his force returning by ship, for which he had guarded his carte-blanche letters of credit from storms and canoe capsizings. For one thing, no ship called during his stay. (One of the great mysteries connected with the Lewis and Clark Expedition is why Jefferson did not dispatch a vessel to rendezvous with him at the Columbia bar.) Nor would he leave a portion of the men to return by sea. "Our party is also too small to think of leaving any of them to return to the U' States by sea, particularly as we shall be necessarily divided into three or four parties on our return in order to accomplish the objects we have in view." The objects were further explorations of the West instead of a simple retracing of their route.

As he ordered the canoes manned and bade farewell to his Pacific post, Lewis wrote, "Although we have not fared sumptuously this winter and spring at Fort Clatsop, we have lived quite as comfortably as we had any reason to expect we should, having accomplished every object which induced our remaining at this place except that of meeting with the traders who visit the entrance of the River."

CHAPTER XVII

———◆•◆———

HOMEWARD BOUND

*All the Indians from the Rocky Mountains to the Falls of
the Columbia are an honest, ingenuous and well-disposed
people. But from the Falls to the seacoast, and along it,
they are a rascally, thieving, set.*
—SERGEANT PATRICK GASS, May 7, 1806

THE MEN made good progress as they started up the Columbia in
the canoes from Fort Clatsop, averaging a gain of 15 miles each
day. But the hunters were dogged by ill luck except at Deer Island, an excellent choice of site by Lewis for a layover. Nor were
the Indians any better off. While Clark explored the Willamette
River, Lewis interviewed many natives who stopped off at his
camp, and all reported the upriver tribes to be nearly starving
and no chance of a salmon run until May. Lewis, however, was
determined to press on, taking his chances in the gameless area
between the Falls and the Nez Percé nation in order to be in a
proper position to cross the Great Divide at the earliest moment
possible. If he waited for the salmon, he might not reach the Missouri before it iced up for the winter or he might not reach the
Nez Percés, who held his horses, before they went east on buffalo
hunts. "We are, therefore, determined to lose as little time as
possible in getting to the Chopunnish [i.e, Nez Percé] village.
. . . We now view the horses as our only certain resource for
food, nor do we look forward to it with any detestation or horror.
So soon is the mind, which is occupied with any interesting object, reconciled to its situation."

225

All the Indians they met as they ascended the river were unmitigated scoundrels and thieves. This was another good reason to put the Columbia behind them as soon as possible. "These people are very unfriendly and seem illy disposed, had not our numbers deterred them. . . . They are great rogues and we are obliged to keep them at a proper distance from our baggage."

When the Americans arrived at the Cascades, rain made cordelling through the "shoots" doubly difficult and rendered the 2,800 yards of portage virtually impassable. By mutual consent, Clark took over the job of hauling the canoes up through the white water, on lines. Lewis gave him all of the men except for a cook, three lame men and Bratton, still sick. These men he posted as guards to protect the baggage from "the greatest thieves and scoundrels we ever met with." For all of Clark's skill, the canoes were damaged by the crushing blows given them by rocks in the rapids and the men were literally exhausted by day's end.

The debilitated condition of the whites gave the Chinooks courage. They threw stones at two soldiers and pushed Shields off the trail. But the last straw for Lewis was when they tried to steal Scammon. A friendly Indian told him that the Newfoundland had been decoyed away. He sent three men in hot pursuit, with orders to fire on the rustlers if they offered the least resistance. The Indians abandoned Lewis's dog and fled. The Virginian reported his anger: "We ordered the sentinel to keep them out of camp and informed them, by signs, that if they made any further attempts to steal our property, or insulted our men, we should put them to death." He added, "Our men seem perfectly well disposed to kill a few of them."

Lewis tried his hand at bringing the last craft, a wooden canoe or pirogue, through the rapids but made a botch of the job. His lack of Clark's skill led the bow to be driven broadside on a rock. Although all hands hauled with every bit of might they possessed, it was a hopeless fight against the river and Lewis reluctantly had to give the order to let go the cable and watch the boat being dashed downstream by the torrent. All he could do was to damn his luck.

When the canoes reached the Dalles, the cordelling, portaging and pushing with poles had to be repeated all over again. The Dalles were much more formidable than in the fall and Lewis decided the pirogues could go no farther since even the light canoes had to be portaged. Since the natives would offer nothing for the pirogues, obviously expecting him to abandon them, Lewis ordered them cut up for fuel. Because the Dalles area was so crowded with Indians of various tribes, Lewis unlimbered his air gun and entertained the onlookers with it while Clark doctored a chief and his squaw ("a sulky bitch"). All this was to the end of securing horses. It worked. Soon, trading kettles for nags, Lewis and Clark had seven animals. But this was not enough and the men still had to function as pack animals, too. Guards kept the animals under close watch as they grazed, hobbled and picketed. They were all restless and wild-eyed stallions and he knew that they were capable of breaking away from the strongest elk-skin reata put on them even without the help of the skulking Indians, of whom Lewis said, "Nothing but our numbers, I believe, prevents their attempting to murder us at the moment."

The wear and tear of three long years of command in the field was having its effect on Lewis. He found that he became irritated more easily than before. His temper grew shorter than ever. When, on April 20th, he learned that the Indians had stolen two spoons and six tomahawks, he reprimanded the chief sharply. The chief, in turn, angrily lectured his people but the diatribe hardly satisfied Lewis, since it did not result in the return of any of the stolen property. So, he recalled, "I ordered the Indians from our camp that evening and informed them that if I caught them attempting to purloin any article from us, I would beat them severely. They went off in rather a bad humour and I directed the party to examine their arms and be on their guard." When he found that yet another tomahawk had been stolen, he decided to spite the thieving Indians. He ordered every paddle, pole and scrap of the chopped-up pirogue put on a fire so that not a particle would be left for the benefit of the natives. When he caught one of the braves stealing an iron canoe-pole socket, he struck him several times and had his troopers kick him out of camp. This was the first time Lewis had raised his hand against an Indian. His patience, indeed, was running out.

Lewis later reflected on his actions. "I informed the Indians that I would shoot the first of them that attempted to steal an article from us; that we were not afraid to fight them; that I had it in my power to kill them all and [to] set fire to their houses, but it was not my wish to treat them with severity provided they would let my property alone. That I would take their horses if I could not find out the persons who had stolen the tomahawks but that I had rather lose the property than take the horse of an innocent man."

After this burst of anger, which seemed to clear the air, Lewis's luck changed—for the better. A friendly Nez Percé not only agreed to guide them to his people's country but to bring two of his own horses. Of the guide, Lewis observed, "He appears to be an honest, sincere fellow. He tells us that the Indians a little above will treat us with much more hospitality than those we are now with." But still the local Indians hung about the detachment's flanks like wolves, waiting for Lewis to abandon his canoes. "The natives had tantalized us with an exchange of horses for our canoes in the first instance but when they found that we had made our arrangements to travel by land, they would give us nothing for them. I determined to cut them in pieces sooner than leave them on those terms. Drewyer [Drouillard] struck one of the canoes and split off a small piece with his tomahawk. They discovered us determined on this subject and offered us several strands of beads for each, which we accepted."

As they traveled the sandy and rocky road east, Lewis was cheered by the changing appearance of both the Indians they met and the horses they ran. Not only did these natives look better, their heads being less flattened and disfigured, but they began to act better. Although their horses almost always had sore backs, Lewis was impressed with the good condition of their mounts otherwise. He credited this to the bunch grass on which they fed. It retained its nourishment as it stood and cured in the sun. "It astonished me," said Lewis, "to see the order of their horses at this season of the year when I know that they have wintered on the dry grass of the plains and, at the same time, [have been] rode [sic] with greater severity than is common among ourselves. I did not see a single horse which could be deemed poor.

Many of them were fat as seals." Both Lewis and Clark bought horses so that they could alternate riding with walking.

In the area of the Umatilla River, at the end of April, the whites fell in with some Walla Wallas. Chief Yellept, to whom they had given a medal the prior October, told them that there was a good road from the Walla Walla village to the junction of the Clearwater and Snake. This confirmed what Lewis's guide said, and meant an 80-mile shortcut for the hungry and tired men and a consequent stretching of their rations. The Walla Wallas pictured the route as passing through a land of milk and honey—or, at least, of water, grass, deer and antelope. Lewis took these glowing reports with a pinch of salt; he hoped for the best but prepared for the worst. His hunters redoubled their efforts and he named Frazier chief dogcatcher for the expedition. Soon the onetime fencing master had ten canines in the larder.

To repay the Walla Wallas for their kindness, both Lewis and Clark doctored them. Clark set, splinted and slung a brave's broken arm while Lewis attended to the many conjunctivitis cases, recording: "We gave them some eye water which, I believe, will render them more essential service than any other article in the medical way which we had it in our power to bestow on them. Sore eyes seem to be a universal complaint among these people. I have no doubt but the fine sand of these plains and river—fishing on the waters, too—contribute much to this disorder." In the evening, Cruzatte contributed medicine for the soul, entertaining the Americans' new friends with a fiddle recital.

The only real criticism which Lewis had of these congenial people was their treatment of horses. "These Indians are cruel horsemasters. They ride hard and their saddles are so illy constructed that they cannot avoid wounding the backs of their horses. But, regardless of this, they ride them when the backs of those poor animals are in a horrid condition." Otherwise, Lewis had nothing but praise for the Walla Wallas. "Some time after we had encamped, three young men arrived from the Wallawollah village, bringing with them a steel trap left behind. This is an act of integrity rarely witnessed among Indians. During our stay with them they had several times found knives of the men which had been carelessly lost by them, and returned them. I think we can justly affirm, to the honour of these people, that they are the most hospitable, honest and sincere people that we have met with in our voyage." Later, an Indian brought Lewis two canisters of powder from a cache which his dog had dug up. The explorer rewarded him for his honesty with a fire steel.

Shortly after meeting the usually friendly Nez Percés on the Clearwater, one of that tribe made the mistake of trying to humiliate Lewis. For a moment the Pax Americana of the Far West hung in the balance. The unfortunate incident was explained by Lewis thus: "While at dinner, one Indian fellow impertinently threw a poor, half-starved puppy nearly into my plate by way of derision for our eating dogs, and laughed very heartily at his own impertinence. I was so provoked at his insolence that I caught the puppy and threw it with great violence at him and struck him on the breast and face, seized my tomahawk and showed him, by signs, [that] if he repeated his insolence, I would tomahawk him. The fellow withdrew, apparently much mortified, and I continued my repast, *on dog,* without further molestation."

This incident was exceptional. The friendly Nez Percés showed Lewis how to secure iron rations from the forest in desperate times. He saw that they ate moss (actually, lichen) on pine trees; he observed how they cut down the long-leafed pine to secure the nuts, or seeds, in the cones, to roast or boil; he learned how to peel pines to find the edible inner bark.

From Twisted Hair, Lewis got his horse herd back. He lost little time in moving out through eight inches of snow to a camp at Kamiah, in northern Idaho. Chief Broken Arm greeted them, offered them dried salmon and camas and cowes roots and, best, a fat young horse to butcher. "This is a much greater act of hospitality than we have witnessed from any nation or tribe since we passed the Rocky Mountains," Lewis noted. "In short, be it spoken to their immortal honour, it is the only act which deserves the appellation of hospitality which we have witnessed in this quarter." After supping on horse beef and smoking in a comfortable lodge provided them, Lewis was not about to change his original high opinion of the Nez Percés, except to enlarge upon it. "As these people had been liberal with us in respect to provision, I directed the men not to crowd about their lodges in search of food in the manner hunger had compelled them to do at most lodges we have passed, which the Twisted Hair had informed me was disagreeable to the natives." On the other hand, Nez Percé courtesy did not forbid their pressing into Lewis's lodge at night and he complained, mildly, "we were much crowded with the Indians in our lodge, the whole floor of which was covered with their sleeping carcasses."

To the Flatheads and Nez Percés, Lewis handed out the last of his medals except for one of the largest "denomination" which he hoarded to give to some grand chief in the highly strategic Yellowstone River region where he hoped an American trading post would be established. He had the help of Charbonneau, Sacajawea and a Snake boy as interpreters but it took half a day to parley with the Nez Percés because of their difficult language and the many steps of translation. It was a long and tiring conference but Lewis felt that his powwow was a great success. (It was; probably no tribe in American history preserved its friendship so long and so completely as the Nez Percés.) He and Clark drew a map, with charcoal, to show the Indians where American trading posts would rise to serve them. The natives, in response, swore that they had but one heart and one tongue on the subject of Lewis's advice; they would follow it. They promised never more to make war on the Shoshones but to receive them as friends. They agreed with all his recommendations except for sending a chief to Washington and they warned Lewis of the Blackfeet and Minnetarees of Fort de Prairie. No peace could be guaranteed as long as the two lawless tribes ranged at large. But Lewis managed to wind up the powwow on a high note by displaying his magnet, compass, watch and trusty air gun. One reason for the friendliness of the Nez Percés was Clark's clinic. He treated up to fifty Indians a day, Lewis noting, "It was agreed between Captain Clark and myself that he should attend the sick, as he was their favourite physician, while I would remain here and answer the chiefs." But another reason was Lewis's prowess with the air gun. The braves were awed by his accuracy when he put two shots into the mark in succession at a full 220 paces.

The impatient Virginian had to quarter his men at Kamiah

from May 13 until June 10, 1806, waiting for the snows to fall back from the Bitterroot passes. But it was a good campsite, as he made clear in his report to the President: "A very eligible spot for defence, it had been an ancient habitation of the Indians. . . . With a good wall of earth, the whole was a circle of about 30 feet in diameter. Around this we formed our tents of sticks and grass, facing outwards, and deposited our baggage within the sunken space under a shelter . . . in the extensive, level, bottom, thinly-timbered with long-leaf pine. Here we are in the vicinity of the best hunting grounds, from Indian information; are convenient to the salmon, which we expect daily; and have an excellent pasture for our horses. The hills to the east and north of us are high, broken and but partially timbered; the soil is rich and affords fine grass. In short, as we are compelled to reside a while in this neighbourhood, I feel perfectly satisfied with our position."

Either Lewis or his Indian inhabitants—and probably both—were overoptimistic. His "best hunting grounds" proved hardly able to keep expeditionary body and soul together. Nor did the salmon arrive on schedule. They did not arrive there at all. The Americans had to buy roots and root bread to put in their bellies, were again afflicted with colic, and almost reduced to beggardom again. The Indians hunted with deer decoys but had little luck. Both whites and red men considered themselves fortunate when a bruin blundered before their gunsights. Lewis examined several, "of the species common to the upper part of the Missouri. They may be called white, black, grizzly, brown or red bear, for they are found of all these colours. Perhaps it would not be inappropriate to designate them the variegated bear." Lewis gave bear meat to the Indians, since it was "a great treat to those poor wretches who scarcely taste meat once a month." He watched them cook it in their fashion, between pine boughs on hot stones. "I tasted of this meat and found it much more tender than that which we had roasted or boiled, but the strong flavour of the pine destroyed it for my palate." He gave the claws of the "grisly" bears to Nez Percé Chief Hohastilpilp because "these bears are tremendous animals to them. They esteem the act of killing a bear equally great with that of an enemy in the field of action. . . . These people will sometimes kill the variegated bear when they can get them in the open plains where they can pursue them on horseback and shoot them with their arrows. . . . The variegated bear I believe to be the same here with those of the Missouri but these are not so ferocious as those, perhaps from the circumstances of their being compelled from the scarcity of game in this quarter to live more on roots and, of course, not so much in the habit of seizing and devouring living animals. [But] the bear here are far from being as passive as the common black bear. They have attacked and fought our hunters already, but not so fiercely as those of the Missouri." To be on the safe side, Lewis gave orders to his men to always hunt *Ursus ferox* in pairs, never alone.

Hunger and illness still stalked the corps. Because Lewis feared his men could not distinguish between the cowes and a species of poisonous hemlock, he forbade their gathering their own roots and bought them from the Indians. He had colts killed for food and a fishing canoe built, then divided up the last of the scanty trade merchandise among the men. Each soldier's stock amounted to but two needles, an awl, a knitting needle, a half ounce of vermilion, a few skeins of thread and about a yard of ribbon—"a slender stock, indeed, with which to lay in a store of provision for that dreary wilderness." The baby, Baptiste or Pomp, had to be doctored with medications and poultices of wild onions and Bratton suffered such a relapse that he could not stand. Had Lewis believed in the efficacy of prayer, he might have sought divine help but, instead, he listened to John Shields who told him of having seen similarly afflicted men restored by violent sweats. He then ordered a sweathouse built, placed Bratton in it and gave him great drafts of horsemint tea, the closest thing he could come up with to the Seneca snakeroot tea which Shields prescribed. After three-quarters of an hour of poaching, Bratton was removed. The next day he was up and around.

So pleased were the two resident physicians of Kamiah with their treatment that they tried to cure a paralyzed chief. Lewis would have preferred using shock treatment—"I am confident that this would be an excellent subject for electricity and much regret that I have it not in my power to supply it"—but the sweatings did improve the chief's condition and Lewis wrote, "He seems highly delighted with his recovery. I begin to entertain strong hope of his restoration by these sweats."

As a horseman of the Piedmont, Lewis admired the Nez Percés. They sat on nicely joined, big, Spanish-style saddles covered with rawhide. Over the *silla* they tossed a buffalo robe. Like the Spaniards, they were adept with the lasso and helped him round up his herd. "Their horses appear to be of an excellent race; they are lofty, elegantly formed, active and durable; in short, many of them look like fine English coursers and would make a figure in any country." He was the first white man to report on their strikingly spotted Appaloosas—"Some of these horses are pied with large spots of white, irregularly scattered and intermixed with the black, brown, bay or some other dark colour."

Sympathy and compassion were hardly the major attributes of the American Indian, and Lewis knew it. Thus, he was most impressed—almost amazed—when Chief Hohastilpilp took pity on the captain's hungering detachment after seeing them butcher the wildest and most vicious of his packhorses. He gave Lewis permission to kill any of the Nez Percé horse herd for food. "This is a piece of liberality which would do honour to such as boast of civilization; indeed, I doubt whether there are not a great number of our countrymen who would see us fast many days before their compassion would excite them to a similar act of liberality." But still Lewis had to send a party to trade with another village for salmon, using all the empty vials and tins he could find, plus uniform buttons, for a medium of exchange. "They returned," he recorded with delight, "with about three bushels of roots and some bread, having made a successful voyage, not much less pleasing to us than the return of a good cargo to an East Indian merchant. Having exhausted all our merchandise, we are obliged to have recourse to every subterfuge in order to prepare in the most ample manner in our power to meet that wretched portion of our journey, the Rocky Mountains, where hunger and cold in their most rigorous form assail the wearied travellers. Not any of us has yet forgotten our suffering in those mountains in September last and I think it is probable we never shall."

From his shady bower, or under the ragged remnant of sail

which had replaced his rotted parfleche lodge, Lewis could see at a single glance winter, spring and summer—and all within fifteen miles. The noon sun bore down hotly on the Clearwater valley while on the hills and the plain swelling up from the river the cooler air kept the vegetation fifteen to twenty days retarded. A little more than a dozen miles away he could see the snowy Rockies, locked in winter still. Observing that the Clearwater was filling but that its level fluctuated markedly, rising by night and dropping by day, he deduced that this phenomenon was caused by the sun melting the snow during the day in the mountains. His camp was distant enough so that the meltwater did not reach it until after nightfall. "I am pleased at finding the river rise so rapidly. It, no doubt, is attributable to the melting snows of the mountains, that icy barrier which separates me from my friends and country, from all that makes life esteemable."

And, as he stared at the snowy mountains, Lewis caught himself muttering to himself, but half aloud, "Patience, patience."

235

CHAPTER XVIII

———◆◆———

EASTWARD HO!

*As we have no time to lose, we will risk the chances and
set out as early as the Indians generally think it practicable,
or the middle of this month. Our party seems much elated
with the idea of moving on towards friend and Country.*
—MERIWETHER LEWIS, on the Clearwater,
June 9, 1806

IT WAS NOW JUNE. Lewis dared not wait much longer to cross
the Rockies or his treacherous old enemy, the Missouri, would
entrap him in winter. He talked to the first party of Indians to
cross the mountains that spring. They had gone to Traveller's
Rest to meet some Flatheads. Lewis felt that if they could make
it, he could. But they warned him of slippery trails, rivers in
flood, and little or no grass. They strongly advised him to wait
two weeks before assaulting the mountain barrier. Lewis debated
their warning with himself but decided to make a tentative start.
He would advance his base closer to the mountains, to a point
where he knew there were camas roots and where, he hoped,
there might be deer. "I begin to lose all hope of any dependence
on the salmon," he sighed. Once in this forward position, he
could make another decision as to whether to commence climbing or not.

Lewis was gratified when the Clearwater began to drop. That
was the signal that the great masses of snow were gone from the
passes ahead. Although the Indians predicted he would not be
able to traverse the Divide for another moon, he determined to

give it a try. "As we have no time to lose, we will risk the chances and set out as early as the Indians generally think it practicable, or the middle of this month. Our party seems much elated with the idea of moving on towards friend and Country. They all seem alert in their movements today. They have everything in readiness for a move and, notwithstanding the want of provision, have been amusing themselves very merrily today in running footraces, pitching quoits, prison base, etc. . . ." He was not rash in his move. "I do not conceive that we are as yet losing any time, as the road is in many parts extremely steep, rocky, and must be dangerous if wet and slippery. A few days will dry the roads and will also improve the grass."

On June 10th, after exchanging some of the horses with the Indians for better animals, Lewis and Clark led their troopers to an advance base on Weippe Prairie, a great meadow filled with blossoming wild strawberry vines and masses of camas flowers. Lewis had no use for the camas root but found the blossoms lovely. "From the colour of its bloom, at a short distance it resembles lakes of fine clear water. So complete is this deception that, on first sight, I would have sworn it was water." Keeping his hunters out, he rested his men for the most difficult leg of the return trip. "We have now been detained near five weeks in consequence of the snows; a serious loss of time at this delightful season for travelling. I am still apprehensive that the snow and the want of food for our horses will prove a serious embarrassment to us, as at least four days' journey of our route in these mountains lies over heights and along a ledge of mountains never entirely destitute of snow. Everybody, [however], seems anxious to be in motion, convinced that we have not now any time to delay if the calculation is to reach the United States this season. *This* I am determined to accomplish if within the compass of human power."

The explorers set out on June 15th with 66 horses, over a slithery trail barricaded, from time to time, with fallen logs. A hard rain wet the men to the skin. Ahead, trudged the hunters, leaving their kill hanging prominently along the route of march, usually at the edges of glades where they knew Lewis would graze the horses. As the men climbed into the rugged, snow-

blanketed foothills, they could see the seasonal clock turn back-
wards. Leaves appeared to retreat into the branches of the small
white maples, and the bloom of the dogwood shrank back into
nothingness as the soldiers climbed to cooler altitudes. The wintry signs did not sit well with Lewis. "These appearances in this
comparatively low region augers but unfavourably with respect
to the practicability of passing the mountains. However, we are
determined to proceed."

Between the North and Middle, or Lochsa, Fork of the
Clearwater, the detachment was stopped dead in its tracks by
snowbanks bulking 12 to 15 feet high, even on the exposed
southerly slopes. "Here was winter with all its rigours," sighed
Lewis. "The air was cold, my hands and feet benumbed." And
there was not so much as a green shrub protruding from the
snowpack to feed the animals. Once more a decision had to be
made and Lewis's mind raced to summon all the factors on both
sides of the question, to proceed or retreat. He took a full two
hours to make up his mind, his men shivering in the icy world of
the high Bitterroots. Although the snow was bearing the weight
of the horses well, he estimated it would take them five days
more to reach the fish weirs at Colt Creek at the very best pace *if*
they could find the right ridges to follow. He turned to his friend,
Drouillard and threw him a questioning look. The *métis* shook
his head. He told Lewis he strongly doubted that they could find
the right route without costly errors and delays. That made
Lewis's mind up. It was too big a gamble. He would fall back
while the horses were still strong and try to keep them in good
condition for a second essay, this time with a guide if one could
be had. Reluctantly, Captain Lewis gave the order to retreat—a
command he had not given before in his Army career. "The
party were a good deal dejected, tho' not as much so as I had
apprehended they would have been. This is the first time since we
have been on this long tour that we have ever been compelled to
retreat or make a retrograde march." Before he fell back to the
plains, Lewis had his men build a deerskin-covered scaffold in
which to cache equipment and thus lighten the loads of the
horses.

After giving the order to fall back, Lewis plotted a plan of action with Clark which they should take in case no Nez Percé came forward as a guide for their next attempt. They could not wait for the snows to melt entirely or they would never make the States by winter. Should no good route to Traveller's Rest present itself, Lewis had another plan up his sleeve. He would fall back and take a roundabout route far to the south which the Shoshones had recommended to him. But this trail would mean a month's delay, at least. He would not use it unless the trail to Traveller's Rest should fail him, and he was sanguine of success. "The snow bears the horses perfectly. It is a firm, coarse, snow without a crust and the horses have good foothold without slipping much. I think the plan we have devised will succeed even should we not be enable to obtain a guide."

The second assault on the mountain range, begun on the 24th, went well. Lewis found the snowbanks shrinking fast, many of them down a full four feet from a week earlier. Much progress was made by the men taking exposed hillsides and low areas between drifts at first, but he found they made even better time on the snow than by trying to pick a trail through the rocky areas free of it. Camps were restful as the small fires drove off the *brûlots,* or eye gnats, and mosquitoes and black flies. Both men and mounts awoke fresh each morning, except the inhabitants of sick bay—McNeal, Clark, Potts and Goodrich. Appetites were fierce during marches of 28 mountainous miles in a day, and even such humble fare as bear oil and boiled roots came to look like "an agreeable dish" to Lewis.

Though the men crossed and recrossed their old trail of the fall, the commander was grateful for his guides, as the trees which he had blazed on the westward march were very hard to find. At the higher elevations, snowfields remained and the horses either slid along on top of them or broke through the crusts to their bellies. The beasts were tired and hungry but there was no forage, so Lewis did not take their packs off but urged them on. When they reached Traveller's Rest in the Bitterroot Valley safely, Lewis called a two-day halt to rest up, recoup the horses, and to allow Shields time to repair the guns damaged on the three-month, 802-mile journey from Fort Clatsop. Meanwhile, he and Clark conferred and decided to split the Corps of

Discovery up to gain a better knowledge of a wider area of the Far West. Lewis would take a party to the Falls of the Columbia and leave three men there to prepare portage carriages while he and six men explored Maria's River. From a large number of volunteers he selected Drouillard, the two Field brothers, Werner, Frazier, and Sergeant Gass to accompany him. The rest of the men would go with Clark to the Jefferson River cache. From there, Ordway would take nine men down the Jefferson in canoes while Clark and the other ten would march to the Yellowstone, build canoes, and descend it to the Missouri. Lewis had a special assignment for Pryor. He and two troopers would take the horse herd, except for the animals with Lewis's party, to Hugh Heney on the Assiniboine River, via Fort Mandan.

The reason for Lewis's apparently munificent gift to the North West Company *bourgeois* was that he hoped to lure him out of British, and into American, service. Lewis wanted him to lead some of the Teton, Yankton and Sisseton Sioux to Washington. Heney would become a U. S. Indian agent and he would trade Lewis's horses for supplies for the trip to the States. With Heney's help, Lewis hoped to impress the Sioux with America's strength (on the East Coast) and remove the barricade which their presence constituted on the Missouri. "Those [Tetons], until some effectual measures be taken to render them pacific, will always prove a serious source of inconvenience to the free navigation of the Missouri or, at least, to its upper branches from whence the richest portion of its fur trade is to be derived. . . . We are positive that she [the United States] will not suffer her citizens to be deprived of the free navigation of the Missouri by a few comparatively feeble bands of savages who may be so ill-advised as to refuse her proffered friendship and continue their depredations on her citizens who may ascend or descend that river.

"We believe that the surest guarantee of savage fidelity to any nation is a thorough conviction in their minds that their Government possesses the power of punishing promptly every act of aggression committed on their part against the person or property of their citizens; to produce this conviction without the use of violence is the wish of our Government; and to effect it we cannot devise a more expedient method than that of taking some of the best-informed and most influential chiefs with us to the United States. They will have an ample view of our population and resources, become convinced, themselves, and on their return, convince their nations of the futility of an attempt to oppose the will of our Government. . . . Should you not succeed in prevailing on the chiefs to go with us, we will make some other arrangements by which you will be enabled, perhaps, to bring them on afterwards, yourself. But it would be preferable in very point of view that they should go with us. The number of chiefs and their attendants must not exceed twelve persons, as we cannot possibly accommodate more." His last words to Heney were warnings to the Sioux: "The mouth of all the rivers through [which] traders convey merchandise to their country are now in the possession of the United States who can, at pleasure, cut off all communication between themselves and their accustomed traders."

Lewis's march started out poorly. First, the commander—who had been named Yo-me-kol-lick, or White Bearskin Folded, presumably because his medicine was like that of the grizzly—fell off a raft into the Missoula River, wetting his chronometer. It was an ill omen for, next, his five edgy Nez Percé guides served notice. They would have to leave. They were terrified of running into Fort de Prairie Minnetarees if they continued with the whites. Lewis set up a camp, lit a smudge fire to relieve the horses from the torture of the mosquitoes and black flies, and attended to a pressing obligation: "I directed the hunters to turn out early in the morning and endeavour to kill some more meat for these people who I was unwilling to leave without giving them a good supply of provisions after their having been so obliging as to conduct us through those tremendous mountains." He was ready to echo Gass's sentiments—"It is but justice to say that the whole nation to which they belong are the most friendly, honest and ingenuous people that we have seen in the course of our voyage and travels . . . good hearted, hospitable, and obliging Sons of the West."

But, alas, Drouillard and the brothers Field had no luck on that Independence Day hunt of 1806. So, in lieu of fresh meat as a parting gift, Lewis presented the Nez Percés with some of the prior day's deer kill, plus a shirt, a handkerchief and some ammunition from his meager store. He smoked a last pipe with them, bade them adieu and *bon voyage,* and sadly watched them disappear from view near the later site of Helena, Montana. "These affectionate people, our guides, betrayed every emotion of unfeigned regret at separating from us; they said they were confident that the Pahkees, the appellation they gave the Minnetarees, would cut us off."

Maintaining a careful watch for these hostiles, both day and night, Lewis led his men through Lewis and Clark Pass to the Medicine, or Sun, River. Indians ran off some of his horses and Drouillard's pursuit of them was in vain. But his return was more important than the missing mounts and Lewis wrote: "His safe return has relieved me from great anxiety. I had already settled in my mind that a white bear had killed him and I should have set out, tomorrow, in search of him." The reduction of his horse pack led Lewis to take only Drouillard and the Field boys with him to Maria's River.

Before Lewis had a chance to set out, McNeal, left to check the caches, was galloping up to him, much shaken, his horse lathered with sweat. He had reached Willow Creek only to run headlong into a grizzly. The animal had so startled his horse that it threw him and he landed, literally, between the very feet of the bear. He managed to scramble to his feet and club the monster over the head with the gun, which he had not had time to aim and shoot. The weapon broke at the breech but stunned the bear and the Scot scuttled away, leaped to his feet and climbed a tree. The grizzly waited at the base of the trunk for three solid hours before losing its patience and wandering off, grumbling. McNeal shinnied down, caught his horse and headed for Lewis like the wind. Lewis, after hearing him out, noted in his log: "These bears are a most tremendous animal. It seems that the hand of Providence has been most wonderfully in our favour with respect to them, or some of us would, long since, have fallen a sacrifice to their ferocity." McNeal's scrape reminded Lewis of his own run of bad luck near the Falls. "There seems to be a certain fatality attached to the neighbourhood of these Falls, for there is always a chapter of accidents prepared for us during our residence at them."

Before he left for Maria's River, Lewis checked the caches near the Falls and found that the river had risen and that water had penetrated his plant specimens, bearskins and medicines, ruining them. But luckily his chart of the Missouri and his other papers escaped with only dampening. Rations were no longer a problem, as he explained. "The Missouri bottoms on both sides of the River were crowded with buffalo. I sincerely believe that there were not less than ten thousand buffalo within a circle of two miles. . . . There are such numbers of them that there is one continual roar." As he and his men hunted the buffalo he noted how many predators were also at work. "The wolves are in great numbers, howling around us and lolling about in the plains in view at a distance of two or three hundred yards. I counted twenty-seven about the carcass of a buffalo."

Should his life and health be preserved, Lewis told Gass, he would meet him at his party at the mouth of Maria's River on August 5th. If he did not arrive by September 1st, the Sergeant should give him up and lead the men to the Yellowstone to meet Clark. He then led his three companions toward Maria's River.

When the quartet crossed the bloody trail of a wounded buffalo near Maria's River, Lewis sent Drouillard to kill it and determine, from any arrows in it, which tribe was roaming the area "The Minnetarees of Fort de Prairie [Arapahos] and the Blackfoot Indians rove through this quarter of the country and they are a vicious, lawless and rather an abandoned set of wretches. I wish to avoid an interview with them, if possible. I have no doubt they would steal our horses if they have it in their power and finding us weak, should they appear to be numerous, would most probably attempt to rob us of our arms and baggage. At all events, I am determined to take every possible precaution to avoid them, if possible." He scanned the plains carefully with his glass but could discern no Indians. Nor did Drouillard report having seen any when he returned, unable to overtake the bloodied buffalo.

The little party of Americans remained uneasy and watchful. On July 18th, Lewis noted: "I keep a strict lookout every night. I take my tour of the watch with the men." But the exploration continued without incident. When Maria's River forked, Lewis ascended the northern branch. By now he doubted that the headwaters would lie as far north as 50°, for he was already in 48° 40' of latitude.

It looked as if luck was staying with Lewis. Drouillard found camps of Indians in the Maria's drainage but the whites managed to steer clear of the warriors themselves. On the 25th Lewis balanced his notebook on his knee at Camp Disappointment on Cut Bank Creek to write, gratefully, before retracing his steps to the Missouri: "We consider ourselves extremely fortunate in not having met with these people."

CHAPTER XIX

TRIUMPHAL RETURN

Thus terminated an expedition conducted and sustained throughout with the greatest skill, courage and fortitude, with the loss of only one man, who died of sickness on their passage up the River, and occasioned the death of only two Indians, who were killed from necessity while in the act of committing a most daring and violent robbery of the horses belonging to a detachment of the main party under the immediate command of Captain Lewis, near the head of the Missouri.

—EDITOR, *Analectic Magazine,* March 1815

EXACTLY one day after congratulating himself on his good fortune in avoiding prowling Minnetarees or Blackfeet, Lewis suddenly spied thirty horses on a hilltop. Upon bringing up his telescope, his fears were confirmed; there were several Indians intently observing Drouillard who, separated from Lewis and the Field boys, was hunting. "This was a very unpleasant sight. However, I resolved to make the best of our situation and to approach them in a friendly manner." He had Joseph Field display the flag as they both advanced. The Indians were so intent in shadowing Drouillard that they did not see Lewis until he was quite close. When they did see him, they hurriedly drove their horses together and grouped themselves as if for a fight. "I calculated on their number being nearly or quite equal to that of their horses [and] that our running would invite pursuit, as it would convince them that we were their enemies. And our horses were so indifferent that we could not hope to escape by flight. Added to this, Drouillard was separated from us and I feared that, his not being apprized of the Indians, in the event of our attempting to escape he would most probably fall a sacrifice. Under these considerations, I still advanced towards them."

When Lewis was within a quarter-mile of the red men, one of their number mounted up and galloped straight at him, full speed. Lewis halted, alighted from his horse, held out his hand in the universal sign of peace and beckoned to the horseman. The rider paid no attention to his sign other than to rein up sharply and then wheel his steed and return to the hillock. In a few moments, the entire party of Indians began to descend the slope. Lewis counted them quickly; there were only eight warriors, but he saw that far more than eight of the ponies were saddled up. "I told the two men with me that I apprehended that these were Minnetarees of Fort de Prairie [they were, actually, Piegan Blackfeet] and, from their known character, I expected that we were to have some difficulty with them; that if they thought themselves sufficiently strong, I was convinced they would attempt to rob us, in which case, be their number what they would, I should resist to the last extremity, preferring death to that of being deprived of my papers, instruments and gun and [I] desired that they would form the same resolution and be alert and on their guard."

At one hundred yards, the Indians halted, except for one warrior who continued his advance. Lewis stopped the Field brothers, likewise but continued his own progress. He shook hands gingerly with the lead Indian and with his companions as they came up. The braves asked to smoke with him so Lewis took advantage of their request to recall Drouillard by a ruse. He told his visitors that his hunter had his calumet. He then sent Reuben Field and one of the Blackfeet to fetch the half-breed. While he waited, he asked the Indians if they were Minnetarees of the North. He thought that they answered in the affirmative. Perhaps they misunderstood him, his silent-tongue expert not being with him at the moment. When he asked if any were chiefs, three of them replied that they were. This he did not believe but nevertheless, in the hope of keeping the peace, he was quite willing to flatter them. So he gave one a medal, the second a flag, and the third a kerchief. As he handed out the presents, Lewis's eyes scanned the horizon for signs of Indian reinforcements. "From none of them appearing, [I] became much better satisfied that we could manage that number, should they attempt any hostile measures." In fact, the braves appeared more alarmed at meeting the whites than vice versa.

After Drouillard and Reuben rejoined them, Lewis invited the Blackfeet to camp with him. "I told them I was glad to see them and had a great deal to say to them." Lewis knew that he could not shake them off in their own country; it would be best to camp right atop them and keep them in plain sight for as long as possible, so that they could not lay an ambush. With apparent kindness, the Piegans invited the palefaces to make use of their buffalo-skin shelter. Lewis and Drouillard accepted but the Field boys preferred to spread out their robes by the fire in front of the lodge. During the early evening, Lewis conversed a good deal with the Indians with Drouillard's help, learning that they were part of a large band camped near the foot of the Rockies. To his surprise, he learned that the main party of Indians was accompanied by some white men.

Since Lewis was woefully short of manpower, he sought to overwhelm his potential adversaries with wordpower. Through Drouillard he gave them a long harangue. "I told these people that I had come a great way from the east, up the large river which runs towards the rising sun, that I had been to the great waters where the sun sets and had seen a great many nations, all of whom I had invited to come and trade with me on the rivers on their side of the mountains. That I had found most of them at war with their neighbours and had succeeded in restoring peace among them; that I was now on my way home and had left my party at the Falls of the Missouri with orders to descend that river to the entrance of Maria's River and there await my arrival." He added, after this lightly veiled reminder of the strength and nearness of his main party, "That I had come in search of them in order to prevail on them to be at peace with their neighbours, particularly those on the west side of the mountains and to engage them to come and trade with me when the establishment is made at the entrance of this river."

The Blackfeet nodded their assent to his request for intertribal peace although some of them pointed out that they had cut their hair in mourning for the members of their tribe who had fallen to Tushepaw arrows. Since he found them very fond of smoking, Lewis was only too ready to fill the bowl; he would let them stupefy themselves if they wished. All the while, till evening, he hammered away at them to ask their chiefs to come to a council which he would hold at the junction of Maria's River and the Missouri. To keep them constantly aware of his own reinforcements, he observed that his many comrades at the confluence would be uneasy over his long absence.

After finishing the long powwow, Lewis took the first watch, waking Reuben Field to relieve him at 11:30. He then went to bed and dropped off into a sound sleep.

A shout and the sound of a scuffle awoke Lewis. Befuddled with sleep, he blinked and rubbed his eyes to find that it was just daylight. As his eyes focused, he saw Drouillard wrenching at his rifle, trying to get it away from the grasp of one of the Piegans. His shout—"Damn you! Let go of my gun!"—had aroused Lewis. The captain found that his nerves and limbs functioned almost automatically in such a crisis. As he later reconstructed the action, "I jumped up and asked what was the matter—which I quickly learned when I saw Drouillard in a scuffle with the Indian for his gun. I reached to seize my own but found it gone. I then drew a pistol from my holster and, turning myself about, saw the Indian making off with my gun. I ran at him with my pistol and bade him lay down my gun, which he was in the act of doing when the Fieldses returned and drew up their guns to shoot him, which I forbade, as he did not appear to be about to make any resistance or commit any offensive act. He dropped the gun and walked slowly off. I picked her up instantly."

A few quick words with his men apprized Lewis of the situation. Joseph Field, on guard duty, had been lulled by the breaking of dawn and the stirring of the camp into life. Carelessly, he had set down his rifle alongside his sleeping brother. The Indian "chief" to whom Lewis had given a medal the evening before,

Side Hill Calf, had suddenly slipped up behind Field and grabbed both weapons. At the same instant, the others rushed to seize Drouillard's and Lewis's rifles. Joseph Field saw these men and turned to grab his own, calling out to his brother at the same time. His cry had not awakened Lewis, but Drouillard's bearish roar had done the trick. While Lewis was still trying to gather his wits, and Drouillard was regaining his rifle, fleet Reuben had leaped to his feet and sprinted after the fleeing Indians. Joseph was already in hot pursuit and the two runners caught up with the Blackfeet in only 50 or 60 paces. They grappled with them, trying to wrestle their guns away from them. When the braves resisted, Reuben drew his skinning knife and stabbed his adversary in the heart. The warrior ran about fifteen steps, then fell dead.

Lewis, continuing the reconstruction of the wild melee, recalled, "Drouillard, having about this time recovered his gun and pouch, asked me if he might not kill the fellow, which I also forbade, as the Indian did not appear to wish to kill us. [But] as soon as they found us all in possession of our arms, they ran and endeavoured to drive off all the horses. I now hollowed [sic] to the men and told them to fire on them if they attempted to drive off our horses. They accordingly pursued the main party who were driving the horses up the river. I pursued the man who had taken my gun, who, with another, was driving off a part of the horses which were to the left of the camp. I pursued them so closely that they could not take twelve of their own horses but continued to drive one of mine with some others. At the distance of three hundred paces, they entered one of those steep niches in the bluff, with the horses before them. Being nearly out of breath, I could pursue them no further. I called to them, as I had done several times before, that I would shoot if they did not give me my horse, and raised my gun. One of them jumped behind a rock and spoke to the other, who turned around and stopped at a distance of thirty paces from me, and I shot him through the belly. He fell to his knees and on his right elbow, from which position he partly raised himself up and fired at me, and, turning himself about, crawled in behind a rock which was a few feet from him. He overshot me. Being bareheaded, I felt the wind of

249

his bullet very distinctly. Not having my shot pouch, I could not reload my piece and as there were two of them behind good shelters from me, I did not think it prudent to rush on them with my [remaining] pistol which, had I discharged it, I had not the means of reloading until I reached camp. I therefore retired leisurely towards camp."

Drouillard met his commander en route. Lewis ordered him to help him round up as many of the Indian horses as possible and to call the Field boys back. Lewis abandoned one of his horses but took four of the best of the Indian mounts. On the fire he placed the attackers' shields, bows and quivers of arrows, plus all other belongings. One of the two guns of the Blackfeet had been left behind so he took it along with some of their buffalo meat. (The surviving Indians were still armed with one rifle, bows and arrows and battle-axes.) He took back his flag but left the medal on the neck of the dead Indian, "that they might be informed who we were."

Lewis ordered his men to push their horses hard in a quick dash for the Missouri River and safety. He was sure that the six savages would arouse the large party to an attack. (David Thompson, as late as 1807, found his path cleared of Blackfeet who were still dropping to the south, hoping to find and punish Lewis. As he put it in his report, "The murder of two Piegans by Captain Lewis of the United States drew the Piegans to the Missouri to revenge their deaths; and this gave me an opportunity to cross the mountains by the defiles of the Saskatchewan River, which led to the headwaters of the Columbia River.")

The treachery of the Blackfeet took place at dawn on July 27, 1806, on the south side of Two Medicine River, about four miles below Badger Creek on what would become, much later, the eastern edge of the Blackfoot Reservation. At 3 P.M. that afternoon, Lewis and his comrades reached the Rose River, 63 miles from the skirmish site. He rested his men and mounts for one and a half hours, then urged them on again for another 17 miles. Halting once more, he rested his party for two hours then proceeded at a less hectic pace, by moonlight, for another 20 miles. Finally, as he later described it, "[We] laid ourselves down to rest in the plain, very much fatigued, as may be readily conceived. My Indian horse carried me very well; in short, much better than my own would have done and leaves me with but little reason to complain of the robbery. . . . As day appeared, I awakened the men and directed the horses to be saddled. I was so sore from my ride yesterday that I could scarcely stand and the men complained of being in a similar situation. However, I encouraged them by telling them that their own lives as well as those of our friends and fellow travelers depended on our exertions at this moment." His companions wished to take a circuitous route to the Missouri but Lewis, afraid the Indians would swoop down on the unsuspecting canoe parties waiting for him, refused. "I told them that we owed much to the safety of our friends and that we must risk our lives on this occasion. . . . It was my determination that if we were attacked on the plains on our way to the point, that the bridles of the horses should be tied together and we would stand and defend them or sell our lives as dearly as we could."

As they neared the Missouri, they thought that they heard the report of a gun, but they could not be certain. Soon, they heard several unmistakable rifle shots. As Lewis put it, "We quickly repaired to this joyful sound." As they reached the bank, thanks to the incredible timing of coincidence, they saw Ordway's canoe just rounding an upriver bend! Lewis and his tired trio abandoned their horses, shook hands warmly with the sergeant and all of his men in relief and gratitude, then threw their gear into the canoes and followed it. They had covered 120 miles in 24 hours of the hardest kind of riding.

Sergeant Gass and his men soon met them. The reconstituted party opened the caches and Lewis examined the hidden red pirogue, pronouncing it unseaworthy from rot. In the white pirogue and the five small canoes, Lewis and his party made very good progress downriver, up to 70 miles a day. To stretch the daily run, Lewis replaced the customary midday stop (for a hot meal) with cold meat lunches, and no stops, and in this fashion added from 12 to 15 miles to an ordinary day's run. There was still time for natural history, however, and the explorer secured four bighorn sheep specimens near Slaughter River. He skeletonized them in order to take the bones back to Washington and

Philadelphia. Hunting was as good as collecting; there were plenty of elk, buffalo, beaver, deer and bear. The men killed two grizzlies, one of them at the campfire itself.

When he landed at the Yellowstone's mouth, Lewis found no Clark, only the remnant of a message from the redhead on a piece of elkhorn—"W.C. a few miles further down, on the right hand side." He pushed off in a now more leisurely pursuit of his comrade, intending to take a noon observation at Burned Hills, the approximate site of later Fort Berthoud, North Dakota, before closing with Clark. It was too late, 12:20, when the boats arrived at the site on August 11th, but Lewis decided to make the stop as planned, only to do some hunting instead of making celestial observations. He took one-eyed Cruzatte with him. They landed on a sandbar thick with willows and elk. The captain's rifle soon brought down a buck and Cruzatte's wounded another. They reloaded and took different routes to seek out the disabled animal.

The next few minutes were as hectic and confused for Lewis as his rude dawn awakening by the Piegans. He eventually put the story together:

"I was in the act of firing on the elk a second time when a ball struck my left thigh about an inch below my hip joint, missing the bone. It passed through the left thigh and cut the thickness of the bullet across the hinder part of my right thigh. The stroke was very severe. I instantly supposed that Cruzatte had shot me in mistake for an elk, as I was dressed in brown leather [i.e., buckskins] and he cannot see very well. Under this impression, I called out to him, 'Damn you! You have shot me!' and looked towards the place from whence the shot had come. Seeing nothing, I called Cruzatte several times as loud as I could, but received no answer. I was now persuaded that it was an Indian that had shot me, as the report of the gun did not appear to be more than forty paces from me and Cruzatte appeared to be out of hearing of me. In this situation, not knowing how many Indians there might be concealed in the bushes, I thought best to make good my retreat to the pirogue, calling out as I ran for the first hundred paces, as loud as I could, to Cruzatte to retreat, that there were Indians, hoping to alarm him in time to make his escape. . . . I still retained the charge in my gun, which I was about to discharge at the moment the ball struck me.

"When I arrived in sight of the pirogue, I called the men to their arms, to which they flew in an instant. I told them that I was wounded but, I hoped, not mortally, by an Indian, I believed, and directed them to follow me; that I would return and give them battle and relieve Cruzatte, if possible, who, I feared, had fallen into their hands. The men followed me as they were bid and I returned about a hundred paces when my wounds became so painful and my thigh so stiff that I could scarcely get on. In short, I was compelled to halt and ordered the men to proceed and if they found themselves overpowered by numbers, to retreat in good order, keeping up a fire. I now got back to the pirogue as well as I could and prepared myself with a pistol, my rifle and air gun, being determined, as a retreat was impracticable, to sell my life as dearly as possible."

After twenty minutes of nerve-racking suspense, Lewis saw his men returning to the beach. Their posture, their air, the handling of their arms, all told him that they had found no sign of hostiles. With them was an alarmed Cruzatte. Sure enough, the sergeants reported no sign of red men on the isle. Cruzatte insisted that he had shot an elk, not Lewis, and he denied having heard any of his commander's calls to him. His pained C.O. successfully kept in check his Welsh temper, for once, acknowledging, "I do not believe that the fellow did it intentionally but, after finding that he had shot me, was anxious to conceal his knowledge of having done so."

With Sergeant Gass's help, Lewis got his bloody buckskin trousers off and dressed his wounds himself, introducing "tents," or bandages, of the newfangled "patent lint" into the bullet holes. "I was happy to find that it [the ball] had touched neither bone nor artery," said the doctor-patient. Gass found the lead ball lodged in the buckskins. Lewis still intended, obstinately, to make an observation but the pain prevented it. He slept fitfully that night in the white pirogue, assailed by pain and a high fever.

The next day, the boats proceeded under the joint command of Ordway and Gass. Lewis was now quite *hors de combat*. Gass noted, "Captain Lewis is in good spirits, but his wound is stiff and sore." Another message from Clark drew the canoes ashore. It advised Lewis that Pryor and his Yellowstone unit had been robbed of all their horses by Indians and had come down the river in skin canoes. This spelled the end of Lewis's plan to exchange horses for merchandise and bring the Sioux to Washington with Hugh Heney.

Next morning, the bowsman spied a camp which he took to be Clark's, but it was that of the first Americans the corps had seen for months. Joseph Dickson and Forrest Hancock, hunters and trappers of Illinois, informed them that Clark had passed them at noon the prior day. Lewis gave them a file and some lead and powder and, from his bed of pain, filled them in on the uppermost Missouri and its tribes and tributaries. Before the corpsmen moved on, the two long-lost hunters, Collins and Colter, rejoined them, to the joy of their messmates. Lewis treated himself. "My wounds felt very stiff and sore this morning, but gave me no considerable pain. There was much less inflammation than I had reason to apprehend there would be. I had last evening applied a poultice of Peruvian barks."

Lewis overtook Clark on August 12th and the corps was finally reassembled. The Virginian relinquished active command to his adjutant and de facto co-commander at the same time that he gave to Clark all responsibility for keeping up the journal of the expedition. He said, "Writing in my present situation is extremely painful to me. I shall desist until I recover." Although he told his friend that his wound was slight and that he expected to be quite well in twenty to thirty days, Clark insisted upon seeing it. "I examined the wound," reported the Kentuckian, "and found it a very bad flesh wound. The ball had passed through the fleshy part of his left thigh below the hip bone and cut the cheek of the right buttock for three inches in length and the depth of the ball."

As they passed on down the Missouri, Clark washed and dressed his friend's wounds frequently. The commander was still weak, Ordway noticed: "Captain Lewis fainted as Captain Clark was dressing his wound." On the 14th, they began to feel much nearer to home. That day they were back among old friends again, the Minnetarees or Gros Ventres and the Mandans. It was just four months and 21 days—and 1,950 miles—after leaving Fort Clatsop in the hands of Chief Comowool. Going west, the 2,529-mile distance had taken them eight months, from April to December 1805. On his return route, Lewis had shaved some 579 miles via his Rocky Mountain shortcut.

Clark had to take over all the diplomatic duties which his fellow officer normally shouldered. It was he who presided at the powwow held on the 15th with the Mandans and Minnetarees. At approximately the same time, Colter asked Lewis and Clark if he could join Dickson and Hancock on their fur-trapping expedition to the Yellowstone. The commanders gave their joint blessing and a discharge, and Lewis, in appreciation of his long and faithful service, outfitted him with a gun, ammunition and what supplies he could spare.

The next day, Lewis and Clark turned the swivel cannon over to Le Borgne, the Cruzatte-eyed chieftain of the Big Bellies. They accompanied the donation with a little ceremony and oratory in order to puff up the importance of this gift to princely proportions in that rascal's mind. They then settled Charbonneau's account and gave him his release. Although he had hardly impressed either officer with his services, they presented him with the blacksmithing tools. Clark offered to raise Baptiste, or Pomp, in civilization, but his parents wished to wait a year before turning the boy over to him. The redhead then picked up Lewis's old friend, Chief Big White of the Mandans, to take him to St. Louis and Washington. With him would go his squaw, Yellow Corn, his son, his interpreter, René Jusseaume, and the latter's wife and two children. Clark revisited all the Indian villages and paid a call on Fort Mandan before shoving off again. He found the bastion a blackened ruin. It had caught fire accidentally and burned down.

At 2 P.M., August 17th, William Clark gave the order to proceed for the United States. By the 19th, he could write, "Captain Lewis is getting much better and we are all in good spirits." As the river swept them effortlessly along, the only real work for the men was bailing when big waves "flacked" into the dugouts. Lewis expected to be up and around in ten days but he was still feeble when the Americans visited the Arikaras and some haughty visiting Cheyennes, so Clark filled in at the council for him again. It turned out to be a critical talk, though neither man realized it then. Perhaps nothing which they could have said would have arrested the decline of Arikara-U.S. relations. The Rees declared that they would not go to Washington with Lewis; they had sent one chief there already and he had never returned. Nor would he ever return. He was dead. The news of his death was just downriver with courier Gravelines, whom Lewis and Clark would soon encounter. The death of Chief Ankedoucharo was the first piece of a pattern of tragedy to fall into position. When all were in place, Lewis too would die.

August 23rd saw a pleased Will Clark take up his pen to write, "I am happy to have it in my power to say that my worthy friend, Captain Lewis, is recovering fast. He walked a little today for the first time." But on the 27th, Lewis, normally a good patient, succumbed to his perpetual impatience. He took too long a walk and hurt himself. He spent a bad night and morning in a real setback. Luckily, the relapse was a brief one and he was soon on the mend again. In fact, on September 1st, when the party heard firing as they reached the area of the treacherous Tetons, he was able to hobble up the bank to form some of the soldiers into a force covering Clark and the rest of the troopers. But the Indians proved to be only friendly Yanktons, plinking with their trade muskets at a keg bobbing in the muddy flood. That day, Lewis and Clark saw their old powwow flagstaff of exactly two years before, to the day, as they floated past Calumet Bluffs.

Below the James, they met the Scots trader of dubious friendship for the United States, James Aird. (He would later dupe Frederick Bates, Lewis's Secretary of Upper Louisiana when the Virginian was governor of that territory, and urge the Indians to war against the United States.) He gave the troopers their first strong drink since July 4, 1805, and briefed the officers on current and not-so-current events. The most exciting news which he passed on was that of the Aaron Burr and Alexander Hamilton duel of July 12, 1804.

Lewis was convalescing well enough now to walk with ease and by the time the canoes reached Floyd's Bluff on September 4th, he was able to pay a visit to the sergeant's lonely grave with

Clark. They found that the Indians had opened the burial and had interred a chief's son with Floyd, to partake of his Big Medicine. They reburied him properly and dropped down to Council Bluffs where Lewis was up to scaling the steep heights which commanded the river.

The Missouri, in Lewis's and Clark's eyes, came to be almost crowded. They met Gravelines, Dorion and one of Chouteau's traders en route to the Loups, Omahas and Sioux. The peddlers spoiled the troopers, plying them with old news and young whiskey. One of the traders whom they met was Captain Robert McClellan, an old Army friend of both Lewis and Clark. Of course, it was little more than his patriotic duty to wet the whistles of all hands with pop-skull whiskey. For the officers, however, he had a real welcoming-home treat, a bottle of wine. The expeditionaries drank in the news, too, almost as avidly as they downed the grain spirits. They learned that one rumor had them wiped out to a man, another had them prisoners of the Spaniards and laboring in the mines of New Spain. McClellan told Lewis that war between Spain and the United States appeared imminent, because word was sweeping the East that Zebulon Pike's men had been killed by the Spanish.

Lewis and Clark examined Jefferson's speech to the Arikaras, carried by Gravelines along with some presents to cover the dead—that is, make amends for their chief's death in the States. He told Lewis that he had been asked to inquire after them, too.

Others bound upriver whom they met included one of the Robidoux family, who carried a trading license unsigned by Governor Wilkinson and unsealed. They were suspicious of him and warned him to see to his credentials. A more pleasant meeting was that with John McClallan, no relation to his near namesake only a few miles upstream. This man, too, was an old friend of Lewis's and they were astonished and delighted at their unexpected meeting. He told Lewis that the people had long ago given him up and, in fact, forgotten him. But not the President, he hastened to add. He told his friend that the Chief Executive, uneasy over Lewis's fate, had asked him to make inquiries as he worked his way west. Like the other traders, McClallan showered gifts on the returning adventurers—biscuits, chocolate, sugar and the liquid which oiled the wheels of empire, corn whiskey. His own private news was of peculiar interest to Lewis. Ostensibly bound for the Platte to trade, he personally planned to start up a trade with Spanish Santa Fe, via the Pawnees and Comanches. McClallan hoped to haul goods by mule train to some point in Louisiana to which the New Mexicans would come to trade. Lewis's mind flickered back to his abortive plan to ride to Santa Fe from St. Louis in 1803.

The first definite sign of civilization for the men (October 20th) was the sight of a small herd of cows grazing on the river-bank. Clark noted that it was a "joyfull sight to the party, and [it] caused a shout to be raised for joy." Shortly, they swept up to the landing of the little outpost of La Charette, or Charriton, where Lewis and Clark's whooping men strained at the oars to get ashore. But, before landing, they asked their commanders if they might fire a salute. With their assent, the corpsmen fired three rounds, followed by a hearty cheer. In the village they were welcomed by two Canadian-Scots traders, but to get whiskey, the heroes had to pay a citizen $8 cash, for two gallons. They knew now, for sure, that they were back in civilization. Clark snorted, "An imposition!" at the price.

The next day the boats reached St. Charles. It was 3 P.M. and the "excessively polite" gentlemen and their ladies were taking their Sunday strolls. After being welcomed ashore, Lewis began to compose a recapitulation of the party's adventures since they had left Fort Mandan. Between St. Charles and St. Louis he drafted a letter for publication which he had Clark copy and sign and direct to his brother. He knew that the news of the expedition's return would appear in the Kentucky papers long before those of the Coast. Since Clark was no writer, Lewis composed the piece. The letter became a news story immediately. It was lifted time and time again after appearing in the Frankfort *Palladium* (October 9, 1806) and, as the first word of Lewis's success, it triggered a revival of interest in the expedition, and in the Far West in general.

On the 22nd and 23rd, Lewis and Clark stopped at Cantonment Bellefontaine, where they were greeted by Colonel Hunt and the saluting guns of Lieutenant Peters's artillery company, before outfitting Big White in American-style clothing for his trip to the Atlantic states.

It was high noon, September 23, 1806, that the explorers made their grand entrance into St. Louis. The great circuit of exploration was completed. Gass wrote, with great restraint, "We were received with great kindness and marks of friendship by the inhabitants after an absence of two years, four months, and ten days." A gentleman who viewed their arrival wrote to friends in the East and his letter was printed in the Philadelphia paper *Poulson's American Daily Advertiser*. The eyewitness said of the corpsmen, "They really have the appearance of Robinson Crusoes, dressed entirely in buckskins."

Captain Meriwether Lewis's formal report on the safe and successful return of his command was in the form of a letter to President Jefferson from St. Louis, dated September 23rd. It began, "It is with pleasure that I announce to you the safe arrival of myself and my party at 12 o'clock today at this place with our papers and baggage." He then came immediately to the point, to relieve Jefferson's suspense. "In obedience to your orders we have penetrated the Continent of North America to the Pacific Ocean and sufficiently explored the interior of the country to affirm with confidence that we have discovered the most practicable route which does exist across the Continent, by means of the navigable branches of the Missouri and Columbia Rivers." He word-sketched the route he had taken; the difficulties of navigating the troubled waters of the Missouri; his belief that sloops could sail up the Columbia as far as the tide itself, 183 miles from the bar and only seven from the Cascades, and that 300-ton vessels could ascend the Willamette safely.

Lewis's enthusiasm for the Northwest Passage aspect of his route was qualified, understandably, by his vivid memory of shoals and chutes and portages. "We view this passage across the Continent as affording immense advantages to the fur trade but fear that the advantages which it offers as communication for the productions of the East Indies to the United States and thence to Europe will never be found equal on an extensive scale to that by way of the Cape of Good Hope." He could not dash completely the hopes which he knew Jefferson held for a practicable Northwest Passage via the Missouri and Columbia rivers, so he added, "Still, we believe that many articles not bulky, brittle, nor of a very perishable nature may be conveyed to the United States by this route with more felicity and less expense than that at present practiced."

Lewis then hurried away from the Northwest Passage to a matter much closer to his heart. He felt that the possibilities of fur trading in the farthest Missouri country were limitless. "The Missouri and all its branches, from the Cheyenne upwards, abound more in beaver and common otter than any other streams on earth." He told Jefferson that he thought it would be best to bring all furs taken by trappers and traders to the mouth of the Columbia by August 1st of each year, including the peltries of the British North West Company, should the U. S. Government wish to handle their catch for transshipment by sea. They would arrive at the market far earlier than pelts sent via Montreal. This kind of competition, assured Lewis, would mean that, soon, nine-tenths of the production of the richest fur country in the New World would travel the President's route. All that must be done was to erect posts on the upper Columbia to transfer East India goods, exchanged for furs by ships calling at the Columbia's mouth, to United States posts on the Missouri. Of course, the exchange would have to be made before the winter freeze-up of Big Muddy. The Columbia was no rival to the Missouri, Lewis asserted, as a fur area. But it was by no means poor. It offered common otter, sea otter, beaver, fox, marten, lynx and three species of bear. The explorer was wildly enthusiastic over the commercial possibilities of the Louisiana Far West—"If the Government will only aid, even in a very limited manner, the enterprise of her citizens, I am fully convinced that we shall shortly derive the benefits of a most lucrative trade from this source and that, in the course of ten or twelve years, a tour across the Continent by the route mentioned will be undertaken by individuals with as little concern as a voyage across the Atlantic is, at present."

Although Lewis let his enthusiasm run away with him, little

dreaming of the roadblocks which would plague American penetration of the Rockies, he was quick to warn Jefferson of the threat of the North West Company to the creation of an American fur trade. "In my opinion, if we are to regard the trade of the Missouri as an object of importance to the United States, the strides of this Company towards the Missouri cannot be too vigilantly watched, nor too firmly and speedily opposed by our Government." He was aware that several Indian nations were in a position to block the Missouri waterway, too. "The embarrassments under which the Missouri at present labours from the unfriendly dispositions of the Kansas, the several bands of Tetons, the Assiniboines, and those tribes which resort to the British establishments on the Saskatchewan, is also a subject which requires the earliest attention of our Government. As I shall shortly be with you, I have deemed it unnecessary here to detail the several ideas which have presented themselves to my mind on these subjects, more especially when I consider that a thorough knowledge of the geography of the country is absolutely necessary to their being understood, and leisure has not yet permitted me to make but one general map of the country, which I am unwilling to risk by the Mail."

He was bringing with him, Lewis advised Jefferson, the skins of sea otters, bighorn rams, and mule deer; also specimens of birds and plants, nine more Indian vocabularies and Chief Big White of the Mandans, in person. He belatedly explained why he had not sent back a canoe with dispatches from the Falls of the Missouri, asserting that by thus lessening the strength of his force he might have hazarded the fate of the whole expedition. So he had "declined that measure, thinking it better that the Government, as well as our friends, should for a moment feel some anxiety for our fate than to risk so much." His position was unassailable; Jefferson, in his instructions, had given him carte blanche to make just such critical decisions in the field.

Giving his itinerary as Cahokia, Vincennes, Louisville, the Crab Orchard, Abington, Fincastle, Staunton and Charlottesville, he told the President that he hoped to make Louisville in ten days' time. He then concluded the historic communiqué: "I

261

have detained the post several hours for the purpose of making you this hasty communication. I hope that while I am pardoned for this detention of the mail, the situation in which I have been compelled to write will sufficiently apologize for having been this laconic. . . . The anxiety which I feel in returning once more to the bosom of my friends is a sufficient guarantee that no time will be unnecessarily expended in this quarter. . . . I am very anxious to learn the state of my friends in Albemarle [and] particularly whether my mother is yet living. With respect to the exertions and services rendered by that estimable man, Captain William Clark, in the course of the late voyage, I cannot say too much. If, sir, any credit be due for the success of that arduous enterprize in which we have been mutually engaged, he is equally with myself entitled to your consideration and that of our common country."

Lewis signed off after a final humanitarian postscript showing his concern for his men. "The whole of the party who accompanied me from the Mandans have returned in good health, which is not, I assure you, to me one of the least pleasant considerations of the voyage."

On the 24th, the two officers dined with Auguste Chouteau, then after dinner they went to a store and bought some material for civilized clothing, which they turned over to a tailor. On the following day, they sunned all their skins and placed them in the storeroom of their St. Louis host, Cadet Chouteau, visited some friends, and wound up the day with a dinner and ball at Chouteau's, honoring their return. At the banquet, such patriotic toasts as the following were raised: "The Territory of Louisiana! Freedom without bloodshed. May her actions duly appreciate the blessing." "The Federal Constitution! May the eagle of America convey it to the remotest parts of the globe and whilst they read, they can but admire." "To the memory of the illustrious Washington, Father of America! May his guardian spirit still watch over us and prove a terror to the engines of tyranny."

Lewis and Clark were also guests at a banquet given in their honor by John B. C. Lucas of St. Louis, at which the first of several poems dedicated to Lewis (not all of which would be complimentary) was read. It was written by Mrs. Lucas, née Anne Sebin, in French. Freely translated, it went thus:

> Captain Lewis, his glory to crown
> To the springs of the Missouri went to drink down.
> From the mount where this River springs forth
> He made his journey to the North.

On the 26th, the two comrades settled down to work again. Clark's laconic entry for that day read, "A fine morning. We commenced wrighting."

Back in Washington, Jefferson, once he was in possession of Lewis's message, commenced some writing of his own. On December 2, 1806, he delivered it, his message to Congress: "The Expedition of Messrs. Lewis and Clarke [*sic*] for exploring the River Missouri and the best communication from that to the Pacific Ocean, has had all the success which could have been expected. They have traced the Missouri nearly to its source, descended the Columbia to the Pacific Ocean, ascertained with accuracy the geography of that interesting communication across our Continent, learnt the character of the country, of its commerce and its inhabitants, and it is but justice to say that Messrs. Lewis and Clarke, and their brave companions, have, by this arduous service, deserved well of their country."

CHAPTER XX

FAVORITE OF FORTUNE

May works be a test of patriotism as they ought, of right, to be of religion.

— MERIWETHER LEWIS, Toast,
January 14, 1807

WHILE THE CHEERS of welcome still rang in his ears, Meriwether Lewis began to plan the writing and publication of his book about the expedition west. He found that his urging of his men to be diarists had borne bitter fruit; two of his detachment, at least, were planning books of their own. The literary troopers were Sergeant Patrick Gass and Private Robert Frazier. Before Lewis could settle down to write the definitive account of the exploration, he had a lot of other, far more prosaic, paper work to attend to during the fall and winter. He had to muster out and pay off the men, award them land grants and, in a number of cases, arrange for their immediate transfer.

Jefferson formally welcomed Lewis back to the U.S.A. with great and obvious relief by writing him: "The unknown scenes in which you were engaged and the length of time without hearing from you had begun to be felt awfully. [I] assure you of the joy with which all your friends here will receive you." He suggested that Lewis and Big White ride over to Monticello from Locust Hill to see the tokens of friendship which the Mandans had sent him via Corporal Warfington.

Jefferson did not reveal his plans in the letter, but he was already considering just what might be a suitable reward for his young friend and agent of national policy, who had carried out his grand design so admirably. He decided upon the governorship of Upper Louisiana as the proper prize. Secretary of the Treasury Gallatin concurred, only cautioning Jefferson to appoint a secretary to govern until Lewis could return to St. Louis from the East. Unwittingly, Gallatin and Jefferson were adding more pieces to the mosaic which, when completed, contributed to Lewis's tragic death.

The return home from St. Louis was a case of "Hail, the Conquering Hero Comes." The two explorers were welcomed to William Henry Harrison's capital, Vincennes, in September. They were in Cahokia in October, where Lewis penned the first account of his narrow escape from the Piegan Blackfeet. In Louisville, they had a visit with George Rogers Clark and the citizens gave them a banquet and ball and lit bonfires in their honor. Lewis arrived at Frankfort, Kentucky, on November 13th and departed on the 15th with Big White, taking the Old Wilderness Road for Washington while Chouteau and the Osage chiefs with him proceeded via the alternate route, through Lexington.

Lewis's triumphal return to the seat of government was interrupted in late November by Colonel Arthur Campbell, in behalf of the Governor of Virginia. Campbell asked Lewis to settle the disputed boundary, Walker's Line, between North Carolina and Virginia. About the 23rd, Lewis took up his instruments and made his observations. He found that Walker had been inaccurate and had run the line too far to the north. North Carolina, therefore, owed Virginia a ten-mile-wide strip of land along their joint frontier. By December 11th, the explorer was in Staunton, with excitement over his coming mounting in the East. Jefferson wrote Charles Willson Peale on the 21st to tell him that he expected Lewis daily and that he would be bringing specimens to the American Philosophical Society. The President hoped that they would end up in his proposed National University. On the day of Christmas Eve, Chouteau reached Washington with his Osages in tow, to announce that his friend Lewis was not far behind. He would be arriving, any day. On Christmas Eve, impatient Peale wrote President Jefferson to say, "Mr. Lewis is richly entitled to a place amongst the portraits of the [Philadelphia] Museum and I hope he will do me the favor of sitting as soon as he arrives here."

It was December 28th, and late in the evening, when Lewis finally reached Washington. (Clark was detained by affairs of the heart and would not come east for weeks.) The Virginian brought Big White, the chief's wife and son, Interpreter René Jusseaume, his Indian wife and their son and daughter. A Washington observer described Lewis's reception on the Atlantic seaboard: "Never did a similar event excite more joy through the United States. The humblest of its citizens had taken a lively interest in the issue of the journey and looked forward with impatience for the information it would furnish. Their anxieties, too, for the safety of the Corps had been kept in a state of excitement by lugubrious rumors circulated, from time to time, of uncertain authorities and uncontradicted by letters or direct information from the time they had left the Mandan towns. . . ."

The evening following his arrival, Captain Lewis took his guests to the theater. Among the many spectators who were far more interested in the explorer and his party than in any onstage theatrics was Sir Augustus John Foster of the British Legation, who observed Lewis's party closely. He discerned that Big White, conscious of the gravity of his chiefly position, tried valiantly to keep a straight face, by picking and pulling at his cheeks to hide his laughter during an exhibit of rope dancing. The squaws, however, each one with a child in her arms, grinned and giggled throughout the performance without inhibition. Jusseaume's wife whispered to her mate that the dancing girls, because of the apparent ease of their contortions, must have had all of their bones removed when they were children. Each feat earned a pronouncement of "Big Medicine!" from her, for she felt that the dancers each bore, within, a great spirit. At intermission, Lewis was persuaded to have his Indians dance. The five Osages and a Delaware squatted on their haunches in a row while Big White, as a truly royal visitor, was given an armchair for a throne. Three of the braves beat on a drum; an Osage rose and postured like a scout discovering an enemy. The three others then leaped about—like frogs, claimed Foster—while still squatting, as if taking up positions behind bushes, in hiding. The men then all stamped about in a war dance, retired and rushed on stage again in a four-man charge, accompanied by shrieked war whoops and hacking at the air with knives and tomahawks.

The Indians asked Lewis if, for a finale, they might not do the calumet dance. He readily assented and the drumbeat was renewed. An Osage danced forward with a pipe, shouting vehemently that he was going to smoke the pipe of peace. Then two of the other braves, naked except for breechcloths, stomped about the stage, crossed calumets, and finally squatted opposite the drummer, to actually pull on the pipes.

The curious Britisher drew the American aside to ask him a number of questions about his exotic wards. Foster was surprised to learn from Lewis that Big White was monogamous. He knew enough of Amerindian customs to be aware that this was rare. He asked the Virginian if cannibalism existed among the Indian nations he had visited. Lewis replied, "Not to my knowledge, sir." In fact, he added, the leaning among the Indians was much to the contrary. That is, not only did they abhor the idea of eating human flesh but, among the tribes with the least contact with whites, it was held wrong to eat the meat of the grizzly—"from the circumstances," said Lewis, "of that animal being known to be fond of the flesh of man." He explained the sole exception to this aversion for human flesh: revenge on an enemy. Should a young warrior avenge the death of his father by killing his slayer, he might eat of the victim's flesh but only a tiny morsel, and it would be consumed strictly for religio-ceremonial purposes, not for nutrition or gastronomy.

On December 30th, President Jefferson received Lewis and Big White and on the following day addressed himself to the Osages.

While Congress sought ways of formally rewarding the Corps of Discovery through a Special Committee of the House headed by Willis Alston, of North Carolina, individuals and groups saluted the heroes with festivity and ceremony. For example, Clark, not yet in Washington, represented Lewis as well as himself in a ceremony at Fincastle, Virginia. Pat Lockhart, chairman of the local reception committee, gave him and the absent Lewis a rousing address of welcome on the 8th of January. He congratulated them on their return and their victory over "bold and unknown rivers . . . [and] mountains which had never before seen impressed with the footsteps of civilized man. . . ." He warmed to his task, saying, "You have surmounted every obstacle which climate, Nature and ferocious savages could throw in your way. You have uniformly respected the rights of humanity and, actuated by principles of genuine philanthropy, you have not sprinkled your path with the blood of unoffending savages." (The two dead Piegans could hardly be considered "inoffensive.") Pat orated on. "Your fame will be as pure and unsullied as of that great man to whom Europe is indebted for a knowledge of our Continent, the extent and importance of which it has been reserved for you to disclose to the world. We conceive it to be a signal proof of the wisdom and attention with which you have conducted the expedition that but one man has been lost to our Country. This fact will afford to future travelers the most salutory instruction. It will teach them that discoveries, apparently the most difficult, may be effected without the effusion of human blood."

Clark responded nobly in behalf of Lewis and himself, thanking the Botetourt County town and its citizens for their hospitality. He promised to hand Lockhart's address to his friend when he met him in Washington.

Amateur orator Lockhart was easily outdone when America's epic poet of the day, Joel Barlow, decided that America's hero of the hour deserved far more than a bonus or a raise in pay. He wrote Jefferson on January 13th to ask rhetorically, "Is there any cogent reason for continuing to call the Columbia River by that name? If not, I should propose to name it Lewis [River] and one of its principal branches, Clarke [sic]." Barlow confirmed to the President that the explorer would never stand for it unless Congress, by act of law, should rename the river, in which case he would bow to the will of the people, like the good democrat he was. "Nothing short of some public authorization will reconcile it with his modesty to give his own name to so great a river." But Jefferson did not like the idea any more than Lewis. Faced with this double negative, the author of *The Columbiad* dropped the idea of rechristening the river and, instead, decided to honor the explorer appropriately and lastingly with a burst of poetry of his own composition.

The undaunted laureate saluted his new hero with a veritable fanfare of poetry. His "elegant and glowing stanzas," to quote the press of the day, were first read at the lavish banquet proffered Lewis on January 14, 1807, to honor him for his safe return and to express the capital city's respect, affection and gratification. Major Robert Brent presided, a Marylander who would shortly be appointed Paymaster General of the Army. Vice-chairman of the proceedings was the Commandant of the United States Marine Corps, Franklin Wharton.

Guests of honor at the dinner, besides Lewis, were Pierre Chouteau, Pierre Provenchère, and Big White. Seventeen scheduled toasts were drunk, plus many of the volunteer variety and all "in a vein of enthusiasm," said the press. Among the toasts were: "To the Constitution, the Ark of our Safety"; "On Captain Lewis's Returning"; Joel Barlow's "To victory over the wilderness, which is more interesting than that over man"; and the punning "May those who explore the desert never be deserted."

The most moving of the toasts was the explorer's own, for in its brevity was distilled much of the essence of the man. The laconic Lewis pushed back his chair, rose to his feet and, extending his glass, proposed, "May works be the test of patriotism as they ought, of right, to be of religion."

Interspersed with the toasts were appropriate songs and instrumental music. Early in this most glorious evening of Lewis's career, Joel Barlow's new poem, "On the Discoveries of Lewis," was read to the assemblage by a Mr. Beckley.

> Let the Nile cloak his head in the clouds, and defy
> The researches of science and time;
> Let the Niger escape the keen traveler's eye,
> By plunging, or changing his clime.

> Columbus! Not so shall thy boundless domain
> Defraud thy brave sons of their right:
> Streams, midlands and shorelands illude us in vain,
> We shall drag their dark regions to light.

Look down, sainted sage, from thy synod of Gods;
See, inspired by thy venturous soul,
Mackensie roll northward his earth-drawing floods,
And surge the broad waves to the pole.

With the same soaring genius thy Lewis descends,
And, seizing the car of the sun,
O'er the sky-propping hills and high waters he bends
And gives the proud earth a new zone.

Potowmack, Ohio, Missouri, has felt
Half her globe in their cincture comprest;
His long curving course has completed the belt,
And tamed the last tide of the West.

Then hear the loud voice of the Nation proclaim,
And all ages resound the decree:
Let our Occident stream bear the young hero's name
Who taught him his path to the sea.

These four brother floods, like a garland of flowers
Shall entwine all our states in a band,
Conform and confederate their widespreading powers,
And their wealth and their wisdom expand.

From Darien to Davis [Strait] one garden shall bloom,
Where war's wearied banners are furl'd;
And the far-scenting breeze that wafts its perfume
Shall settle the storms of the world.

Then hear the loud voice of the nation proclaim,
And all ages resound the decree:
Let our Occident stream bear the young hero's name
Who taught him his path to the sea.

Although Barlow was obstinate and had "the loud voice of the Nation" on his side, the Occident stream's name was not changed and the Columbia continued to roll seaward under the same name as before. However, Secretary of War Henry Dearborn was so caught up in the spirit of the times that he proposed to Congressman Alston's Committee that the enlisted men not only be given 320 acres besides their regular Army compensation, but that Clark be awarded 1,000 acres and Lewis 1,500 and, finally, that double pay be given to all of Lewis's command. It is not known whether Dearborn was impressed by the attentions of prominent men like Barlow or was simply embarrassed by his 1803 refusal to promote Clark to captain at Lewis's request. In any case, Lewis got the ear of the Secretary and persuaded him to make further amends. Dearborn informed the Congressional Committee: "It may be proper of me to remark that, in a conversation with Captain Lewis, he observed that whatever grant of land Congress might think proper to make himself and Lt. Clark, it was his wish that there should be no distinction of rank so noticed as to make a difference in the quantity granted to each, and that he would prefer an equal division of whatever quantity might be granted to him." Dearborn stuck stubbornly to his guns, however, in insisting that Lewis was commander and Clark his first officer, *not* co-commander. And his recommendation remained 1,000 acres for Clark and 1,500 for Lewis.

Captain Lewis formally complimented his entire detachment, asserting that the men had given him ample support in the field, had served with manly firmness, and had borne up under the fatigues and sufferings of the long march with both patience and fortitude. He asked the Government for a just reward for all. But he had something special to say (either good or bad) of only ten of the 29 names on the roster he handed Dearborn for forwarding to Congress. First, there was Corporal Richard Warfington, whom he had persuaded to stay on in his service after his enlistment ran out because he needed him to command the keelboat on its return from Fort Mandan. "It would seem," said Lewis, "that, when rewards are about to be distributed among those of the party who were engaged in the enterprise, that his claim to something more than his pay of 7 dollars per month, as corporal, cannot be considered unreasonable." There was the curious case of John Newman, about whom Lewis had such mixed feelings. His ambivalence was due to his having had to court-martial and punish Newman for mutiny in 1804. Ashamed of his actions, Newman had worked hard all winter to atone but Lewis had not dared to allow him to make the march to Oregon. Although he "stood aquitted" in Lewis's mind, for reasons of discipline the

271

commander had to send him back. But he wanted to put in a good word for Newman with Congress. And Lewis strongly urged that Sergeant Floyd's father be given some gratuity in consideration of the loss of his son on the expedition, "a young man of much merit."

As C.O., Lewis made negative statements about only two of his men—Toussaint Charbonneau, although he admitted that Sacajawea's husband had been of some use as an interpreter, and Jean Baptiste Lepage. The latter he damned gently by describing him officially as a man "entitled to no peculiar merit."

Rather strangely, Lewis was noncommittal about Patrick Gass, John Ordway and Nathaniel Pryor, the sergeants three of the expedition. (Could he have perhaps feared them as potential literary rivals?) But a number of enlisted men stood out in Lewis's appreciation. For instance, there was François Labiche. Of him, Lewis advised Dearborn, "He has received the pay only of a private though, besides the duties performed as such he has rendered me very essential services as a French and English interpreter; therefore, I should think it only just that some small addition to his pay as a private should be added, tho' no such addition has, at any time, been promised by me." John Shields was also singled out for special mention as blacksmith, gunsmith and armorer-artificer. "He has received the pay only of a private. Nothing was more peculiarly useful to us in various situations than the skill and ingenuity of this man as an artist in repairing our guns, accoutrements, etc., and should it be thought proper to allow him something as an artificer, he has well deserved it."

Three of the enlisted men loomed, in Lewis's eyes, head and shoulders above the rest of the rankers. They were Drouillard and the Field brothers. He called Joseph and Reuben Field "two of the most active and enterprising young men who accompanied us. It was their peculiar fate to have been engaged in all the most dangerous and difficult scenes of the voyage, in which they uniformly acquitted themselves with much honour." If Frémont was the Lewis of forty years later, his Kit Carson was but another Drouillard. The half-breed is one of the major (but largely forgotten) figures of the Far West. Of this interpreter-scout-hunter, second in his esteem only to Clark, the commander said, "A man of much merit, he has been peculiarly useful for his knowledge of the common language of gesticulation, and his uncommon skill as a hunter and woodsman. Those several duties he performed in good faith and with an ardour which deserves the highest commendation. It was his fate also to have encountered on various occasions, with either Captain Clark or myself, all the most dangerous and trying scenes of the voyage, in which he uniformly acquitted himself with honour. He has served the complete term of the whole tour and received only 25 dollars per month and one ration per day, while I am informed that it is not unusual for individuals in similar employment to receive 30 dollars per month."

While Congress mulled over Lewis's recommendations, the stories in the *National Intelligencer* and other newspapers about the "well spread board" of January 14th fed the public interest in him. Charles Willson Peale, quite out of patience by February 10th, wrote his old friend, Jefferson, "I long to see Captain Lewis. I wish to possess his portrait for the [Philadelphia] Museum." Peale felt that a picture of Meriwether Lewis was essential to the Museum because the captain had enriched its collections so much. Jefferson responded on the 12th by saying that he expected his young friend to leave Washington for Philadelphia at the close of the Congressional session. But it was April before Peale met Lewis. He dined with him then, as a guest of Dr. Caspar Wistar, and Lewis soon sat for a portrait by Peale.

On Valentine's Day, Jefferson forwarded to Dearborn a list of the articles which Lewis pronounced most valuable for trading with the Indians. There were but eight items, topped by the blue beads which had bedazzled all Indian eyes from the Otos to the Tillamooks. Lewis reported that, if he had the exploration to do over again, he would make up from one-half to two-thirds of his stores, in value, in the bluish beads. Other desiderata of the Plains, Rockies and Pacific Coast tribes ranged from brass buttons, knives, battle-axes and tomahawks to saddler's-seat awls and glover's needles for sewing moccasins and buckskins, iron combs, arrow points and nests of camp kettles, preferably of brass rather than iron.

Two weeks later, Jefferson nominated Lewis to fill the position of Governor of the Territory of Upper Louisiana. The nomination was approved by the Senate and on March 9th Clark was named Lewis's Superintendent of Indian Affairs. On the day of his gubernatorial confirmation, Lewis resigned from the Army, which he had served for thirteen years. Jefferson signed his commission and, at the same time, Lewis was made a general of the Louisiana Militia. In asking Dearborn to accept his resignation from the Regular Army, Lewis ended, "In doing this, Sir, I beg leave to express the pleasure I feel in acknowledging the justice, propriety and confidence which has ever been evinced towards me by your Department."

The Act of Congress compensating Lewis and Clark and their men was signed by the President on March 3rd. By it, the officers received 1,600 acres each, Congress having ignored Dearborn to accede to Lewis's request of equal compensation. The enlisted men and noncoms, besides their double pay of $10 and $16 per month, were awarded 320 acres of donation land, parcels of public land lying west of the Mississippi. The bill underwent considerable debate in the House before being passed 62–23 on February 28th. It was passed speedily in the Senate, without amendment and almost without debate. On March 6th, Lewis and Clark endorsed all of their men's warrants as attorneys-in-fact, Lewis signing all but six of them. A gratified country even saw to it that the ragged and weathered Crusoes who returned from the Pacific were outfitted properly in new uniforms.

Not so pleasant an attention was paid Lewis by the *Monthly Anthology* of Boston in the form of a satirical poem in its March issue. Titled "On the Discoveries of Captain Lewis," it was a witty but stinging Federalist parody of Barlow's enthusiastic ode. The verse was unsigned and Lewis perhaps never learned that the anonymous author was none other than John Quincy Adams. The Federalist Bramin's answer to the eulogistic stanzas of Barlow was eloquent proof of the correctness of Captain Henry Ellis's 1750 claim. Captain Ellis, author of *Considerations on the Great Advantages Which Would Arise From the Discovery of the North West Passage,* wrote: "It is the general fate of such as propose making discoveries for the publick service to be treated with ridicule."

Good people, listen to my tale,
Tis nothing but what true is,
I'll tell you of the mighty deeds
Achiev'd by Captain Lewis—
How, starting from the Atlantick shore
By fair and easy motion
He journied *all the way by land*
Until he met the ocean.

Heroick, sure, the toil must be
To travel through the woods, sir;
And never meet a foe, yet save
His person and his goods, sir!
What marvels on the way he found
He'll tell you, if inclin'd, sir—
But *I* shall only now disclose
The things he *did not* find, sir.

He never with a mammoth met
However you may wonder;
Not even with a Mammoth's bone,
Above the ground or under—
And, spite of all the pains he took,
The animal to track, sir,
He never could o'ertake the hog,
With navel on his back, sir.

And from the day his course began
Till even it was ended,
He never found an Indian tribe
From Welchmen straight descended:
Nor, much as of Philosophers
The fancies it might tickle;
To season his adventures, met
A Mountain, sous'd in pickle.

He never left this nether world—
For once still he had his reason—
Nor once the waggon of the sun
Attempted he to seize on.
To bind a *Zone* about the earth

He knew he was not able—
They say he did—but, ask himself,
He'll tell you tis a fable.

He never dreamt of taming tribes,
Like monkeys or like bears, sir—
A *school,* for teaching floods to flow,
Was not among his cares, sir—
Had rivers ask'd of him their path,
They had but mov'd his laughter—
They knew their courses, all, as well
Before he came as after.

And must we then resign the hope
These elements of changing?
And must we still, alas!, be told
That after all his ranging,
The Captain could discern nought
But Water in the Fountains?
Must Forests still be form'd of Trees?
Of Rugged Rocks the Mountains?

We never will be so fubbed off,
As sure as I'm a sinner!
Come—let us all subscribe, and ask
The HERO to a dinner—
And Barlow stanzas shall indite—
A bard, the tide who tames, sir—
And if we cannot alter *things*
By God, we'll change their *names,* sir!

Let old Columbus be once more
Degraded from his glory;
And not a river by his name
Remember him in story—
For what is *old* Discovery
Compar'd to that which new is?
Strike—strike *Columbia* river out,
And put in—River Lewis!

Let dusky Sally henceforth bear
The name of Isabella;
And let the mountain, all of salt,

Be christen'd Monticella—
The hog with navel on his back
Tom Paine may be, when drunk, sir—
And *Joël* call the Prairie-dog
Which once was called a Skunk, sir.

And when the wilderness shall yield
To bumpers, bravely brimming,
A nobler victory than men;—
While all our heads are swimming,
We'll dash the bottle to the wall
And name (the thing's agreed on)
Our first-rate ship *United States*
The flying frigate *Fredon.*

True, Tom and Joël, now, no more
Can overturn a nation;
And work, by butchery and blood,
A great regeneration;—
Yet, still we can turn inside out
Old Nature's Constitution,
And bring a Bable back of *names*—
Huzza! for REVOLUTION.

Most of the jibes of Adams's poem were meant more for
Jefferson and his enthusiastic naïvete in regard to salt mountains
and hairy mammoths than at Lewis. The Federalists called the
president a philosopher, but in derision. They could neither
suffer him nor his common men ("Jacobins"), nor his scientific
explorers. The *Connecticut Courant* described once, to Federal-
istic satisfaction, a procession of the President's followers and
friends in the political poetry which seemed only second nature
to New Englanders:

> And now across the Green
> A motley throng there pours,
> Drunkards and whores
> And rogues, in scores.

But Adams's devasting doggerel stung Lewis, too, although
the Bostonian in the litter of tongue-in-cheek footnotes which

accompanied his stanzas explained that he meant no deprecation of Lewis's public services. He was only criticizing bombast in politics and poetry, and Barlow's effort, he said, fell neatly into both categories. But the Virginian could not help smarting under Adams's wicked wit in such notes as the following: "Here the young HERO is exhibited in the interesting character of school-master to a river; and the proposition that the river should take his name by way of payment for his tuition, appears so modest and reasonable that one should make no objection were it not that the wages must be deducted from the scanty pittance of poor Columbus. He has already been so grossly defrauded by the name of this hemisphere that we cannot bear with patience a proposal to strip him of that trifling substitute of a river."

Lewis had enough on his mind to keep himself from brooding over the attacks of Federalists. He was engaged in cleaning up the loose ends of the expedition, starting on his book, and making his gubernatorial plans. Clark left for St. Louis to fill his post as Superintendent of Indian Affairs in March. Lewis turned over to his friend $6,896.34 of the money due the corpsmen. After the redhead left, Lewis, knowing his friend's tendency to worry over him, sent a note flying after him to allay his fears, for Lewis was hagged by ill health. "I took some pills last evening after your departure, from which I have found considerable relief and have no doubt of recovering my health perfectly in the course of a few days." He fully expected to be in St. Louis by October 1st and asked Clark to get Charles Gratiot to fix the garden, steps and piazza of his house since he expected to rent it.

Most of the Governor's time was spent in working up his field notes and journals for publication. He wrote a public letter and a prospectus both of which were printed in the *National Intelligencer* on March 18th and in several subsequent issues. Lewis first warned the reading public of unauthorized, and possibly spurious, publications on his tour of the West which were being prepared. His intention was to warn people, to put them on their guard so that the books would not depreciate his own, which would take much time and labor to complete. However, he hoped to have his map published in October and the first of his volumes of narration by January 1808, with two more to follow as soon as possible.

To only one member of his party had Lewis given permission to publish a journal. That individual was Frazier, and Lewis came to regret his approval as he saw him hurrying it into print. When Frazier's prospectus was submitted to him, Lewis managed to expunge from it all promises that it would carry information on natural history, since Frazier knew nothing of the subject. But the would-be publisher, less fearful of Lewis's wrath than of the loss of sales to naturalists and amateurs of science, restored the text, forcing Lewis to publicly decry Frazier as only a private, entirely unacquainted with celestial observations, mineralogy, botany and zoology. "He cannot therefore possibly give any accurate information on these subjects, nor on that of geography, and the whole which can be expected from his Journal is merely a limited detail of our daily transactions." This letter to the public may have been the reason for the death, a-borning, of Frazier's masterpiece. In any case, the book never went to press.

To discourage others of his campfire scribes, he ended his *National Intelligencer* letter, "With respect to all publications relative to this voyage, I presume that they cannot have stronger pretensions to accuracy or information than that of Robert Frazier." He bought Ordway's journal, to forestall that sergeant turning author, and if any of the other more literate troopers considered publication, this article by Lewis scared them off. All but one. Patrick Gass was an Irishman and therefore stubborn. He did not scare. The carpenter-sergeant turned author in spite of Lewis's admonition. Worse, his intended publisher, David McKeehan, was a hotspur who immediately began to fire a barrage of letters denouncing Lewis for his monopoly on the story of the expedition.

Pleasant news at this time came to Lewis. Clark and Julia Hancock were engaged to be married. Clark wrote him, banteringly, of his matrimonial prospects. "My friend, your choice is one I highly approve but should the thing not take to your wish, I have discovered a most lovely girl. Beautiful, rich, possessing those accomplishments which is calculated to make a man happy. Inferior to you, but to few others, the daughter of C_____.

His politics is in opposition to yours. I understand the father of my [Julia] is also a Fed, which I did not know until the other day. I took him to be a good, plain Republican. At all events, I will hope to introduce some substantial, sincere Republicanism into some branch of the family, about January."

Lewis chuckled over the letter from his happy friend and proceeded to wind up his Washington business. He was tiring of the attacks on his book and himself, the snide remarks of Federalists who wished to deflate the importance of the expedition in order to humiliate Jefferson. He hurried off seeds to the Philadelphia nurseryman, Bernard McMahon, and to William Hamilton for his Schuykill River estate. To Frederick Pursh, Hamilton's German botanist, Lewis sent dried plants to examine and describe for his proposed book. He gave Pursh an advance of $70 to prepare drawings of the plants for the book, then hired John James Barralet, for $40, to make a drawing of the Great Falls of the Missouri to illustrate his narrative. Charles Willson Peale was also busy on natural history illustrations for the volumes.

Pursh was much impressed with Lewis as an amateur botanist, saying, "The collection of plants . . . was small, being made on their rapid return trip. The much more extensive one made by Lewis on the way West was lost by being deposited [i.e., cached] among other things at the foot of the mountains. The loss of this first collection is the more to be regretted when I consider that the small collection communicated to me, consisting of about one hundred and fifty specimens, contained not above a dozen plants well-known to me to be natives of North America, the rest being either entirely new or but little-known, and among them at least six distinct and new genera."

Even more impressed than Pursh was the pioneer American ornithologist, Alexander Wilson, who, in his magnum opus of 1811, *American Ornithology,* recalled, "It was the request and particular wish of Captain Lewis, made to me in person, that I should make drawings of such of the feathered tribes as had been preserved, and were new. That brave soldier, that amiable and excellent man, over whose solitary grave in the wilderness I have since shed tears of affliction, having been cut off in the prime of his life, I hope I shall be pardoned for consecrating this humble note to his memory, until a more able pen shall do better justice to the subject."

Once in Philadelphia, Lewis visited John Conrad, his choice as publisher, who estimated the cost of bringing out the book as $4,500. While he was staying at Mrs. Woods's boardinghouse in early April, he received proofs of the formal prospectus from Conrad. The prospectus was soon issued as a single-sheet broadside and as an announcement in the columns of the *National Intelligencer*. According to it, Lewis's narrative would be in two parts but in three octavo volumes because of its length. The first 400–500-page volume of the three-decker would contain an account of the voyage, a map, Barralet's view of the Great Falls, and plans of both the Missouri and Columbia falls. He promised to include remarks on the navigation of the two great waterways for future traders, also an itinerary of the shortest and most practicable route between the heads of the two rivers. He intended his second volume to deal with geographical matters, the fur trade, a description of the rivers, mountains and Indians of the West. Volume three would treat his new love, scientific research, particularly natural history. He promised, "It will contain a full dissertation on such subjects as have fallen within the notice of the author and which may properly be distributed under the heads of Botany, Mineralogy and Zoology." He would explain the origin of the prairies, of the so-called volcanic and other phenomena, and the mysterious cause of the excessive muddiness of the Missouri. (The cause, he would reveal, was the constant *eboulement*, or caving in, of its banks.) Finally, the third volume would contain a table of twenty-three Indian vocabularies he had gathered and a number of natural-history plates. Separate from the bound volumes would be the large-scale "Lewis and Clark's Map of North America."

Conrad and Lewis promised delivery of the books "at the most respectable commercial towns" on the fairest of terms—no money down, no payment until actual delivery. Since Lewis did not know the exact number of engravings, he could not set a price on the set. But, shifting to the third person, which passed for the editorial "we" in 1807, he wrote, "He therefore declares to the public that his late voyage was not undertaken with a view to pecuniary advantages and pledges himself that the estimate which he will in this instance set on his literary labours shall be of the most moderate description. His principal reason, indeed, for proposing a subscription at all is that he may be enabled to form some estimate of the number of copies to be struck off." (Finally, he was able to estimate the cost of the three-volume set as $31.)

Response to the announcement was immediate but not all of it kindly. Waspish McKeehan, Gass's publisher, on April 7th shot a sharp note to the Governor, attacking his "illiberal and indelicate" notice. He criticized Lewis for his rapid advancement to power and wealth (!), his change from polite and respectful language to commands and dispensation of favors, his deprivation of Frazier of all benefit from his book by purging it of scientific matter. He then accused Lewis of overstating the hazardous nature of the enterprise and the courage necessary to undertake it. "I have no doubt but had Government given an invitation, hundreds as daring, enterprising and capable as Your Excellency would have offered to engage in the expedition and for compensation much smaller than were received by yourself and the other persons composing the Corps." The publisher then turned scurrilous. He accused Lewis of pocketing his pay as Presidential secretary and "master of ceremonies" at the Executive Mansion while leading the party west. This was an unblushing lie, of course; Lewis was succeeded at the White House by, first, Lewis Harvie and, second, William Burwell. McKeehan then dug at the President, likening him to a Prince rather than a Republican and calling all the praise of Jefferson mere "tinsel." He suggested that the President's hobbyhorse had bolted and run away with its rider.

After taking it upon himself to suggest that "prudent, firm and courageous" Clark was undoubtedly blushing at the attitude of the man whom he had "once" called his friend, McKeehan protested that Lewis had no right to censor his soldiers' diaries, since they were private property. The publisher then became shrill and almost hysterical as he goaded his pen on. He pictured Lewis as an arrogant "His Excellency-in-embryo." He felt he was privileged to read the Governor's mind, too, for he put these words into Lewis's mouth: "I'll squeeze, I'll squeeze the nation first and then raise a heavy contribution on the citizens individually; I'll cry down those one-volume journals and frighten the publishers and no man, woman or child shall read a word about *my* tour unless they enter their names on *my* lists, and pay what price I shall afterwards fix on my three volumes and map." He accused the Virginian of living in a glass house, of being no more a man of letters than Frazier, and insisted he had degraded his companions: "It is to be regretted that the wealth and honours heaped upon you so soon rendered your heart callous toward the companions of your 'fatigues and painful sufferings!' "

The Pittsburgher, not content just to picture Lewis as a hound of Hades, next tried to destroy him as a writer. "I am of opinion it [Gass's book] will be more interesting and useful to readers generally than the volume of your own which is to be 'confined exclusively to scientific research,' for, while Your Excellency was stargazing and taking celestial observations, he was taking observations in the world below."

Finally, pulling all stops, the publisher stooped so low as to, ridiculously, accuse Lewis of not only overstating the gravity of his skirmish with the Piegan warriors but of shooting himself in the rump solely so that "the young hero might not return without more scars."

Although Lewis was eager to get to St. Louis, he doggedly kept at work on his book and in settling the last accounts of the expedition. William Simmons, a War Department accountant, pestered him for more receipts and accounts. More pleasant interruptions to his labors were the sittings for portraits by Charles Willson Peale and C. B. J. Fevret de Saint-Mémin. He had to postpone his appointment with Peale several times but the artist forgave him, writing Jefferson that, despite his impatience, "I am not sorry to have had a little time for improvement of my hand before Captain Lewis shall do me the favor of sitting." Some time before May 5th, Peale finished a pencil sketch of Lewis which eventually became an oil portrait on a wood panel, showing a dark-blond Virginian with short sideburns, ruddy of visage—even apple-cheeked. Lewis's appearance was deceptive; a strong nose could not entirely offset a softness of face which would have been more appropriate to a city dandy than the leader of America's greatest exploring expedition. While he painted, Peale continued work on his natural history drawings for the book which Lewis was tentatively calling *Lewis and Clark's Tour of the Continent of North America, Performed by Order of the Government of the United States During the Years 1804, 1805 and 1806.*

Saint-Mémin completed a crayon portrait of Lewis, Big White and several of the Osages, using a device called the physiogno-trace, invented by John I. Hawkins of Philadelphia, to get more accurate profiles.

On the 9th of May, Lewis paid a call on Dr. Benjamin Smith Barton, to return a borrowed book to him. But first he inscribed it to his scientific tutor: "Dr. Benjamin Smith Barton was so obliging as to lend me this copy of Monsr. Du Pratz's History of Louisiana in June 1803. It has since been conveyed by me to the Pacific Ocean through the interior of the Continent of North America on my late tour thither and is now returned to its pro-prietor." The volume is now in the hands of the Library Com-pany of Philadelphia.

Charles Willson Peale wrote his son, Raphael, on June 6th that he was busy mounting the animals which Lewis had brought to the Philadelphia Museum and that he had finished drawings of three of them, which were much to Lewis's satisfaction. Lewis himself apparently helped him when he was not working on his journal. On the 19th of June, the explorer met with the members of the American Philosophical Society to ask for the use of some of the specimens he had given the Society. He was confident he would soon have his book in print, so much so that Peale gra-ciously withdrew the drawings and text of a paper on the prong-horn antelope which he was about to submit for the Society's *Transactions,* because Lewis would present a much fuller de-scription of the *cabri* in his forthcoming book.

Lewis was still in Philadelphia at the end of June, running errands for Jefferson including the resetting of General Dear-born's ring and the repairing of Jefferson's and John Randolph's watches at Henry Voigt's horological shop. He also corresponded with the President and sent him more seeds. The Chief Executive hoped to see him in the capital on Independence Day but Lewis, regretfully, had to tell him that he would not be able to get back to Washington until the 15th of July, on his way to St. Louis to assume his governorship.

But still Lewis tarried in the Southeast, now apparently detained by Cupid. On November 3rd he was no farther west than Albemarle. He wrote his old friend Mahlon Dickerson of Philadelphia and Morris County, New Jersey, to introduce his half brother, John H. Marks, and to ask him to look after him while he was in Philadelphia attending medical lectures. Lewis, as ever, was short of cash. But he gave John $60 and a bill of exchange on the Bank of the United States, payable after he drew his governor's pay in January. He asked his friend to supply Marks with money up to $300. "I pledge you my honour it shall be returned immediately on notice of the advance being made. I have enjoyed a great share of health since I had the pleasure of seeing you last and am now on the eve of my departure for St. Louis. So much for business, now for the girls."

Lewis then made clear why his progress west had been so slow. "My little affair with Miss A-n R—h has had neither beginning nor end on her part; *pr. contra,* on my own it has had both. The fact is that, on enquiry, I found that she was previously engaged and, therefore, dismissed every idea of prosecuting my pretentions in that quarter and am now a perfect widower with respect to love. Thus, floating on the surface of occasion, I feel all that restlessness, that inquietude, that certain indescribable something common to old bachelors, which I cannot avoid thinking, my dear fellow, proceeds from that void in our hearts which might, or ought, to be better filled. Whence it comes, I know not, but certain it is that I never felt less like a hero than at the present moment. What may be my next adventure, God knows, but on this I am determined, to get a wife.

"Do let me hear from you as frequently as you can and when you have no subject of more importance, talk about *the girls.* You see already, from certain innate workings of the spirit, the changes which have taken place in my dispositions and that I am now so much unlike my former self that I speak of those bewitching gypsies as a secondary consideration. I sincerely wish, my dear fellow, that candour would permit me to say as much with respect to Miss E—— B——y of Philadelphia, whose memory will still remain provokingly important in spite of all my philosophy. Have you heard from her? Have you seen her? How is she? Is she well, sick, dead or married? Oh! I had forgotten you have no particular acquaintance with her. Ask your coadjutor, R. Rush, and tell me. Adieu. Direct to me at Louisville, Kentucky, until the last of this month, and after that period forward your letters to St. Louis."

The "old bachelor" was finally done with wooing and was off to his beloved West. But, once again, his progress was slowed by a woman. When he visited Fincastle, the home of Clark's betrothed, Lewis met Letitia Brackenridge and was smitten again. His brother, Reuben, was with him and approved highly of the comely, "accomplished, and beautiful" Letitia. In fact, Reuben wrote she was "one of the most beautiful women I have ever seen, both as to form and features. She is a very sweet looking girl and I should like to have her as a sister." Perhaps Letitia overheard these sentiments of Reuben's; in any case, she panicked at the attentions of the Governor and fled to Richmond. Lewis did not follow her. This love affair, if it was that, may have been Meriwether Lewis's last, although he later bantered with Clark about Clark's lovely niece, Miss Anderson, whom the Kentuckian and his bride brought with them to St. Louis in June 1808.

Although Captain Lewis was no longer present in the flesh on the Atlantic Coast, his effigy remained. At the end of the year, Peale finished his wax sculpture of the explorer for display in his Museum. Captain Henry Massie was much impressed with the waxwork figure of his fellow Virginian. "A good one," he commented, "the dress very curious; the likeness excellent." It was no wonder that the effigy's face was a dead ringer for Lewis's own; the painstaking Peale had created the visage by taking a mold of Lewis's face and casting a life mask from it. Peale dressed the figure in a Snake Indian ceremonial robe trimmed with 140 ermine skins and on January 29, 1808, reported on his accomplishment to Jefferson. "My object in this work is to give a lesson to the Indian who may visit the Museum and also to show my sentiments respecting wars. I am pleased whenever I can give an object which affords a moral sentiment to the visitors of the Museum."

At the foot of the wax statue, Peale affixed an explanatory tablet which purported to carry Lewis's very words to Sacajawea's brother, Chief Cameahwait of the Shoshones. Actually, the words were not Lewis's; Peale created the speech almost out of whole cloth, as he admitted to President Jefferson. But they were worthy of Lewis, the explorer-peacemaker. "Brother, I accept your dress. It is the object of my heart to promote amongst you, our neighbours, peace and goodwill that you may bury the hatchet deep in the ground, never to be taken up again and that, henceforward, you may smoke the calumet of peace and live in perpetual harmony, not only with each other but with the white men, your brothers, who will teach you many useful arts. Possessed of every comfort in life, what cause ought to invoke us in war? Men are not too numerous for the lands which we cultivate, and disease makes havoc enough amongst them without deliberately destroying each other. If any differences arise about lands or trade, let each party appoint judicious persons to meet together and amicably settle the disputed point."

Of the inscription, Peale wrote the President, "Lewis is supposed to say this; such, I believe to be the sentiments of our friend, Lewis, and which he endeavoured to instill in the minds of the various savages he met with in his long and hazardous tour."

---◆◆◆---

CHAPTER XXI

HIS EXCELLENCY

A considerable time intervened before the Governor's arrival at St. Louis. He found the Territory distracted by feuds and contentions among the officers of the Government, and the people themselves divided by these into factions and parties. He determined, at once, to take no side with either but to use every endeavour to conciliate and harmonize them. The even-handed justice he administered to all soon established a respect for his person and authority and perseverance, and time wore down animosities and reunited the citizens again into one family.
— THOMAS JEFFERSON, 1814

MERIWETHER LEWIS did not realize what he was getting into as Governor of Upper Louisiana. The old Franco-Spanish town of St. Louis which he had known was gone, revolutionized during his absence by the immigration of Americans from across the Mississippi. Daily the little capital became more sophisticated, turning its political face toward Washington rather than westward up the Missouri. Politicians, speculators and out-and-out peculators crowded into the territory to fatten on the new pickings there in land fraud and Indian trade. Violence, deceit and character assassination became the guidelines of sociopolitical activity with, as always, basic economic motives lying at the bottom of every scrape.

Even crafty James Wilkinson had had his hands full as Governor. He could not control the Balkans-like brawling of the territorial capital; all he could do was to complain to Washington of pettifoggers and renegadoes. He came to be hated and Jefferson finally had to remove him. This he had accomplished by ordering him, as a general in the Army, to the southern frontier. Wilkinson left St. Louis in August 1806 and his Secretary, Joseph Browne, took office as Acting Governor; thus the post was open when Lewis returned from his successful expedition and Jefferson was casting about for a suitable reward for his young friend. On March 3, 1807, one day after Senate confirmation of the appointment, the President named Meriwether Lewis Governor of Upper Louisiana for a three-year term, also Commander in Chief of Militia and Superintendent, ex officio, of Indian Affairs. A month earlier Jefferson had chosen a new Secretary for Louisiana, Frederick Bates, and on March 7th the President appointed William Clark Agent for Indian Affairs. Two days later, Dearborn ordered Clark to take whatever measures were necessary to return Chief Big White to the Mandans. This was to be his, and Lewis's, first order of business because it was a matter of great personal concern to the President.

Secretary Bates wasted no time in Washington. He was in St. Louis by April 1st, informing Lewis on the political and Indian situations as the Governor had ordered. There was less disaffection in Upper Louisiana than he had expected. "The people have already received intimations that you are probably before this time appointed their Governor and, from the least information which I have been able to collect, it will be in your power to reunite the contending parties. Even the friends of Wilkinson will be satisfied and perhaps pleased with your Government, since they are to lose their General. . . . Harmony, I am sure, can be easily restored. It requires nothing but integrity, firmness, and a good understanding among the officers of government. And I cannot avoid considering it as particularly unfortunate that the strength of the administration should have been impaired in the imaginations of the people and its name brought into disrepute by the dissensions of the former officers. I take pleasure in expressing the opinion that you have a fair opportunity of establishing a lasting reputation in Louisiana by composing the unhappy divisions of her inhabitants. When these people saw the agents of the General Government quarrelling among themselves, it is not at all to be wondered at that those agents would fall into contempt."

Luckily, the Indians of the territory were quiet for the moment. Indian Agent John B. Treat took some credit for this, claiming that it was due largely to the four traders whom he had sent to reside with the tribes. They kept the redskins well supplied with goods, content and tractable. But the era of good feeling which followed Lewis's expeditionary powwows was coming to an end. Factor Rudolph Tillier, at Bellefontaine, reported that white agents were stirring up the Indians by asserting that France and Spain, and even Britain, were going to wrest Louisiana away from the United States. These reports alarmed Dearborn enough for him to ask Lewis to look into them the moment he should arrive in St. Louis.

Lewis tried to run his unruly territory from Washington. This was an impossible task, an incredible folly. Letters flew between Bates and Lewis and, at times, Jefferson and Dearborn took a hand in the correspondence. The Governor was able to attend to many routine matters from afar, such as securing data on Burrist activities in his territory and approving the formation of a military school and militia unit in Mine à Burton. But he could not control local politics or Indian affairs from the eastern seaboard. Bates wrote him for information or advice on Indian matters, an area in which it soon was apparent to Lewis that his Secretary floundered when hardly getting his feet wet. Although he possessed an air of vast self-confidence, it was superficial and Bates confessed his insecurity and timidity to the Governor in several ways. Apparently highly fearful of criticism, he wrote that he hoped never to commit a serious error or make a personal enemy in St. Louis. He hid behind his lawbooks, saying, "I shall endeavour to remain behind the ramparts of the laws and hope that there I shall be unassailable." And on that most pressing problem of Louisiana government, the handling of the Indians, he revealed his bewilderment. "On the Indian subject I have had little more than the law to guide me and that, you know, is general. . . . I very often find myself totally in the dark on subjects of very material consequence. For instance, with respect to Indian trade on the Missouri. Shall licenses be granted to trade among those nations with whom the United States has, heretofore, had no intercourse? And shall the right to deny to foreigners a participation in the trade west of the Mississippi be enforced? Lewis's answer, of course, was "no" to the first question, and "yes" to the last. He wanted the law enforced to the letter and an end put to Wilkinson's indiscriminate granting of *congés,* or licenses.

Although he had William Clark and the Territorial Militia to back him up, Bates told Lewis that it was impossible for him to offer protection to Lewis Rogers, the white chief of a band of Shawnees and Delawares on the upper Meramec, who had come to him for help after being threatened by Osage horse thieves. The Secretary could only lamely report that he looked forward to the return of Pierre Chouteau, the man most influential over the Osages, to settle the problem—perhaps.

Lewis heard directly from Nicholas Boilvin that the British were stirring up the Sioux of Rock River to attack St. Louis. According to his information, only Boilvin's warning that they would face ruin if they struck deterred them. Clark reported that the more distant Sioux, those closest to British posts on the Assiniboine, were the most hostile. He wanted Pierre Dorion kept on as subagent to the Sioux. Though a very troublesome fellow, Dorion was useful in keeping the peace. Lewis agreed. But the Kentuckian did not let the press of other Indian business distract him from his Number One charge, the return of Big White to his people. He sent Nathaniel Pryor, now an ensign, with an escort of fourteen soldiers, young Pierre Chouteau, and twenty-two traders, on May 18, 1807. With them went $400 worth of presents. Dearborn approved of this method of bolstering the military force by attaching civilian traders, armed with government powder, lead and ball.

Ensign Pryor's first independent command was a disaster.

The return of Big White should have been a minor and uneventful sequel to the Lewis and Clark Expedition. Instead, it would take two expeditions and two years of time to restore the Mandan chief to his village, plus the loss of several lives and the loss of much face by the U. S. Government in Indian eyes. It would also lead directly to the death of Meriwether Lewis.

Pryor felt little worry about safely delivering Big White. The Teton Sioux, the only tribe on the river to make any trouble for Lewis, had been awed by his show of strength and determination. The Arikaras had given Lewis little trouble in 1804. Neither Pryor nor anyone else realized how the attitude of the Rees had changed since Gravelines brought the news to them of the death of their chief in the white man's country. Arikara suspicion smoldered into burning hostility and when Pryor arrived at their villages, September 9, 1807, they fell upon him to avenge the mysterious (to them) death of their sachem. Pryor put up a spirited defense but was defeated and driven down the river. Three of Chouteau's traders were killed, ten more men, both soldiers and traders, were wounded and one of them died later. Among the wounded was Pryor's old comrade of the Lewis and Clark Expedition, George Shannon. He was hurt so badly in one leg that it had to be amputated.

Meanwhile, in St. Louis Bates was growing fond of the topmost governmental office and loath to surrender it to Lewis. His pride and jealousy soon festered into hatred. He wrote the Governor, "Contrary to my first expectations, you must expect to have some enemies." (He neglected to add that he was among them.) He began to indulge in controversial acts, one of which was relieving John Smith T. as a justice of the peace. He described Smith to Lewis as a desperado who wore two pistols and a dirk and carried a rifle. The charge was that Smith had resisted a public officer in the proper discharge of his duty. Bates also fired James Richardson, Deputy Surveyor of the District of St. Louis, and was about to remove Sheriff Henry Dodge of Ste. Genevieve, but reconsidered.

By infrequent mail, Lewis tried to keep apprized of affairs 700 miles away in St. Louis. He soon became completely dismayed by his Secretary's handling of Indian matters and told him to keep his hands off this policy, letting Clark, Chouteau and himself attend to it. Bureaucrat Bates skillfully hid his resentment and delivered a predictable reply: "In compliance with your advice, I shall decline all interference in the affairs of the Indian Department, unless it should become necessary to take measures for the defence of the Territory or unless those gentlemen, themselves, should ask my interposition." Whether he was sincere or not, he speedily forgot this promise. A short time later he was reporting to Dearborn that he had given presents to Osages whom the Spaniards were trying to lure away from American friendship, but lectured them, and sent them on their way. "I do not think we have danger to apprehend," said Bates. "Every precautionary measure will be adopted and should it make its appearance, we will endeavour to repel it." Inept in his dealings with the Indians, it was all talk and no action with Bates. But at least he accepted Lewis's insistence on stricter control on trading licenses. He reported to the Governor that he would license no British traders west of the Mississippi until he had orders from Lewis to act otherwise.

In July 1807, Bates alerted Colonel Hunt at Bellefontaine to the rumors of a border war due to erupt when the corn should ripen. It was being planned by an alliance of tribes from the Great Lakes to the Mississippi and Missouri valleys. Bates said that he did not put much stock in the story, although it had been given him by William O'Bannon, the interpreter. But at the same time that he told Hunt not to worry, he sent Boilvin and the treacherous James Aird to check on the rumors of British-inspired war preparations by the Indians. He also secured ammunition from Bellefontaine. Boilvin reported that British agents were poisoning the minds of the Indians against the United States but that no war seemed imminent, so Acting Governor Bates turned on O'Bannon and accused him of peddling a wild rumor, even insisting that the Irishman had a private motive for doing so.

By August 12th, the pendulum had swung back and Bates was worried again. He was now convinced that there really was a plot afoot and that it had been simmering for some time. Yet, when Boilvin suggested that a few stands of arms be sent to exposed settlers on the Des Moines River, Bates refused, saying, "If our citizens disperse themselves so widely, they ought to encounter the hazzards and not expect to be followed by protection in all their erratic enterprizes." While Lewis envisaged a great territory and eventual state opening up the untapped West, Bates was, already in 1807, committed to the status quo.

The erratic Bates continued with his vacillating Indian policy. At one moment he would tell Colonel Hunt that the frontier alarms were genuine; the next moment he would dismiss them as false. He pontificated that the Indians of the Mississippi and Missouri rivers could never cooperate in a war. Perhaps this was because White Hair, Lewis's old theatergoing companion of Washington days, promised him that the Osages would never join an anti-U.S. coalition. Boilvin, who trusted and respected Bates in Indian matters even less than did Lewis or Clark, contacted the Governor directly about the British machinations. This bypassing made Bates furious. He complained to Dearborn, writing accusingly that Boilvin, "from a strange perversity of thinking, sometimes acts with much indiscretion."

When Moses Austin, of later Texas fame, suggested to Bates that a legionary corps be formed for frontier defense, the Acting Governor appeared to agree but told him that the time was not ripe. When Samuel Hammond, Jr., asked that the outlying settlements be armed, along the lines of Boilvin's suggestion, Bates demurred. He wrote Hammond that the settlers should take care of themselves and that scattering arms all over the territory was wasteful.

Clark, way over in Louisville, Kentucky, heard rumors of an impending Indian war on the Missouri frontier. But Bates wrote him, "I disbelieve the whole of them." However, the Secretary reported that he had mustered one-third of the militia. He apologized for the act: "This I did to silence the clamours of those ravens who are perpetually croaking about the tomahawk and the scalping knife."

Bates was receiving plenty of information and advice about the Indians all of this time. Louis Lorimier warned him of an attack, because British Agent Alexander McKee of Malden, Canada, was sending letters to chiefs, promising them a concerted war plan. Lewis, Clark, Boilvin and Chouteau also contributed to the pool of information. The Secretary of War, apparently convinced by Lewis's arguments against the buying of captives from Indians, suggested to the Acting Governor that he try to release prisoners held by the Osages by getting their strongest neighbor tribes to put pressure on them. Bates affected (or perhaps had) no opinion on the matter; he hid behind his ignorance of Indian affairs and blamed Boilvin and Chouteau for giving him conflicting advice.

By October, however, Bates was pushed by the deteriorating Indian situation, dramatized by Pryor's defeat, to ask Rudolph Tillier, at Bellefontaine, for $1,200 to $1,500 worth of trade goods to use in wooing the Mississippi red men away from their Canadian traders. He conveniently forgot his earlier denunciation of O'Bannon and informed Dearborn that he planned to set up two posts, one at the Des Moines River and the other at Prairie du Chien. Although he had told Hammond that he did not want Regular Army men patrolling the frontier, he now called on Colonel Hunt for troops. But the Colonel turned him down, writing, incredibly, "It is not in my power to have anything to do with the Indians. It's out of my power. I cannot consent to spare a man from this cantonment to go on an expedition of the kind and I believe my principle as a military man, in trust, to be right." Rebuffed, Bates dropped his plan although he reminded Lewis that the Sauk and Fox Treaty of 1804 stipulated that trading posts would be established and that Jefferson, in an 1806 greeting to an Indian delegation, had reiterated the promise.

Back and forth wobbled Bates. But, at least, he was diligent in reporting Indian affairs to Lewis. He warned him that the Spaniards were building forts on the Platte and in the Pawnee Republic. In December, he proposed that Boilvin winter on the Des Moines with a small supply of trade goods, in lieu of a post. Unfortunately, as he drifted further and further away from his promise to Lewis not to meddle in Indian matters, he also became more defective in judgment in this area. He had trusted the treacherous, anti-American Scot, James Aird, as an Indian informant; his next blunder was almost disastrous. He granted a trading license to another Britisher, Robert Dickson, describing him as a "man of honour" to Governor Lewis. He could not have picked a worse person to trust. The Briton conned him completely with a cock-and-bull story of the sacrifices he had made for the United States. Bates's noble response to Dickson was, "Our Government will not treat you with ingratitude. You shall have a [trading] license."

Bates wrote Lewis: "I rely greatly on Mr. Dickson. By him we shall be correctly informed of whatever passes among the Sioux of River Des Moines and the Iowas. He will do whatever we may reasonably desire of him, and return to St. Louis with intelligence when necessary. He has been our friend, uniformly, and his deportment and professions when this singular indulgence was conceded him, convince me that he will cooperate most heartily in all our Indian measures." Thus, in one stroke, Bates wrecked the political climate of the Indian nations of the Missouri Valley over which Lewis and Clark had labored so hard. Never was Bates so inept in a decision. He was completely hoodwinked by the Britisher who used Bates's "singular indulgence" to work unceasingly to turn the Indians against the United States. This *agent provocateur* helped the War of 1812 become an Indian war, threatening Louisiana-Missouri as well as Indiana and Illinois. Among his converts to outright war on the United States was Chief Black Hawk of the Sauks, for whom the later Black Hawk War would be named.

The bewildered Bates, after clasping the British spy to his bosom, then turned on his own agents, such as Boilvin and O'Bannon, denouncing them to Clark. He next alienated the militia. When his proclamation urging men to volunteer for service fell largely on deaf ears, he damned the Franco-Spanish settlers, blindly ignoring the services of militia officers Chouteau, Delaunay, Lorimier, etc., by saying, "They are blameless and inoffensive for the most part, but they know nothing of the duties of a soldier and could never be *dragged* into action either with Spaniards or Indians." When William H. Ashley, later to win great fame in the fur trade, resigned his militia captaincy, Bates remarked, "A stupid captain of militia sends me his commission because, says he, 'I do not feel disposed to serve under the present administration.' "

Meriwether Lewis's year-long procrastination in assuming his duties as Governor was absolutely inexcusable. In a very real sense he was as responsible as Bates for the deterioration and chaos of Indian affairs. No amount of romantic dalliance, attendance at Burr's treason trial as the President's personal reporter, social or scientific activity in the American Philosophical Society circle, or editing of his journals for publication (and not one line of copy reached publisher Conrad) justified such a monumental error. No man, not even a Machiavellian genius, could rule such an unruly province 700 miles distant, particularly with such a hostile proxy as Bates on the scene. This man, upon whom Lewis had to depend, became an enemy almost from first acquaintance although his brother, Tarleton, was a good friend of Lewis's. The roots of jealousy and hatred were deep, extending back to 1801 when Jefferson chose Lewis to be his Presidential secretary. Bates's father had had his heart set on his son winning the post. On May 4, 1801, he had written him to say that Lewis had received the appointment and that "my golden dreams have been delusive."

Lewis and Bates were seldom in agreement. They disagreed on personalities and appointments, planning and policies. In Indian matters they were poles apart. Bates felt humiliated because Lewis not only took his ex-officio Superintendency of Indian Affairs seriously but bypassed him to deal directly with Clark. And Clark went along with Lewis, not Bates. A particular nuisance to Bates was Lewis's old friend, Big White. Tiring of his quarters at Cantonment Bellefontaine, the Mandan insisted on coming to St. Louis. Pierre Chouteau, not Bates, took care of him in Lewis's absence but the chief annoyed the Secretary with his sensitivity and pride, as when he publicly announced that he was "a brother of the President, not just a son."

Eventually, Bates came to oppose all of Lewis's policies. If the Governor wanted restrictions on Indian trade, Bates wanted it open. If Lewis wished *congés* cut back, Bates wanted to broadcast them like handbills. The Governor, like his brother Reuben and his best friend, Will Clark, was deeply committed to the American fur trade. But Bates made clear his sentiments on the trade shortly before he arrived in St. Louis. "As long as we are Indian traders and hunters, our settlements can never flourish and, for my part, I care not how soon the savage is left to traverse in solitude his own deserts until the approach of civilization obliges him to retreat into more gloomy recesses."

Reuben Lewis reached St. Louis on February 25, 1808, with his brother's carriage and three cases of furniture and other possessions. Suspicious Bates grumbled, "Governor Lewis has a brother in this country for whom, I suppose, some provision must be made." The Governor himself arrived on March 8th and took over the reins of authority at once. He found that Bates had done a good job, aside from Indian affairs. He had acted with administrative ability, had compiled and revised the territorial codes, had selected able subordinates for the most part, and Lewis retained most of them in office.

The Virginian was given a good welcome. There was still a warm reservoir of good will in St. Louis despite his long and aggravating absence from his post. The territory was quiet, too, save for local discontent at the Ste. Genevieve mines and a few marauding Osages on the frontier. One of those who greeted him was Moses Austin, who then warned him of attempts by friends of Colonel Smith T. to blacken Bates's character and create a breech between Governor and Secretary. In fact, opined Austin, this, "as said and impressed on the minds of the people, has already taken place and Governor Lewis has expressed his dissatisfaction of the Secretary's conduct." But Austin could not believe that Lewis would be taken in for long by the wiles of desperado Smith. "My confidence in the correct views of Governor Lewis are such that, until I am convinced by seeing Smith clothed with the ensigns of his office, I will not believe him reinstated in the confidence of the Governor, altho' proclaimed by a thousand tongues." Lewis did not restore Smith T. as a justice of the peace, but he did show his displeasure with Bates by removing one of his appointees, Court Clerk Thomas C. Scott, and reappointing Joseph McFerron, whom Bates had fired.

Perhaps typical of the warm greetings of welcome which Lewis received was that of Michel Amoureux, an old French revolutionary living in New Madrid. He expressed the belief that all the French of Louisiana would close ranks behind Lewis to put an end to the rivalry of factions which originated in "the unruly and misguided ambition of only a few men." His enthusiasm for Lewis was refreshing: "I avail myself of this opportunity to express the satisfaction I feel, in common with all Louisianans, by the choice made of your person to govern over this Territory. Thanks be given to the wise and virtuous Magistrate who presides over the Union!"

The Governor lost no time in plunging into work. One of his first acts was to confirm Daniel Boone as justice of the peace of Femme Osage. He offered a similar post to explorer James Mackay (who declined it) and stole a leaf from Clark's book by bringing René Jusseaume's thirteen-year-old son to St. Louis to raise and educate him. He also brought a newspaper to the frontier by financing Joseph Charless's *Missouri Gazette,* which printed its first issue on July 22, 1808.

But Lewis was apprehensive; all reports reaching him suggested not only a deterioration in Indian affairs but the distinct possibility of a large-scale war. Besides prowling and plundering Osages, Marpack, the chief of the Potawatomis, was poised to strike—probably at the very Osages. The Sauks, Foxes and Iowas were becoming obstreperous; the Arikaras had, effectively, closed the Missouri River by routing Pryor's command. But Lewis skillfully mixed force with friendship. He inspected Cantonment Bellefontaine and sent forty men in hot pursuit of Osage raiders, but he also hired his old corpsman, Alex Willard, as government blacksmith to the Sauks and Foxes. No smithy had been promised them by their 1804 treaty but since one had been given to the Osages by their treaty of 1808, Lewis thought that such a concession was just good diplomacy. He appointed Willard smith for twelve months at $30 per month, furnished him with transportation, tools, fuel, a shop, and "a hand to strike."

A month later he dictated to Bates one of his first formal proclamations (April 20th), organizing what amounted to an Indian Territory, access to which by whites would be controlled by him. Because of the difficulties in executing territorial laws and protecting settlers in the scattered settlements on Indian land far to the west, and to enable the frontiersmen to better resist unprovoked Indian aggression, Lewis stated, "I have thought it proper to issue this, my proclamation, prohibiting all persons whomsoever under the penalties of the law from establishing dwellings on, or cultivating the lands of the United States to which the Indian title may or may not have been extinguished. . . ." Lewis then ran the metes and bounds for his Indian Territory, ordered all men beyond the pale to return by June 15th, and empowered the territory's sheriffs to act as federal marshals to remove any people who might fail to comply with his proclamation. The only exceptions were citizens who bore written licenses from the President or himself to reside beyond the line.

Lewis worked to correct the bad political situation in St. Louis but the squabbling in the political rookery of the territory worried him far less than the unprotected frontier facing the Indian nations. Whereas Bates faced east, Lewis faced the West, and always would. His interests were upriver—exploration, science, trade, Indians, furs. He relished the word from the President that John J. Astor was preparing to carve a slice of the fur trade away from Great Britain by a million-dollar American Fur Company. But first the river route must be pacified. Dearborn, for all his incompetence, was not so blind that he did not see, too, how unprotected were the borders of the new territory, although he knew that Clark was trying to shape the 2,447-man militia into a real fighting force. On May 17th he ordered Colonel Thomas Hunt to establish forts on the Osage and Des Moines rivers. They were to serve as both military garrisons and as trading posts. He wanted a stockade, blockhouse and barracks, garrisoned by thirty men, at each establishment and he asked Clark and George Sibley, the factor-designate to the Osages, to set out at once with a party to start building the posts.

Hunt consulted with Lewis on the matter before moving out and the Governor advised him to suspend the move, telling him that he would write to Dearborn and explain the postponement of the operation. He then laid before Hunt his substitute plan of action, on which he had been working when Dearborn's orders arrived. He would first send out his most trusted Indian agent, Nicholas Boilvin. "To insure a favourable reception to our messenger, Mr. Boilvin," he told the Colonel, "and to give the speech the best effect, I have thought it advisable that he should be accompanied by a military escort. The murderer of one of our

300

citizens at Portage des Sioux will be demanded of them [the Sauks and Foxes]. If he is delivered, it will be necessary that he be conveyed to this place in order that he may be delivered to the civil authority. Should the murderer not be delivered, I have given orders to Mr. Boilvin to bring with him from those nations all public property of every description; this cannot be effected but by the accommodation of a large boat and a number of hands. Such an equipment would cost the Government a considerable sum if undertaken by private individuals and could not be expected, even then, to have so good an effect as if executed by the Regular Troops under your command. I have, therefore, thought proper to call on you for a detachment of one subaltern, one sergeant, and twenty-five privates, and a barge equipped with provisions for twenty-eight persons for fifty days."

The Governor's orders to Boilvin were explicit but they left him a necessary freedom of action. Lewis first convinced him that the Government's policy of spending the taxpayers' money to bribe Indians into peace was misguided. It was not founded on right, justice or even good sense. "I hold it a consequence inevitable that should we continue to pay the aggressors for their forbearance to aggress, and the injured to abstain from retaliation, we at once encourage war among the tribes and tax ourselves with the expenditure of considerable sums to defeat one of the primary objects of our present philanthropic administration in relation to those unfortunate people, which is to induce those tribes in amity with the U States and residing within our limits, to remain in peace with each other.

"You will, therefore, be guided in future with respect to expenditures under this head," he continued, "as we cannot with complacency think of paying for disobedience to our will. I do not, however, positively interdict you from making such expenditures in extreme cases and where there may be some important object to be obtained thereby, but they must always be made with that sound discretion which I feel confident you possess. You will, no doubt, perceive that this custom of 'covering the dead,' as it is called, or giving something to the injured nation, originated in the defenceless state of the traders who resided among the Indians formerly, and the pretext which such an occurrence gave the Indians for plundering them. The Indians flattered the traders by assuring them that they looked up to them for protection; the traders received their adulation and promised them that protection which they could not give. . . .

"As the Government of the United States has thought proper now to extend their protection as well to the Indians as to the traders, they must both be held obedient to its will or suffer the penalties. You will urge the Indians by every argument you can suggest to live in peace with their neighbours and assure such as will not conform to our wishes in this respect that no traders can be permitted to bring them merchandise and that, consequently, they will thus be deprived of the means either of making war or defending themselves from the retaliation of others whom they may have injured. Tell them that no prisoners will hereafter be bought by the United States from any Indian nation and that if they wish to profit by our protection, they must take our advice." Finally, Lewis ordered Boilvin, "Should the Sauks and Foxes refuse to deliver the murderer, themselves, and, at the same time assure you that they will not protect him, or that you are at liberty to take him, you will in such case seize the murderer and, if he attempts to escape, put him to death."

Colonel Hunt had no authority to detach troops from his garrison at the Governor's request. But he complied, although he had refused Bates's similar request of October. He immediately informed Dearborn of his action, however, stating that he had acted for the good of the country. Dearborn endorsed his action but grudgingly. He made it clear that he did not want it repeated. Then he fired off a note to Lewis to remind him that, except in the direst of emergencies, the Governor had no right to detach troops from posts without the approval of the President. He obviously did not like Lewis's new plan, either, for he feared that Boilvin would interfere with his Indian agent at Prairie du Chien, John Campbell, in whom he had more confidence than had Lewis. He could not hide his displeasure with the Governor's interfering with his orders, and he chided Lewis for not keeping in touch with Washington, saying that if Hunt had not informed him he would not have known of the change of plans.

Dearborn's sharp letter crossed with one of Lewis's bearing a full statement on his actions. He stated in this July 1st letter that he had moved the location of the Osage trading post from the Secretary of War's choice of a site on the river. "The Osage River at present has not sufficient depth of water to admit a pirogue or small boat to ascend ten miles, nor will it be in a navigable state until the fall rains commence, which usually happen in the latter end of September or beginning of October. The fluctuating and uncertain navigation of that River during the winter and the spring season also renders it, comparatively with the Missouri, ineligible for permanent trading establishments. If this establishment has in view the trade of the Osage nation, as I have supposed, there is a site on the Missouri much nearer their villages than you can approach at this season by way of the Osage River. The point I allude to is the Fire Prairie [about a dozen miles east of Independence, near Sibley, Missouri], situated on the southwest side of the Missouri, about 300 miles from its mouth and about fifty-five or sixty miles from the Osage villages. From this place, we can ascend or descend at pleasure while on the Osage River, the difficulties of the navigation are such that, even admitting the Indians were friendly, as would embarrass the trade considerably. The Fire Prairie is also convenient to the Kansas [Indians], as well as the principal hunting grounds of the Iowas and Sauks. I think the site an eligible one in other points of view. By compelling several nations to trade at the same establishment, they will find it absolutely necessary to live in peace with each other, and consequently, this establishment, from its situation, would in the course of a few years be very instrumental in bringing about a permanent peace between the nations on the lower part of the Missouri. It will not interfere with the establishment of the Council Bluffs, as it is near 400 miles below it.

"The band of the Great Osage, on the Osage River, have cast off all allegiance to the United States," warned Lewis, "and, with a few exceptions, no longer acknowledge the authority of their former leader, White Hair. They have threatened the lives of the inhabitants of the Territory, have taken several prisoners and, after retaining them for some days, insulting and otherwise maltreating them, dismissed them, destitute of provisions and nearly so of clothes, at a considerable distance from the inhabitants. They have stolen a large number of our horses and wantonly killed our cattle. They have also plundered our frontier inhabitants of their clothes, household furniture, &c., destroying such articles as were not portable and, from the information received of the traders as well [as from] White Hair, himself, who is now with me, I have every reason to believe that so soon as they have returned from their summer hunt in the latter end of September, that other, exaggerated, depredations may be expected on our frontier.

"Early in April last I ordered all the traders, hunters and other white persons in the towns and country of the Osages to return. The traders I positively directed to destroy their gunpowder provided there was any danger of its falling into the hands of the Indians. They succeeded in bringing off the balance of their powder and the nation is, by this time, no doubt destitute of ammunition. At the time my orders reached the Osage villages, the River was so low that it was not until several weeks after that the traders could descend. They were charged to conceal their intended movements from the Indians but some of the more incautious *engagés* disclosed their design and it was with much difficulty that their lives were saved by the interference of the Little Osages and the adherents of White Hair.

"The principal chief of the Little Osages; White Hair; and four warriors are now with him. The Little Osages have behaved extremely well and I believe they are sincere in their determination to adhere to their connection with the Government of the U' States. White Hair informs me that he cannot govern his people and that we must, therefore, take such measures with respect to them as we deem most proper. The arrangement I have made with these chiefs is that they are to return immediately to their nations. White Hair is to withdraw the well-disposed part of his band, join the Little Osages, retire to the Fire Prairie, and leave the malcontents to their fate. This arrangement has been known to the Shawnees, Delawares, Kickapoos and other friendly nations of our vicinity, who have promised me that they will not do any injury to those who, thus, withdraw themselves. With respect to the malcontents, I have, in several councils with the Shawnees,

Delawares, Kickapoos, Iowas and Sioux, declared them [the Great Osages] no longer under the protection of the Government of the U' States, and that they were at liberty to wage war against them if they thought proper, under this resriction only—that they should attack in a body sufficiently large to cut them off completely or drive them from their country."

Lewis reported that the friendly tribes had sent runners to their kin in Indiana Territory to join the anti-Osage crusade and that a Shawnee chief had told him that by about August 10th some 2,000 braves would assemble at an island in the Missouri just above the Gasconade, to march on the Osages, who were only 700-strong. "War appears to me inevitable with these people," concluded Lewis. "I have taken the last measures for peace, which have been merely laughed at by them as the repetition of an old song."

According to the Governor, the Osages were sure that the United States could no more control its traders in the field than Spain had been able to control hers and that the traders would continue to supply them with arms and powder, in order to secure peltries. Moreover, they considered themselves independent of traders *or* Government and strong enough to fall on the frontier inhabitants if they chose war. "In order to put an end to these evils," Lewis went on, "some plan must be adopted by which to command the traders before we can possibly govern the Indians. To effect this, I can devise no method more effective than that of assembling them at established posts where they can be placed under the view of correct, impartial and judicious agents of the Government, who shall be invested with sufficient powers to compel their obedience to the laws.

"Big Track's band of the Great Osages on the Arkansas River have not been much less active in committing depredations on our frontier than those on the Osage River. Within the last eighteen months, they have killed one of our citizens and have stolen a number of our horses. Their hostile disposition towards us at present is such that I have refused all applications for licenses to trade with them and have given orders for arresting all unauthorized traders who may attempt to ascend the Arkansas to their villages." The Kansas, Great Pawnees, Loups, Omahas,

Poncas and Pawnee Republic Indians had declared in favor of Spain, reported Lewis, and only the Little Osages, the Missouris and a part of the Great Pawnees were still friendly toward the United States, perhaps 1,000 warriors in all. "In the course of the last winter," he added, "the Omahas killed two *engagés,* robbed their traders and sent me an insolent message. The Kansas have robbed their traders and have been extremely insolent. The Indians of these hostile nations have been lying in wait to intercept the traders on the Missouri at an unusual season. Several boats and pirogues have been fired on. In one instance, two men were killed in descending, at the entrance of Grand River. The [guilty] nation is not known, but the Iowas are suspected. Measures have been taken to ascertain the fact and obtain the murderers.

"Such appeared to be the hostile disposition evinced by the great majority of the Indians on the Missouri that I determined, early in June, to grant no licenses to trade on the Missouri until a sufficient force was sent to establish permanent trading posts. The traders complained of this measure as arbitrary and injurious to the country. Such is their blind infatuation for the possession of peltry and fur and such their total indifference for the safety of the frontier or the lives of the *engagés,* whom they employ. However, I believe that they are now pretty well satisfied with the measures I have taken, as all those except one small crew of five persons, who had previously received licenses to ascend the Missouri, had been fired on and compelled to return. None have been killed but several have received balls through their clothes."

Finally, the Governor warned Dearborn that, at the very moment of writing, the Osages, Pawnees and Kansas were gathering at a council called by the Spaniards on the Great Saline River, 300 miles to the west of the Osage villages. "The result of this council it cannot be expected will be favourable to the quiet of our frontier. Some measures are, therefore, necessary for their defence." Since he had no authority to call out the Regulars, Lewis asked to be allowed to organize three companies of spies (scouts) of 70 men each. He wanted to pick men superior to those turned up by recruiting sergeants in the Atlantic states. He asked for 500 stand of muskets, 300 rifles, 120 swords, 60 pairs of pistols and 1,500 to 2,000 pounds of gunpowder. "If this is granted, I am ready to vouch for the defence of the Country."

Lewis also took the time to brief Governor William Henry Harrison of Indiana Territory on his Indian program. "I have in several late conferences with the Shawnees, Delawares, Kickapoos, Sioux, Sauks, Iowas, etc., declared the Osage nation no longer under the protection of the Untied States and set them at liberty to adjust their differences with that abandoned nation in their own way, but have prohibited their attacking them except with a sufficient force to destroy or drive them from our neighbourhood." Ironically, this letter was picked up and printed by a Philadelphia newspaper and came to Jefferson's attention *before* the Governor's dispatches reached Washington. Where Lewis's silence had puzzled the President before, his lack of correspondence with him now hurt Jefferson. Dearborn heard next to nothing from Lewis; Tarleton Bates complained, "Meriwether Lewis is silent, though he promised to write weekly." A coolness developed between Lewis and Amos Stoddard, too, as a result of his incommunicativeness, and the major managed to write an entire book on Upper Louisiana without mentioning his erstwhile friend.

Just what preoccupied Lewis so much is not clear, unless it was simply his Indian policy and political harassments. Perhaps he was swallowed alive by his work. He was unable to delegate except to Clark. He dared not depend on Bates, now his implacable enemy.

It was August 24th before Lewis finally allowed the Dearborn-plan expedition to march. He had Boilvin accompany it to the Des Moines, with the Sauk annuity. Preceding this detachment by several days was George Sibley's party, en route to the Osages to set up the Fire Prairie establishment, escorted by Captain Clemson's Company. Bellefontaine was doing so poorly as a trading post that Lewis split its supply of trade goods between Sibley and John Johnson, the factor of Des Moines. He also ordered out 80 militiamen, 20 riflemen and 60 dragoons, under Clark's command, to move to the Osage site, timing their march so that they would arrive at the same time as Clemson's command because he felt that all, not just a part, of it should have been dispatched as a show of force.

Lewis took other precautions, reporting, "Three spies have been provided and will be sent off in a few days to learn more minutely the designs of the Indians, and the substance and result of the Spanish council at the Great Saline, and the machinations of the British traders to pass into the Missouri. . . . The designs of the Indians are soon changed by interest; the Spaniards have no merchandise to attach them firmly to them; the British have it, and it is to them I look more particularly for all pending evils on the frontier, and I sincerely hope that the General Government in their philanthropic feelings towards the Indians, will not lose sight of the safety of our defencelsss and extended frontiers. The Michilimackinac Company, or a great majority of them, had formerly become bankrupts in the Indian trade; the North West Company, on whom they are now absolutely dependent, associated them for the purpose of monopolizing the trade of the Missouri, and the western branches of the Mississippi, thus, desperate in their fortunes, unprincipled from their habits, and hostile in the extreme to our Government, they become a fit instrument under the direction of the North West Company to mar our best arrangements for the happiness of the Indians and the tranquility of the frontier."

Lewis blamed the recent Indian difficulties on the Britishers and urged blockhouses to keep both Indians and their English teachers under control. "Without some more efficient check on the Indians, who have for fifteen years and upwards derived advantages from practicing those lessons of rapacity taught them by those traders, [they] cannot in a moment be brought back to a state of primitive innocence by the united efforts of all those people, however sincere they might be in the work of reclamation. I hold it an axiom incontravertible that it is more easy to introduce vice in all states of society than it is to eradicate it, and this is still more strictly true when applied to man in his savage than in his civilized state."

Lewis found Indian affairs on the Mississippi only little less dangerous than on the wild Missouri. Not only were the Sauks unwilling to hand over the murderers among them, they killed several Iowas and Sioux in the Des Moines area while rustling horses. He knew they would respect force, and only force. He demanded the horses in a very positive manner and they gave up the animals, with bad grace. But they then joined the Foxes to bring their strength up to 800 braves and raided the Government's agricultural settlement opposite their old village. "I learned that the British agents were tampering with them at their new station," Lewis reported to Dearborn, "and that 300 warriors under a chief called Black Eagle, had already set out to join the British on the Lakes. In this situation, I laid a scheme which has in view to retain the Sauks and Foxes or to divert them from a close alliance with the British, to recover from them the Sauk murderer, also to obtain the Iowa murderers, should it prove to be them who killed the *engagés* on the Missouri, and to restore peace among the Sauks, Foxes, Sioux and Iowas." Lewis had nothing less in mind than a great prairie peace; perhaps it was this which absorbed all of his time and led him to neglect his correspondence. He based his program on economic-military strategy, occupying the controlling positions on routes of trade and travel.

"In order to carry my plan into operation," continued Lewis, "I found it necessary to use the influence of Old Dorion to withdraw from the employment of the British merchants two of his sons whom I have taken into the pay of the U' States as interpreters at the rate of one dollar per day. Also a very active, intelligent man who was also in the employment of the British merchants, by the name of [Maurice] Blondeau, who has much influence with the Sauks and Foxes. To this man I have promised a sub-agency with the pay of one dollar and fifty cents per day. This man has more influence with the Sauks and Foxes, or rather possesses their confidence to a greater degree, than any man in the country. These persons, with Old Dorion, I have sent up the Mississippi some weeks since to commence the work."

But, concluded Lewis, "To Mr. Boilvin, the principal part of the duties of this affair are assigned. I sent him up to the Sauks and Foxes with a speech. . . . On the success he meets with, or the information he brings, will very materially depend the future arrangements I shall make for the defence of the Territory or the measures I shall recommend to you in relation of fixing the site for the factory in that quarter. My present impression is that if the Indians surrender the murderers and the Sauks return to their old village with professions of contrition for past offenses, that it will be best to establish a factory at the Rapid Des Moines on the southwest side of the Mississippi near their village. . . ." There, Lewis would station fifteen troopers while the balance of Bissell's Company would erect a post at the entrance of the Wisconsin River or at the Dog Prairie, and House's Company would guard the entrance of the Illinois River against British incursions. "Although the Sauks may not be friendly, yet I do not believe that they would oppose by force of arms a full company from ascending the Mississippi unless their object was made known to them. Until the return of Mr. Boilvin, I have advised Col. Hunt to make no movement but to have all matters in readiness to proceed when he shall receive your further instructions or previously thereto should the state of the Indians in that quarter warrant his carrying into effect those [orders] he has already received."

Placing great faith in Boilvin, Lewis nevertheless also enlisted the services of Denis Julien and Julian Dubuque to woo the Indians away from the British. He had a lower estimate of Indian Agent John Campbell, a Dearborn favorite, but was careful in his handling of him. "I took care not to enlist his pride against me by neglect. I well know how tenacious those people are of what is called their influence over the Indians and the mania with which they are frequently seized for acquiring Indian popularity. This always costs them much and is frequently of short duration, not extending beyond the hour in which their liberality has been dispensed. Indian popularity, like bank stock, is readily transferred, with this difference, however. That the proprietor possesses no control over the act of transfer. He often deceives himself and then deceives others; he hugs the shadow when the substance has fled. The Government should therefore, in my opinion, trust with caution for the government of the Indians to the imagined influence of the individuals.

"If I understand the Indian character at all, I do know that there are but two effective cords by which the savage arm can be bound; the one is *love of merchandise* and the other is the *fear of punishment*. Whatever may be the previous standing of any individual among them, if he neither possesses the means of gratifying the one or inflicting the other, he becomes as Samson with his locks shorn, and I will venture my reputation as a politician in Indian affairs that any system which may be laid down or adopted for their government, if not bottomed upon one or both of those principles, will in practice prove abortive. . . . Unless the Government of the United States does support their agents by placing it in their power at all times to distribute rewards and punishments among the Indians, they will soon become as weak as other men; and too much confidence ought not to be placed in the individual influence of any person unsupported by these aids."

Lewis's long and detailed defense of his course of action, so obviously well thought out, was largely negated by his delay in transmitting it to Washington. During this silent interim, his reputation was done irreparable damage. Dearborn complained to the President about Lewis's overriding his orders. Jefferson, for his own part, expressed disappointment that his friend had not written him, saying, "It is astonishing we get not one word from him." He began to fear the Governor had been too precipitate in committing the United States to force in the Osage dispute. He wrote Lewis to express his regret at the rupture of Osage-American relations, urged patience in the cases of the Sauk and Fox murderers, and requested that complete interdiction of trade with the two tribes be used only as a last resort. The President abhorred war and put his trust in trade to win over the Indians. "Commerce is the great engine by which we are to coerce them, and not war," he was fond of repeating to his friend. Nevertheless, he recognized the weakness of Louisiana's frontiers and approved Lewis's recruiting of three special companies of mounted scouts, the Louisiana Spies, the predecessors of the dragoons and cavalry of the later Indian Wars.

The Governor was stung by the rebuke of Dearborn and the crossness of Jefferson. He wrote Dearborn that he must not have received his letters of May 3rd, July 1st and July 16th. He reminded him of the slowness of the mails by pointing out that the

Secretary's letter of castigation had taken forty-two days to reach him. However, he promised to be responsible to Washington's will. "I trust that the proper motives will be ascribed to my acts by the Executive of the U' States, whose orders and arrangements both duty and inclination will ever induce me to further by every means in my power. Nothing has been done as yet or through my recommendation by the military but what may be readily undone, if not approved, and I shall in future, unless discretionary or specific powers be granted me on this subject, be as cautious with respect to my requisitions on the Regular troops as you can possibly wish me. . . . [But], surrounded as I am with numerous faithless savage nations, many cases will arise which require my acting before it is possible I can consult the Executive of the United States." He promised not to misuse his authority in this respect, however. "In future, if it be deemed inexpedient to grant me a discretionary use of the Regular troops, I shall have only to regret the measure and make the best defense I can with the Militia. . . . I have thought it better not to act, at all, than to act erroneously and I shall certainly not lay myself liable, hereafter, to the censure of the Executive under this head, tho' I shall ever feel a pleasure in exercising to the best of my judgment and abilities such discretionary powers as they may think proper to confide to me."

The Governor's program was bearing fruit. Fort Osage was garrisoned and the Des Moines post, Fort Madison, was being constructed by Pryor and Lieutenant Alpha Kingsley. It worried the Sauks and Foxes so much that Black Hawk was on the point of raiding it before it dominated his people. But it was too late. In his autobiography the chief mentioned the lost opportunity— "Had our party got into the fort, all the whites would have been killed, as the British soldiers had been at Mackinac many years before." Clark returned from Fire Prairie with a good treaty with the Great and Little Osages, one which ceded lands to the United States and set up a boundary line. To enforce the treaty, Clark appointed the Governor's brother, Reuben Lewis, as Osage subagent. The Governor was not completely satisfied with the treaty, however, and after conferring with Clark, sent Pierre Chouteau to negotiate another in October 1808. Clark explained to Dearborn that the second treaty would be more in line with Government wishes and that it was in order because some of the prominent chiefs had been absent at the time of the first treaty and protested it. It was a very satisfactory treaty to Lewis.

Chouteau's powwow went as smooth as suet and the Osages adopted the treaty on November 10th. (It was ratified by the U. S. Senate, unanimously, on April 28, 1810.) The thorny Osage problem was apparently solved.

Noted Lewis, "This draft of a treaty, you will observe, contemplates something more than the restoration of peace. It gives to the Great and Little Osage the most efficient security in our power to bestow. It assures to them, for their exclusive use, the lands west of the boundary line. It separates those who sanction it from the vicious and the profligate, whom no treaties can bind, whom no menaces can intimidate, and by whose ungovernable conduct the peace of both nations is perpetually endangered. It enables us, also, to reduce to submission, without bloodshed, those who persevere in hostility, by witholding from them the merchandise necessary for their support. By these arrangements we shall obtain a tract of country west of our present settlements and east of the hunting boundary of the Osage sufficient for the purposes of our white hunters and for such Indian nations as have long been on terms of intimate friendship with us. Thus will our frontier be strengthened and secured with the least possible expense to the Government. The establishment of a boundary line has long been desirable and the want of one, settled by treaty, has never ceased to create doubts and, sometimes, embarrassments of the most serious nature in our courts of justice."

While the Governor was as stubbornly vigilant as a watch crow over Indian affairs, he did not neglect other gubernatorial duties. He prohibited bold stakery, claim jumping and illegal pre-emption of mining claims; enacted a law to permit villages to incorporate as towns; laid out a road from St. Louis to Ste. Genevieve, Cape Girardeau and New Madrid; and attended to a myriad other matters, including the erection of a shot tower and the exploration of saltpeter caves. Personal affairs took much of his time, too: his Masonic lodge; his concern over Drouillard, tried for murder (and acquitted); his reception of Clark and his new bride. By now, he and Bates were no longer on speaking terms. After a real row, Bates wrote his brother, "We now understand each other much better. We differ in everything, but we will be honest and frank in our intercourse." A riot in the perennially turbulent lead mines caused Lewis to order Justice of the Peace James Austin to arrest the men responsible and to command: "If any resistance be made by an armed force, the Militia are to be called to your assistance. In the event of a continued forcible opposition, they are hereby ordered to fire upon the lawless banditti employed in the resistance." This drastic order won Lewis few friends and Bates commented, "I lament the unpopularity of the Governor but he has brought it on himself by harsh and mistaken measures. He is inflexible in error, and the irresistible Fiat of the people has, I am fearful, already sealed his condemnation."

Lewis was well aware of Bates's hostility but not sure of its cause. He called on the Secretary to ask for an explanation. Bates insisted that although he differed with him on civil government measures, there was no personal hostility involved. "Well," said Lewis, "do not suffer yourself to be separated from me in the public opinion. When we meet in public, let us, at least, address each other with cordiality." Bates assented, writing his brother, "However I may have disapproved and continue to disapprove the measures of the Governor, as a man I entertain good opinions of him." But soon the venom was flowing again from his pen: "He [Lewis] has fallen from the public esteem and almost into the public contempt. He is well aware of my increasing popularity. . . . How unfortunately for this man that he resigned his commission in the Army. His habits are altogether military and he never can, I think, succeed in any other profession. . . . He has been spoiled by the elegant praises of [Samuel Latham] Mitchell and [Joel] Barlow and overwhelmed by so many flattering caresses of the *high and mighty* that, like an overgrown baby, he began to think that everybody about the house must regulate their conduct by his caprices. . . . I never saw, after his arrival in this country, anything in his conduct toward me but alienation and unmerited distrust." Launching into poesy, Bates wrote, "Oh, Lewis, how from love I pity thee! Those who stand high, have many winds to shake them and if they fall, they dash themselves to pieces." Faced with such a pious fraud as Frederick Bates, Lewis could have used a poet, himself, as an ally— such a one as Emerson, who wrote, "Do not say things. What you are stands over you the while and thunders so that I cannot hear what you say to the contrary."

At this time Lewis was doing a little writing of his own, but not poetry. He expanded his Indian policy into an article in the *Missouri Gazette*, titling it "Observations and Reflections on the Subject of Governing and Maintaining a State of Friendly Intercourse With the Indians of the Territory of Louisiana," and signed it with the nom de plume Clatsop. In it he criticized the defects of both the Spanish and American systems of handling the Indians, particularly the handing out of licenses and the granting of credit to the Indians. "This credit," he wrote, "was nothing less than the price of his [the trader's] passport, or the privilege of departing in safety to his home." Small wonder, observed Lewis, that the prevailing sentiment in the Sioux and Kansas camps was scorn for the whites—"The white men are like dogs; the more you beat and plunder them, the more goods they will bring you and the cheaper they will sell them."

But he reserved his severest criticism for, as usual, the plotting British traders. "If we permit the British merchants to supply the Indians in Louisiana as formerly, the influence of our Government over those Indians is lost. For the Indian in possession of his merchandise feels himself independent of every government, and will proceed to commit the same depredations which they did when rendered independent by the Spanish system. The traders give themselves but little trouble at any time to inculcate among the Indians a respect for governments, but are usually content with proclaiming their own importance. When the British merchants give themselves trouble to speak of governments, it is but fair to presume that they will teach the natives to respect the power of their own. And, at all events, we know from experience that no regard for the blood of our frontier inhabitants will influence them at any time to withhold arms and ammunition from the Indians, provided they are to profit by furnishing them."

Once again, Lewis pointed to the weaknesses of the savages—their love of gain and their fear of punishment. He urged that punishment take the form of the withholding of trade goods from them. "This species of punishment, while it is one of the most efficient in governing the Indians, is certainly the most humane, as it enforces a compliance with our will without the necessity of bloodshed. But in order to compass the exercise of this weapon, our Government must first provide the means of controlling their traders. No government will be respected by the Indians until they are made to feel the effects of its power or see it practised on others; and the surest guarantee of savage fidelity to any government is a thorough conviction in their minds that they do possess the power of punishing promptly every act of aggression which they may commit on the persons or property of their citizens.

"If both traders and Indians throughout Upper Louisiana were compelled to resort to regulated commercial posts, then the trader would be less liable to be pillaged and the Indians deterred from practising aggression, for when the Indians once become convinced that, in consequence of their having practised violence upon the persons or property of the traders, that they have been cut off from all intercourse with those posts and that they cannot resort to any other places to obtain merchandise, then they will make any sacrifice to regain the privilege they had previously enjoyed. I am confident," concluded Lewis, "that, in order to regain our favour in such cases, they would sacrifice any individual who may be the object of our displeasure, even should he be their favourite chief; for their thirst of merchandise is paramount to every other consideration and the leading individuals among them, well knowing this trait in the character of their own people, will not venture to encourage or excite aggressions on the whites when they know they are, themselves, to become the victims of its consequences."

CHAPTER XXII

———◆◆———

LAST JOURNEY

Our Governor Lewis, with the best intentions in the world is, I am fearful, losing ground. His late preparations for Indian War have not been popular. He acted for the best. But it is the fate of great men to be judged by the results of their measures. He has talked for 12 months of leaving the country. Everyone thinks that he will positively go, in a few weeks.

—FREDERICK BATES to James Abbott,
July 25, 1809

Should Governor Lewis leave this quarter, I fear from what I hear among the Indians all would not be quiet long. They would be dissatisfied at the departure of their Father Lewis, as they style him since his visit to them on his voyage up the Missouri.

—NICHOLAS BOILVIN to William Eustis,
April 21, 1809

MANY MATTERS besides writing articles for the *Missouri Gazette* kept Governor Lewis busy during the fall and winter of 1808. As founder and Master of the first Masonic lodge in the West, he kept active in that sphere; he made many appointments of territorial officials; he laid the foundations of the State of Arkansas by cutting the Arkansas District away from the too-large New Madrid District of Louisiana. But his main concern remained the Indians. The presence of Tecumseh's brother, the Prophet, gave him much uneasiness. Lewis's intelligence network frus-

317

trated surprise moves by the Winnebagos against Fort Bellevue and its successor, Fort Madison, as he quickly reinforced the Des Moines frontier with militia and artillery.

When Jefferson asked the nation to raise 100,000 men because of strained relations with Great Britain, Louisiana's quota was a mere 377 men but Lewis set about organizing the force as if the safety of the entire republic depended on it. He drafted men from militia corps and tried to fire up the lukewarm patriotism of the Franco-Americans with a full blast of oratory: "We are called upon, fellow citizens, to bear a part, when the effort shall be necessary, in defending our liberties and our Country from the unhallowed grasp of the modern barbarians of Europe who, insatiate with the horrid butcheries of the eastern world, are now bending their course towards our peaceful and happy shore. We must be prepared to meet them; the cup of accommodation has been drained; the delusion of their friendly professions has been poured out and leaves exposed, in characters too legible to be mistaken, the base motives which form the rule of their actions towards us. With them, power begets right, and justice is laughed to scorn. With them, those laws founded in justice and in natural right, which have so long bound the civilized nations of the earth in confidence and a decent respect towards each other, are now obsolete, and the foot of power rests without remorse on the shattered remains of the most sacred institutions of those nations whose only crime has been the want of strength to resist oppression.

"From enemies thus destitute of magnanimity and virtue, what have we to expect? Naught but the repetition of those wrongs practiced on others. National degradation and oppression await a state of inactivity and want of zeal to defend our country and our liberties. Shall we, then, at a crisis like this, be the last to volunteer our services in defence of our national rights? Shall we acknowledge the goad of the law necessary to stimulate us to the defence of those rights, of which, when bereft, existence itself forms but a barren waste? Forbid it, ye genius of America. . . . Danger flies before the ardent hero and when he has gained the prize he sought, he is astonished that it has cost him so little. Shrink not, therefore, fellow citizens, from the task.

Shielded with the justice of our case, we are doubly armed. United and firm, let us obey the call of our Country and be prepared to set at nought the machinations of those sanguinary bands of hirelings when they shall dare assail our rights or liberties."

Lack of zeal by Gallic militiamen was not the only headache for Lewis, in protecting the territory from British and Indians. He was also frustrated by the U. S. Army's unwillingness to cooperate with him. Captain George Armistead stated that Lewis had no authority to interfere with the movement of Indians, nor would he respect Cherokee lands. As far as the captain was concerned, whites could settle where they pleased. He belligerently added for Lewis's benefit that he would like to see who would prevent it. He boasted he would not obey any order given him by the Governor. "But," he added, "if the Governor made a polite request, I would then go as far as I thought proper." He would not recall illegal traders unless they were peddling whiskey to the Indians. "If I were in your place," Armistead advised Indian Agent John B. Treat, "I would not be directed by any information from him [Lewis]. You have your information and instructions from the Secretary of War and not from Governor Lewis." Treat dryly replied, "I shall not ask your advice on my business, nor any other person. I have received the Governor's letter, which I shall be guided by."

Indian Agent James McFarlane also warned Lewis not to depend on his militiamen in Arkansas, since many of them were engaged in illegal trading with the Indians. He reported white incursions into Indian lands and violent disputes. Settlers were letting their cattle run among the stock of friendly Indians, then killing animals without distinction as to ownership. This caused very bad feelings among the normally pro-American Cherokees. Reported McFarlane, "There are, at present, families settled one hundred and fifty miles up the River Arkansas, for no purpose but to harbour horse thieves and murderers. I hope you will approve this and have them removed."

The next play of the Army game was insane. When McFarlane got some Osages to start for St. Louis and a parley with the Governor, Colonel Thomas Hunt tried to get other Indians to intercept them at White River, telling them they were at liberty to kill the travelers. Luckily, the Indians considered Hunt to be a big liar and they contacted McFarlane, telling him, "We know that you are going to see Our Father [Lewis]; we, therefore, will let you pass."

While the Army blocked Lewis, the British continued their machinations. Boilvin told Clark that they were advising the Indians at Detroit that the Americans planned to seize all Indian lands and game, giving them not so much as a blanket in return. Not all of the Indians were taken in and the most powerful tribe, the Sioux, dealt British plotters a blow when they announced they would acknowledge no white leader but their American Father. Tension slowly began to taper off as summer waned in 1809; and Bernard Pratte reported the frontier quiet except for pig-stealing Iowas. On July 6th, in fact, the border was so quiet that Lewis discharged the troops he had called out in November, "all immediate danger from the Indians on our frontier being happily subsided."

In the meantime, Meriwether Lewis's great military-commercial expedition, under the command of Pierre Chouteau, was wending its way up the Missouri. As long before as February 24th, he had signed a contract with the nascent St. Louis Missouri Fur Company's partners, William Clark, Manuel Lisa and Silvestre Labadie, to do the job of finally restoring Big White to his people. Lewis himself was probably a silent partner in the firm. Clark was a partner and the Governor's brother, Reuben, was an officer of the company. Thomas James said he was a partner; Robert Lucas said he was the company's patron and benefactor. It all amounted to the same thing. He was determined to wrest a portion of the fur trade of the Upper Missouri away from the British.

With the failure of Pryor very much in mind, Lewis built up a strong force even without Army help. He not only wanted to return Big White, as he had promised Jefferson so long before, but to open up, and keep open, the Missouri now blocked by the Arikaras. He wanted a force powerful enough to give the British pause in their take-over of uppermost Louisiana Territory, too. Since his militiamen were not well armed, and enlisted for only a six-month hitch, he decided to use mercenaries. Lewis paid the company $7,000 to supply a force of at least 120 men, of whom 40 must be Americans armed with rifles and plenty of ammunition—"The quantity and quality of which shall be approved of by the Governor of this Territory." He charged this small army to protect Big White by force of arms and at the risk of life. Should they fail to deliver the chief safely home, the $7,000 would be forfeited to the United States. Pierre Chouteau was to command the military portion of the expedition—that is, as far as the Mandan villages. From there, it became a commercial enterprise with Lisa in charge.

Lewis's orders to Chouteau were clear and specific. "I consider the honour and good faith of our Government pledged for the success of this enterprise. You will, therefore, consider its accomplishment as paramount to every other consideration connected with the expedition and will, consequently, take such measures on your voyage as may appear best calculated to insure its success.

"That the Arikara nation should be severely punished for their unprovoked attack on the party under the command of Ensign Pryor in September 1807 is also devoutly to be wished, as well for the reputation of our Government as for the security which it would give to the future navigation of the River Missouri. . . . The hostility of the Arikaras renders it necessary that you should adopt war measures in the commencement, or at least that you should meet them with a force sufficiently strong to insure a successful issue should a decision by arms become necessary to terminate the existing differences between us or to effect the safe return of the Mandan chief." Lewis felt Chouteau's force was "sufficient not only to bid defiance to the Arikaras but to extirpate that abandoned nation, if necessary."

If the Rees wanted peace, they were to surrender those who had killed Pryor's men. If they could not single out the guilty parties, they were to surrender hostages. Here, Lewis showed a ruthless streak in his nature. "These murderers, when delivered, will be shot in the presence of the [Arikara] nation." Should they not wish peace, Chouteau had carte blanche. "You will take such measures as you think best calculated to surprise and cut them off." Should his force be weakened by desertions to the point where he could not force a showdown of arms, Chouteau was to avoid the Rees and act on the defensive. But on one point the Governor was adamant. "In no event whatever are you to make such terms with them as will commit the honour of our Government or such as will prove a bar to their being thereafter punished in an exemplary manner for the atrocities of which they have been guilty."

Governor Lewis was pleased when the first section of the expedition got under way, some 160 riflemen, including 80 Delawares, Shawnees and white hunters in the van. On May 17th, a second party of 110 traders set out and Lisa led the third group of 80 men onto the last of the 13 keelboats and barges on June 17th.

Although desertions were many, because of Lisa's hard-driving ways, it was a powerful armada which reached the Arikaras and Chouteau found them, suddenly, meek as mice. He lectured them sternly and moved on to deliver Big White to his village on September 24th, where he was received as if risen from the dead.

While everything was going well on the Missouri, all was not quiet along the Potomac. William Eustis had succeeded Dearborn as Secretary of War. He was an urbane man, devoted to Jefferson, but a politician completely lacking in real ability or vision. His mind could no more understand the importance of Lewis's pacification of the Missouri Valley than it could grasp the extent of the great sweep of prairies and high plains rolling up toward the Shining Mountains. He was a loyal party man, a bureaucrat. During the critical antebellum years of 1809–11 he would pinch pennies so zealously that the War Department decayed into a stagnant bureau of eight clerks, completely unprepared for "Mr. Madison's War" of 1812. Public criticism of his inane policy would lead to his resignation in 1812, but in 1809 Eustis was firmly in charge.

That summer of 1809, rumor swept St. Louis that Washington was displeased with the Governor, leading Boilvin to write both Eustis and the President. He warned Madison of the British agents tampering with the Indians of Prairie du Chien and urged him to carry out Lewis's recommendations of the establishment of a post, the handing out of presents, and the exclusion of British traders. Otherwise, the British might triumph and, "God only knows what might be the consequence of such an event!" he exclaimed. He wrote Eustis of his work in spying on British intrigues and praised Lewis's vigilance, which had saved hundreds of settlers from Indian tomahawks. "His Excellency, Governor Lewis, who is always on the watch, received information of what was fermenting among the Indians [and] ordered me to visit the nations *mal intentionnées.*" Boilvin, aware of Lewis's troubled situation, could not forbear leaping to the Governor's defense. If the interior and remote parts of the territory were as well run as Lewis administered the capital, good order would be assured, he said. And, he added, "Should Governor Lewis leave this quarter, I fear from what I hear among the Indians all would not be quiet long. They would be dissatisfied at the departure of their Father Lewis, as they style him. . . ."

Boilvin's appeal was too late. On a hot summer's day in Washington, a clerk in the Department of State, named T. Smith, scrawled across a letter of Lewis's the words "The bill mentioned in this letter, having been drawn without authority, it can not be paid at this Department." The bill in question, a draft of February 6th for a mere $18.70 in favor of Peter Provenchère for translating the laws of the territory for publication, was the result of a felony trial with which Judge Lucas could not proceed. Although he was unauthorized to pay for such services, Lewis had gone ahead. "I did not hesitate to cause the copies of those laws to be made out and furnished him. I was compelled to take the course which I have, or suffer a fellow to escape punishment."

His words had no effect on Washington and Lewis had to pay Provenchère in cash from his own pocket. This seemingly minor incident worried the Governor; there was a lot more involved than $18.70. "This occurrence has given me infinite concern as from it the fate of other bills, drawn for similar purposes, to a considerable amount cannot be mistaken. This rejection cannot fail to impress the public mind unfavourably with respect to me, nor is this consideration more painful than the censure which must arise in the mind of the Executive from my having drawn public monies without authority. A third, and not less, embarrassing circumstance attending the transaction is that my private funds are entirely incompetent to meet these bills, if protested."

Although the handwriting was clearly on the wall, Lewis was not prepared for the shock of Eustis's letter of July 18th. It burst on him like a grenade, shook him badly, and proved to be his death warrant. Perhaps because he had just been praised by John Mason, the Superintendent of Indian Affairs, for his Indian program, Lewis was unprepared for the letter from the pennysniffing Eustis. In it he caustically reminded Lewis that the Department had advanced him $7,000 to convoy Big White home and, therefore, he could not honor Lewis's additional bill for $500, dated May 13th, for presents of tobacco, powder and trade goods for the Indians.

Eustis—whom both Henry Clay and Albert Gallatin pronounced utterly incompetent in any field—assumed a posture of outraged officialdom and pronounced judgment on Lewis's Indian policy, about which he knew nothing. He proceeded to lecture Lewis sarcastically: "It has been usual to advise the Government of the United States when expenditures to a considerable amount are contemplated in the Territorial Governments. In the instance of accepting the volunteer services for a military expedition to a point and purpose not designated, which expedition is stated to combine commercial as well as military objects, and when an Agent of the Government appointed for other purposes [Chouteau] is selected for the command, it is thought the Government might, without injury to the public interests, have been consulted. As the object and destination of this force is unknown and more especially as it combines commercial purposes, so it cannot be considered as having the sanction of the Government of the United States, or that they are responsible for [its] consequences."

Lewis was dumfounded; he had sent the contract, signed by Clark, Chouteau, Lisa, Hempstead and James Wilkinson, Jr., to the War Department. It clearly stated the purpose of the expedition.

Eustis, before closing his damning letter, pointedly reminded him that Jefferson was no longer in office and that remonstrances at the Executive Mansion would do Lewis no good. "The President [Madison] has been consulted and the observations herein contained have his approval."

An angry and embittered Lewis replied on August 18th, saying of the accusing letter, "the feelings it excites are truly painful." He reminded the Secretary he always accompanied his drafts with explanatory letters. "If the object be not a proper one, of course I am responsible but if, on investigation, it does appear to have been necessary for the promotion of the public interest, I shall hope for relief." Doubtless, as Lewis wrote, the words of Jefferson echoed in his ears—"I am uneasy hearing nothing from you about the Mandan Chief nor the measures for restoring him to his country. That is an object which presses on our justice and our honour and, farther than that, I suppose severe punishment of the Ricaras indispensable."

But Jefferson was out of office so Lewis did not belabor the point. Instead, he reminded Eustis, "I have never received a penny of public money but have merely given the draft to a person who had rendered public service, or furnished articles for public use, which have been, invariably, applied to the purposes expressed in my letters of advice. . . . To the correctness of this statement, I call God to witness."

Was Bates's fine hand to be seen in this affair? Lewis continued, "I have been informed [that] representations have been made against me. All I wish is a full and fair investigation. I anxiously wish that this may reach you in time to prevent any decision relative to me. . . . I shall leave the Territory in the most perfect state of tranquility which, I believe, it has ever experienced. I find it impossible, at this moment, to explain by letter and to do away by written explanations the impression which, I fear, from the tenor of your letter, the Government entertains with respect to me and shall, therefore, go on by the way of New Orleans to the city of Washington with all dispatch. I shall take with me my papers, which I trust, when examined, will prove my firm and steady attachment to my country as well as the exertions I have made to support and further its interests in this quarter.

"I most solemnly aver that the expedition sent up the Missouri under the command of Mr. Peter Chouteau is a military command, has no further object than that of conveying the Mandan

Chief and his family to their village and, in a commercial point of view, that they intend only to hunt and trade on the waters of the Missouri and Columbia Rivers within the Rocky Mountains and the plains bordering these mountains on the east side and that they have no intention, with which I am acquainted, to enter the dominions of or do injury to any foreign nation." Apparently, the person who was spreading tales in Washington was tarring him with a Burrite brush, suggesting that Chouteau's expedition was a filibustering maneuver against Spain. To this Lewis was led to say acidly, "Be assured, Sir, that my country can never make 'a Burr' of me. She may reduce me to poverty, but she can never sever my attachment to her."

Lewis's reference to impoverishment was not purely rhetorical. He reported to Eustis that the two contested bills had sunk his credit and brought in all his private debts, totaling $4,000, on the run. To do justice to his creditors, Lewis handed over to them, as security, what land he had acquired in Louisiana. "The best proof of which I can give of my integrity," he wryly reminded his superior, "as to the use or expenditure of public monies, the Government will find at a future day by the poverty to which they have now reduced me. Still, I shall do no more than appeal to the generosity of the Government by exposing my claims. I had sooner bear any pecuniary embarrassment than attempt in any manner to wound the feelings or injure in the public opinion the present Executive or either of the Heads of Departments [War and Treasury] by complaining of injuries done, other than in friendly expositions. I am convinced that the motives expressed in the latter part of your letter are those which have actuated you." Here he referred to Eustis's insistence that he had written only out of public duty. "But, at the same time, I trust that the motives which induced me to make the expenditures will be found equally pure."

The Governor then explained why he spent more than the original amount. "Some weeks after making the contract with the Missouri Fur Company for taking the Mandan Chief to his village, I received information through the Sioux and Omahas, that the Cheyennes had joined the Arikaras and were determined to arrest all boats which might ascend the river. I conceived it necessary, in order to meet the additional force and to insure the success of the expedition conveying the Mandan Chief, to make a further advance with a view that, should it become necessary to engage an auxiliary force among the friendly nations through which they would pass, that Mr. Chouteau, the Commanding Officer, might be enabled to acquire such aid by means of those supplies."

To his letter, Lewis attached another copy of the contract. He asked that Chouteau be retained as Osage agent (Eustis planned to fire him), explaining, "The reason for wishing Mr. Chouteau not to be displaced is that if the event takes place before one or the other of the Osage treaties are ratified, there will, in my opinion, be war with that nation."

Word that Lewis was coming east reached the ex-President at Monticello. On August 16th he wrote Lewis, in an attempt to re-establish their old camaraderie. English botantist John Bradbury was to hand Jefferson's missive to Lewis, personally. It doubled as a letter of introduction. Jefferson wrote, "I have so long promised copies [of Lewis's projected book] to my literary correspondents in France that I am almost bankrupt in their eyes. . . . Your friends here are all well and have long been in expectation of seeing you. I shall hope, in that case, to possess a due portion of you at Monticello." But Bradbury did not arrive in St. Louis until December 31, 1809, long after Lewis's death.

Governor Lewis hurried his last-minute travel preparations, naming his "three most intimate friends," Clark, Alexander Stewart and William C. Carr, as possessors of his power of attorney so they could sell any of his property to settle bills. He owned some dozen parcels of land near St. Louis. On August 30th he presided over the Territorial Council. Finally, two days after ordering John B. Treat to reopen trade on the Arkansas River, Lewis left St. Louis for Washington by boat, via New Orleans. It was September 4th.

Bates was sure that Eustis's letter to Lewis was tantamount to recall. "He has been too unfortunate to expect a second nomination," the Secretary gleefully wrote a friend. Unable to woo support for himself, he backed Judge John Coburn as Lewis's successor. Then Clement Penrose crossed him, suggesting that

327

Bates's quarrels with Lewis were not the result of honest differences of opinion but from the Secretary's "barbarous conduct," caused by his aspiration to the highest territorial office. Bates lashed out at the Pennsylvanian, ranting, "You will say that I have been and am the enemy of the Governor and that I would be very willing to fill that office myself. I told you this morning that it was *false*—and I repeat that it is an impudent stupidity in you to persist the assertion. In return for the personal allusions with which you have honored me, I tender to you my most hearty contempt." After blustering and hectoring Penrose further, he ended, "I pledge my word of honour that if you ever again bark at my heels, I will spurn you like a puppy from my path."

Bates took advantage of Lewis's departure to hurry letters off to Eustis, carping, "The Governor has never confided in me the wishes of Administration on this [Indian Affairs] or, indeed, on any other subjects. . . . It is not in my province to arraign the conduct of Governor Lewis and it is surely as distant from my inclination as it is from official decorum. Yet, in speaking of the present situation of Territorial business, it is scarcely possible to forbear a retrospect into the past. . . ." After maligning Lewis's administration, he wrote to Gallatin to destroy the latter's confidence in Lewis by damning the Governor for a do-nothing record in regard to the bold stakery and other lead mine difficulties, although, said Bates, he acted "as if he had brought with him all the views of Administration in his portfolio."

Lewis, busy dropping down the Mississippi, had no exact idea of what Bates was up to but he must have known his enemy would seize the opportunity to strike at him. So, he set his personal affairs in order, probably at New Madrid. On September 11th he made out his last will and testament, witnessed by F. S. Trinchard. "I bequeath all my estate, real and personal, to my Mother, Lucy Marks, after my private debts are paid, of which a statement will be found in a small minute book deposited with Pernia, my servant."

On September 15th, the boat reached Chickasaw Bluffs and Fort Pickering where the fort's C.O., Captain Gilbert C. Russell, met him. According to the latter's statement, made long after

(1811), Lewis was put ashore in a state of mental derangement apparently brought on by illness and fever, after having twice attempted to kill himself. Russell ventured that the mental illness was due to Lewis's "indisposition." Some writers have taken this to mean alcoholism but Sam Johnson's dictionary usage probably applied—simply "disorder of health; tendency to sickness; slight disease," with no connotation of delerium tremens, or other aspects of alcoholism. Russell took over, forbade Lewis all grain spirits and confined him to claret and light wine while he was in the care of Surgeon's Mate W. C. Smith at the fort. Lewis remained in bad mental and physical health for five days but on the sixth day, in Russell's own words, "all symptoms of derangement disappeared and he was completely in his senses and this continued for ten or twelve days." At the end of that time, Lewis swore off hard liquor.

The day after his arrival at the fort, Lewis wrote President Madison a letter which was rough, containing eighteen erasures, but hardly the incoherent babbling of a man suffering (according to some writers) from neurosis. "I arrived here yesterday about 2 o'clock, P.M.," wrote Lewis, "very much exhausted from the heat of the climate. But, having taken medicine, [I] feel much better this morning. My apprehension from the heat of the lower country and my fear of the original papers relative to my voyage to the Pacific Ocean falling into the hands of the British has induced me to change my route and proceed by land through the state of Tennessee to the city of Washington. I bring with me duplicates of my vouchers for public expenditures, etc., which, when fully explained—or, rather, the general view of the circumstances under which they were made [being explained]—I flatter myself they will receive both approbation and sanction. Provided my health permits, no time shall be lost in reaching Washington. My anxiety to pursue and fulfill the duties incident to the internal arrangements incident to the Government of Louisiana has prevented my writing you more frequently."

Perhaps because of a recurrence of fever, Lewis did not write again till the 22nd, when he penned a note to Stoddard. "I must acknowledge myself remiss in not writing you in answer to several friendly epistles which I have received from you since my return from the Pacific Ocean. Continued occupation in the immediate discharge of the duties of a public station will, I trust, in some measure plead my apology. I am now on my way to the City of Washington and had contemplated taking Fort Adams and [New] Orleans in my route but my indisposition has induced me to change my route and [I] shall now pass through Tennessee and Virginia. The protest of some bills which I have lately drawn on public account form the principal inducement for my going forward at this moment. An explanation is all that is necessary, I am sensible, to put matters right. In the meantime, the protest of a draught, however just, has drawn down upon me at one moment all my private debts, which have excessively embarrassed me. I hope you will, therefore, pardon me for asking you to remit as soon as is convenient the sum of $200 which you have informed me you hold for me. I calculated on having the pleasure of seeing you at Fort Adams as I passed but am informed by Captain Russell, the Commanding Officer of this place, that you are stationed on the west side of the Mississippi. You will direct to me at the City of Washington until the last of December, after which I expect I shall be on my return to St. Louis."

Before resuming his journey, accompanied by Major James Neelly, Chickasaw Indian agent, Lewis also sent a land warrant to New Orleans to be sold and the money used to pay his creditors.

Then, on September 29th, a pale and shaky Lewis borrowed $99.58 from Russell, feeling his cash resources ($120) were insufficient for his journey to Washington and back. He secured a saddle horse and two pack animals from Russell and Neelly, the pack animals to carry his two trunks and portfolio, jammed with public and private papers including sixteen red morocco-bound journals of the expedition. He left two trunks and a bundle with Russell to be forwarded to him in Washington by boat. Lewis carried two pistols, a dirk and a pipe-tomahawk, as he set out.

As far as the Chickasaw Agency, at Big Town, where the Memphis Road joined the Natchez Trace, near modern Houston, Tennessee, Lewis, Neelly, Pernia and Neelly's slave were accompanied by an Indian interpreter and several Chickasaws. (There is a persistent rumor that a Negro servant, Tom or Captain Tom, accompanied Lewis, too.) Lewis, unwell, rested two days at the intersection of the trails and sent word with a traveler to hold his trunks rather than send them by boat. He would send Russell further instructions from Nashville, he said. At the Agency, or Old Factor's Stand, Lewis was probably delirious again, for Neely described him as deranged from time to time. Recovered again, the Governor and his companions rode up the Trace on the 6th, making excellent time for a sick man (if Neely's figures were correct), 50 miles a day. They crossed the Tennessee River on the afternoon of the 8th or the morning of the 9th, traveled throughout the day and camped at Dogwood Mudhole. Two of the horses escaped that night and Neely remained behind, next morning, to retake them while Lewis and the servants rode on northeast. The Governor promised to halt and await the Indian agent at the first white habitation he might encounter.

Near Little Swan Creek in the bosky hill country of south-central Tennessee, Lewis turned his horse off the shallow swale of the Natchez Trace where it skirted a hacked-out clearing in the oaks. From this new meadow rose a haze of chimney smoke, mingling with the soft light of sunset. As he left the canopy of oaks and maples, Lewis saw a pair of rude log cabins, at right angles, joined by a 12- or 15-foot dogtrot or breezeway. He greeted the lone woman who stood awaiting him and learned that this was Grinder's Stand, seventy-two miles from Nashville and on the very border of Indian Territory. Lewis dismounted, took off the loose robe, or duster, striped blue and white like mattress ticking, which he wore, and looked over the establishment. The cabins were rude, indeed, and the only other signs of civilization were a barn and stable and the stumps of cut trees in the clearing. But it would do.

The woman identified herself as Mrs. Robert Grinder and explained that her husband was away, helping with the harvest at their Duck River farm, some 20 miles distant. Lewis inquired if he might have lodging. Mrs. Grinder assented, of course, but asked, "Do you come alone?" No, the Governor told her, his servants would be along shortly. After taking his saddle into the cabin which the woman indicated would be his, the Virginian asked Mrs. Grinder for a glass of whiskey. But when she brought it, he drank very little. Shortly, the servants rode up and Lewis asked one of them about powder for his pistols, saying that he was sure he had some handy in a canister. The servant's reply was indistinct but Lewis, instead of seeing to the priming of his arms, began to pace back and forth before the rude oak door of his cabin, obviously upset, talking to himself. At times, he would walk up almost to his startled hostess, then wheel on his heel and stride away, wrapped in thought and anger as he rehearsed his upcoming confrontation with Secretary of War Eustis.

When Mrs. Grinder announced that supper was ready, the Governor sat down at the table but did not lose his agitation. After eating only a few bites, he started up, his face flushed with a fit of anger, muttering something to himself as he considered anew the injustice of his treatment by Washington. Finally, he lit his pipe and drew a chair close to the door, remarking, "Madam, this is a very pleasant evening." He smoked for a time, then got up and resumed his impatient pacing, traversing the yard this time. Regaining his composure once more, he took his seat, filled his pipe and lit it. Blowing clouds of smoke and staring toward the west, he observed, "What a sweet evening this is!"

In the meantime, Mrs. Grinder was preparing a bed for her guest in the cabin. However, the Governor stopped her, explaining that he preferred to sleep on the puncheon floor. He sent one of the servants for his bearskins and buffalo robe, which were spread on the floor. Since it was now dark, Mrs. Grinder took her leave of the gentleman in order to make her own bed in the kitchen while the servants headed for the stable to bed down in the hayloft, 200 yards away. But Mrs. Grinder did not sleep. According to her later testimony, the frenetic and puzzling pacing of her visitor so unnerved her that she lay awake for a long time, during which time she could plainly hear Lewis talking aloud, "like a lawyer," as he walked back and forth in the adjoining cabin.

Suddenly the woman was brought fully awake by the loud report of a firearm nearby. It was followed by a thud in Lewis's cabin, like the sound of a heavy object hitting the floor. Then she heard the words, "Oh, Lord!" followed by the explosion of another shot. A few minutes later, she heard her guest at the kitchen door, crying out pitifully, "Oh, madam! Give me some water, and heal my wounds!"

It must have been 3 A.M. when the woman peered through the chinks between the logs of the kitchen wall. She saw Governor Lewis staggering backward in the dark, to fall against a stump left by Grinder between the kitchen and the sleeping cabin. Then he crawled on hands and knees a short distance to a tree and, with its support, pulled himself painfully up into a sitting position. After resting thus for a moment, he lurched and shuffled his way through the shadows and back into the cabin. But he was soon at her door again, scratching feebly at it, not speaking now. She next heard him scraping in the bucket with the gourd as the gunshot wounds made his body beg for water. But there was not even to be the solace of water for Lewis. The bucket was empty.

Mrs. Grinder, as she later told her story, was terrified. In any case, she did *nothing* for the dying man who scratched at her bolted door, begging help. At daybreak, hours later, she sent two of her children to the barn to arouse the servants who had, apparently, heard nothing.

Pernia and the Negro came up to find Lewis lying on the bed which he had spurned the night before. He was wounded in the head and side by pistol balls (and perhaps cut with a knife or razor; the accounts differ), was in great pain and fitfully conscious. According to one of the several versions which Mrs. Grinder gave interrogators, Lewis uncovered his side to show them the dreadful wound where a bullet had entered. In addition, a pistol ball had torn off a portion of his forehead, not causing much bleeding but exposing part of the brain. Lewis, according to Mrs. Grinder, begged them to take his rifle—presumably because he had emptied his pistols into his own body—and blow out his brains. If they would do this for him, he said, he would give them all the money he had in the trunk. According to the strangely timid frontierswoman, the Governor, who had been unable to kill himself with two heavy-caliber pistols, begged

Pernia not to be afraid of him, assuring the Creole that he would not hurt him.

Meriwether Lewis's last words on earth came as the rising sun tinged the treetops to the east with light. They were, "I am no coward, but I am so strong. It is so hard to die."

CHAPTER XXIII

———◆•◆———

POST-MORTEM

His [Lewis's] death was greatly lamented. And that a fame so dearly earned as his should be clouded by such an act of desperation was, to his friends, still greater cause of regret.

CAPTAIN GILBERT RUSSELL,
November 26, 1811

In the death of Governor Lewis, the public behold the wreck of one of the noblest men. He was a pupil of the immortal Jefferson, by him he was reared, by him he was instructed in the tour of the sciences, by him he was introduced to public life when his enterprizing soul, great botanical knowledge, acute penetration and personal courage soon pointed him out as the most proper person to command a projected exploring party to the Northwest Coast of the American Continent.

Democratic Clarion (Nashville),
October 20, 1809

WORD of Lewis's tragic death reached the public when Major James Neelly wrote to Jefferson, October 18th, from Nashville. He began, "It is with extreme pain that I have to inform you of the death of His Excellency, Meriwether Lewis, Governor of Upper Louisiana, who died on the morning of the 11th instant and, I am sorry to say, by suicide." It was this report by Lewis's erstwhile traveling companion, whom the ex-President had no reason to suspect or distrust, which convinced Jefferson that the man who had almost been a son to him had taken his own life.

It is not known exactly when Neelly finally rode up to the inn; how long he stayed (some say two nights, some say he rode on with Lewis still unburied); whether he, or a mysterious mail carrier, Robert Smith, discovered the body; whether he examined the body for powder burns, which would have strongly suggested suicide; whether he even examined the Governor's pistols to see if they had taken his life. If it was a case of foul play, and not suicide, Neelly himself may have been involved; if it was foul play and he was not a part of it, close questioning by him of the woman would probably have trapped her in inconsistencies. He intimated that he found the Governor's arms to be the weapons used when he said that Lewis had "shot himself in the head with one pistol and a little below the breast with the other."

In his letter to Jefferson, Neelly also passed on as gospel the words which, supposedly, Mrs. Grinder or Pernia told him Lewis had used when they entered the cabin. "I have done the business, my good servant. Give me some water."

Neelly concluded by saying he had had the Governor buried as decently as possible in that lonely clearing. With no coffins or even lumber to be had, apparently, Lewis was buried in a crude box of hewn oak planks, fastened with iron nails made by Robert M. Cooper at his nearby (15 miles away) smithy. Neelly asked what he should do with Lewis's belongings. He stated he had two trunks, filled with papers, "amongst which is said to be his travels to the Pacific Ocean and, probably, some vouchers for expenditures of public money for a bill which he said had been protested by the Secretary of War and of which act, to his death, he repeatedly complained. I have also in my care his rifle, silver watch, brace of pistols, dirk and tomahawk"—none of which Neelly ever returned to Lewis's family of his free will, though the rifle was eventually recovered. The major made no mention of the cash Lewis was carrying. His body, supposedly, was found with only twenty-five cents in his pockets.

Neelly, if he had been hunting the horses while Lewis was dying, had not done a good job of it, for he wrote from Nashville on the 18th, "One of the Governor's horses was lost in the wilderness, which I will endeavour to regain. The other I have sent on with his servant who expressed a desire to go to the Governor's mother and to Monticello. I have furnished him with fifteen dollars to defray his expenses to Charlottesville." (John Brahan, a friend of Lewis's, added $5 to Neelly's $10.) "Some days previous to the Governor's death, he requested of me, in case any accident happened to him, to send his trunks, with the papers therein, to the President, but I think it probable he meant to you. I wish to be informed what arrangements may be considered best in sending on his trunks."

Pernia, or John Pernier, apparently visited Locust Hill (after all, Lewis owed him money—$240), delivering some of Meriwether's effects to Lucy Marks. On November 26th he rode Lewis's horse over to Monticello, where Jefferson gave him enough money to get to Washington with a letter from the ex-President to Madison. But not one word, alas, of Jefferson's conversation with the Creole has come down to us. Certainly, however, Pernia confirmed Neelly's claim of suicide (whether rightly or wrongly), so that Jefferson never even considered murder to be a possibility.

Whatever Jefferson thought, and whatever the public was told by the press, local folk were not convinced that it was suicide. In the last seventy-five years the belief that Lewis was the victim of robbery and murder has grown. The scrapbook in Bill Alderson's Tennessee State Library on the death has fifteen clippings for murder to two for suicide.

As stories of Lewis's mysterious death proliferated, they grew more varied. Mrs. Grinder told her story in at least three different versions; Captain Russell made two differing reports; a Negro servant and a white girl, a cook, materialized to claim having been at Grinder's that dreadful night and to offer some fine apocrypha. Soon, Lewis was said to have not ony been shot in the forehead and side, but in the mouth, under the chin and in the intestines. In one version of his last night, he is said to have had his wallet stolen early in the evening. In another, he is claimed to have told his servant when Mrs. Grinder summoned him after the deed was done, "I have done the business, my good servant. Give me some water." Further, his body was said to have been cut with a razor or sharp knife on the arms (wrists), on one thigh, and at the neck. The knife-wounds story spread quickly. It was in the Nashville *Democratic Clarion* on October 20th in columns edged in mourning black for "the untimely end of a brave and prudent officer," in the Frankfort, Kentucky, paper and the *National Intelligencer.* Russell passed it on; on November 19th, Charles W. Peale told his son, Rembrandt, "Governor Lewis has destroyed himself. . . . He shot himself by two shots. This not being effective, he completed the rash work with a razor."

No government inquiry, official or otherwise, was made into Lewis's death. Incredibly, no official even so much as visited the scene. Apparently, Clark never made the pilgrimage although in his later years, according to his niece, he insisted that his friend had not taken his own life. Lewis's grave was neglected and forgotten. His half brother, John H. Marks, eventually visited the scene and looked up Neelly's wife. He was able to secure Meriwether's rifle from her but had to leave without his brother's pistols and knife which Neelly, absent, always wore. It was the opinion of some, such as Alexander Wilson's biographer, that the Government actually hushed up the entire matter of Lewis's death.

But Wilson would not allow the matter to remain hushed up. He apparently heard a rumor that no information was available on Lewis's death because of accusations that the Governor was involved with treacherous Wilkinson. It is possible, however, that Jefferson wished the affair forgotten. Convinced it was suicide, he saw the end of the great explorer, who had been the son never born to him, as shameful. Madison would, of course, have gone along with his wishes. Wilson was actually preparing plans for a walk with William Bartram from Philadelphia to St. Louis, to visit their mutual friend after observing and collecting specimens on the way, when the news of the Governor's death reached Philadelphia on November 10th. Bartram's enthusiasm for the trip now vanished (he was seventy years of age) but Wilson determined to go ahead with his plans, substituting a visit to Lewis's grave for the hoped-for reunion. He and Lewis had become close friends as members of the circle of artists and scientists which revolved around engraver Alexander Lawson in 1806 and 1807. At his home they had met Lawson's daughter, Malvina, who, all her life, remembered the two as remarkably alike—shy and silent but observant in intelligent company. It was at this time that Lewis gave the young student of birds the greatest encouragement he had had to that time, by presenting the Scot with the birds he had brought back from the West. In Wilson's words, it was "the request and particular wish of Captain Lewis, made to me in person, that I should make drawings of such of the feathered tribes as had been preserved and were new." (These included the Louisiana tanager, renamed the western tanager; Clark's crow; and Lewis's woodpecker.) From Lewis, Wilson learned that the raffish blue jay was to be found far up the Missouri, that the thieving red-winged starlings roamed the Missouri Valley in great sweeping flocks (at which the Indians launched their arrows), and that the passenger pigeon was seen as far west as the Great Falls. Lewis put Wilson in touch with Ordway, too, and the sergeant was the source of many anecdotes for the ornithologist. From him, for example, Wilson learned that the magpies of the prairie were so greedy that they swooped down to feed on the hunters' kill while the men were still skinning out the animals.

From Nashville, Wilson dropped southwest toward Grinder's Stand but, perhaps fearful of what he might find there, he put up for the night at a new inn, Dobbin's Stand, just six miles north of Grinder's. The next morning, he climbed up from a branch of Little Swan Creek to the 1,000-foot wooded mesa, the Flat Woods, where he found the death site. He met Grinder, told him that he was a friend of Lewis's, and asked to see the grave. Grinder was not only taciturn, he was as unfriendly as he was uncommunicative and was obviously resentful of the tales of Lewis's death being a murder in which he was probably implicated. He agreed to care for the grave, for a fee, and led the ornithologist to it, an earthen mound where the trail joined the partially cleared flat. A few fence rails piled atop the mounded hump identified Lewis's last resting place. Wilson wrote a friend of the scene: "He lies buried close by the common path with a few loose rails thrown over his grave. I gave Grinder money to put a post fence around it, to shelter it from the hogs and from the wolves, and he gave me his written promise."

The innkeeper then took him to the cabin and left him with Mrs. Grinder before the fireplace where Lewis had died. Wilson found her voluble; no questions were necessary, she poured out her story with great graphic detail and power as the scientist took notes. She seemed to be an observant and imaginative woman—even eloquent—but intense and embittered. He came to feel that the dolorous events of the predawn hours of October 11th—and the persistent rumors of homicide—had preyed on her mind.

Finally, it was time to go. "I left this place in a very melancholy mood, which was not much allayed by the prospect of the gloomy and savage wilderness which I was just entering, alone," Wilson wrote his friend. Once out of sight of the cabins, he broke down and wept for his dead friend. A little later, the birdman turned poet and composed a brief *adieu* to his friend:

> The anguish that his soul assailed,
> The dark despair that round him blew,
> No eye, save that of Heaven beheld,
> None but unfeeling strangers knew.
>
> Poor reason perished in the storm
> And desperation triumphed here!
>
> For hence be each accusing thought,
> With him my kindred tears shall flow,
> Pale Pity consecrate the spot
> Where poor lost Lewis now lies low.
>
> Love as these solitudes appear
> Wide as this wilderness is spread,
> Affection's steps shall linger here,
> To breathe her sorrows o'er the dead.

Below Grinder's, Wilson was covering the ground which Lewis had passed, only in reverse direction. It became rougher with rocky climbs, thickets and fords, and Wilson began to suspect Neelly's account of the Governor's journey. Nobody could make 50 miles a day through this country, felt Wilson. The major's timetable was all wrong; he was either a poor memorizer or a liar. Wilson ended up convinced that the horses must have strayed far beyond the point which Neelly had reported. Therefore, the major's convenient disappearance had taken place much closer to Grinder's than he had said and if foul play there had been, by Pernia, the Grinders, or others, Neelly could have been a party to it.

On his ride, Wilson encountered a mockingbird which was singing its own sweet song, not the borrowed melodies of other birds which the feathered mimes adopted so easily. He wondered if perhaps the bird had sung for Lewis. He knew well how rarely the bird's own song was heard and he knew the folklore of it—that when one heard the unique song of the mock-bird, it was a signal of death.

Aside from Wilson, and John H. Marks, few came to pay homage to Jefferson's agent of empire at Grinder's Stand. Because of his quasi recall; his bankruptcy (creditors flocked like buzzards to his poor estate, including McFarlane, Chouteau, Pernia and even Jefferson, reducing it to a shocking $9.43½ before they were through); and the shame of his (supposed) suicide—Lewis's fame was as effectively sunk as his fortune. Thus, when the editor of his journals, Paul Allen, praised him to Jefferson in 1813 it was in a rather faint eulogy:

"The hazardous expedition is the only part of Captain Lewis's life which, were he now alive, he would be willing, probably, to submit to public notice. It was on one occasion only that his great talents were put to the proof and then were found adequate to the emergency."

Jefferson, his mind made up for him by Neelly and Pernia, and a statement of Captain Russell's—that Lewis "destroyed himself in the most cool, desperate and Barbarian-like manner"—said little and what he did say tended to damn Lewis as an insane suicidist. He wrote Russell on April 18, 1810, for example: "He was much afflicted and habitually so, with hypochondria. This was probably increased by the habit into which he had fallen [intemperance] and the painful reflections that would necessarily produce in a mind like his." When he wrote Benjamin Smith Barton in October of that year, he was so restrained that all he could say was, "His [Lewis's] family cherish his memory with all the fondness his singularly valuable qualities merited. To them, he was ever most affectionate and devoted." Barton, in writing Jefferson (October 16th), was far more open: "During the Governor's last visit to Philadelphia, there was some difference between him and me, originating *wholly* in the illiberal conduct of some of my enemies here who laboured, not without some effect, to excite uneasiness in his mind as to my friendship for him. I cherish with respect the memory of your friend. . . . His fate was, indeed, melancholy and unhappy; but similar have sometimes been the fate of the best and wisest men."

Dr. Samuel L. Mitchell had none of Jefferson's agonizing doubts about his old friend. When running for a Congressional seat himself, he stated that Lewis could have ably filled the highest office in the land, the Presidency.

After the brief flurry of eulogies immediately following his death there came the embarrassment of the supposed manner of his passing, and Lewis slipped into oblivion. No one noticed when, in March 1812, the contested bills of exchange which had led directly to his death were, ironically, admitted by the War Department and Lewis's actions in behalf of Big White (and in behalf of Thomas Jefferson) vindicated.

It was up to Jefferson to set things right, to make amends for his country's shabby treatment of its greatest explorer; of his name; even of his virtually unmarked grave. But he failed. Doubtless this was because his adopted son had, he felt, *failed him* by taking the coward's way out of difficulties. Jefferson later became convinced of a strain of insanity existing in the Lewis lineage—a strain no historian before or since has ever turned up.

When Jefferson was called upon to preface the published journals of the Lewis and Clark Expedition in 1814, he first maligned Lewis's memory by reiterating the unproved, unfounded tales of "hypochondria" and "sensible depressions of mind" which he had observed, he said, in his secretary. (Yet he had entrusted him with the carrying out of his great design of discovery and acquisition of the West!) "During his Western years," Jefferson wrote, "the constant exertion which that required of all the faculties of his body and mind suspended these distressing affections, but after his establishment at St. Louis in sedentary occupations they returned upon him with redoubled vigour and began seriously to alarm his friends. He was in a paroxysm of one of these when his affairs rendered it necessary for him to go to Washington." In my opinion this is utter nonsense; Bates watched Lewis like a hawk, ready to pounce on any weakness or misstep, in order to report it to Washington and get the removal of the man who drove him to fury by coolly ignoring him, as if he were not within 2,000 miles of St. Louis. Not once did he mention insanity or depression until he heard the Neelly-Russell tale from John B. Treat.

Jefferson's next words all but sealed the fate of Lewis's reputation: "About 3 o'clock in the night, he did the deed which plunged his friends into affliction and deprived his country of one of her most valued citizens; whose valour and intelligence would have been now employed in avenging the wrongs of his Country [in the War of 1812] and in emulating by land the splendid deeds which have honoured her arms on the ocean. . . ."

When finally, Jefferson evaluated the worth of his dead friend, it was too late. The damage was done. But his words deserve to be remembered:

"Of courage undaunted, possessing a firmness and perseverance of purpose which nothing but impossibilities could divert from its direction, careful as a father of those committed to his charge, yet steady in the maintenance of order and discipline; intimate with the Indian character, customs and principles, habituated to the hunting life, guarded by exact observation of the vegetables and animals of his own country against losing time in the description of objects already possessed, honest, disinterested, liberal, of sound understanding and [of] fidelity to truth so scrupulous that whatever he should report would be as certain as if seen ourselves. With all these qualifications, as if selected and implanted by Nature in one body for this express purpose, I could have no hesitation in confiding the enterprise [the Expedition] to him."

The plinth of the weathered Lewis Monument, erected so belatedly by the State of Tennessee in 1848 over the explorer's remains, bears a paraphrase of Jefferson's words under an epitaph

343

which reads: *Immaturis obit, sed tu felicior annos. Vive meos. Bona Republica! Vive Tuos.* The Volunteer State, in borrowing from Jefferson, stated the case for a rescue of Lewis's reputation which was in 1848—and which still is in 1964—long overdue. "His courage was undaunted. His firmness and perseverance yielded to nothing but impossibilities. A rigid disciplinarian, yet tender as a father to those committed to his charge; honest, disinterested, liberal, with a sound understanding and a scrupulous fidelity to truth."

Was Meriwether Lewis murdered? Yes.

Is there proof of his murder? No.

Could Lewis's death have been a suicide? Yes. Not only because the analysts today will insist that *anyone* is capable of self-destruction, given the right set of circumstances, even a man of courage like Lewis, but because the Governor was fatigued, depressed, sick and, at times, delirious. (No one has ever suggested that Lewis killed himself while in full possession of his senses.) And, where there was no proof of murder, there was "evidence" of suicide at Grinder's Stand.

Is it likely that the cause of Lewis's death was self-murder? Not at all. If there is such a person as the anti-suicide type, it was Meriwether Lewis. By temperament, he was a fighter, not a quitter. Much has been made of his introspection but a line-by-line analysis of his long journals and letters show his thirty-first birthday reveries (always pounced upon by suicide theorists) to be an almost unique example of moody soul-searching or excessive introspection. Sensitive he was; neurotic he was not. Lewis was one of the most positive personalities in American history.

Not enough has been made of the factors weighing against his taking his own life. His courage; his enthusiasm; his youth (thirty-five); his plans—to return to St. Louis, after seeing his mother and setting things straight in Washington; to engage in the fur trade with his brother, Reuben, and his best friend, Will Clark. His book he was eager to finish, too, and he gave a man at Curry's Stand, en route to Grinder's, a prospectus and promised to send him a copy as soon as he finished it.

The damage of the contested bills has been overstated by those who feel his death was a suicide. These meant no wrecked career; they were par for the military and governmental course of the day. Similar accusations of impropriety, incompetence, etc., and contested vouchers by pennysniffing clerks in Washington plagued many associates of Lewis, including Captain Russell, Zebulon Pike and James Neely. Moreover, although his credit was torpedoed by Eustis, Lewis was setting about to restore it by selling parcels of land. Even had his bills not finally been approved, as they were in 1812, he would never have put a pistol to his head for such a ridiculous reason.

Nor was he *persona non grata* in Washington. Commanding General Jonathan Smith was planning to consult with him in regard to the Sioux and other matters of which Boilvin had written him, and Secretary Eustis told Pierre Chouteau that he would take up the Osage Agency matters with Lewis before making any decision.

Zealous researchers like Elliott Coues, O. D. Wheeler, Reuben Thwaites, John Bakeless, Vardis Fisher and Donald Jackson all lean toward the murder theory though all seem unsure of exactly what did take place in the dogwood- and azalea-brightened Flat Woods of Tennessee on that dread morning of October 11, 1809. Only Dawson Phelps of the writers and researchers seems completely convinced of the case for suicide.

Yes, it was murder. And, as the coroner's jury of 1809, whose records have all been lost, must have felt, by a person or persons unknown. Since there was no evidence to implicate anyone, and the stage was set for suicide, Foreman Samuel Whiteside and his jury decided that their inquest could legally bring forth only a verdict of apparent suicide.

The killer could have been Pernia, Lewis's servant. But, if so, his fellow loft-lodger, Neely's servant, must have been a very sound sleeper, bribed or terrified into lasting silence, or an accomplice in the crime. Perhaps both Neely and his man were in on the plot. The Creole wanted the money which his master owed him. He is said to have put on the Governor's fine garments immediately after his death and, according to some macabre and incredible accounts, to have dressed the bloody corpse in his own shabby clothes.

The guilty party might have been one of the Grinders; the inn-keeper, lurking in the woods, or his hard-bitten woman, who spurned a dying man's cries for water, by her own admission. If the Grinders were the assassins, they were stupid but lucky in committing the bloody deed on their own property. Or were they so completely sanguine of their murderous skill, like Kate Bender and her Kansan kin of later days, that they preferred to murder at their very hearth?

Over the years, the two major suspects have been Grinder and Pernia. The former abandoned the tragic Stand after Lewis's death, but he did not go far, only to his old farm on Shipp's Bend of the Duck River, near Centerville. He prospered, but slowly. It was not until 1814 that he could pay $250 down on a piece of land he wanted. (Or, did he patiently hoard Lewis's $120 and add to it?) There was no trial of Grinder, any more than there was of Pernia or anyone else, nor was an indictment ever handed down. Pernia was said to have been accosted by Lewis's sister on the streets of Mobile or New Orleans, wearing the silver watch given the explorer by William Wirt and carrying Meriwether's rifle. But Isaac Coles was sending the watch to Jefferson in 1810; rifles were not usually carried on city streets in 1810, and John Marks secured the weapon from Neelly's wife in 1812. So the story is mere legend. If Pernia had a hand in Lewis's murder he did not profit by it. He disappeared and it is tantalizing to think he was murdered to seal his lips, though Jefferson wrote William D. Meriwether on August 21, 1810, of the servant's suicide. "You will probably know the fate of poor Pierney, his [Lewis's] servant, who lately followed his master's example." Jefferson learned of the Creole's death when the latter's landlord, John Christopher Suverman of Washington, informed him that an impoverished and despondent Pernia had killed himself on April 29th with laudanum.

Did Neelly commit the deed? Did he ransack the trunks? They were found in great disarray when inventoried in Nashville. A meticulous and methodical man, Lewis would hardly have jumbled together private and public papers in the chaos in which they were found. And Neelly did mention the trunks' contents in his letter to Jefferson. He certainly stole the Governor's rifle, horse, pistols, dagger and pipe-tomahawk. It is not known who took Lewis's money, missing only a shilling on the corpse, but it could have been Neelly as well as Pernia or the Grinders. The major was dismissed from his Indian Agency shortly after Lewis's death, at the request of his Chickasaws, and was denounced as an accomplice in Lewis's death by Captain Gilbert Russell in angry letters to Jefferson. The captain did not actually claim that Neelly pulled the triggers but, instead, wrote that the Indian agent had stolen the Governor's side arms "and perhaps some other of his effects for some claim he pretends to have upon his estate. He can have no just claim for anything more than the expenses of his interment unless he makes a charge for packing his two trunks from the [Chickasaw] Nation—and for that he can not have the audacity to make a charge after tendering the use of a loose horse or two, which he said he had to take from the Nation [to Nashville], and also the aid of a servant."

Russell also insisted that Neelly had no money when he set out with Lewis yet he gave Pernia $15 later. Was it from Lewis's pocket? Russell accused Neelly of being both a drunkard and a thief, and Lewis' half brother, John H. Marks, was never able to get Meriweather's pistols and dagger back from the major. The gravest charge which Russell made was that Neelly plied Lewis with liquor. "After leaving this place, by some means or other, his [Lewis's] resolution left him and this Agent, being extremely fond of liquor, instead of preventing the Governor from drinking or putting him under restraint, advised him to it and from everything I can learn, gave the man every chance to seek an opportunity to destroy himself. And, from a statement of Grinder's wife, where he killed himself, I can not help believing that Purney was rather aiding and abetting in the murder than otherwise."

What about Russell, himself, as a suspect? He was no paragon of virtue. On November 5, 1809, Surgeon's Mate W. C. Smith, who had taken care of Lewis while he was sick at the fort, wrote to Secretary Eustis that Russell had arrested him on "charges frivolous in their nature," had confined him to close quarters and caused him to fall ill. More indications of Russell's lack of stability were in Eustis's communiqué to General Wade Hampton, pointing out that the Indian factor at Russell's post had also complained about him. Said Eustis, "With the degree of culpability attached to him by the informant, I am not acquainted. It is possible he may be imprudent and not experienced." On November 3, 1811, Russell, now a major, solicited Neelly's Chickasaw Agency, should it become vacant. On December 9th, charges were preferred against Russell by Lieutenant Colonel Robert Purdy, who asked for his arrest. By December 30th, Russell had prepared countercharges against Purdy. In 1815, now a colonel, Russell received an honorable discharge from the Army.

The motive in Lewis's death was robbery, not politics, although Jonathan Daniels's belief in a rather complicated plot, with Bates, General Wilkinson and Pernia all involved, is not beyond possibility. The contents of an obviously sick and delirious gentleman's pockets and trunks were fair game for every cutthroat on the Natchez Trace, especially if the desperado thought, as did ex-Governor Gilmer of Georgia and others, that Lewis had found a gold mine in the West and was carrying a map and ore samples in his baggage.

If Lewis was shot from behind, as some of the descendants of the coroner's jury have insisted, then it was murder, pure and simple, even if his own brace of pistols did the work. If he was badly slashed with a knife or razor, too, as Russell believed and as the newspapers of the period reported, then the odds on suicide drop even lower.

Who, then, if not Pernia, Grinder, Neelly or Russell, was Meriwether Lewis's murderer? His assassin, I am convinced, was either an unknown land pirate of the ilk of the Harpe brothers of bloody Natchez notoriety, or the mysterious Runnion, suspected by Whiteside's coroner's jury because his mocassin tracks and the impression of the butt of his unusual rifle were found in the dirt near Lewis's cabin. Planned as a murder by night, followed by the abduction and secret burial of the body, the homicide was bungled because of the stout resistance Lewis put up in the darkened cabin. Ironically, through sheer luck—Lewis's record of illness and temporary mental disorder—a hastily conceived frameup of suicide, made necessary by Lewis's tenacious hold on life and the arrival of either Neelly or the mysterious postrider, Robert Smith (who claimed to have found the body), worked to perfection.

Only nine days after Lewis's death, Major Neelly wrote Washington that there were white intruders on the Indian lands. On November 25th, he wrote again to protest these interlopers, who were not amicably disposed, and by December 30th was asking Wade Hampton for a detachment of dragoons to dislodge them from Chickasaw Territory. On November 18, 1811, the War Department wrote him about a stolen horse and an attempted murder, ending, "You may also pay the demand of those Indians who apprehended and delivered up to you the man who attempted to murder his fellow-traveler." Neelly reported on June 5, 1812, that a murder was committed at his Agency by a Kentuckian and that the Creeks were dancing with white scalps. On the 12th he repeated his warnings of thefts and dangerous intruders and again asked for troops to police the Natchez Trace. Washington's answer was to replace him as Chickasaw agent. But his reports show how dangerous was the Natchez Trace when Lewis rode it in 1809.

With Thomas Jefferson's stamp of approval on the suicide contention, however, it is small wonder that even William Clark was led to exclaim, when he heard the news of his friend's end, "I fear, Oh! I fear the weight of his mind has overcome him!" But a few doubters persisted, like Indian Agent John Burke Treat, who wrote Frederick Bates on October 31, 1809. "Certainly the short acquaintance I had with him [Lewis] at St. Louis in June last wholly precludes my having any reason to offer for his committing such an act so very extraordinary and unexpected." The doubters are legion, today.

It must be remembered that not even Mrs. Grinder ever claimed she saw Lewis shoot himself. The evidence for suicide, apparently overwhelming, was circumstantial. The only witnesses other than the men involved in the killing were Solidago, Cornus Florida, Carya Glabra and Acer Rubrum. And, for all that they could tell, they never have talked. For these are not the names of the shadowy Chickasaw chiefs who rode out of Fort Pickering with Meriwether Lewis, but the mute trees and shrubs who witnessed Lewis's dying moments—the goldenrod, flowering dogwood, hickory and red maple of Grinder's Stand.

In a democracy such as ours—to which Meriwether Lewis was so strongly dedicated—it is held in the courts of justice that a man is presumed innocent of a crime until proved guilty. Meriwether Lewis has not been proven guilty of self-destruction at Grinder's Stand in the early hours of October 11, 1809. Therefore, let him be found NOT GUILTY of the charge—the crime of suicide.

ACKNOWLEDGMENTS

THIS BIOGRAPHY could not have been written without the help of an American Philosophical Society research grant which made it possible for me to travel to the East Coast and to research in the libraries of the Society and other institutions.

Individuals who helped me to puzzle out Lewis's life were legion but memory will arrest and detain only the following. For particular moral support, I would like to thank Jonathan Daniels, Allan Nevins, Donald Jackson and Vardis Fisher. For help in running down information, for verification or interpretation, my thanks go to Anne Freudenberg and Elizabeth Ryall of the University of Virginia Library; Gertrude Hess and Murphy Smith, Doctors George W. Corner, Richard Shryock and Whitfield Bell, all of the American Philosophical Society; Mrs. Frances H. Stadler and Mrs. Ruth K. Field of the Missouri Historical Society; Howell Heaney, Ellen Shaffer and Emerson Greenaway of the Free Library of Philadelphia; Mrs. Gerald May of the New Jersey Historical Society; Doctors Edwin Carpenter and John Pomfret of the Henry E. Huntington Library, *et* Librarian Robert Dougan; Herman Friis, National Archives; Oliver Wendell Holmes, National Historical Publications Commission; Gerald McDonald and Glenn Read of New York Public Library; Michael Kennedy, Historical Society of Montana; William Alderson, Mrs. Gertrude Parsley and Isabel Howell of the Tennessee State Library; Nyle Miller, Kansas Historical Society; Irene Payne, Oregon State Highway Department; Margaret Currier, Peabody Museum, Harvard; Tom Vaughan and

Harry Lichter, Oregon Historical Society; Jim Bear, Monticello; Carl Dentzel, Southwest Museum (Los Angeles); Colton Storm and Holden Hall, Newberry Library; Dr. Leo Stanley; Dr. Lawrence Kinnaird; Dr. Abraham Nasatir; Glenn Skillin, John Carter Brown Library; Michael Harrison; Henry H. Clifford; William S. Powell, University of North Carolina Library; Edwin Wolfe, The Library Company, Philadelphia; Joe Ewan, Tulane; Ed Castagna, Enoch Pratt Library; Dr. Roy F. Nichols, University of Pennsylvania; Stephen T. Riley, Massachusetts Historical Society; Ruby El Hult; Lee Ash; Milton Kaplan, Library of Congress; Arlene Hope; Warner Wood; Sy Mantell; Ray Baker Harris and Mrs. Inge Baum, Librarians of the Supreme Council, 33°; Ludwig Emge; and my patient and long-suffering wife.

RICHARD DILLON

BIBLIOGRAPHICAL NOTE

This book lacks a bibliography not because the author did not ponder hundreds, literally, of books and manuscripts in the researching and writing of Meriwether Lewis's biography, but solely because he finds himself unable to better the thirteen-page bio-bibliographical appendix to Donald Jackson's remarkable collection of *Letters of the Lewis and Clark Expedition, With Related Documents, 1783–1854* (Urbana, University of Illinois Press, 1962).

This excellent work by Jackson is one of the three absolutely essential keys to a study of Lewis. The book has astonishingly few weaknesses. The author, possibly, overlooked a few documents; he mentioned but (alas) did not transcribe some others which he felt were less important than those he published; he excluded others, still, because they did not fit within his frame of reference which was the Expedition, per se.

The second great source is Reuben Gold Thwaites's *Original Journals of the Lewis and Clark Expedition, 1804–1806 . . .*, published in New York by Dodd, Mead in eight volumes in 1904 and 1905. (There is also a deluxe, large-paper and extra-illustrated edition of this work by Thwaites, and Bernard De Voto's popular condensation of the *Journals* into one volume is based on Thwaites. De Voto's book is useful chiefly for the editor's annotations.)

The last of the essential trio is the weakest—Milo M. Quaife's *The Journals of Meriwether Lewis and Sergeant John Ordway . . .* (Madison, Historical Society of Wisconsin, 1916), since it is quite limited in scope, covering only Captain Lewis's down-Ohio voyage from Pittsburgh to Wood River, in 1803.

The original, authorized account of the expedition is useful, of course, although it is in the paraphrase of Nicholas Biddle rather than in the words of either Lewis or Clark. This Nicholas Biddle-Paul Allen *History of the Expedition Under the Command of Captains Lewis and Clark* . . . (Philadelphia, Bradford and Inskeep, 1814), has been reprinted many times. As annotated by Elliott Coues in 1893 it is most helpful, especially for identifying geographical sites, Indian tribes and natural history specimens. Patrick Gass's bowdlerized version of the expedition, *A Journal of the Voyages and Travels of a Corps of Discovery Under the Command of Captain Lewis* . . . is disappointing but worthwhile. It was first published in Pittsburgh by Zadok Cramer in 1807 and has gone through many subsequent editions. The several unauthorized or spurious accounts of Lewis's great endeavor which preceded to press the Biddle-Allen authorized account are of limited worth in a volume of this kind but important to the story of the effect of the expedition on the public.

Monographs of great value include Olin D. Wheeler's *On The Trail of Lewis and Clark, 1804–1904* (New York, Putnam, 1904), and Albert and Jane Salisbury's *Two Captains West* (Seattle, Superior, 1950), the latter lavishly illustrated with photographs. Both are excellent aids for tracing the exact route of Lewis and Clark. Among other specialized books, Abraham Nasatir's *Before Lewis and Clark* (St. Louis, St. Louis Historical Documents Foundation, 1952) is outstanding. Fine books, also, are Raymond D. Burroughs's *The Natural History of the Lewis and Clark Expedition* (East Lansing, Michigan State Unitersity Press, 1961), and Elijah Criswell's *Lewis and Clark, Linguistic Pioneers* (University of Missouri Studies, Volume XV, No. 2, 1940).

The greatest mass of resource material is to be found in periodical articles, but most of this is chaff. Generalized rehashes of earlier accounts of the expedition are common and of little or no research value. But among the serial literature articles are some gems, such as the various specialized studies of the medicine, maps and firearms of the Expedition. Highly important are such articles as Charles G. Clarke's "The Roster of the Lewis and Clark Expedition," in the *Oregon Historical Quarterly,* Volume 45 (December 1944), pp. 289–305, and Dawson Phelps's "The Tragic Death of Meriwether Lewis," in *William and Mary Quarterly,* Series 3, Volume 13 (July 1956), pp. 305–18.

Far and away the most complete biographical account of Captain Lewis, until the appearance of the volume in hand, is John Bakeless's *Lewis and Clark, Partners in Discovery* (New York, William Morrow, 1947). Thomas M. Marshall's *The Life and Papers of Frederick Bates* (St. Louis, Missouri Historical Society, 1926) sheds much light on Lewis's role as Governor of Louisiana Territory, as do Volumes 13 and 14 of Clarence C. Carter's *Territorial Papers of the United States* (Washington, Government Printing Office, 1948–1949).

Vardis Fisher's *Suicide or Murder?* (Denver, Alan Swallow, 1962) is an exhaustive study of the puzzle of Lewis's death. Various standard works on Jefferson and his writings, such as Julian Boyd's volumes, are helpful in understanding Lewis, and the better histories of the fur trade, such as Hiram Chittenden's, suggest his role in launching Uncle Sam into the peltry business on the Upper Missouri.

The primary sources of original manuscript materials, and contemporary newspaper accounts, are: The Missouri Historical Society; Alderman Library, University of Virginia; the National Archives; Library of Congress; American Philosophical Society; Tennessee State Library and Archives; Kansas State Historical Society; Massachusetts Historical Society; Henry E. Huntington Library; Wisconsin Historical Society; Historical Society of Pennsylvania; Oregon Historical Society; and the Bancroft Library.

INDEX